Care Ethics in the Age of Precarity

Care Ethics in the Age of Precarity

Maurice Hamington

Michael Flower

Editors

University of Minnesota Press

Minneapolis

London

Published by the University of Minnesota Press
111 Third Avenue South, Suite 290
Minneapolis, MN 55401–2520
http://www.upress.umn.edu

ISBN 978-1-5179-1186-7 (hc)
ISBN 978-1-5179-1187-4 (pb)

Library of Congress record available at https://lccn.loc.gov/2021023219

Printed on acid-free paper

UMP KEP

For Breonna Taylor
whose precarity, like that of many Black Americans, was so extreme
that she was murdered in her own home by those
charged with protecting the public

Black Lives Matter

In memoriam
Elena Pulcini
(1950–2021)

The ethics of care was not only pivotal for her research, but also at the heart of her teaching, mentoring, and social commitment. It became palpable, above all, in her great capacity not only to diagnose and analyse, but also to listen and to encourage.

—Christine Unrau

Contents

Acknowledgments

We would like to acknowledge the 150-plus scholars who participated in the inaugural Care Ethics Research Consortium (CERC) Conference in Portland, Oregon, on September 27–28, 2018. The conference theme was care ethics and precarity, and the discussions there directly led to this volume, although the chapters here were independently developed by a handful of participants into intellectual explorations beyond their brief presentations. In particular, we recognize Sophie Bourgault, Veronica Hotton, Carlo Leget, Neera Malhotra, Monica Mueller, Sarah Wolf Newlands, Inge van Nistelrooij, Vicki Reitenauer, and Merel Visse for their roles in helping to make the conference a fertile space for innovation, compassion, and thoughtfulness. We also thank Pieter Martin, senior acquisitions editor at the University of Minnesota Press, for his guidance and advice in framing this collection as well as the outstanding copy editors employed by the Press.

Introduction

A Care Movement Born of Necessity

MAURICE HAMINGTON AND
MICHAEL FLOWER

> Measuring the importance of care for human life means recognizing that dependence and *precarity* are not accidents that happen only to "others."
>
> —Sandra Laugier, "The Ethics of Care as a Politics of the Ordinary"

"Precarity" is a challenging term because it both names a threat that is real and pervasive and is comprised of many elements crucial to individual being. Judith Butler describes precarity as "a politically induced condition in which certain populations suffer from failing social and economic networks of support and become differentially exposed to injury, violence, and death" (2010, 25). And what is more, in her introduction to *State of Insecurity: Government of the Precarious,* Butler makes it clear in her agreement with the book's author, Isabell Lorey, that this pervasive condition is a matter of the long haul: "Precarity is not a passing or episodic condition, but a new form of regulation that distinguishes this historical time." Precarity "has itself become a regime, a hegemonic mode of being governed, and governing ourselves" (Lorey 2015, vii). In one sense of the term, all life is precarious because, by definition, the concept of life is juxtaposed against death. To have life is to exist with the ever-present possibility of death as well as to have ongoing requirements for survival.

Ostensibly, for any living creature, death can occur at any time. Moreover, living creatures have needs for sustenance that vary, the deprivation of which can cause warranted anxiety. This volume is not a consideration of all varieties of precarity but rather addresses broadly construed forms of market-induced precarity. This type of precarity is not a "natural" result of existence. Rather, market-based or what we are labeling "neoliberal precarity" describes a politically fashioned reality; the precarity we see and experience results from how the complex processes of neoliberalization construe and assign value. In particular, this value is reflected in how people are organized economically and politically to distribute wealth and value in societies—a politically fraught process. And in this context, more than "the financialization of everything" is at play. As Wendy Brown has recently argued, "Neoliberalism's attack on democracy has everywhere inflected law, political culture, and political subjectivity"; understanding the terrain of precarity as well as assembling an effective resistance to the forces shaping it surely means "appreciating the rise of white nationalist authoritarian political formations as animated by the mobilized anger of the economically abandoned and racially resentful, but as contoured by more than three decades of neoliberal assaults on democracy, equality, and society" (2019, 8). Thus, although we might wish to see the purpose and efficacy of our social organizing to be the minimization of precarity for its members, the chapters in this volume suggest that dominant forms of social arrangement have increasingly failed to sustain large segments of the population; the demands of austerity are inequitably distributed as a matter of policy and not as a "natural" and thus necessary outcome of a free market. Note how both the brief Laugier ("not accidents") and Butler ("politically induced") quotes above express a concern for the intentionality of precarity.

Humans can socially organize themselves in many different ways, but a neoliberal approach favors free markets that minimize outside controls on the nature and shape of economic enterprise.[1] William Davies describes four common aspects attributed to current neoliberal thought: (1) neoliberalism attempts to build something new rather than return to any laissez-faire environment of the past; (2) neoliberal policy endeavors to privatize traditionally nonmarket institutions or disband them altogether; (3) neoliberalism solicits an active state-sponsored role in privatization; and (4) neoliberal thinking portrays inequality as a necessary by-product of the ultimate goal of high productivity—"Competition and inequality are valued positively under neoliberalism" (2014, 310). It is the latter acceptance of inequality, and by extension precarity, combined with the social hegemony of neoliberal thinking that concern so many social observers. Extending the analysis of Michel Foucault, Wendy Brown describes emergent knowledge authority within neoliberalism as "an intensification of the market as a state of veridiction . . . the market becomes *the*, rather than *a* site of veridiction *and* becomes so for every arena and type of human activity" (2015, 67). Nothing is left untouched—a point richly illustrated by William Connolly (2012, n.p.) in a passage quoted in full:

> What, then, are some of the political movements and modes of state activism supported by neoliberalism? They include, with varying degrees of support from different leaders, laws to restrain labor organization and restrict consumer movements; corporate participation on school and university Boards; favorable tax laws for investors; corporate ownership and control of the media; court decisions that treat the corporation as a "person" with unlimited rights to lobby and campaign; demands for bankruptcy laws that favor corporations at the expense of those working for them; special corporate access to state officials to maintain inequality and restrain unemployment benefits; extensive discipline of the work force; the legal defense of corporate, financial power to limit consumer information about the policies that affect them; the ear of state officials who regulate credit and the money supply; use of the state to enforce debt payments and foreclosures; huge military, police and prison assemblages to pursue imperial policies abroad and discipline the excluded and disaffected at home; meticulous street and institutional security arrangements to regulate those closed out of the neoliberal calculus; huge state budgets to promote the established infrastructure of consumption in the domains of highway expenditure, the energy grid, health care, and housing codes; state clean up of disasters created by under-regulated financial and corporate activity; and state/bureaucratic delays to hold off action on global climate change.

Thus does neoliberal capitalism dominate social truth in the way religious truth once did. Diminishing the value of living actors, market-based approaches create "winners" and "losers" without proportionately valuing the pain and suffering of those who are objectified participants. This is neoliberal precarity: a human-made insecurity and dis-ease with micro-level implications for individual beings and macro-level significance for ecosystems. As Nancy Fraser and Rahel Jaeggi describe, "One implication is that our crisis is not only economic. It also encompasses care deficits, climate change, and dedemocratization" (2018, 3).

Care Ethics

The fundamental question addressed by the authors in this volume is how those employing care theory can effectively respond to the prevalent reality of neoliberal precarity. Feminist scholarship coalesced around a concept of care ethics in the 1980s as a relational approach to morality that values context, emotion, and action over the abstract external ethical rationality that dominates Western philosophical thinking. Although still a minority position that is marginalized among some philosophers, care ethics has evolved into interdisciplinary and international theories of care. Scholars in divergent fields have found care theory a robust means of understanding human interaction and imagining a better world. Care thinking has been applied to political, economic, aesthetic, and environmental realms. Participating in new approaches to viewing existential reality in relational, nonauthoritative, and postmodern ways, some scholars working in the emergent fields of performance philosophy (Thompson and Fisher 2019) and posthumanism (Bozalek 2016) have found connection to care theory. Thus, care ethics is growing in popularity and exploration at a time when the threat of neoliberal precarity is dramatically on the rise. The juxtaposition of care and precarity is both intellectually fascinating and morally compelling.

Definition is an important consideration when it comes to "care." There have been many evils historically wrought in the name of care, thus making distinctions important. Fiona Robinson, for example, describes how colonial encounters framed oppression in terms of paternalistic care: "When care is understood as benevolence, charity, or attention to the 'victims' or the 'vulnerable' in societies, an ethic of care could serve to reinforce existing patterns of domination and dependency within and among societies and at the global level" (2011, 165). Although the precise understanding of care varies by scholar (as witnessed among our contributors), the care addressed in this volume is generally understood as a practice of informed responsive actions on behalf of the one cared for and authentically aimed toward their growth and flourishing. Although "care" is a common term, informed responsive practices preclude a purely subjective understanding of care. In other words, just because someone labels what they are doing as care does not mean it aligns with the understanding of care theorists.

The most commonly quoted definition of care ethics is offered by Joan Tronto and Berenice Fisher:

> On the most general level, we suggest that caring be viewed as a species activity that includes everything that we do to maintain, continue, and repair our 'world' so that we can live in it as well as possible. That world includes our bodies, ourselves, and our environment, all of which we seek to interweave in a complex, life-sustaining web. (1991, 40)

This definition is true if a bit vague. One can see in this definition how care is in fundamental opposition to precarity, given that care aims for people to live "as well as possible." Caring does not neatly fit into traditional Western moral thinking and has alternatively been described as a virtue, duty, labor, practice, and/or disposition. Although "care" is a common and familiar term as a moral approach, it is profoundly complex such that it defies simple description. For example, Virginia Held offers a definition that addresses care as both practice and value:

> As a practice it shows us how to respond to needs and why we should. It builds trust and mutual concern and connectedness between persons. . . . Care is also a value. Caring persons and caring attitudes should be valued, and we can organize many evaluations of how persons are interrelated around a constellation of moral considerations associated with care or its absence. (2006, 42)

Some theorists are troubled by the lack of a clear and concise definition for care ethics. In *The Core of Care Ethics*, Stephanie Collins laments the lack of a "core slogan" (2015, 3) for care ethics in the manner that, for example, the happiness principle of creating the greatest amount of happiness for the greatest number of people is associated with utilitarianism. However, the quest for clarity should not come at the sacrifice of accounting for the complexity of human experience. In her exploration of care, Peta Bowden resisted the impulse to "produce a consensus, or to catch the essence of care, nor yet to unearth some hidden truth that shows that there has been implicit agreement all along about the meaning of caring." She advanced the claim "that it is precisely these kinds of aims that tend to lead understanding astray, and to cause us to overlook the complexity and diversity of the ethical possibilities of care" (1997, 183). Despite complexity, a working definition can serve as a guiding principle that clarifies a starting point for analysis. To that purpose, care can be characterized as responsive inquiry, empathy, and action. Care is always a response to the particularity of someone's circumstance that requires concrete knowledge of their situation, entailing imaginative connection and actions on behalf of their flourishing and growth. The circumstances of precarity constitute a state wherein a caring response is called for.

Another significant aspect of care theory is its feminist origins and its basis in women's experience. Feminist social theory gives care theory an attentiveness to the dynamics of power and privilege in society. Gender identity played a driving role in the development of care ethics. Although sometimes unfairly associated with gender essentialism, Carol Gilligan's (1982) originary work on care ethics highlighted masculine tendencies toward individuation and feminine propensities toward connection that initiate different dispositions toward caring relationships. In regard to today's neoliberal precarity, gender, and masculinity in particular, is not only still relevant but dramatically so. Certain manifestations of masculinity can be viewed as contributing factors to fomenting and maintaining unnecessary precarity. For example, "hypermasculinity" or "toxic masculinity" can participate in proclivities toward violence and war. Bonnie Mann argues that pervasive gender shaming creates a form of masculinity that fetishizes and fantasizes invulnerability, thereby creating a powerful sense of "sovereign manhood" that "disrupt critical cognition and moral concern" (2014, 114).

Under these conditions, going to battle and engaging the enemy are important aspects of displaying invulnerability and masculine sovereignty. Of course, war and violence are a powerful means of spreading precarity, whether it be the long-term physical and psychological impact on the combatants who survive, family members of combatants, or those affected by collateral damage and destruction of infrastructure. Neoliberalism is strongly implicated in modern warfare, as arming and rebuilding are lucrative pursuits supported by many industries. War is not the only expression of masculinity, but it is anathema to care. An intersectional analysis reveals how precarity can impact differently privileged identities in complex ways. For example, Susanne Y. P. Choi (2018) addresses how precarious work can emasculate some men, given that their gender identity is tied up with their vocation. Nevertheless, to ignore the role of some manifestations of masculinity in the fomenting of precarity is to participate in the modern tendency to ignore the damage wrought by certain forms of manliness.

A Care Movement?

Given the forces contributing to widespread neoliberal precarity on the one hand and the rise of relational scholarship on the other, perhaps the time is ripe for social need and the scholarly reconceptualization of morality to coalesce into a care movement. History has demonstrated that ideas can lead social and political change. Intellectual movements of empathy and inclusion have cooperated with social and political activism in the past to bring about lasting social transformation. Several authors of late have observed that despite countervailing narratives, and high-profile incidents of brutality, the long-term trajectory of history demonstrates that the world is becoming more empathetic and connected (Rifkin 2009) and less violent (Pinker 2012). However, the human capacity for care requires intellectual and physical support to reach fruition. There have been periods of time when rich ideas and willing individuals have helped spark human progress toward greater empathy and understanding. Two such periods of intellectually fueled social change in recent human history include the Progressive Era and the hippie movement.

In the late nineteenth and early twentieth centuries, Progressivism sparked local activism and policy change in an effort to improve society on the heels of free-market capitalism's industrialization, urbanization, and labor migration. Progressive Era enthusiasts held an abiding confidence that social well-being could be improved through intentional organizing and action as witnessed in the social settlement movement of the time.

The corollary intellectual movement in the Progressive Era was "pragmatism" as manifested in the work of John Dewey, William James, and Jane Addams, among others. These public philosophers emphasized the centrality of human experience, pluralism, democracy, education, and social improvement. Addams exemplified the spirit of cosmopolitan hope when she described democracy as social ethics:

> We are learning that a standard of social ethics is not attained by travelling a sequestered byway, but by mixing on the thronged and common road where all must turn out for one another, and at least see the size of one another's burdens. To follow the path of social morality results perforce in the temper if not the practice of the democratic spirit, for it implies that diversified human experiences and resultant sympathy which are the foundation and guarantee of Democracy. (2002 [1902], 7)

Although sometimes naïve and manifesting its own unconscious bias, the legacy of the Progressive Era includes lasting social and political reforms such as the Universal Declaration of Human Rights, the New Deal, environmental advances, business and economic reforms, and protections for women, children, and laborers, as well as advances by men and women of color. Ultimately, the social optimism was suppressed by the political realism of two world wars, but the influence of the period remains.

In the 1960s, another eruption of compassion and social improvement emerged in the countercultural movement that embraced peace and love as embodied in the hippie lifestyle. A reaction to unpopular and prolonged war, repressive social mores, environmental degradation, and materialism, the hippies rejected authority as manifested in age and formal social hierarchies. The countercultural movements also had an intellectual base in what became known as the New Left. Many academics such as Angela Davis, Frantz Fanon, and Herbert Marcuse influenced and were influenced by hippie ideas. For example, Marcuse (1969) described hippies as "the only viable social revolution" of the time in their rejection of materialism, war, and "competitive performances." The legacy of the 1960s includes advances in women's rights, civil rights, gay rights, and environmental advocacy. Many progressive efforts today can trace their genealogy to the social and intellectual environment of the 1960s.

One might argue that the widespread unnecessary neoliberal precarity signals that it is time for another international social movement infused with empathy and compassion that reconnects people separated by identity-based discrimination, disparate resources, and oppressive violence. The world seems weary of social and political approaches guided by abstract hierarchical moralities that can be co-opted by concentrated power whether financial, religious, or military. Too many people have become inured to fearmongering narratives, social fractionation, and violence. Care ethics reaffirms our interconnected humanity. Perhaps care represents "the only viable social revolution" in the face of today's neoliberal precarity. Accordingly, Carol Gilligan frames care ethics as a tool for a resistance movement: "A feminist ethic of care is integral to the struggle to release democracy from the grip of patriarchy . . . A feminist care ethic encourages the capacities that constitute our humanity and alerts us to the practices that put them at risk" (2011, 177).

Chapters in This Volume

Care Ethics in the Age of Precarity is made up of eleven chapters from social and political theorists representing Canada, Italy, Japan, the Netherlands, and the United States. All of the authors address how care theory can respond to precarity, especially the tenuous circumstances fomented by market-driven neoliberalism. However, each contributor takes a unique approach to the theme, often by defining terms in sometimes conflicting and sometimes congruent ways. A number of the chapters deepen current analysis of care and precarity by synthesizing and refining ideas such as vulnerability, dependency, empathy, and relational ontology. Other chapters introduce care thinking to new realms of intellectual discourse such as ethical temporality, multiverse political thinking, the role of eros, and feminist new materialist analysis by offering inquiry into the work of scholars not normally associated with care ethics.

The volume begins with one of the most prominent voices in care theory, philosopher Eva Feder Kittay, addressing precarity through the lens of her signature concern for ability. However, her chapter,

"Precarity, Precariousness, and Disability," extends the analysis of care and precarity beyond the differently abled to the plight of the disability worker. Kittay distinguishes between precarity and precariousness: "Precarity is a socioeconomic notion and is produced in a given political economy. Precariousness is an existential condition that we all face, but it is one that I believe is intensified by disability." She implicates neoliberalism for its role in valorizing citizenship marked by independence and productivity. For Kittay, the measure of a society is how it takes care of its vulnerable members—something for which the market is ill-equipped to accomplish, particularly for those who lack resources. Kittay claims that "at the heart of all social organization is the care and protection of dependent people. All else is built around this." Accordingly, care in the face of precarity is not a social nicety or peripheral political concern but rather central to a healthy, functioning society.

In the second chapter, "Neoliberalism, Moral Precarity, and the Crisis of Care," Sarah Clark Miller pushes us to rethink what a "crisis of care" really means. After addressing the hazards of neoliberalism, Miller explores what the commonly invoked moniker "crisis of care" entails. She draws attention to two interrelated and undertheorized aspects of a crisis of care: the moral precarity of caregivers and the relational harms of neoliberal capitalism. The former describes the tension many caregivers can find themselves in knowing what the one being cared for needs but being unable to provide it. Miller finds this kind of distress to be a moral injury inflicted by neoliberalism's approach to resource allocation. The real human beings providing care who are ensnared in this predicament experience exhaustion and burnout. However, Miller finds a second stage to the moral precarity of caregivers in the damage it does to caring relationships: "Two possible forms of relational harm can result from moral injury: harm to intrapersonal relationships, or the relationships we hold with ourselves, and harm to interpersonal relationships, represented in the connections we hold with others." Sometimes, it appears that care theory is running on at least two tracks: one personal and phenomenological and the second a critical political philosophy of care. Miller links them together in her interrogation of the meaning of a crisis of care. In the conclusion, she strikes a wary note regarding social reproduction. The more neoliberal values influence practices, the more widely inculcated is this trajectory: "The myriad ways neoliberalism exacerbates our moral precarity accumulate through the crisis of care until ultimately the very fabric of our interdependence is at stake." Care has always connoted more than normative adjudication, and Miller's cautionary tale signals how care is a necessary way of being in the face of forces that seek to divide and imperil society.

In "Vulnerability, Precarity, and the Ambivalent Interventions of Empathic Care," philosopher Vrinda Dalmiya also expresses concern that care theory is too often associated with vulnerability. Noting the international flow of care labor from the South to the North, Dalmiya's apprehension is geopolitical: "Care, grounded as it is in responses to an all-pervasive vulnerability, ends up talking past socioeconomically caused precarities." She draws upon Eva Kittay's notion of "secondary dependency" to address the precarity of those who care for the precarious. Dalmiya seeks an approach that bridges the political and the personal. Specifically, she offers "affective solidarity" that respects difference as an outgrowth of imaginative empathy that can cross borders to create political coalitions. Dalmiya is anything but romantic about the role of empathy. She cites empathetic failures, including examples of volunteer tourism, which reveal how challenging empathetic care is. Nevertheless, Dalmiya still contends that caring can be "politically transformative if its empathic moment triggers such entangled intersubjectivity." Dalmiya weaves a cautionary yet compelling argument for the central role of empathy in a political theory of care that enables solidarity to confront precarity.

For those new to the subject of precarity, Andries Baart provides a comprehensive overview of the topic in "Precariousness, Precarity, Precariat, Precarization and Social Redundancy: A Substantiated Map for the Ethics of Care." A pioneering Dutch philosopher of presence and medical ethics, Baart draws upon experiences in the Netherlands as well as international political movements to interrogate the lexicon of precarity and to offer a practical road map for care theorists. His provocative primary concern is that in the process of providing aid, caring social efforts "reproduce the process of precarization" through the normalization of precarious existence. Baart views the problem as pervasive, and he casts a wide net for his analysis: "Precarity pertains to much more than poverty, unemployment, bad housing, or unhealthy working conditions. Fundamentally, it is about pervasive uncertainty: you do not have any idea whether you will be able to survive until tomorrow." Baart provides the most systematic review of the precarity literature found among the chapters in this volume. He briefly overviews the works of Pierre Bourdieu, Robert Castel, Guy Standing, Oliver Marchart, Judith Butler, and Kathleen Millar. From this analysis, Baart acknowledges the contested nature of the term and draws together some common threads of understanding. Baart offers a "map" to demonstrate the forces and impact of late modernization. He makes an intriguing comparison between precarity and social redundancy—the notion that increasing numbers of us are unnecessary to the economy. Baart contends that both social phenomena have helped to spur the current round of populism witnessed around the world, and he contends that it is up to care theorists to describe how to disrupt the process of precarity production and reproduction he has suggested.

No one can escape the fragility of human life. Tragically, contributor Elena Pulcini passed away from COVID-related health issues while *Care Ethics in the Age of Precarity* was in production. She was an internationally known Italian care theorist and social philosopher who added a great deal of heart to the care ethics literature through her work on moral emotions. Her chapter, "Global Vulnerability: Why Take Care of Future Generations?" extends her impressive intellectual legacy. In the chapter, Pulcini takes up how care can address precarity by transcending the challenges of time and place. Pulcini notes the temporal dimension of precarity created by neoliberal globalization, given that much of precarity is worry about the future: the next meal, next month's rent, the lives our children will have, and so on. She finds all the existing normative approaches inadequate to the task in that they fail to take into account the moral subject and their motivation to act: "All of the major theories of justice—Rawls and neoliberalism, utilitarianism, and communitarianism—have hit a wall or failed outright to justify the obligation toward the future generations by proposing the same abstract and rationalistic assumptions." Pulcini reformulates the problem of caring for distant others by considering issues of vulnerability, debt, and reciprocity in ways that recenter ethics around the caring subject in order to understand what motivates action. She returns to the theme of empathy to argue that proximity is not necessary to trigger empathy. The relational ontology of care theory, which expands the notion beyond abstract normative considerations, is crucial for Pulcini. She elegantly concludes, "The strength of the ethics of care lies in it sinking its roots not in normative precepts or deontological imperatives but indeed in a form of life, in material and symbolic forms of organizing one's life and one's world." Pulcini will be missed as a scholar and as a friend.

Italian care theorist and scholar of pedagogy and medical research epistemology Luigina Mortari offers a prosaic chapter, "Care: The Primacy of Being," which continues the theme of viewing care ethics as more than a normative formula for moral adjudication but rather care as a way of being. Mortari claims that not only is care imperative for our existence, but it also structures who we are and what we do. She suggests that care "could be defined as a *fabric of being*." In an unconventional genealogy, Mortari turns to ancient philosophy to find that in *The Republic*, Plato suggested that philosophers were obliged to care for citizens in the art of living. Unfortunately, care has been largely overlooked in the history of philosophy until the present. Mortari seeks a natural language definition of care through the ontological reality of fragility and vulnerability. In interrogating these concepts, Mortari develops a threefold notion of care that responds to precarity as an "ontological necessity." For Mortari, "the practice of care is implemented in three ways: by procuring things to preserve life, by fostering being through the cultivation of each person's potentiality, and by healing the wounds each person has sustained both in body and in spirit." In Mortari's sweeping analysis, we find a notion of care for the precarious that is not dictated by external moral norms but rather that finds its foundation in our fundamental connection to our nature, making care a realization of our humanity.

The assumption thus far among all of the chapters in this volume, and for most considerations of precarity, is that it is a negative and uncomfortable position to be mitigated in society as much as possible. In "Deliberate Precarity? On the Relation between Care Ethics, Voluntary Precarity, and Voluntary Simplicity," Carlo Leget, a care ethics scholar and a leader in advancing care ethics research worldwide, provokes the reader to reframe conventional thinking about precarity by asking what can be learned about precarity from those who have intentionally chosen a precarious lifestyle. Leget explores examples of deliberate precarity from the thirteenth, twentieth, and twenty-first centuries, as well as current decisions by some to live with voluntary simplicity. Although recognizing that the earlier historical contexts were quite different from those of the present day, Leget finds a number of potential benefits from intentional precarity, including spiritual, epistemic, symbolic, instrumental, and transformative outcomes. Such acts and attributes can be "examples of a lifestyle that shines as a protest against . . . neoliberalism." In the final sections of the chapter, Leget analyzes the philosophy behind voluntary simplicity movements. He draws upon the work of German sociologist Hartmut Rosa to suggest that today's precarity points to a deeper issue than just caring for the needy in the acceleration and churning that markets cause when they seek more and more growth. Leget, through Rosa, claims that "neoliberalism, with all its perverse effects on caring relationships, is the wrong answer to a deeper and more fundamental problem. It is the wrong answer because it sustains the process of acceleration that turns the world we live in into a 'mute' world: a great heap of dead and meaningless raw material." Leget concludes by making it clear that voluntary precarity or simplicity is not intended as a mainstream lifestyle choice, but he does offer significant insights for how to care for one another without ignoring underlying causal dynamics.

In "Precarious Political Ontologies and the Ethics of Care," political scientist and feminist theorist Maggie FitzGerald also challenges the reader to think about care ethics and precarity differently through the nascent theoretical framework of the pluriverse. Although care theory is often associated with a relational ontology, FitzGerald describes a pluriverse approach as reframing political ontologies to "consist of the ongoing, shifting, dynamic, and (de)stabilizing practices and relations that bring worlds into existence." Accordingly, rather than understanding politics as a static competition of constituent values and interests, the concept of the pluriverse views political ontologies as enacted or performed and entangled with one another in a complex and changing social environment. FitzGerald suggests that care theory provides an effective means of engaging the political pluriverse. She employs an extended case study of the Māori people of New Zealand and their relationship to the Whanganui River to demonstrate the clash of political universes. For the Māori, the Whanganui River is a living entity. Their political universe came into conflict with that of the state, which considered the river a natural phenomenon instrumental to human needs. The Māori had to overcome the differences in political ontologies to have the Whanganui River given identity status in the law.

For FitzGerald, the Māori example epitomizes a marginalized political ontology. With this example as a backdrop, FitzGerald describes precarity as enhanced vulnerability, although the relationship between marginal and privileged political ontologies is not straightforward. She describes an interrelated entanglement: "Precarity, as developed here, highlights those worlds at the margins of the global political economy, specifically those that have been excluded, purposefully reshaped, devalued, and even erased, while also equally emphasizing that even apparently 'stable' or 'hegemonic' worlds are vulnerable and unstable, dependent upon marginalized worlds, and susceptible to falling precarious themselves." The responsive epistemic resources in care theory allow for a method of navigating the political pluriverse and the ever-present potential for precarity.

While FitzGerald innovatively pushes care theory into the contemporary discussions of political pluriverse, political scientist and theorist Sacha Ghandeharian provides another fresh approach to thinking about subjectivity within care theory in "Care Ethics and the Precarious Self: A Politics of Eros in a Neoliberal Age." Taking neoliberal presuppositions head on, Ghandeharian claims that a careful analysis of the relationship between care and desire or eros can "broaden our understanding of the relational and ethical self and its inescapable precariousness." For Ghandeharian, eros provides a robust understanding of subjectivity that is simultaneously a critique of neoliberalism. Drawing heavily upon Luce Irigaray's work on eros, and the notion that "our very being, as subjects, depends on a *becoming-between-two*" in a responsive, non-homogenizing way, Ghandeharian suggests that our fundamental relationality results in "self-inflicted precarity." He also turns to the work of Kelly Oliver who frames subjectivity as a "witnessing structure." Ghandeharian juxtaposes these relational understandings of subjectivity with the achievement subjectivity demanded by neoliberal thinking. Neoliberalism undermines the fundamental relationality of subjectivity by framing the subject relation as a matter of commodity; Ghandeharian views such commodification as doomed to failure. Engaging the writings of Byung-Chul Han to understand eros as motivating political care, Ghandeharian advances a key claim—that we meet precarity with precarity. Ultimately, Ghandeharian offers a novel approach to viewing care theory as an antidote for neoliberal thinking.

Continuing the theme of care theorists engaging in new and innovative political narratives witnessed in the previous two chapters, sociopolitical thinker, feminist philosopher, and qualitative researcher Emilie Dionne thrusts care ethics into contemporary posthumanities discussions in "Resisting Neoliberalism: A Feminist New Materialist Ethics of Care to Respond to Precarious World(s)." Extending the work of Karen Barad, Dionne frames feminist new materialism (FNM) as recentering analysis around matter that she describes as ontologically indeterminate. Ultimately, Dionne claims that FNM can expand care theory's ability to "participate in the work of healing, alleviating, or transforming precarity and its multifarious effects on people's lives." To accomplish this connection, Dionne begins by offering a lexicon for the field of FNM and, in particular, Barad's notion of agential matter, agential realism, and intra-action. She then utilizes Judith Butler and Isabell Lorey's conceptualization of precarity to contend that neoliberalism works to embody a precarious ontology: "when precariousness and precarity *matter* and come to stay through the effects of governmental precarization, they also become a self-sustaining and new ontology-making process that becomes ingrained and incredibly difficult to change or counteract." Dionne offers some concrete tools for care theorists by analyzing several extended illustrations of how neoliberalism foments precarity. Dionne finds hope in new feminist theories leveraging the liminality of care theory: "Care ethics is enriched by considering FNM's views of a world that is increasingly agential in light of its new, constantly increasingly, situation of shared, mutually entangled, and complexifying conditions of globalization, growing sickness, fragile ecological transformations, and the various insecurities that trouble us." Put crudely, in some ways, FNM puts another nail in the coffin of androcentric modernism as reflected in the messiness described in the above quote. From its origins in resisting the categories laid out by Lawrence Kohlberg in the Heinz Dilemma, care has eschewed traditional ethical frameworks. Perhaps Dionne has helped to show that new feminist thinking is providing an appropriate theoretical constellation from which care can reach its full potential.

The volume concludes with a more personal account of precarity and policy: "Precariousness, Precarity, and Gender-Care Politics in Japan" by feminist political theorist Yayo Okano. In an extended localized case study, Okano juxtaposes natural disasters in Japan, including typhoons and earthquakes (not to mention the Fukushima Daiichi Nuclear Power Plant disaster), with political policies that weaken social welfare but which are instigated under the guise of strengthening the nation. She wonders whether care ethics can provide any resources for resisting the precarity wrought by the policy changes. In the midst of recurring natural disasters, the country has also faced economic stagnation and turned to the market to fix its woes: "Because the structural reform launched in the mid-1990s adopted neoliberalist rhetoric, workers in Japan have been facing deregulation of labor conditions in order to pay the price necessary to stimulate the national economy." According to Okano, the result of these policies is that young people, women, and the less educated find themselves with more tenuous labor prospects. Further exacerbating the circumstances is that for the past decade, the government has diverted funds for building a stronger military defense, for example, by lowering corporate taxes and increasing consumption taxes. Furthermore, in the effort to build the Japanese army, government leaders used images of the vulnerable—women and children—to make the case that a strong army is needed to protect them. The irony of utilizing this justification is not lost on Okano: "Japan has been in a vicious circle of impoverishing people's welfare and, at the same time, heightening insecurity, anxiety, and precarity among people." Okano offers us an example of a destabilization witnessed repeatedly around the world and for which care becomes an act of resistance.

Note

1. As William Connolly (2012) remarks, "Perhaps the quickest way, then, to dramatize the difference between classical market liberalism and contemporary neoliberalism is to say that the former wanted the state to minimize interference with "natural" market processes as it purported to leave other parts of civil society to their own devices, while the latter campaigns to make the state, the media, schools, families, science, churches and the corporate estate be ordered around neoliberal principles of being."

Works Cited

Addams, Jane. 2002 [1902]. *Democracy and Social Ethics.* Urbana: University of Illinois Press.

Bowden, Peta. 1997. *Caring: Gender-Sensitive Ethics.* London: Routledge.

Bozalek, Vivienne. 2016. "The Political Ethics of Care and Feminist Posthuman Ethics: Contributions to Social Work." In *Values and Ethics in Social Work*, edited by Richard Hugman and Jan Carter, 80–96. London: Palgrave Macmillan.
Brown, Wendy. 2015. *Undoing the Demos: Neoliberalism's Stealth Revolution*. Brooklyn, N.Y.: Zone Books.
Brown, Wendy. 2019. *In the Ruins of Neoliberalism: The Rise of Antidemocratic Politics in the West*. New York: Columbia University Press.
Butler, Judith. 2010. *Frames of War: When Is Life Grievable?* London: Verso.
Choi, Susanne Y. P. 2018. "Masculinity and Precarity: Male Migrant Taxi Drivers in South China." *Work, Employment and Society* 32 (3): 493–508.
Collins, Stephanie. 2015. *The Core of Care Ethics*. London: Palgrave Macmillan.
Connolly, William. 2012. "Steps Toward an Ecology of Late Capitalism." *Theory and Event* 15 (1): n.p.
Davies, William. 2014. "Neoliberalism: A Bibliographic Review." *Theory, Culture and Society* 31 (7/8): 309–17.
Fisher, Berenice, and Joan C. Tronto. 1991. "Toward A Feminist Theory of Care." In *Circles of Care: Work and Identity in Women's Lives*, edited by Emily Abel and Margaret Nelson, 35–62. Albany: State University of New York Press.
Fraser, Nancy, and Rahel Jaeggi. 2018. *Capitalism: A Conversation in Critical Theory*. Edited by Brian Milstein. Cambridge: Polity.
Gilligan, Carol. 1982. *In a Different Voice: Psychological Theory and Women's Development*. Cambridge, Mass.: Harvard University Press.
Gilligan, Carol. 2011. *Joining the Resistance*. Cambridge: Polity.
Held, Virginia. 2006. *The Ethics of Care: Personal, Political, and Global*. Oxford: Oxford University Press.
Laugier, Sandra. 2015. "The Ethics of Care as a Politics of the Ordinary." *New Literary History* 46 (2): 217–40.
Lorey, Isabell. 2015. *State of Insecurity: Government of the Precarious*. Brooklyn, N.Y.: Verso.
Mann, Bonnie. 2014. *Sovereign Masculinity: Gender Lessons from the War on Terror*. New York: Oxford University Press.
Marcuse, Henry. 1969. An essay on liberation. https://www.marxists.org/reference/archive/marcuse/works/1969/essay-liberation.htm.
Pinker, Steven. 2012. *The Better Angels of Our Nature: Why Violence Has Declined*. New York: Penguin.
Rifkin, Jeremy. 2009. *The Empathic Civilization: The Race to Global Consciousness in a World in Crisis*. New York: Jeremy P. Tarcher/Penguin.
Robinson, Fiona. 2011. *The Ethics of Care: A Human Approach to Human Security*. Philadelphia, Pa.: Temple University Press.
Thompson, James, and Amanda Stuart Fisher, eds. 2019. *Performing Care: New Perspectives on Socially Engaged Performance*. Manchester, UK: University of Manchester Press.

CHAPTER 1

Precarity, Precariousness, and Disability

EVA FEDER KITTAY

The neoliberal political economy promotes the liberal ideal of the citizen and worker as independent and self-sufficient. While liberalism can, at least in theory, accommodate a more or less generous support system for those who must depend on another's care, neoliberalism drains those systems, leaving puny and punitive policies in its place. Those who cannot "measure up," which many of us cannot at some time in our lives, are denigrated as dependents and, with the possible exception of the very young, are subject to stigma and shame. The disabled person who depends on another's care and the caregiver exist in an economic, social, and political order that relegates "inevitable dependencies"[1] to the private domain and makes each of us carry what I will call the "burdens of (inevitable) dependencies" individually rather than collectively. This state of affairs is heightened in neoliberal political economies.

While neoliberalism has created a situation where precarity characterizes a vast class of workers, precarity has always been the condition of the dependency worker who does hands-on care for a dependent or supports a dependent person in some essential ways. The precarity of the care worker arguably has ill effects on those who depend on their care.

With the rise of neoliberalism and the advent of the disability movement, disabled people, who were one class of adults who were previously exempted from the ideal of self-sufficiency, are now expected to be "independent and productive." Although the advocates for disability will often adopt the same ideal, the undercutting of social supports that neoliberalism ushered in has turned that aspiration into a condition of precarity for the disabled person—one especially damaging, given a feature of disability that I refer to as "precariousness."

Vrinda Dalmiya observes: "Bodies are associated with dependency on the world and on others. This 'opening up' to the outside introduces fragility on multiple registers."[2] It is the fragility and dependency of the body, especially when it is impaired in ways that come to be considered a "disability," and the fragility of those who care for dependent bodies in ways that make them derivatively dependent, that constitute the point of intersection. If our thinking starts from the fragile and dependent body, we can remark that as it "opens up to the outside," the extent to which a disabled person experiences her well-being and her life as precariousness very much turns on the precarity of the caregiver.

In this chapter, I discuss the relationship between the precarity of dependency workers and the precariousness of living with a disability. Precarity is a socioeconomic notion and is produced in a given political economy. Precariousness is an existential condition that we all face, but it is one that I believe is intensified by disability. The approach I adopt, as I explain later in the chapter, is shaped by a commitment to "social-welfare feminism"—a feminism focused on supporting women, the great bulk of care workers, in their dependency work, but in turn also aspiring to promote conditions that avoid turning the precariousness of disability and inevitable dependencies into an added precarity for the disabled person.

There are two important links between the precariousness of disability and the precarity of care workers. The first, I claim, has to do with the inadequate conceptualization of dependence. A better conceptualization is provided by an ethic of care. The second, I argue, involves the failure of providing adequate support, primarily public support, which is key to undoing an ever-tightening knot between precarity and precariousness. Here again, an ethic of care that becomes a politics of care ethics can help us understand the sort of approach to public support that is required.

The argument is that the precariousness that characterizes disabled life, along with the precarity of the care worker, turns the precariousness of disability into an added form of parity for the disabled person.

This is a condition that is made worse by the withdrawal of support and exploitation by neoliberalism of the ideology of the worthy citizen as productive and independent. Rather than effectively supporting the aspiration of those disabled people who are able to be integrated into productive labor, the withdrawal of care support undermines those aspirations, and it makes life still more precarious for those for whom the ideal is meaningless.

Until we have a system of justice that is designed to take dependency seriously, the already precarious well-being of disabled people will be made that much more precarious by the precarity that caregivers face. A conception of justice that takes dependency seriously will be one that takes an ethic of care to be a—if not the—central moral theory directing our conception of what is just. I will not be able to go into all these ideas with the depth of consideration they deserve, but I will try to lay down the lines of the argument. Turning to an ethic of care reveals not only how problematic the developments of neoliberalism are, but also what placing care at the center of society can contribute to ameliorating the situation for disabled people and caregivers alike. The argument will proceed in five steps, each developed in a separate section of the chapter.

In the first section, I defend the view that while the life of a disabled person is not inherently a life with lesser well-being, it is one that is precarious in ways, or to the extent that others are not. Furthermore, I make the case that precariousness in general is not necessarily opposed to a good level of well-being. Precarity, on the other hand, insofar as it is associated with a felt level of insecurity, is more directly tied to a diminished level of well-being. In the second section, I show how the precariousness of disabled people can (though it need not) slip into a precarity that is inevitably disadvantageous.

Then, in the third section, I shift to the precarity of care workers: those tasked with assisting a disabled person, whether in the form of family members, care workers in aggregate settings, or personal assistants. The condition of care workers, I show, epitomizes the situation of what Guy Standing calls the precariat. In the fourth section, I consider how the precarity of the care worker contributes to creating precarity in the lives of the disabled. Furthermore, the precariousness of the disabled, when coupled with the assumption that the life of a disabled person has lesser well-being, can be used to justify the precarity of the caregiver and the disabled alike. Finally, in the fifth section, I consider the implications of the argument for a social and political order to which we should aspire where precariousness does not result in or aggravate precarity.

Before embarking on the argument, it is important to note that I am not a member of the precariat. Nor am I a disabled person. I have, however, been a caregiver to a disabled family member. Yet, I have been more privileged than most caregivers of disabled family members and more advantaged than most paid caregivers. I have employed many caregivers for my daughter and have come to know the many caregivers who have assisted my daughter who have been employed by the agency that is now responsible for her daily care. I have a deep relationship with a disabled person: my now adult daughter. My daughter is not a member of the precariat either, at least not strictly speaking. This is largely because she is not properly a member of a workforce in any meaningful sense. Because of her very significant cognitive as well as physical disabilities, she is not representative of the adult disabled person who may wish to live independently.

Her care is now largely supported by the government and by our own financial contributions. And while my own relationship to precarity is at an arm's length, I have witnessed the precarity of the many caregivers who have helped my daughter live the good life she has been privileged to live. So, while some of what I have to say comes from firsthand knowledge, the rest is second hand or the product of research. I signal these facts because I am so enmeshed in my life with my daughter that I may well fail to appreciate very different experiences with disability, and I welcome correctives to my own relatively narrow horizon. Now to consider the above points one by one.

Disability and Precariousness

How we define disability reflects the ways in which we think of disability and the individuals we include among the disabled. Let us accept that disability is a constructed concept: the construction differs relative to the time, place, and purpose for which it is employed. We can also accept that the individuals who come to be included under the concept may belong to groups that bear only a family resemblance to one another. Disabilities may be cognitive, psychological, physical, or sensory, and each of these may be of various sorts and degrees. Some disabilities are congenital; others are acquired or the consequence of old age. Some impairments are lifelong, others affect us only in one period of our lives. Others still are episodic disabling. Some are invisible; others are strikingly visible. Disability is found in all races, among people of different sexual and gendered lives. These intersections will result in different outcomes for people with similar disabilities. The impact on functioning is wildly different, though most always inflected by other social and economic standing. Still most all disabled people meet stigma and discrimination and face a battle to make the world more accommodating to their bodies and minds.

Most disabled people also encounter bodily, economic, and social situations that make their attainment of a good life more *precarious*. Note that I did not say that they are less likely to have a good life. To say that the attainment of a good life is more precarious is just to say that the hold on having a good life is more tenuous. I will explain how and why these are two things different. But first let me address the question of why I say that a disabled life is not a life of lesser well-being, or at least is not a life of lesser well-being because of the disability itself, for this is not the received wisdom.

The claim, made and argued for by many disabled people, is that the "dis" in disability, unlike what some believe, is not that the disabled have lesser well-being or lesser capacity for well-being when compared to another person in a comparable situation (same family background, culture, financial security, race, gender, social status, profession, etc.). That is, the "dis" does not or should not be taken to stand for the idea that disability is a "bad" difference.[3] This is not to say that having a disability in certain circumstances and for certain people might not be bad for them, but rather that disability as such is not something that is inherently bad.

Proponents of what has become known as the social model of disability claim that the difference that exists in the body or mind of a disabled person is disadvantageous only when there is a lack of fit between the body and the environment. That disability, as opposed to the impairment in the body, is a social factor often caused by built physical environment that can, if the political will is there, be built differently. Sometimes, the environment needs to be taken in a broader sense than the merely physical, as the obstacles that disable may be social: discrimination, neglect of needs and important services, social stigma, and an intentional exclusion from participation in normal life, that is, the social technologies that fail to accommodate disabled people.

Elizabeth Barnes (2016) goes still further, arguing that even though people with disabilities have to endure the disadvantages society imposes, even these social "bads" do not necessitate considering life with a disability a lesser life. If they were the defining feature of a disability identity, then the idea of disability pride would make little sense. The point becomes clearer using the analogy of the African American struggle.

When African Americans proudly proclaimed that "Black is beautiful," they made it clear that the problem with being Black in America was not the color of one's skin but the discrimination and lack of rights. But that is not what made blackness what it is. The blackness of one's skin was more than skin deep: there was a culture, a heritage, certain values, and ways of life that came along with being American of African descent, and this was to be celebrated.

In a similar fashion, these disabled activists, scholars, and just ordinary folk want to say that there is a pride to be taken in one's disability—that blindness or deafness or being a wheelchair user will continue to define the person partially, even if society is no longer discriminating, and that there is something positive about one's identity as a disabled person (or as being a person with a particular disability). This is a difficult claim to accept from the "horizon of ability" where disability looks only like a lack.

Stephen Kuusisto, a blind writer and poet, is happy to disabuse us of that mistake. He writes:

> There are landscapes inside us. Introverts know it. Artists see them. When you're blind these lands are persistent and strange: where you've been and where you might go become fanciful. I see the meadow where a little girl played a flute for me when I was four years old. We were in Finland. I was the blind kid who saw only colors and shapes. The meadow was the girl's music; music was sky. I whirled around birches in buttercup light. Whenever I hear a penny whistle I think of yellow air and a yellow girl. Many of my blind friends report the same thing: the spaces before us and the spaces behind are rich and alive within. We navigate by memory and creativity. (1998, 162)

Although there is a disadvantage to being disabled in an ableist society, writings such as these give those who are not disabled at the moment an insight into why people speak of disability pride.

I have been quite convinced by writers with disabilities who propound this view, and as the mother of a person with a disability, I have seen that people with disabilities are able to achieve a level of well-being that is commensurate with those who are not disabled. In other words, a disabled life is not inherently a lesser life in terms of well-being or goodness, unless perhaps one builds in having certain capacities as an essential feature of well-being or a good life. Such definitional rigging, however, is unwarranted if we are to believe the many testimonials and biographies of disabled people. And not to believe them is a striking example of epistemic, and in particular testimonial, injustice.

So, if it is not the functional limitations or even the disadvantage of living in an ableist society, what is the "dis" in disability? I suggest that the "dis," if it is justifiable at all as a statement about something negative about disability, resides in the various forms of precariousness that people with disability face. Precariousness, while a feature of all human life, is still more present in the life of a disabled person. But if one's well-being is precarious, it need not be lesser simply because the well-being is more precarious. How so?

It is easy enough to see that (1) having a good life and (2) having a life in which that goodness is precarious are entirely compatible. We can simply note that (a) many people can claim to have good lives, that is, a life of well-being, and (b) *everyone's* life is precarious (in ways I will elaborate below). If (1) and (2) were incompatible, then no one could claim to have a good life. Might we nevertheless say that if one life is more precarious than another, then the more precarious life will have a *lower* level of well-being? So, if disabled people live more precarious lives than those who are not disabled, then disabled people live lives of lesser well-being. To show that this is false, we have to dig deeper to see how precariousness affects well-being, if it does so at all.

Consider some of the ways that lives are precarious. Our bodies are frail and vulnerable. No matter our age, health, and good lifestyle choices, we all are subject to disease, accidents, or random acts of violence: we can be struck down by some accidental wind that throws a killing tree branch down on us or receive a fatal blow from a reckless driver. Furthermore, our well-being is dependent on others: most of us do not hunt, fish, or grow our own food and thus are dependent on food producers, markets, and so forth.

Similarly, we are dependent on others to assure that our air is breathable and our water drinkable. Not only are we vulnerable insofar as the skin on our bodies extends and dependent on others for the necessities of food, clean air, and drinkable water, we are also vulnerable in our attachments: the people we love, the people we depend upon, the people who depend on us, and the people we care about. We can be torn from or lose any of them, and we can feel the loss or hurt they may feel if they lose us.

All these contingencies remind us that no matter how well someone is protected—by other people, by wealth, by privilege, by good health, by a strong physique—everyone is susceptible to having that good life, that sense of well-being, snatched from them. These irrefutable facts of human life are like the floor we stand on; we are not aware of it until it is no longer beneath our feet. As these are always unwelcome thoughts, we delude ourselves into thinking that we are much more safe and secure in our life, our loves, and our well-being than we truly are.

But does all that unavoidable precariousness reduce the level of our well-being? Consider the procurement of food. In a modern industrial society, most of us do not grow our own food, nor do we process it. We are nonetheless able to procure that food, as long as we are not totally impoverished. Most of us, if we are not very young children, do not depend on others to put that food in our mouths or bellies. We are part of a highly interdependent web of food production and food ingestion. There are the farmers, distributors, and retailers. There are those who enable us to purchase or otherwise attain the food. Then, there are those who convert the raw products into edible food. Should there be a disruption, our access to food will endanger our well-being and even our lives. Yet, as long as we are secure in our expectation that food will make its way to our table, we do not suffer a lower quality of life if we purchase the food than if we had grown it ourselves. (In fact, we may have a higher quality of life because our dependence on another to grow the food allows us to do other things we might value.)

There are, however, significant numbers of people other than infants who do suffer a lower quality of life—people who are very ill, or have certain sorts of disabilities, or who have grown very frail in old age—and they may not be able to procure, process, or even ingest food without another's aid. Must their life be of a lower quality? Once again, not if we have good reason to feel secure in our expectation that those we depend on will come through.

Situations may look precarious when we consider all the possibilities that can go wrong. Still, that precariousness need not affect our quality of life, again, as long as we have reason to feel relatively secure that we can get what we need. *Precariousness reduces well-being when that precariousness is not countered with a security that we can either procure or receive from another what we need.* Security, however, is always relative security.

In disability, we encounter more occasions where we face the possibility of losing the form of well-being we have achieved or encounter more obstacles as we strive for a good life. We may need a personal assistant, and we can be at the mercy of the state to provide the means to hire one. A shift in the political winds and the financing for personal assistants is cut. We may require technologies that are more fine-tuned to our particular needs than those that most people use, and they may be more essential to our ability to participate in society. Technologies, no less than people, can fail or disappoint and so incapacitate us.

Our bodies may fail us more easily, given medical frailties that are at times associated with certain disabilities. We may lack means to communicate our particular pains and sensations so that by the time others notice, we are in fact very ill. (This is something my daughter Sesha who is disabled in a number of ways has to cope with.) Because of disability, we may be more prone to bodily failures that are life-threatening, more dependent on medical interventions, more exposed to social stigma, and more in danger of being excluded from social, economic, or political participation. *Yet, once again, such precariousness, when coupled with reasonable expectations that we can be secure in avoiding the harms they entail, need not affect our quality of life.* Therefore, even if disability can make one's hold on well-being more precarious, the added precariousness does not necessitate a lower level of well-being.

Someone may retort, "But if you think a disabled life is more precarious than a nondisabled life, and since being precarious, being insecure, is not a good thing, there is at least one measure by which a disabled life is inherently a worst life." But this is as incorrect. A point too often overlooked is that the *richer* our life is, the more people who are precious to us and thus make our life better, the more precarious is our hold on the goodness of that life (Wolfe 2016). Well-being is one thing. Precariousness is another.

What, then, are some of the implications of the claim that the "dis" in disability is the heightened precariousness of a disabled life? What will it allow us to say? It allows us to claim that the precariousness of a disabled life will be experienced as something bad just when the disability makes important things we depend on undependable. While we acknowledge that even in a world without ableism, not all that is undependable can be vanquished, there is still no reason to think that acknowledging the precariousness of disability confirms the view that disability is a "bad" difference.

Now, if we agree that disability is not inherently a bad difference, then we can insist that disability should not be used to justify infanticide, lesser medical treatment, or any other treatment based on the assumption that a disabled person's life must have diminished well-being.

Furthermore, to speak of precariousness of disability as compatible with a good level of well-being helps to solve a puzzle—one often called the paradox of disability—namely, that those with disabilities experience no difference in the level of well-being when compared to those without a disability. If it is not the level of well-being that is impacted by disability, but rather the precariousness of that achievement, then the conundrum is resolved.

This is because, as I mentioned above, we recognize that we do not walk around with a present consciousness of the precariousness of life. Just as we can know enough about quantum mechanics to realize the illusory nature of solidity, we still do not worry about the next step we take. We feel reasonably sure our foot will land on the ground. Likewise, the knowledge that life and limb are always vulnerable to destruction, decay, and injury rarely paralyzes us. The additional precariousness of disability similarly recedes from the consciousness of disabled people. People with mechanical wheelchairs do not utilize this equipment with the constant fear and expectation that the chair will fail and breakdown. It is something to consider when taking the vehicle on unknown terrain, just as we may worry about breaking a limb when we go on difficult hiking trails or worry about losing our lives when we go to war. But most of the time, those things that are precarious in our lives do not have an impact on our happiness or even on most of our choices in life. The same is true irrespective of whether we are disabled.

Finally, understanding that the "dis" in disability is due to a precariousness that need not diminish our well-being prompts us to ask under what conditions does this precariousness turn into an insecurity that blights our ability to flourish? Attention to precarity helps provide a way to approach this question. While precariousness is compatible with a good life, the same cannot be said about precarity. Precarity has a subjective component; at the forefront of the mind, it is experienced as insecurity. Our precariousness need not be experienced as insecurity, that is, until we find ourselves at the edge of a cliff. That is to say, the precariousness of disability can slide into precarity.

Precarity and Disability

Precarity is perhaps most closely associated with labor and economic insecurity. Millar (2017) identifies three theorists who, she says, represent three distinct meanings of the term. For Bourdieu, precarity is a labor condition; for Guy Standing, it is a class category; and for Judith Butler, it is an ontological experience. For the moment, we will bracket Butler's use. The many forms of precariousness that disabled people face all have as a predictable consequence the enforced poverty and lack of employment that characterizes disability today.

One can associate the two different uses of the term "precarity" with the two prominent models of disability, each of which plays a role in the different forms of legislation pertaining to disability that we find in the United States. Precarity as a characterization of a labor condition, or more precisely an unemployment condition, aligns with the medical model of disability that is utilized in disability policies known as Social Security Disability Insurance (SSDI) and Supplement Security Income (SSI). The idea of precarity as a condition of a class is operative in the social model of disability that undergirds the American for Disabilities Act (ADA) and the Individuals with Disabilities Education Act (IDEA).

The first set of policy provisions understands disability as a medical condition, and the criteria for claiming the entitlements that the policy provides for are medical. It is an individualistic model, and the government intervenes only to ensure that a person with a disability is not made abjectly poor by virtue of the disability. Thus, under SSDI or SSI, a person qualifies for benefits only if the individual meets the medical criteria certifying that the person has a disabling condition, if the disability has a duration of twelve months or more, and if the disability prevents a person from working and earning an income. The remedial response is to provide some cash support, which falls far short of replacement income and, in the case of SSI, is means tested.

On the other hand, the ADA and the IDEA were formulated on a social model, which conceives of disability less as a feature of the body and more as a feature of socially constructed obstacles that prevent the person from working or otherwise participating fully in society. Its remedial response is to make the workplace, the educational environment, and other public spaces accessible to the disabled person, and to make accommodations that enable the disabled person to participate fully in social, political, and economic life.

Notice the direct conflict between these different government policies. While SSI and SSDI require that people get their bone fides as disabled people by demonstrating that they are *incapable of working* (for medical reasons) and therefore in need of assistance, the ADA requires that a person who has received a diagnosis that qualifies them as disabled to receive the accommodations that will *enable them to work*. If a person is disabled, they can *either* receive supplemental income under SSDI or SSI or make demands in accord with the ADA that the working (or social) conditions be altered in ways that accommodate the disability. When one hears government officials complain about the growing numbers of "disabled," they are generally referring to disability in the SSDI or SSI sense not in the ADA sense (although there is significant griping about needing to make accommodations as well; Chana Joffe-Walt 2013a, 2013b).

However, following Guy Standing as speaking of precarity as a new class, the precariat, his discussion of people with disabilities (whom he takes to be members of the precariat) is oddly conceived, or better, it is oddly confused. He writes:

> The notion of "the disabled" is unfortunate. . . . In today's electronically charged world of instant diagnosis and communication, it is easier to identify and categorise an individual's impairment and to tag that

> person for eternity. This means many more are sized up for classification, for treatment or for neglect. (2011, 86–87)

As we have just pointed out, many people with disabilities do not find "the notion of 'the disabled'" unfortunate. What is unfortunate is the discrimination.

Standing goes on to say:

> This is how disability and the precariat come together. . . . In labour market terms, they [the state] have institutionalised quota systems, specialised workplaces, anti-discrimination laws, equal opportunity workplace amendments and so on. And they have increasingly tried to sift out the deserving poor. In the 1980s, many countries resorted to incapacity benefits, . . . to move people from unemployment to being out of the labour force altogether. By the beginning of the twenty-first century, governments were looking at the mounting benefit bills with sceptical fiscal eyes and set out to reduce them by re-medicalising disability, by seeking to make more of the disabled "employable" and by pushing them into jobs. Many joined the precariat by the side door. (2011, 87)

Standing throws specialized workshops, anti-discrimination laws, and equal opportunity workplace amendments, medicalizing disability and seeking to make more disabled people "employable," into a single cart, then designates them all as "side doors to the precariat. Standing conflates disability as a condition (sometimes temporary) that prevents one from "gainful employment" and disability that calls for modifications of the physical and social world to allow for the inclusion of people with disabilities. The first is often associated with pain and tragedy, with stigma and shame. The other is a political stance that rejects the tragic view of disability, eschews stigma and shame, and encourages disability pride. The first view leaves the putatively disabled person open not only to pity but also to suspicion, given they make claims for cash stipends and medical/therapeutic services. Disabled people viewed in this light are subject to all sorts of questions. Are they really unable to take a job? Are they faking it because they don't want to work? Are they poor enough to qualify to receive handouts from the public coffers? Are they really among the "*deserving* poor?" Being the object of such wariness induces a kind of precarity on the subject of the mistrust: the precarity of the marginalized who live on a pittance and who cannot be full participants in the social and economic life of their society.

The second view, which regards disability as a misfit between one's environment and one's body, requires a variety of responses, depending on how that misfit comes about and remains in place. Disability on this model fits better with the notion of class: the struggles of disabled people to change their condition are analogous to civil rights and political struggles. The claims of disabled people may still raise misgivings, but this is because their demands impose demands on employers, educators, restauranteurs, realtors, and others to alter their environments, make exceptions, and give special consideration when such accommodations are reasonable. Treating disability in this fashion should remove the precarity that comes with worries about being the deserving poor. Unfortunately, this view of disability still struggles to take hold, and it too requires policing the boundaries between the "truly disabled" and those who are faking it to receive the benefits of "special treatment." The precarity here comes more from outright discrimination and less from the tragic, but suspicious, view that characterizes the first kind.

Although both positions can leave the disabled person squarely among the precariat, the first view asks whether they are pitiful enough to be treated specially. In a world in which this view of disability takes hold, the lives of the disabled are precarious, and that precariousness inevitably translates into precarity in political and economic life. In contrast, the second view acknowledges that not only is disability a construct—a response of an ableist society to certain impairments—but also that ability itself is no less a construct (Reynolds, forthcoming, 2018). Both are based on a relationship that holds between a "majority body" and the natural and social world in which it exists, rather than in the impairments or prowess of a body. Vary the natural environment or the social world in relevant ways and our "able" person is disabled. On this view, where accommodation, invention, and a relaxation of constrictive norms is the appropriate response to disability, there is no inevitable pairing of the disabled and the precariat: precariousness and precarity come apart. Yet, this view also misses something important.

The many forms of precariousness that disabled people face all have as a predictable consequence the enforced poverty and lack of employment that characterizes disability today. The ADA with its civil rights approach to disability has been disappointing in this respect. According to an NPR report aired in July 2015:

> If you have a disability in the U.S., you're twice as likely to be poor as someone without a disability. You're also far more likely to be unemployed. And that gap has widened in the 25 years since the landmark Americans with Disabilities Act was enacted. (Fessler 2015)

The year 2015 was only seven years after the Great Recession, and most working Americans were still recovering from the economic backslide it created. It may be that the widening of the gap between the employment status of the disabled and the nondisabled has been partially due to this wide economic failure.[4] Yet, the widening of the gap also demonstrates how the disabled are particularly prone to precarity: prejudice (which is not yet undone by the ADA) combined with the various forms of precariousness that disabled people already face make the disabled the poster children for job insecurity.

The portrait of Emeka Nnaka, a former semipro football player from Tulsa, Oklahoma, who broke his neck making a tackle, illustrates how easily employment opportunities are frustrated and how the only options available are low paid, part-time, and insecure. Nnaka recently was able to get an accessible van to transport him to work. Prior to that, Nnaka said, "I'd spend about three hours in transportation daily when I was riding the lift. So, think about three hours out of your day in which you're not doing anything" (Fessler 2015).

But even with the van, the handicapped parking space was too narrow for the ramp to unload his wheelchair, the front door of his employer had no button to push the door open, the elevator was too narrow for him to turn around to push the button of his floor . . . and this was an employment office specializing in getting jobs for disabled people. As long as the ability to be employed is frustrated by things that are such small inconveniences for others, the free movement and true inclusion of people with disabilities remains a utopian fantasy.

Furthermore, some supports that are in place may be counterproductive—a direct consequence of the competing conceptions of disability that inform different policies. Neither set of policies is adequate in itself, and both together can augment the problems with each of them rather than complement the deficiencies of the other. Michael Morris, Executive Director of the National Disability Institute in Washington, D.C., remarks that if recipients of federal disability payments save more than $2,000, they risk losing their benefits, including medical care. Morris says, "The decision becomes, 'Wow, I think I'm going to just stay put where I am.' Which is the equivalent of a life sentence of poverty" (quoted in Fessler 2015). Still worse, because the ADA is in place, many will think that there is no longer a problem—legally, obstacles have been removed. It appears, then, that those who are disabled who cannot find a way out of the precariat are themselves failures in the modern economy. The fault redounds to them. Civil rights alone do not take the precarity out of precariousness. And the political struggle needs to be broader than the rights of disabled people. The missing part of the story is the caregiver and the role of care or, if you will, the promotion of an ethic of care as integral to an adequate conception of justice.

Precariousness of Disabled People as Derived from Precarity of Caregivers

We have pointed out that the precariousness faced by people with disabilities (like the precariousness faced by all) comes in many forms. The first form that comes to mind when able people think of disability is failure of the body, and one cannot deny that many people with disabilities have impairments that makes their health more precarious or which subject them to hazards that people without these impairments may more easily avoid. Many hazards can be minimized, and some eliminated, if the world we live in is attuned to what such hazards might be and appropriate accommodations or adjustments are made. To site a common example, where traffic is controlled by visual signals only, crossing a street presents a special hazard if your sight is impaired. If audio is used as well, the hazard is reduced. But the precariousness of disability also comes from an erratic adherence to good practices. Maneuvering a wheelchair up and down curbs makes moving along sidewalks more hazardous to wheelchair users. Curb cuts help alleviate such concerns. However, once curb cuts are widely available, encouraging people in wheelchairs to venture out, one can easily happen upon just that one street where these accommodations have not been made. Then, an entire day can be spoiled by something as monumental as a serious accident or as irritating as a missed appointment.

Health issues loom large in the lives of people with certain disabilities. Someone with epilepsy, for instance, can wind up in hospital more easily than most with life-threatening aspiration pneumonia. Worse still, once the person with significant disabilities gets treatment, she may find lax medical attention by providers who wonder if aggressive treatment is "worth it," given the disability. Ableism in a profession meant to return people to full health and full functioning is an occupational hazard, making every illness, irrespective of whether it is related to their specific disability, that much more precarious for the disabled person. Insofar as these forms of precariousness impact a person's economic position, they can bring the disabled person face to face with precarity.

We have already mentioned the precariousness that comes from dependence on technologies critical to a disabled person's well-being. We saw the importance of the van in the life of Emeka Nnaka. But for many, dependence on others to assist with matters of daily life is a sine qua non. The folks who step in with this assistance are the care workers, personal assistants, or dependency workers of some sort. But for many disabled people, their ability to function, to thrive, and even to survive will depend on a dependency worker and their availability, cost, competence, reliability, considerateness, adherence to the rights of disabled people, and so forth. Unpaid dependency workers might be family members or sometimes friends. Paid dependency workers might be home health aides, babysitters for children, state or private employed personal assistants, or care workers in aggregate settings. This list is not exhaustive.

At the outset, we mentioned three forms of precarity and said that we would hold in abeyance that sense that is most closely associated with an ontological condition. It is time we consider this aspect of precariousness and precarity. Both the precariousness associated with bodily frailty and the precariousness that comes from our dependence on others are a part of our ontological precariousness. Judith Butler holds that as an ontological status, we are all equally precarious, while precarity is not evenly distributed. But if I am right to say that in disability we are in a state of added precariousness, then Butler is wrong. Precariousness, no less than precarity, is not evenly distributed, even if we are all in a state of precariousness, all vulnerable to precarity, and to joining the precariat.

Nowhere is this clearer than in the precariousness we face because we are dependent on others. When we speak of the dependence we have on others for care, it is clear that this relational aspect is a subset of the precariousness that is simply a part that we all face, given our inevitable dependence, our inextricable interdependence, and the inexorable need human beings have for deep and meaningful connections with others. Such connections, if lost, are a source of profound sorrow and profoundly impact on our well-being. And yet, disabled people (along with others who are inevitably dependent) have an added level of precariousness, and those who are inevitably dependent are still more vulnerable to precarity because their ability to have an acceptable level of well-being is tied to the precarity faced by care workers.

Dependency workers are often the bulwark between people with disabilities and the precariousness of disability that can come from socioeconomic status, broader political conditions, or heightened bodily vulnerabilities. In other work, I have spoken of dependency workers as derivatively dependent. They become dependent when, in meeting the needs of others, they require others to help them meet their own needs. In a somewhat analogous fashion, we can say that the precariousness of disability is kept at bay, often to the extent that dependency workers are themselves secure in their ability both to do their work and to have their needs met. Perhaps we should say that the added precariousness of disability is, in part, at least a derived precariousness—derived from the precarity of the dependency workers who answer to their needs and wants.

Dependency Workers as Paradigmatic Members of the Precariat

Dependency workers are in many ways paradigmatic of those who find themselves in the precariat. This is true of both dependency workers who are paid caregivers and those who are familial dependency workers. Who are the dependency workers? Paid dependency workers include home health aides, nannies, personal assistances, and hands-on care workers in residential settings. For the most part, these are women, people of color, members of minority ethnic groups, and immigrants or migrants. Nine out of ten of all home care workers are women, whose median age is forty-five. People of color make up half of all home care workers, although people of color are only a quarter of the total U.S. workforce. More than one-quarter are immigrants, and 90 percent are U.S. citizens. (These figures do not include those in the gray economy, who do not pay taxes and receive no social security.) More than half have no formal education past high school (PHI 2015).

Most dependency work, however, is done by family members, usually women, but not exclusively. They are spouses or partners, daughters (and sometimes sons), mothers (sometimes fathers), grandmothers, aunts, and friends.[5]

In defining the precariat, Standing remarks: "The precariat was not part of the 'working class' or the 'proletariat,' " that it is "a new phenomenon even if it had shades of the past," and that it is "globalisation's child" (2011, 5).

Dependency workers are not "a new phenomenon," nor are they necessarily the product of globalization (although the migrant domestic worker is). Yet they fit well under the characterization of workers who are neither "working class" nor "proletariat." If we examine seven forms of labor-related security that Standing maintains the precariat lack and that identify those in the precariat, we see that criteria are each fulfilled by paid and familial dependency workers. As we look at each form of labor insecurity, we see how well dependency workers fit the description.

1. "*Labor market security*—Adequate income-earning opportunities; at the macro-level, this is epitomised by a government commitment to 'full employment' " (Standing 2011, 10).

   Paid dependency workers frequently do not belong to groups of workers who are recognized by the government, and who feature in their employment figures. They tend to belong to what is sometimes called the shadow economy: they are often not paid "on the books," and so not only do they not pay taxes, but their work does not get counted toward their social security (an apt metonym for their insecurity). Familial dependency work is not counted at all as employment; that work garners the carere no social security or other benefits of full-time work.

2. "*Employment security*—Protection against arbitrary dismissal, regulations on hiring and firing, imposition of costs on employers for failing to adhere to rules and so on" (Standing 2011, 10).

   Paid dependency workers have no such protection. They are hired and fired at the employer's will for any or no cause. There are no costs to employers who do not follow the rules, and there are usually none to follow. There is one exception to this lack of protection. This is when a dependency worker is hired through an agency that does have rules that are somewhat protective for the dependency worker. Moreover, the work is erratic, and two-thirds of home care workers work part-time or for part of the year (PHI 2015).

   Familial dependency workers have no employment security either, although mothers can be reasonably secure that they will be expected to continue mothering, even with little or no support from the father or the state. Other family members who care for someone do not even have that.

3. "*Job security*—Ability and opportunity to retain a niche in employment, plus barriers to skill dilution, and opportunities for 'upward' mobility in terms of status and income" (Standing 2011, 10).

   There is no job security for paid dependency workers and none for familial dependency workers. There is no niche in employment to secure, and there is no ladder.

4. "*Work security*—Protection against accidents and illness at work, through, for example, safety and health regulations, limits on working time, unsociable hours, night work for women, as well as compensation for mishaps" (Standing 2011, 10).

   Such protections exist only at the employer's discretion. The uninsured rate of home care workers is 26 percent, most relying on Medicare or Medicaid. The passage of the ACA increased the rate of coverage by 14 percent (PHI 2015). Wives can make some of these demands on their husbands, but it is a privilege that comes via a marriage rather than a demand based on their role as familial dependency workers.

5. "*Skill reproduction security*—Opportunity to gain skills, through apprenticeships, employment training and so on, as well as opportunity to make use of competencies" (Standing 2011, 10).

   Again, there is no such security. This is true, even though the demand for home care workers is increasing and will continue to increase as the population of adults older than sixty-five years of age grows. There will be need for more specialized knowledge, but there is no attempt to create educational or learning opportunities for dependency workers (PHI 2015).

6. "*Income security*—Assurance of an adequate stable income, protected through, for example, minimum wage machinery, wage indexation, comprehensive social security, progressive taxation to reduce inequality and to supplement low incomes" (Standing 2011, 10).

   Domestic work continues to be exempted from minimum wage law in some states (HomeWork Solutions 2018). Employed families with children can get reverse income credit. Payment for home health care has not kept up with inflation. In 2005, the average pay was $10.21, and adjusting for inflation. According to the Bureau of Labor statistics latest posted data, in 2018, the mean was $11.99, and the average was $12.62.[6] With the demise of the Assistance to Families with Dependent Children, women with dependents have a five-year lifetime limit to receive cash assistance. Other familial caregivers lack even this, although their dependents may receive SSI or Medicaid, which can pay for home health aides or pay salaries for those who work in institutional settings.

7. "*Representation security*—Possessing a collective voice in the labour market, through, for example, independent trade unions, with a right to strike" (Standing 2011, 10).

   Domestic workers are just now beginning to unionize, led primarily by the Service Employees International Union.

Organizing care workers who work in private homes is especially challenging, and efforts to unionize are met by resistance, even at the government level.

On the characterization of the precariat above, dependency workers fit squarely into this class. What bearing does all this labor-related insecurity for paid and unpaid dependency workers have on the precariousness of dependents, particularly the disabled (including the frail elderly)? It has immense repercussions in at least six ways, detailed below.

a. *Skills and competence*—Home care workers and dependency workers dealing with disabled, ill, or frail charges need to assist with the activities of daily living, prepare meals, manage medications, help people go to work, and be involved in activities. Most of these requisites involve skills and competences that are scarcely taught. It continues to be assumed that such knowledge just resides in the extra X chromosome possessed by approximately half of humankind. Alternatively, such skills are thought to be coaxed out of us by our love and devotion (especially if we are familial caregivers). But both notions are simply false. Good caregiving is skillful caregiving. It involves what is often a steep learning curve, and much is at stake in getting things right. There is also a much called for skill to handle the work in a way that the one needing assistance feels themselves neither to be a burden nor to be unduly in debt.[7]
b. *Quality and willingness of workers who enter the field*—Because no training is viewed as necessary and because the pay and status of care work is so poor, it is not infrequently a job taken by those for whom it is the only job (save something such as prostitution) that a woman (or even some men) with a limited education, poor language skills, or an arrest record can get. But being cornered into taking this poorly paid job does not make a person qualified to do care work. If someone takes this job only because they could not get anything better, we cannot be surprised if poor care, indifference to one's work, heavy turnover, as well as a low

skill level are the result. To leave an already precarious population, those who are in need of care, in the hands of an underqualified and poorly motivated workforce is to perpetuate an unhappy and even dangerous situation.

c. *The steadiness and reliability of the workers*—Many workers who are already dealing with poverty or health issues both for themselves and for their families turn over frequently and may not, despite their best efforts, be reliable or go to work with a clear head. A sick child, a bad cold, the need to visit a child's school, the need to go to social services to collect benefits—all these and more interrupt the regularity with which a person can be reliable in showing up for work. The precarious of disability often hangs on these sorts of interruptions of care. A disabled person who needs assistance to get to work, an ill person who needs medication, a person who needs to be properly positioned—all the small and large things that make our lives go well are imperiled.
d. *Possibility of abuse*—Although dependency workers can be abused by the people they care for, especially if there are important class and racial hierarchies in play, the disabled and elderly are more vulnerable than most to abuse, including sexual violation, by caregivers who are unsuited and improperly vetted. The very dependency of an inevitably dependent person may even give some, who might otherwise feel powerless, the sense that they now have power, which, when unrestrained by adequate oversight, can be abused and used to harm vulnerable people.
e. *Frustration of familial caregivers*—Familial caregivers are not trained and often not well equipped to care for people with significant disabilities who have some inevitable dependencies. Even though the emotional attachment and the will to care may be there, without the competence to respond properly to needs and the ability to tolerate resistance to one's care, things can go very wrong. This can endanger the very relationship that is the motivating force for the care. Furthermore, family caregivers can suffer ill-health

associated with their caregiving and become unable to provide the needed care.

f. *The impact of economic struggle*—When combined with the poverty that people with disabilities already face, the constant economic struggle of familial caregivers adds precariousness to an already precarious situation.

I hope I have made a sufficiently compelling argument that the precarity faced by caregivers, paid and unpaid, in general, carries over to the disabled person, transforming the precariousness of disability into a form of precarity for the disabled person. Just as dependencies are nested, so are levels of security and insecurity. My security that my needs will be met hinges, at least in part, on the caregiver's own security. This is especially true in familial caregiving. It is less true in the case of the paid caregiver, since paid caregivers are more fungible, but it is still powerful. I may be able to fire an inept caregiver or a caregiver who cannot show up because her child gets ill and cannot come into work, but if my work, well-being, or medical condition depends on being able to depend on this inept caregiver at this time, the consequences for me can nonetheless be grave.

Upshot

My claims at the outset—that the increased precariousness that people with disabilities face in achieving and holding on to a good quality of life, whatever their disabilities, and the precarity that marks a set of labor conditions that creates economic insecurity and social and political marginalization of care workers—are linked (1) by the issue of dependency and (2) by the need for adequate supports for dependency-related needs. The ways in which dependency is a linchpin has, I think, been covered in the remarks I have already made. But the need to address systems of support for disabled people and caregivers needs more elaboration.

What I mean by "supports" are, first, political structures and social policies that make accommodating the needs of people with disabilities a nonnegotiable demand in a wealthy society. In a significant part of the world, we are not in a condition of scarcity or even relative scarcity.

There is enough to go around for each in an affluent society to live a decent life. I venture to say that if all programs for people with disabilities were adequately funded and physical accommodations were made uniformly adequate, the affluent societies of today would scarcely feel squeezed. What such funding would do is provide a peace of mind that should we become disabled through accident, illness, or frail old age, we would not find ourselves in a situation of precarity. Our important needs and legitimate wants would still be attended to. And should we become family members who have a dependent person in our care, we too would not fall into a state of precarity. Living with a disability would still involve a more precarious hold on well-being, but it would not result in precarity, that is, in a state of insecurity that can blight our prospects for flourishing. The precariousness that we all face as human beings, as I pointed out earlier, need not impinge on our ability to live our lives well if we can be sufficiently secure in our belief that the next step we take will not plunge us into an abyss.

Just as important as providing the policies and funding that will support the needs of people with disabilities, so a just society must take a radically different stance toward caregivers. Their needs as well as the needs of dependents must take priority in state funding. But we have to do more.

Today, most paid caregiving that is done is state funded. Yet, wealthy corporations that today benefit from a growing precariat and see little need to accommodate the needs of familial caregiving or any dependency needs must assume some social responsibility for meeting these needs. Just as corporations depend on a tax paid for infrastructure for their smooth functioning, so they depend on someone taking care of children or assisting disabled relatives, of attending to sick family members, and of helping their frail and ailing elders for their workers and their consumers. Today, they free ride on the mostly female, mostly immigrant and migrant, Black and brown labor force of dependency workers.

Johanna Brenner (2017) in critiquing Nancy Fraser's attack on "progressive neoliberalism" writes:

> The dominant politics of feminism through the 1970s and '80s was defined neither by radical or socialist feminism nor by classic liberal

> feminism. Rather, the feminist politics of this period was characterized by what I would call social-welfare feminism. (4)

This feminism she defines as:

> Social-welfare feminists share liberal feminism's commitment to individual rights and equal opportunity, but they go much further. They look to an expansive and activist state to address the problems of working women, to ease the burden of the double day, to improve women's and especially mothers' position in the labor market, to provide public services that socialize the labor of care, and to expand social responsibility for care (for example, through paid parenting leave and stipends for women caring for family members). (4)

Brenner (2017) claims that the program of social-welfare feminist was overtaken in the "tsunami of capitalist restructuring." My aim in bringing up this discussion here is not to enter the fray between Johanna Brenner and Nancy Fraser, both of whom express much with which I agree. Rather, we need to keep alive the ideals of social-welfare feminists until the ground for implementing such policies becomes realizable, though I do not pretend to know how to make the ground fertile for such change. Nonetheless, too many programs for social change, many inherently valuable, continue to marginalize the concerns raised by social-welfare feminists.

I plead guilty to being a social welfarist feminist. Welfare feminism, as I understand it, is concerned with bringing us a world that approximates the form of justice that I have called Doulia. Doulia begins with the fact of inevitable dependency and depends on an acknowledgment of our inextricable interdependency. We begin with the relationship that we have all found ourselves in, being fully dependent on a caring person. And that caring person is herself dependent on other individuals and social, economic, and political systems that she requires to sustain herself, her dependent, and the relatedness that dependency care demands.

What I mean by beginning with the fact of inevitable dependency is that any adequate political/social/economic system will need to acknowledge that at the heart of all social organization is the care and protection of dependent people. All else is built around this.

Somehow—and there are any number of plausible origin stories—women came to be charged with the care of children, and the social technologies that made use of this labor assignment have given us a variety of patriarchal structures and systems—a set of variable instantiations of social life that effectively occlude the founding dependency relations that lie at the center of our social, political, and economic institutions.

By addressing inevitable dependencies and the nested dependencies that build on the *ur* dependency we all experience as infants, I found in writing *Love's Labor* (1999) that I could bring together the concerns of the mother who needs to depend on state welfare, the caregiver who is subject to domination and exploitation whether her labor is paid or unpaid, and people who are inevitably dependent due to a disability—people such as my daughter. In a homologous fashion, I believe, we bring together the condition of the precarity of the worker within neoliberalism and the precariousness that is particular to disability. A just society that concerns itself with the one must have the resources to concern itself with the other. And those resources reside in an embrace of an ethic of care as forming the heart of a conception of justice not predicated on independent, equally empowered, and equally situated individuals who come together to form a fair system of social cooperation. Instead, it is founded on the recognition of asymmetrical relations that exist alongside symmetrical ones, on the indispensable need for care—a need that may not be equal among all but which ought to be met as that need manifests itself, and on the aspiration to create a society in which people with different degrees of precariousness, need, and dependency can live together on terms that are fair to all.

An ethic of care, as we know, is an expensive ethic: the attention and resolve to act on another's behalf is such that we can only care for a *limited* number of people. Within an ethic of care, however, care is the central value. It is the summum bonum or, perhaps still better, the foundational good—the good upon which all other goods depend. If care is such a good, then it is a good not only for me and those I care for but a good for all. Now, if we take the value of care as an ultimate value, then we must care not only about those whom we can take care of, but also about *care*. To care about care demands of us certain duties. There is a negative duty: that in caring for those we are charged to care for, we do not prevent others from receiving the care they need. There is also a positive duty: to promote a social, political, and economic order in which those who need care can receive it, and those who need to care for another are not depleted, exploited, or dominated as a consequence of their care for another. Together, these constitute a fundamental regulative ideal embedded in an ethic of care.

An ethic of care, then, has as its mission, as part of the valuing of care itself, the building of the theoretical and practical apparatus to realize that regulative ideal. By looking at the relationship between precariousness—especially the heightened precariousness of those who are disabled or who are otherwise particularly vulnerable and dependent on another's care—and precarity—the state of insecurity brought on by economic and political conditions—we have, I hope, another handle to identify pressure points in our body politic—one that is still far from realizing the ideals of an ethic of care.[8]

Notes

1. I discuss "inevitable dependency" in my book (Kittay 1999). See also Fineman (1995).

2. "Different DeCenterings: Corporeality and Care in a Comparative Context," presentation at Care Ethics Research Consortium Conference, University of Ottawa (online), May 3, 2021.

3. This view is eloquently articulated and argued in Elizabeth Barnes (2016). Barnes makes the case for physical disabilities only, but it can arguably be extended to cognitive and possibly psychological disabilities as well.

4. More recent data confirmed that the gap remains: "The Equality and Human Rights Commission (EHRC) 2017 report found that the disability pay gap—the difference between what non-disabled and disabled workers earn—is 13.6%. On top of that, disabled people are significantly more likely to be unemployed, lose a job and be in low-waged work than non-disabled people" (Ryan 2018).

5. Extending the notion of precarity to work that is outside the waged labor economy shows us that critiques of precarity need not be attached to "the taken for granted valorization of waged work as an economic necessity, social duty and moral practice" (Kathi Weeks 2011, quoted in Millar 2017).

6. Labor Statistics Bureau, https://www.bls.gov/oes/2018/may/oes311011.htm#nat. It was $11.71 in 2020, according to the website (https://www.payscale.com/research/US/Job=Home_Health_Care_Worker/Hourly_Rate).

7. For an excellent discussion of this point, see Rivas (2002).

8. This chapter is based on a keynote presentation delivered at the inaugural conference of the Care Ethics Research Consortium (CERC) held in Portland, Oregon, in September 2018. I thank Maurice Hamington and Michael Flower for their useful editorial advice.

Works Cited

Barnes, Elizabeth. 2016. *The Minority Body: A Theory of Disability.* 1st ed. Studies in Feminist Philosophy. Oxford: Oxford University Press.

Brenner, Johanna. 2017. "There Was No Such Thing as 'Progressive Neoliberalism.'" *Dissent.* https://www.dissentmagazine.org/online_articles/nancy-fraser-progressive-neoliberalism-social-movements-response.

Fessler, Pam. 2015. "Why Disability and Poverty Still Go Hand in Hand 25 Years after Landmark Law." *All Things Considered.* https://www.npr.org/sections/health-shots/2015/07/23/424990474/why-disability-and-poverty-still-go-hand-in-hand-25-years-after-landmark-law.

Fineman, Martha Albertson. 1995. *The Neutered Mother.* New York: Routledge.

HomeWork Solutions. 2018. "State Minimum Wages." Last modified December 2018. https://www.homeworksolutions.com/knowledge-center/state-minimum-wages/.

Joffe-Walt, Chana. 2013a. "Millions of Americans Don't Work due to Disability, and the Number Is Growing." *All Things Considered.* https://www.npr.org/2013/03/22/175072446/millions-of-americans-dont-work-due-to-disability-and-the-number-is-growing.

Joffe-Walt, Chana. 2013b. "Unfit for Work: The Startling Rise of Disability in America." Planet Money, *This American Life.* https://www.npr.org/sections/money/2013/03/22/174194673/unfit-for-work-the-startling-rise-of-disability-in-america.

Kittay, Eva Feder. 1999. *Love's Labor: Essays in Women, Equality and Dependency.* New York: Routledge.

Kuusisto, Stephen. 1998. "Don't Tell 'Em You Can't See, Just Go On Out There . . ." In *Planet of the Blind,* 162. New York: Bantam Dell.

Millar, Kathleen M. 2017. "Toward a Critical Politics of Precarity." *Sociology Compass* 11 (6). https://doi.org/10.1111/soc4.12483.

PHI. 2015. *U.S. Home Care Workers: Key Facts.* New York: PHI. https://phinational.org/wp-content/uploads/legacy/phi-home-care-workers-key-facts.pdf.

Reynolds, Joel Michael. 2018. "The Extended Body: On Aging, Disability, and Well-being." *The Hastings Center Report* 48:S31–36.

Reynolds, Joel Michael. Forthcoming. *Ethics After Ableism: Disability, Pain, and the History of Morality.* Minneapolis: University of Minnesota Press.

Rivas, Lynn May. 2002. "Invisible Labors: Caring for the Independent Person." In *Global Women: Nannies, Maids and Sex Workers in the Global Economy,* edited by Barbara Ehrenreich and Arlie Russell Hochchild, 70–84. New York: Henry Holt and Company.

Ryan, Frances. 2018. "We Know about the Gender Pay Gap. But What about the Disability Pay Gap?" *Guardian US Edition,* April 11, 2019.

Standing, Guy. 2011. *The Precariat: The Dangerous New Class.* London: Bloomsbury Academic.

Wolfe, Katharine. 2016. "Together in Need: Relational Selfhood, Vulnerability to Harm, and Enriching Attachments." *The Southern Journal of Philosophy* 54 (1): 129–48.

CHAPTER 2

Neoliberalism, Moral Precarity, and the Crisis of Care

SARAH CLARK MILLER

Neoliberalism has long been on a collision course with care. Scholars from a wide array of disciplines have considered how caretaking practices and policies have been negatively affected under neoliberal principles and institutions. Economists (Wrenn and Waller 2017), geographers (Lawson 2007; Smith 2005), philosophers (Fraser 2016; Gary 2021), sociologists (McGee 2020), anthropologists (Nguyen, Zavoretti, and Tronto 2017; Povinelli 2011), political scientists (Tronto 2013), and gender studies scholars (Glenn 2010) have all examined the crisis of care under neoliberalism. In different ways, they have acknowledged the complicated and troubling ways in which the need for care has increased just as social and institutional structures that support care have withered. While an abundance of excellent investigations into the economic, social, and political implications of neoliberalism already exists, moral critiques of neoliberalism are less plentiful.[1] I address this lacuna by offering an analysis of the crisis of care informed by care ethics. In doing so, I aim to detail both the moral precarity and the relational precarity that threaten the necessary practices of giving and receiving care under neoliberalism.

While scholars critical of neoliberalism regularly employ precarity as a lens of analysis, it represents a newer addition to the ethics of care—one that is deserving of further exploration. Care ethicists often begin with a strong focus on the needs, vulnerability, and dependency of individuals, that is, individuals who are in need of care and, in turn, those who provide care to them. Given this perspective, one might think that the next logical step for care ethicists who wish to emphasize the concept of precarity would be to home in on the precarity of human lives, as scholars external to care ethics have done, in order to consider how best to care for precarious others. While there is value in this approach, I proceed in a different direction. My attention initially turns to the moral precarity of caregivers in neoliberal regimes and, thereafter, to the precarity of relationships and relationality itself. This analysis stands in distinction to the more common method of examining the precarity of individuals who constitute relationships, on the one hand, or the systems in which such individuals are situated, on the other.

After offering an opening consideration of the hazards of neoliberalism, I address the general shape of the crisis of care that has evolved under its auspices. Two aspects of this crisis require greater attention: the moral precarity of caregivers and the relational harms of neoliberal capitalism. I first consider the moral precarity that caregivers experience by drawing on a concept rooted in the experiences of healthcare workers and combat veterans, namely, moral injury. Through this concept, we can see how caregivers in late-stage capitalism face a seemingly unavoidable violation of their own significant moral beliefs. Second, I examine how the crisis of care results not only in individual harms of moral injury but also in harms to relationships themselves as I continue to track the impact of moral injury on our intrapersonal and interpersonal lives. Ultimately, I argue that an important facet of the crisis of care is how it operates as a crisis of relationality in which our intrapersonal and interpersonal connections are placed under practical and moral strain. In taking a broader view, we can see how the fraying of particular intrapersonal and interpersonal connections can accumulate, resulting in the unraveling of wider webs of interdependency just when we need them most. Throughout the chapter, I concentrate on the moral implications of the crisis of care driven by neoliberalism, featuring the damage that caregivers and their relationships sustain when situated in morally precarious ways. In doing so, I stress the point that the crisis of care under neoliberalism is as much a moral and relational crisis as it is a political and economic one.

Lastly, a note regarding my use of the term "neoliberalism": "neoliberalism" operates somewhat flexibly in this article in an effort to represent and accommodate the multiple senses of the concept currently in circulation. While it might be too strong a charge to say that neoliberalism is a full-blown conceptual shapeshifter, it does appear to morph somewhat, depending on context. As Springer, Birch, and MacLeavy note, it is "a slippery concept, meaning different things to different people" (2016, 1). Economist Dani Rodrik observes that "even its harshest critics concede [that] neoliberalism is hard to pin down. In broad terms, it denotes a preference for markets over government, economic incentives over cultural norms, and private entrepreneurship over collective action" (2017). We can add an ethical layer to this group of concepts by underscoring how neoliberalism's ideology emphasizes individual responsibility while downplaying collective or institutional responsibility (Bloom 2017). To put it more bluntly, neoliberalism sometimes appears infused with an ethical sense of personal responsibility on steroids, paired with a form of hyper-individualism (Ward 2015).

Springer, Birch, and MacLeavy offer the following consensus on the definition of neoliberalism: "At a very base level we can say that when we make reference to 'neoliberalism', we are generally referring to the new political, economic, and social arrangements within society that emphasize market relations, re-tasking the role of the state, and individual responsibility. Most scholars tend to agree that neoliberalism is broadly defined as the extension of competitive markets into all areas of life, including the economy, politics, and society" (2016, 2). In addition, neoliberalism imprints the values that sustain competitive markets upon ethical life, shaping and reshaping what we believe constitutes not only the good life but also right action. Neoliberalism requires and gives rise to new ethical arrangements to sustain it just as much as it requires new political, economic, and social arrangements to do the same. Finally, neoliberalism is not the only term used to describe this cluster of economic, political, social, and ethical tenets. Other descriptors (all of which do have their own different flavors and senses, which are not the focus of my work here) include "free-market capitalism," "late-stage capitalism," or simply, "late capitalism." I will draw on these terms somewhat interchangeably.

The Hazards of Neoliberalism

Neoliberal principles and institutions impinge upon individual flourishing in many serious ways, including increased poverty, exploitation, illness, and inequality. For the vast majority of people, existence in a neoliberal context is marked by a heightened sense of vulnerability and dependency, where they are at greater risk of a wide variety of harms. Getting one's basic needs met can prove impossible in a neoliberal world. In essence, neoliberalism fails to countenance the type of beings that care ethicists have long recognized us to be: ones born into serious and abiding dependency, ones with needs, ones who, in short, require care throughout the entirety of our lives.

One characteristic commonly associated with neoliberalism is the precarity it produces. Judith Butler describes precarity as "the politically induced condition in which certain populations suffer from failing social and economic networks . . . becoming differentially exposed to injury, violence, and death" (2009, 25). Our current circumstances are run through with the threat of failure—of our democratic political systems, supply chains, economic structures, healthcare systems, and much else central to human need fulfillment. The threat of such failures places many populations in a vice-like grip of risk and the unrelenting anticipation of injury upon injury. The compromise of individual agency and well-being become commonplace. In late capitalism, whole systems and the individuals situated within them teeter on the edge of collapse.

This picture of the hazards of neoliberalism is perhaps familiar. Yet, it is incomplete in at least two significant ways. It fails to consider (1) the precarity of relationships and (2) moral precarity. In addition to the ways in which neoliberalism imperils individuals, the broader populations of which they are members, and the systems in which they exist, it also endangers a vital source of human connection positioned between individual and structural levels, namely, relationships. Neoliberalism heightens the always already existing precariousness of relationships. In jeopardizing relationships, it subjects not only people but their intimate connections with others to injury and instability, which can ultimately push those relationships to the point of rupture. Moreover, the very conditions of cultivating relationships arguably shift under neoliberal capitalism's "political logic of radical individuality, self-responsibility, and independence" (Shaw and Byler 2016), yielding a broader context in which the moral value of relationships is undermined and occluded or in which there is an inability to value relationships in noninstrumental ways in the first place.

The second insufficiently theorized aspect of neoliberalism's hazards concerns the moral precarity that caregivers must sometimes endure. Moral precarity arises in circumstances where fulfilling the responsibilities one takes to be central to one's sense of ethical identity proves circumstantially impossible without also incurring considerable and unavoidable harm. When experiencing moral precarity, it becomes increasingly difficult and ultimately unfeasible to adhere to the ethical principles that comprise the core of one's integrity. The moral precarity that caregivers encounter under neoliberalism can, in part, be characterized through the concept of moral injury, which originates in scholarly work about the crises that healthcare workers and combat veterans often face. Moral injury exposes a major moral failing of neoliberalism with regard to care.

In addition to the exposing caregivers to moral injury, the crisis of care under neoliberalism results in harms not only to them as individuals but also to their relationships. The notion of relational harm captures this connected representation of the moral precarity of caregivers in neoliberal circumstances and also also highlights the distinctive precarity of relationships under neoliberalism. Relational harm encompasses forms of harm that individuals sustain to their relational capacities, as well as harms inflicted on their relationships with themselves and others, where relationships are taken to be entities of significant moral value distinctive from the value of the individuals comprising such relationships.

In order to explore these moral dimensions, I begin with the crisis of care under neoliberalism, which serves as the backdrop for identifying more precise moral harms. Both ramifications of neoliberalism for care—the moral injuries that attempting to care in late capitalism necessarily involves and the relational harms that neoliberalism inflicts on caregiving relationships—underscore the various dimensions of moral precarity and demonstrate, each in its own way, the precarity of relationships within neoliberal norms and institutions.

The Crisis of Care

In order to understand the role of neoliberalism in producing and maintaining the crisis of care, a system-level perspective is needed. According to Nancy Fraser, the crisis of care arises in what she calls "the third regime" of "social reproduction-cum-economic production in capitalism's history" (2016, 104). This third regime is "the globalizing financialized capitalism of the present era," which she describes as follows:

> This regime has relocated manufacturing to low-wage regions, recruited women into the paid workforce, and promoted state and corporate disinvestment from social welfare. Externalizing carework onto families and communities, it has simultaneously diminished their capacity to perform it. The result, amid rising inequality, is a dualized organization of social reproduction, commodified for those who can pay for it, privatized for those who cannot—all glossed by the even more modern ideal of the "two-earner family." (2016, 104)

Fraser sets forth the mechanisms that give rise to various individual experiences of the crisis of care. Women, who traditionally perform most unpaid dependency labor in the home, enter the paid workforce outside the home. This move is met not with increased support for the realities of caregiving, as would actually make sense, but rather with government and corporate structures weakening social welfare programs, resulting in an increased demand that dependency labor will be carried out by families and their communities just as families are less able to complete such work (Robinson 2015; White 2015). Unable to take on the necessary care work in full themselves, families who are fiscally able pay others to perform caregiving labor for them. With this reality in mind, we can see why Fraser argues that the crisis of care "is best interpreted as a more or less acute expression of the social-reproductive contradictions of financialized capitalism" (2016, 99).

This formula sets the conditions for a crisis of care as multiple interlocking forces compound: neoliberalism calls more women into the workforce while placing increased dependency labor onto families under conditions of eroding support for social welfare. As women have tended to bear the greatest expectation of and responsibility for care, they bear the brunt of the moral harms of a diminished capacity to care, as I will detail in the pages that follow. To be clear from the start, when looking for a way through this morass of issues, there are multiple ready solutions that should be avoided on account of their moral dubiousness. As sociologist Micki McGee explains, "Capitalism's care problem leaves anticapitalists and other social justice advocates with an even more difficult problem: how to develop new forms of care provision that refuse racist, patriarchal, capitalist schemes for supply. . . . How do we ensure that we do not rely on the discounting of labor based on the traditional gendered and racial social hierarchies, on the fantasies of self-sufficient individuals whose self-making work of maximizing capacities and potential will insulate them from a devastating lack of community, or on the fantasy of an 'infinite supply' for those who stay positive?" (2020, 55). McGee calls to mind how a viable solution cannot be to create greater opportunities for women to return to exclusively performing dependency labor in the home. That such dependency labor has long been their assumed and assigned primary responsibility in no way means that it should continue to be. Nor should the solution be to offload care labor on women of color and migrant workers, futher exacerbating already existing racial hierarchies. Nor should it rest upon the assumptions that care workers not be paid a living wage or granted the benefits and protections that citizenship affords. Exposing the moral dimensions of the crisis of care for relationships—and the setting forth of the serious harms it entails—is intended to initiate a call for more creative solutions on individual, relational, social, and structural levels. In order to begin to generate better solutions, however, we need to fully grasp the forms of moral harm that the crisis of care inflicts on caregivers, which is why I now turn to moral injury—the first of two major harms.

Moral Precarity and Moral Injury

One important tool for understanding how neoliberalism exposes caregivers to moral precarity in the midst of the crisis of care is the notion of moral injury. The concept of moral injury originally arises in the literature concerning the strains that healthcare workers and combat veterans experience in fulfilling their professional obligations.[2] It proves useful in unpacking the deeper moral implications of the crisis of care that neoliberalism brings about. According to Dean, Talbot, and Dean, "Moral injury occurs when we perpetrate, bear witness to, or fail to prevent an act that transgresses our deeply held moral beliefs. In the health care context, that deeply held moral belief is the oath each of us took when embarking on our paths as health care providers: Put the needs of patients first" (2019, 400). For example, in circumstances of limited medical resources—be those resources equipment or time or medicines—doctors and nurses may not have the means to uphold the firmly ingrained moral principle of beneficence, which entails helping patients or, depending on the circumstances, preventing and limiting harm to patients. Moral injury captures a particular dilemma, one of "simultaneously knowing what care patients need but being unable to provide it due to constraints that are beyond our control" (401). The problem is not a lack of knowledge regarding what might be needed or what one should do. To the contrary, the full knowledge of what is needed absent the ability to meet those needs is the crux of the problem.

In such circumstances, what moral injury induces is clinician distress. Clinician distress is more than burnout (Talbot and Dean 2018). Burnout implies a kind of complicated exhaustion at the individual level suggesting that an individual practitioner who is feeling burnt out needs extra support and perhaps a shift in level of responsibility. The form of distress clinicians experience that the concept of moral injury highlights, however, is more expansive. It captures a sense of the moral friction arising in interactions between individual and organizational levels (Padgett and Ascensao 2019, 502), thus foregrounding the dynamic between individuals and institutions. Clinician distress gives expression to "the agony of being constantly locked in double binds when every choice one makes yields a compromised outcome and when each decision contravenes the reason for years of sacrifice" (Dean and Talbot 2019). The distress arises from there being no way to clear the remainder of harm that necessarily results from the insufficiencies of individual beneficent action in the context of a system with complex limitations. The closely related concept of "moral distress," found in the nursing literature, is also relevant to clarifying the moral harms of the crisis of care. McAndrew, Leske, and Schroeter hold that moral distress occurs "when a nurse cannot follow through with moral actions and compromises professional integrity" (2018, 552; cf. Jameton 1993;

Corley and Minick 2002; Corley et al. 2005). In such circumstances, a nurse judges that there is an ethically correct course of action, but a serious obstacle or set of obstacles prevents him from taking that course. This represents an important aspect of moral injury.

Drawing on moral injury as articulated in the healthcare literature can help to make sense of the moral precarity that neoliberal caregivers face. One place to begin in order to understand this sense of moral injury is with the everyday experiences of those attempting to engage in caregiving practices in the midst of free-market capitalism. Caregivers undergo the crisis of care in personal and intense ways. Neoliberalism makes caring for those we love very, very difficult. Caring for others within the framework of late capitalism is peppered with impossible choices. And, as we scramble to meet others' needs in the face of multiple obstacles, it can make caring for ourselves outright impossible.

The moral precarity of caregivers' daily experience in a crisis of care gives rise to a sense of incessant pressure: we are pressed for time, squeeze in chores at home before work, force ourselves to complete work of importance late at night while those we care for sleep, and are sandwiched between the unrelenting, sometimes unpredictable needs of our littles and our elders—between the children we are raising and the aging parents we are seeing through to the end. And ultimately, the deck is stacked against us: our hearts are crushed when we inevitably fail to care well for those others (not to even begin to mention ourselves) in a context of the untenable, competing demands of work and family. From this perspective, work-life balance is a fiction, time poverty is real, and exhaustion is unending. The governing myth of the quotidian crisis of care is that if we were more efficient, we could do it all.

When events turn more dire, the true depth of moral injury, as well as the distress caregivers experience, emerges. The particular distress of not being able to care for one's own is excruciating. Those crushed hearts can be rendered fully pulverized when we face impossible dilemmas of care under conditions of finitude, equipped with no good choices. The COVID-19 pandemic—a global health crisis, it must be noted, arguably sustained if not created by neoliberalism (Navarro 2020)—is perhaps the best recent example of the amplification of the crisis of care to levels that guarantee seemingly unending moral injury. Caregivers are faced with unthinkable choices that force the balancing of fiercely competing needs. Do I travel to visit my critically ill elderly parent in the hospital, risking exposure to a virus that other family members at home cannot sustain? Do I ration attention to my child struggling with remote schooling in order to open up space in my schedule to help my struggling students? Do I cut much-needed time to connect with my spouse in order to catch up with professional commitments key to attaining professional goals? And in the midst of all of this, how do I continue to care for a community in crisis? Dear friends who are sick with COVID-19? Struggling financially? Deeply lonely? In such an environment, where the amount of need present so completely outstrips the finite capabilities we have, we face an unavoidable and excruciating apportioning of harm to those whom we firmly believe it is our responsibility to protect and keep whole. We are faced with choices no one should have to make and feel weighty culpability attached to the responsibility of harm distribution. In such circumstances, we assume responsibility for that which is well beyond our control. The governing myth in this instance is perhaps even more dispiriting than the first: that if we were morally better, we could avoid tragedy for those we love.

Thus, to see our inability to achieve work-life balance as evidence of a broken system run through with tensions between capital and care is true, but perhaps not true enough. Yes, we are exhausted because we are often unable to keep up with the unreasonable dual demands of workplace labor and dependency labor. Yes, this is a symptom of the ways in which neoliberalism as a system is deeply problematic. But to stop at this level of observation is to fail to appreciate the deeper moral significance of this scenario. What caregivers experience is not merely "a failure of resourcefulness and resilience" (Talbot and Dean 2018). Caregivers are plenty resourceful and have proven their resilience over centuries. Caregivers are not simply burnt out (though, surely, they are this too). The moral significance of this phenomenon is more complex, and arguably even more damaging and difficult. Beyond exhaustion and burnout, what caregivers risk losing when they endure forms of moral injury under neoliberalism is their ability to uphold their own sense of morality—the core beliefs that make them who they are. This amounts to the risk of losing their very sense of identity as caring individuals.

Care ethics can help us perceive the significance of those core beliefs and what it means to violate them, hence further elucidating the nature and extent of moral injury that caregivers often suffer under neoliberalism. At the core of care ethics, one finds certain responsibilities that emanate from key concepts within the theory and practice of care. Vulnerability and dependency are two such key features of moral life. Enacting responsibilities related to vulnerability and dependency in daily life is what it means to be a caring person. If you identify as a carer, you will understand yourself to have a responsibility to protect those for whom you care in accordance with their vulnerabilities to injury, as well as a responsibility to support them in their dependency by meeting their needs. Moreover, as a caregiver, you likely understand that there are important moral differences in how one cares for others, expressed through the manner in which you meet others' needs (Miller 2012, 73–96). Caring well for others requires focus, emotional connection, and time. Others' needs can be met, their vulnerabilities tended to, and their dependency supported in ways that are cursory rather than robust. Caring often and well will both be central to the self-conceptions that caretakers adopt. Seeking shortcuts to caregiving runs counter to the very nature of what it means to care well, and this is just the kind of pressure neoliberal institutions exert over individuals in their caregiving capacities. Caring well is exactly what neoliberal capitalism places just out of reach.

When structural conditions increase both the vulnerabilities and dependencies of those for whom you care in seemingly exponential ways, as neoliberalism does, something will break. (To be totally honest, lots of things will break, but my focus here is on the aspects of morality that such conditions can shatter.) What is vital to recognize in order to grasp this point are the specifics of the moral precarity that is in play. That for which you understand yourself to be responsible increases within a context where two other crucial factors loom large: (1) your own levels of vulnerability and dependency are increasing because you, too, are intertwined with the same neoliberal system; and (2) your buy-in to that neoliberal system in the form of work outside of the home significantly reduces your ability to fulfill your increasing responsibilities. Welcome to the moral crucible of the crisis of care, where moral injury is inevitable.

In the midst of the crisis of care, there are few, if any, decent options available, and to the extent we have choices within the oppressive structures birthed by neoliberal principles, we are often forced to choose which aspect of our moral integrity we will sacrifice. Competing demands for care that cannot be simultaneously met (e.g., the conflicts that emerge when caught between meeting the needs of one's aging parent or one's growing child) mean that caregivers often face the hard choice—the integrity sacrificing choice—of whom to let down, of whose well-being to compromise on this occasion. One simply cannot do it all, at every moment, overwhelmed as many of us are by the press of needs, including our own. There is no way to emerge from such scenarios with your moral integrity fully intact and with the clear feeling that one cares well for those one loves. This crisis of care, fueled and underwritten by neoliberal institutions, exposes the depths of our moral precarity.

Continuous and inescapable double, even triple, binds are bad enough on their own, when they are properly conceived as beyond the control of those caught within them. But the knife of moral injury twists deeper still within neoliberalism with its ever-present prescription for personal responsibility. (As a side note, the autonomy myth [Fineman 2005] of the self-sufficient individual is perhaps all the more insulting when one is suffering so fully in the midst of currently unavoidable failures of care.) The moral upshot is that the moral injury is doubly layered as caretakers come to hold themselves responsible for the moral injuries they suffer. The moral responsibilities of care that they are unable to fulfill appear to be a matter of individual failure, rather than resulting from a system in which there is no winning. A significant aspect of the moral injury is being unable to meet the needs of others in the context of a system that makes you believe that you should be able to do so. Thus, not only do they suffer a very serious moral blow in the form of an undermining of their most dearly held moral principles and of failing to be who they thought they were morally. They also may well believe it is nobody's fault but their own.

Returning to one place where the concept of moral injury originated—in scholarly work on combat veterans—adds a final important element to this increasingly complex picture of the moral precarity inherent in being a caregiver in the midst of a crisis of care. Shelia Frankfurt and Patricia Frazier explain that within this framework, "the moral injury construct has been proposed to describe the suffering some veterans experience when they engage in acts during combat that violate their beliefs about their own goodness or the goodness of the world" (2016, 318). Such acts are perceived as moral transgressions so serious that they can produce forms of trauma. Veterans who experience moral injury often feel guilt, shame, and a sense of betrayal of both self and others. Moral injury can result in a sense of losing one's moral moorings and bearings, thereby feeling morally disoriented.

While the claim that the moral injury sustained during the crisis of care reliably results in trauma, as combat can be a step too far, observing that caregivers experience guilt, shame, and a sense of betrayal when they encounter what they perceive to be their failures to care surely is not. Attempting to fulfill the role of caregiver in neoliberal contexts can fully upend a caregiver's sense of the goodness of herself and her world. What is more, the inability to care well can feel like a form of moral transgression worthy of self-recrimination expressed through feelings such as guilt, shame, and a sense that she has betrayed not only those she loves but also herself. Thus, the ultimate result of moral injury for combat veterans and caregivers can perhaps surprisingly be said to be very much the same in one regard: in undergoing significant moral injury, both caregivers and combat veterans have "experienced repeated insults to their *morality*" and therefore question "whether they [are] still, at their core, moral beings" (Dean, Talbot, and Dean 2019, 400, emphasis in the original). The point of drawing this connection is not to suggest that the contexts of combat and caregiving under neoliberalism are similar, let alone the same. Rather, it is to recognize that there are resonances between their moral outcomes.

In morally hazardous[3] caregiving contexts, if the nature of compromise of one's personal values is serious enough and the practical outcomes dire, it is not going too far to say that something like trauma can result from moral injury. Examples of this currently abound under the particular conditions of caregiving during a global pandemic, for both healthcare workers and caregivers alike. This collision of caregiving and tragedy is, of course, not new. As Nancy Scheper-Hughes, author of *Death without Weeping: The Violence of Everyday Life in Brazil* (1993) acknowledges, "Throughout much of human history . . . women have had to give birth and to nurture children under ecological conditions and social arrangements hostile to child survival, as well as to their own well-being" (1989, 14). Yet, the particular way in which this plays out in late capitalism adds additional dimensions of moral precarity. There is a real sense in which neoliberalism weaponizes care: it uses the desire many have to take care of others and warps it into a hyper-individualized matter of personal responsibility. When things go completely belly up, neoliberalism further warps the inability to care well into a matter of personal failing.

Neoliberalism's Relational Harms

On one level, the harm that befalls caregivers who experience moral injury is a direct harm to individuals. They suffer a series of negative consequences in light of not being able to enact a core part of their moral code. Yet, another aspect of moral injury that requires exploration is how it results in harms not only to individuals but also to relationships, which is to say, it inflicts relational as well as individual harm.[4] Relational harm results when the relational capacities of individuals are compromised or when relationships themselves sustain harm. My focus here will be on the harms that relationships sustain, where relationships are understood as entities with moral value that is distinctive from the moral value of the individuals who make up any given relationship. Two possible forms of relational harm can result from moral injury: harm to intrapersonal relationships, or the relationships we hold with ourselves, and harm to interpersonal relationships, represented in the connections we hold with others. These forms of relational harm reveal another dimension of the moral precarity that arises in light of neoliberalism while also providing additional insight into the relational precarity manifest in neoliberal societies. In essence, the precarity that neoliberalism creates for individuals and systems extends to relationships, too, as a notable yet relatively unexplored outcome. Investigation of such harms will ultimately help us gain a crisper understanding of the intersection of the moral and relational significance of neoliberalism.

An illuminating way to discern what happens when caregivers suffer moral injury is to examine how it impacts the way in which they relate to themselves. When caregivers are unable to uphold moral principles of importance to them in caring for others under the pressures of neoliberalism, they sustain harm to their intrapersonal relationships. This harm can take multiple forms. In the face of the disintegration of their moral integrity, a sense of distrust in their own moral abilities and agency can arise. If you understand yourself to be guided by a principle of care and you fail repeatedly to uphold that principle, you may come to question your own moral commitments. If this happens while locked into a neoliberal ethical perspective of personal or individual responsibility, you may fail to apportion appropriate causal responsibility for this failure to the economic and political systems in which you find yourself. Instead, you will believe that you cannot carry out the moral commitments you undertake. Such a situation may further impinge upon your ability to respect yourself not only as a moral person in general but also as a carer in particular. To employ the language of more traditional moral theories for a moment, this amounts to a violation of a duty to self. You fail to respect yourself. More extreme cases may involve an undermining of a sense of your own moral standing, as repeated violation of one's fundamental moral code may compromise your understanding of yourself as an entity worthy of others' reciprocal care.

The crisis of care, with the dual demands it makes on caregivers to carry out dependency labor in the home while also performing workplace labor outside of it, inflicts further intrapersonal harm on their personal identities. The self-conception that caregivers have as moral beings guided by a principle of care, while important, is far from the sum total of their identity. The crisis of care is a crisis for both home life and work life. While my primary focus in this chapter has been on the moral injury that caregivers sustain in attempting to care for others under neoliberalism, recognition of the harms to their concept of self beyond that of a carer is equally important. Attempting to care for others in late capitalism can undermine persons' abilities to be self-determining in the sense of being able to set and work toward life goals of significance to them, many of which will involve professional pursuits. This can result in a violation not only of their moral self-conception but also of other crucial aspects of their personal identity. Again, in more traditional (and admittedly Kantian) moral language, this amounts to a violation of duty of self-perfection. They neglect their given talents and, in doing so, can fail to pursue life goals of considerable significance to them. This undermines their self-trust and self-respect in slightly different ways, but the result is the same: a compromised relationship with themselves. If they have yet to understand work-life balance as the neoliberal fiction that it is, they may assume personal responsibility for the inability to "juggle" an overload of competing demands and can come to see how they defect on the life goals they have set for themselves as a form of abandoning themselves—a form of abandonment for which they are responsible.

In the preceding section, I focused on how caretakers' inability to provide satisfactory care in societies regulated by neoliberal capitalism results in those caretakers sustaining moral injury. Central to such moral injury is the undermining of their belief in their own fundamental moral decency as they assume responsibility for care failures largely beyond their control. Yet, the concept of moral injury overlooks how the precarity of neoliberalism extends to relationships between people, too, as evidenced by the direct harms to interpersonal caregiving relationships that also ensue. It matters that individual caregivers experience moral injury under neoliberalism. Of equal importance is how neoliberalism can disrupt the relationships caregivers hold with those for whom they care. Those threads of connection can become so frayed that they ultimately break, unable to sustain the stress that late capitalism inflicts upon both individuals and collectives. The fraying results not only from the caregiver's experience of not being able to care well for others but also from the care recipient's experience of not being well cared for. When you possess needs that are someone else's to meet—be it a matter of duty, love, or both—and they fail to meet those needs or fail to do so lovingly and with respect, even if their failures occur for reasons you know are beyond their control, the bond you share can begin to fracture. When care negligence occurs repeatedly over time, that relational bond can crumble beyond repair. The destruction of such relationships is the collateral damage of the economic gains that neoliberalism delivers to a relatively small minority. In calculating the sum total of neoliberal capitalism's damages, the harms our relationships sustain should count just as much as the harms we incur as individuals.

The Significance of Social Reproduction

The precarity that neoliberalism engenders affects whether we understand ourselves to be decent, caring people capable of upholding our own moral code; it affects the degree of self-trust and self-respect present in our intrapersonal relationships; and it affects the strength and sustainability of our most cherished interpersonal relationships. Before closing, there is one final relational repercussion of neoliberalism with which to reckon. The forms of moral precarity I have discussed coalesce to produce an overarching relational precarity evident in the way in which neoliberalism generates relational vulnerability, instability, and unpredictability. Why does this matter? When relational precarity is felt and experienced on a wide enough scale—and perhaps especially when the precarity of caring relationships in a crisis of care results in a larger sense and reality of relational precarity—troublesome and potentially disastrous outcomes can result for the core mechanisms of social reproduction.

What is social reproduction? According to Fraser, social reproduction "is about the creation and maintenance of social bonds. One part of this has to do with the ties between the generations—so, birthing and raising children and caring for the elderly. Another part is about sustaining horizontal ties among friends, family, neighborhoods, and community" (Leonard and Fraser 2016). Historically speaking, social reproduction has primarily been "women's work." Through reproductive labor, women have built and maintained vertical lines of social reproduction from generation to generation. Through emotional labor, they have created and maintained horizontal lines of social reproduction, sustaining networks vital to our survival and holding out the promise of our thriving.

Grasping the importance of social reproduction will help us to see why the strain of moral and relational precarity that neoliberalism generates is so weighty. In short, we need robust and well-functioning systems of caretaking to sustain social reproduction. When carers suffer moral injury and their relationships suffer harm, their abilities to care well and participate fully in the work of social reproduction are hampered. Fraser explains why this is so important: "This sort of activity is absolutely essential to society. Simultaneously affective and material, it supplies the 'social glue' that underpins social cooperation. Without it, there would be no social organization—no economy, no polity, no culture" (Leonard and Fraser 2016). Through Fraser's comments, a clearer picture of why the crisis of care under neoliberalism is such a significant problem snaps into focus.

It is not just the case that reduced social reproduction labor results in fewer babies and in people who are less emotionally satisfied. Rather, the myriad ways neoliberalism exacerbates our moral precarity accumulate through the crisis of care until ultimately the very fabric of our interdependence is at stake. This wider sustaining tapestry of interdependence begins to unravel. Our webs of relationality, which have always been much more fragile than perhaps we cared to realize, start to tear. As fabric and web give way, institutions undergirded by cooperative sociality—the economy, political institutions, and ultimately aspects of culture—are jeopardized, threatening the social contract itself. And this is ulitimately why the moral injuries of neoliberalism deserve our careful attention and why the moral precarity of the crisis of care is so deeply consequential.

Notes

I would like to acknowledge Maurice Hamington, Michael Flower, and Lori Watson for providing helpful comments on this chapter.

1. Some examples of such analyses include Bloom (2017), Wrenn and Waller (2017), and Nguyen et al. (2017).

2. There are multiple ways that moral injury is used in the philosophical literature (Wiinikka-Lydon 2019). Jean Hampton's (2007) discussions of moral injury represent one important use of the term that I will not be employing in this article. Carol Gilligan (2014) has also written recently on moral injury and care ethics, claiming that care ethics is "the ethic of resistance to moral injury" (90).

3. I intend this phrase here in a moral rather than economic sense.

4. See Miller (2009) for a more comprehensive discussion of the nature of relational harm.

Works Cited

Bloom, Peter. 2017. *The Ethics of Neoliberalism: The Business of Making Capitalism Moral*. New York: Routledge.

Butler, Judith. 2009. *Frames of War: When Is Life Grievable?* New York: Verso Books.

Corley, Mary C., and Ptlene Minick. 2002. "Moral Distress or Moral Comfort." *Bioethics Forum* 18 (1–2): 7–14.

Corley, Mary C., Ptlene Minick, R. K. Elswick, and Mary Jacobs. 2005. "Nurse Moral Distress and Ethical Work Environment." *Nursing Ethics* 12 (4): 381–90.

Dean, Wendy, and Simon G. Talbot. 2019. "Moral Injury and Burnout in Medicine: A Year of Lessons Learned." *STAT*. https://www.statnews.com/2019/07/26/moral-injury-burnout-medicine-lessons-learned/.

Dean, Wendy, Simon Talbot, and Austin Dean. 2019. "Reframing Clinician Distress: Moral Injury not Burnout." *Federal Practitioner* 36 (9): 400–402.

Fineman, Martha Albertson. 2005. *The Autonomy Myth: A Theory of Dependency*. New York: New Press.

Frankfurt, Shelia, and Patricia Frazier. 2016. "A Review of Research on Moral Injury in Combat Veterans." *Military Psychology* 28 (5): 318–30.

Fraser, Nancy. 2016. "Contradictions of Capital and Care." *New Left Review* 100:99–117.

Gary, Mercer E. 2021. "Care Robots, Crises of Capitalism, and the Limits of Human Caring." *International Journal of Feminist Approaches to Bioethics* 14 (1): 19–48.

Gilligan, Carol. 2014. "Moral Injury and the Ethic of Care: Reframing the Conversation about Differences." *Journal of Social Philosophy* 45 (1): 89–106.

Glenn, Evelyn Nakano. 2010. *Forced to Care: Coercion and Caregiving in America*. Cambridge, Mass.: Harvard University Press.

Hampton, Jean. 2007. "Righting Wrongs: The Goal of Retribution." In *The Intrinsic Worth of Persons: Contractarianism in Moral and Political Philosophy*, edited by Daniel Farnham, 107–50. New York: Cambridge University Press.

Jameton, Andrew. 1993. "Dilemmas of Moral Distress: Moral Responsibility and Nursing Practice." *AWHONN's Clinical Issues in Perinatal and Women's Health Nursing* 4 (4): 542–52.

Lawson, Victoria. 2007. "Geographies of Care and Responsibility." *Annals of the Association of American Geographers* 97 (1): 1–11.

Leonard, Sarah, and Nancy Fraser. 2016. "Capitalism's Crisis of Care." *Dissent*. https://www.dissentmagazine.org/article/nancy-fraser-interview-capitalism-crisis-of-care.

McAndrew, Natalie Susan, Jane Leske, and Kathryn Schroeter. 2018. "Moral Distress in Critical Care Nursing: The State of the Science." *Nursing Ethics* 25 (5): 552–70.

McGee, Micki. 2020. "Capitalism's Care Problem: Some Traces, Fixes, and Patches." *Social Text* 38, no. 1 (142): 39–66.

Miller, Sarah Clark. 2009. "Moral Injury and Relational Harm: Analyzing Rape in Darfur." *Journal of Social Philosophy* 40 (4): 504–23.

Miller, Sarah Clark. 2012. *The Ethics of Need: Agency, Dignity, and Obligation*. New York: Routledge.

Navarro, Vincente. 2020. "The Consequences of Neoliberalism in the Current Pandemic." *International Journal of Health Services* 50 (3): 271–75.

Nguyen, Minh T. N., Roberta Zavoretti, and Joan Tronto. 2017. "Beyond the Global Care Chain: Boundaries, Institutions and Ethics of Care." *Ethics and Social Welfare* 11 (3): 199–212.

Padgett, Lynne, and Joao L. Ascensao. 2019. "Reframing Clinician Distress: Moral Injury not Burnout." *Federal Practitioner* 36 (11): 502–4.

Povinelli, Elizabeth A. 2011. *Economies of Abandonment: Social Belonging and Endurance in Late Liberalism*. Durham, N.C.: Duke University Press.

Robinson, Fiona. 2015. "Care Ethics, Political Theory, and the Future of Feminism." In *Care Ethics and Political Theory*, edited by Daniel Engster and Maurice Hamington, 293–311. New York: Oxford University Press.

Rodrik, Dani. 2017. "The Fatal Flaw of Neoliberalism: It's Bad Economics." *The Guardian*. https://www.theguardian.com/news/2017/nov/14/the-fatal-flaw-of-neoliberalism-its-bad-economics.

Scheper-Hughes, Nancy. 1989. "Death without Weeping." *Natural History* 98 (10): 8–16.

Scheper-Hughes, Nancy. 1993. *Death without Weeping: The Violence of Everyday Life in Brazil.* Berkeley: University of California Press.

Shaw, Jennifer, and Darren Byler. 2016. "Precarity." *Cultural Anthropology.* https://journal.culanth.org/index.php/ca/catalog/category/precarity.

Smith, Susan J. 2005. "States, Markets and an Ethic of Care." *Political Geography* 24 (1): 1–20.

Springer, Simon, Kean Birch, and Julie MacLeavy. 2016, "An Introduction to Neoliberalism." In *Handbook of Neoliberalism,* edited by Simon Springer, Kean Birch, and Julie MacLeavy, 1–14. New York: Routledge.

Talbot, Simon G., and Wendy Dean. 2018. "Physicians Aren't 'Burning Out.' They're Suffering from Moral Injury." *STAT.* https://www.statnews.com/2018/07/26/physicians-not-burning-out-they-are-suffering-moral-injury/.

Tronto, Joan C. 2013. *Caring Democracy: Markets, Equality, and Justice.* New York: New York University Press.

Ward, Lizzie. 2015. "Caring for Ourselves? Self-Care and Neoliberalism." In *Ethics of Care: Critical Advances in International Perspective,* edited by Marian Barnes, Tula Brannelly, Lizzie Ward, and Nicki Ward, 45–56. Bristol, UK: Polity.

White, Julie Ann. 2015. "Practicing Care at the Margins: Other-Mothering as Public Care. In *Care Ethics and Political Theory,* edited by Daniel Engster and Maurice Hamington, 208–24. New York: Oxford University Press.

Wiinikka-Lydon, Joseph. 2019. "Mapping Moral Injury: Comparing Discourses of Moral Harm." *The Journal of Medicine and Philosophy* 44 (2): 175–91.

Wrenn, Mary V., and William Waller. 2017. "Care and the Neoliberal Individual." *Journal of Economic Issues* 51 (2): 495–502.

CHAPTER 3

Vulnerability, Precarity, and the Ambivalent Interventions of Empathic Care

VRINDA DALMIYA

Is Precarity a Problem for Care Ethics?

The concept of vulnerability is importantly different from that of precarity, though both foreground notions of fragility. Vulnerability is cashed out in terms of frailties associated with human embodiment. Care ethics can thus be billed as an ethics of vulnerability because responding to "inevitable dependencies" of old age, sickness, and death constitutes its normative foundations. The moral refashioning toward care, after all, occurs "when we view the *vulnerability of dependency*, rather than interference of others into our lives as the chief moral concern" (Kittay, Jennings, and Wasunna 2005, 454; emphasis mine). Within the distinctively relational framework of care, what we owe to others and why is motivated by needs arising from being human with a body. But then, can an ethics based on universal corporeal dependencies address situational sufferings that we *do not* share? The idea of precarity, unlike vulnerability, signals exclusionary political orders and ideologies that render some more vulnerable than others. We all fall sick, for instance, but many cannot access health care, and their suffering is disproportionately greater because of poverty. Thus, there is a gap between ontological conditions of fragility requiring "care" and political conditions of precarity requiring ideological and social change. Estelle Ferrarese (2016) therefore distinguishes vulnerability as a "state" and precarity as a "process" created by policies of exclusion often identified with neoliberal agendas. The worry then is that care, grounded as it is in responses to an all-pervasive vulnerability, ends up talking past socioeconomically caused precarities, just as claims of "all lives mattering" elide the unique circumstances of Black lives. From this point of view, far from being an "alternative" to the troubles created by neoliberalism as some have claimed it to be (Tronto 2017), the care perspective could well be irrelevant to it.

When caring is situated geopolitically, another wrinkle tangles vulnerability and precarity in especially pressing ways. Studies show that migrants coming in from poorer nations to address the "crises of care" in the North routinely fall prey to oppressive policies in their host countries (Weir 2005). The latter are due to "privileged irresponsibilities" sanctioned by the neoliberal ethos in the receiving states (Tronto 2013). Parvati Raghuram, on the other hand, stresses how neoliberal policies undergird global chains of caring from the opposite end. Structural adjustment programs, opening up to foreign capital, and removal of state subsidies in the sending states "has squeezed the life of women in the Global South, forcing them to pursue alternative survival strategies, particularly migration" (2016, 513). Hence, in the global context, the very process of meeting *vulnerability* needs through care is embroiled with *precarities* experienced by (migrant) care workers. The question, then, is whether the care ethical perspective can redress unique sufferings arising *because* of a response to vulnerability needs across national borders. Such entanglement of vulnerability and precarity in the context of globalization resurrects older concerns about the troubled relationship of care to class and race and its extension outside domains of intimacy. This chapter explores whether resources within the perspective of care—resources in intimacy itself—enable care to step beyond an engagement with all-too-human vulnerabilities and speak to pains caused by neoliberal policies not equally shared by all.

One move toward making the care framework more inclusive could be to understand the precarity of migrant care workers in terms of Eva Kittay's notion of "secondary dependency" (Kittay 1999). Kittay has shown how caregivers themselves become vulnerable when responding to basic vulnerabilities or the "inevitable dependencies" of the cared for. For example, the affective labor of attending to the "primary" physical needs of a disabled child leaves the mother unable to attend to her own needs, thereby making her dependent on others. But as Kittay goes on to argue, since care ethics calls for responsiveness to dependency, it is logically committed to addressing these ("secondary" or created) dependencies of caregivers as well. In this way, the precarity of migrant care workers—their situationally caused needs arising because they take care of vulnerabilities in the Global North—could be folded into the normative world of care and redressing them would become an obligation within that framework. However, the subsequent question is what is at issue here. Can the responsibility to attend to such caring-induced precarity be operationalized in terms of the care perspective itself? Kittay's (1999) "analogical move" in *Love's Labor* that calls for extending infant care to a caring for global caregivers is too thin to answer this question. The fragility of precarity is of a different kind: after all, transnational caring, often involving "affective after-lives of colonialism, slavery and racism" (Pedwell 2013, 22), is complex in a different way and requires sensitivities other than and beyond those of mothers being attuned to the corporeal fragility of infants. Thus, conditions of responding to an ontological state (vulnerability), on the one hand, and to politically induced circumstances (precarity), on the other, can fall apart. While *Love's Labor* goes a long way toward incorporating precarity as a moral responsibility within the care framework, one may need to step outside the world of care in order to make the political adjustments that redress these injustices. Noting that care work bleeds into the political sphere is an important step. But it is a different move to then claim that institutional changes also involve the conceptual pillars of care. Spelling out sociopolitical transformations in terms of "care concepts" is not the same as claiming that caring requires these changes. The endeavor here is to see whether care can go deep enough to reach the latter domain.

In her later work, Kittay herself (Kittay, Jennings, and Wasunna 2005; Kittay 2008, 2009) bridges the gap between addressing vulnerability and the political concerns of redressing precarity by using the relational self to ground a "right to care." Since the self in care ethics is constituted by intimate bonds to un-substitutable others, the dignity of a migrant care worker gives her a right to care for her own children in and through affective relations with them: her very selfhood generates an entitlement that she be able and allowed to "take care" of them in this way. However, ensuring this right requires large-scale adjustments in global policy. For instance, either economic conditions in the home country improve so that the worker is not forced to migrate to provide the resources needed to care for her family back home, or changes in immigration policies and pay structures in the host country open up the option of her family to accompany her so that taking care of them face to face can continue. In this way, a fundamental principle of care ethics—the affective bonds of the relational self—serves as the hinge for macro-level adjustments that reduce precarity associated with migrant care work. Of course, Kittay's terminology is that of responding to the "unique harm" of such labor, but the uniqueness here clearly gestures toward precarity over and above vulnerability.

I find this move ingenious. However, care "travels" in a globalized world in multiple ways other than the migration of professional care workers. Such alternative mobilities are linked to a host of harms not spoken for by the right to care, or any other "right" for that matter.[1] Therefore, my discussion moves away from injustices associated with the "global heart transplant" and looks at caring across nations in what is termed "volunteer tourism" and "celebrity humanitarianism." This is a radically different form of transnational care in that the direction of the flow is from the North to the South, is sporadic, and does not particularly generate precarities in the tourist caregivers who offer care in the countries they visit. Yet, the phenomenon brings to light the slippage between addressing (corporeal) vulnerabilities of transnationally based cared fors and redressing their precarities, that is, the politically motivated insecurities framing their experience of vulnerabilities. Failure in addressing such precarities in these instances of cross-border caring helps focus on whether care can at all respond to complicated inequities caused by colonization and oppressive histories between nations. In fact, help/aid structured by neoliberal practices perpetuate neocolonial precarities that necessitate aid.

Similar conundrums seem pervasive. Kittay appeals to an "eros of social relations" (Weir 2008)—the affective ties constituting a relational self—in order to reach into the precarity of migrant care workers. The alternative explored here taps into the resources of affective care work by specifically focusing on *empathy*. Of course, there are doubts whether empathy is significant for ethics in general (Prinz 2011) and for care ethics in particular (van Dijke et al. 2019). I sidestep those debates in order to begin with empathy as an umbrella concept that captures the emotional dimensions of an ethics that is non-rule based, relational, and geared to responding to particularized needs. Redressing specific needs requires understanding them. This in turn often depends on alternative knowledge sources to access the mind of concrete care recipients (Hamington 2017). Empathy is one such epistemic resource. However, it runs into a problem. On a "processual" understanding, neoliberalism (Peck and Theodore 2019) is an adaptable political rationality that reaches beyond the market and insidiously (re)constitutes subjectivities. This governing rationality of competition and individualism distorts the workings of affect and empathy in volunteer tourists attempting to reach out to the vulnerabilities of global others. Their empathic care then replicates and serves to further entrench colonial hierarchies responsible for the very needs (in the South) that the tourist caregivers seek to mitigate. The point here is that neoliberal forces can run as deep as the resources of care and distort the very mechanisms (in this case empathy) used to mitigate the precarities caused by the latter ideology.

My strategy of pushing back against the "corporatization" of empathic care is first to rethink empathy in the light of Dan Zahavi's articulation of the process within the discipline of phenomenology (2014a, 2014b, 2015; Zahavi and Rochate 2015) and then to explore whether this can enable transnational care to elide the corrupting forces of a shape-shifting neoliberaliz*ation* mentioned above.[2] I will argue that a rearticulated empathic "caring for" across the North/South divide can become a moment of resistance by grounding political solidarity for structural change. This reframing of empathy—a crucial constituent of care—therefore becomes aligned both with responses to precarity and with "politicizing" care ethics.

Maurice Hamington has also drawn attention to the political efficacy of empathy in the context of care. As a form of "embodied knowledge" necessary for caring, he argues that empathy is an "outgrowth of imagination that works from the body's resources" (2012, 60). Since embodiment is shared even among those we do not know, there is a potential for empathic caring across social divisions. In a bid to "negotiate powerful narratives of socially constructed otherness," he casts caring as a bodily "performance" (2015, 79). Appealing to dramaturgical exercises and reflective character acting, he shows how the skill of empathic caring can be trained to generate understandings of (and hence responses to) intersectionally complex identities different from ours. Even though Hamington is not explicitly concerned with caring in international contexts in these articles, the skills of negotiating entanglements of race, class, gender, and other socially articulated vectors of identity that he does address might well be portable and also help care ethics speak to transnational precarities.

The "spirit of empathetic understanding" (2015, 95) emerging from Hamington's novel dramaturgical/performative reading of care is grounded in an iterative dynamic of imaginative and embodied care shaping a certain kind of moral identity—a caring selfhood skilled at being attuned to intersectional differences. But these abilities or imaginative/empathic dispositions are honed by concentrating on an ontologically common denominator: the body. The strategy is to mobilize this corporal base to reach imaginatively into socially constructed otherness. But I wonder if this can go all the way with radical difference. In the memoir of her travels for international humanitarian projects, for example, Angelina Jolie (whose significance for our argument will become clearer shortly) repeatedly confronts limits to a presumed commonality when she says, "I *can't imagine* what they must be feeling" (2003, 34) and "I *don't know* what I am feeling" (51), and even "it (i.e., what people are going through all over the world) is *worse than I had imagined*" (75; all emphases mine). Instead of relying on imaginative extension of a universal corporeality, this chapter explores the strategy of beginning with differences that are foregrounded (paradoxically) by empathy. Imagination comes in to negotiate the contradictory pulls and dissonances of conflicting emotions revealed by empathic reaching outs. Thus, rather than a pre-given, shared sameness, an "affective solidarity" across borders *emerges* through the cooperation of empathy and imagination and goes on to becoming a stepping-stone for political coalitions.

This also indicates how empathy here differs from Michael Slote's use of the notion as the "primary mechanism of caring" (2007, 4). Claiming that "the care-ethical approach can be used to understand all of individual and political morality" (2), Slote's empathy-based criteria for social justice parse central moral concepts in terms of differences in empathy. However, to the extent that empathy is the source of moral motivation, Slote wants to expand our empathic range (and hence, care) by cultivating the capacity of "having the feelings of another (involuntarily) aroused in ourselves" (13). But as the musings of

Jolie above show, in the context of uneven power between empathizers and empathized, this is not always possible. In fact, it is not even desirable, given how empathy actually goes awry in an unequal social world. These dangers point us to explore an alternative understanding of empathy in relational terms as a *space of tension* between subjects. This, rather than "having the feelings of another," can function as a critical resource for both self- and social transformations.

The Failure of Transnational Empathic Care

Let us begin with an obvious *failure* of transnational empathic care because of intrusions of a neoliberal creep. In the contemporary phenomenon of "volunteer tourism," nongovernmental organizations (NGOs) in the South working to ameliorate vulnerability needs of local populations invite volunteers from the North to come and help in their developmental agendas. The idea is to provide privileged individuals from the North an "immersive" and "meaningful" experience of a foreign (usually poor) country. Traditional "sight-seeing" is sidestepped, while "doing" and "feeling" are encouraged. As Mary Mostafanezhad (whose fieldwork and analysis I rely on here) says, "Through discourses of sentimentality volunteer tourism is re-packaged as a seemingly more 'real' experience . . . and highlights affective and empathic encounters with local people" (2014, 115). Intimate face-to-face exchanges constitute "taking care" of (most often) the needs of underprivileged children within the organizational structure of a particular NGO. Such niche tourism has become attractive, usually for students on a "gap year," partly due to the media hype over celebrity involvement in international aid (e.g., Angelina Jolie). Volunteers construct themselves as "giving back," "making a difference," or "helping."

While there is a clear action component of "taking care" in such encounters, the intermingling of "cognitive empathy" and "emotional empathy"[3] that is the hallmark of care ethics is also at work here. The emotional dimensions of the exchanges are highlighted and considered to be life changing. Jackie, a twenty-three-year-old American, volunteering in Thailand, had this to say: "I just really loved working with the children and the young women. I don't want to seem all emotional but it totally was an emotional experience. I feel like their mother. I really feel like they love me too. It was such a fulfilling experience for me. I will never forget their faces. It was just so authentic" (Mostafanezhad 2013, 494). Jackie "feels" the love of the recipients of care, which motivates her to respond to their needs "like their mother." This basic core of sentimentality, however, takes on an interesting (and problematic) shape as we dig deeper into the discourses of tourist/volunteer participants. For instance, Sally, a twenty-three-year-old German volunteer, says, "You don't need to know anything necessarily; you just need to know, okay, this kid needs a hug and I can do that. I think that, that just gives you a feeling like, alright, if I can do this then anyone can, and well, there are lots of things I can do" (Mostafanezhad 2013, 490). And Natalie, a twenty-four-year-old from Canada goes further in explaining, "I only want to take care of the children because that is where you can make the most difference. Children are where we need to focus our attention. And, I am a woman and so I know how to do that. . . . Plus, it is good for me because I am studying to be a pre-school teacher and someday I want to have kids of my own" (Mostafanezhad 2013, 490).

What, if anything, is troubling about privileged tourist volunteers articulating their care in the above manner? Mostafanezhad sums it up in the concept of a "humanitarian gaze," which can be teased out in different ways. Besides the problematic gendering of care, the mother–child nexus in these comments is concerning on many other levels. First, volunteer tourism revolves around helping *children*. It is deemed "hard to work with adults because they have more complicated needs" and also "they are harder to develop relationships with" (2014, 115). However, the "child" is a trope for innocence. The focus on children also infuses the "helping/caring" of the tourist volunteers with a veneer of innocence. But in effect, this slips into preserving age-old imperialist hierarchies of "us" and "them" where the Global South becomes the infantile native forever in need of "us." Second, as markers of the "real" and the "authentic," these empathic encounters become the basis of a "felt truth" (Pedwell 2012b, 165). Tourist caregivers claim to be sources of authority on the basis of their "immersion" while the "Third World other" remains the passive object of empathy. This once again reinscribes the entrenched hierarchy of some who can know/give/help and others who are simply recipients of redemption and care. Finally, and most importantly, when compassionate volunteer tourists who "choose" to give (and hence, insidiously claim the power not to do so) are projected as the solution for social ills, the historical causes of poverty are elided. This invisibility of larger structural contexts goes hand in hand with a lack of awareness that historico-social particularities of the volunteers themselves are responsible for producing the problematic conditions that they try to redress. These contentious histories live on in the memories of "adults" in the Global South; traces left on their affective profiles result in the "difficulty" of relating to them in transnational exchanges that we are talking about. Thus, when the NGO–humanitarian–tourist nexus actively avoids engaging with forces that have caused a large number of people to lead precarious lives, pockets of incomprehension are created that quickly become the fault of the others.

In volunteer tourism, then, care work is explicitly and exclusively framed as a response to vulnerability needs of transnational care recipients—the generic desire for "hugs" that "anyone" can give and everyone needs. But attention to universal corporeal wants misses the fact that current vulnerabilities of "Third World children" are embedded in histories of exclusion and that their suffering includes *precarities* resulting from power plays between nations. An occlusion and willful ignorance of this fact is aided and abetted by thinking of cross-border exchanges as relations between independent individuals. Self-styled agents of change fail to see the background structures of privileging that poise them to be "helpers." The importance of structural conditions is erased by articulating caring as the individual's effort, competence, and responsibility to make the world better. Empathy, in such constructions, becomes one more "technology of knowing the other"—a skill for vitae building, which, in turn, quickly turns into a marketable resource. After all, banks and corporations "care" for their customers too! Students with immersive experiences in the developing world not only become good homemakers (the future mothers and preschool teachers in Mostafanezhad's studies) but also can sell themselves as "sensitive managers" to corporations with profit-oriented goals. Care allies itself with an "emotional capitalism" (Illouz 2007, 5) defined as "a culture in which emotional and economic discourses and practices mutually shape each other" (5) and where "affect is made an essential aspect of economic behavior and in which emotional life—especially that of the middle classes—follows the logic of economic relations and exchange" (5). We see here how the functioning of empathy is subsumed under neoliberal mantras of individualized responsibility and independence as well as the market rationality of corporate, entrepreneurial subjectivities.

In her analysis, Kittay, too, linked the perils of migrant care work to the transformation of care into a "commodity." Something similar happens to empathy in volunteer tourism. Affective immersions become the means to further market-oriented agendas: "feelings" consume the cultural other, transforming them into actors within a capitalist logic. But of course, empathy in transnational care work, even when constructed in this way, does help to alleviate some vulnerabilities—providing medicines and food and school supplies motivated by compassion is not unimportant. And the "good" of a "mothers-without-borders" kind of performance by, say, Jolie remains ambiguous and cannot be completely dismissed. However, the point is that more often than not such empathic care work ends up eliding and reinscribing precarities and is without the teeth to redress those causalities even as it addresses corporeal and general needs.

Despite these pitfalls, many feminists and anti-racist theorists (Meyers 1994; Chabot Davis 2014; Pedwell 2013) see empathy as central for social justice. Even Jolie, in the first chapter of her journal, notices her attitude as shifting from "studying people in a zoo" (Jolie 2003, 11) to wanting "to take each and every one of them home" (27) to the realization that their needs would not be met "unless all the right bureaucratic paperwork and process is done properly" (71). She asserts "I am forever changed" (xi) because of her immersive transcultural experiences. But is this change once again fated to be a piece of a neoliberal "self-improvement" feeding into emotional capitalism? Is it simply acquiring the individual capacity to feel and connect with exotic others, or can it be pushed to seeing "the structures of feeling and feeling of structure" (Pedwell 2012a, 294) that underlie our being caring subjects in the first place? It is fruitful to explore empathy with these questions in mind to see if it can open up radically different kinds of encounters between the North and South. Thus, "if we were to argue *against* neoliberalism from the standpoint of care" (as Joan Tronto [2017, 28] would have us do), and if there is no "outside" to a forever shifting neoliberal*ization*, then care has to be able to push back against these distortions and co-options of its voice from the *inside* as it were. Does empathy involved in the process of caring contain subversive resources to flip the system? This is what leads us to take a harder look at the transformational potential of immersive encounters valorized by volunteer tourism.

An Alternative: The Complex Intentionality of Affective Encounters

The dominant model of empathy in care ethics relies on identificatory gestures such as "mirroring," "transparency," or "putting oneself in the shoes of the other." Dan Zahavi (2014a, 2014b), however, following phenomenologists such as Edith Stein and Husserl (and recent work in cognitive science), rejects claims of a first-personal replication of another's mental states. Rather, empathy is said to be a sui generis capacity of directly accessing the minds of others but only as *their* conscious experiences. Just as I immediately grasp my mental states (in introspective self-knowledge), I can also directly know mental states experienced by another subject (in empathy). It is a prejudice, according to Zahavi, to categorize all mental states that are "directly" accessed as being housed in the subject's own mind. While the empathic grasp of another's, say, grief remains "mine," its intentional content, the sorrow, is experienced as belonging to someone else. If I see that you are agitated, I do not have to feel it as my own agitation. Empathy thus retains the difference between the empathizer and the empathized.

This model is useful in understanding face-to-face encounters of "immersion" in transnational contexts where the gap in viewpoints of the subjects involved may sometimes be unbridgeable. Targets of transnational empathy, as independent subjects of experience, can now have a radically different orientation to the world, and their experiences remain noncongruent with their empathizer's, even in the moment when the latter empathizes. This also allows the empathized to have a different perspective on the *empathizer* as part of their world. For instance, "*your* take on the world" includes "your take on *me*" as part of your world. Consequently, my empathic encounter with you has a triadic epistemic structure. In accessing the other's mind, the privileged tourist empathizer is pulled along to see both the *world* and *herself* differently as an "object" in the eyes of the relatively disadvantaged, cross-cultural or racial other. This nicely captures the import of Maria

Lugones' "playful world-travelling." The latter, after all, according to Lugones, is partly constitutive of cross-cultural and cross-racial love that involves entering into another's world so that "we [can] understand what it is to be them and *what it is to be ourselves in their eyes*" (Lugones 1989, 287; emphasis mine).

According to Zahavi, a triadic relation between me, you, and your take on the world stems from a connection between *two yous* and can be richer still. While "*your* take on the world" includes "your take on *me*" as part of your world, such self-othering does not exhaust the complicated intersubjectivity here. A distinct form of "being with others" called a "we-intentionality"—an experience of togetherness or a kind of sharing that brings in a "special reciprocity"—can emerge and is crucial for our argument here.

Think of the couple, Jane and Mary, enjoying a movie "together." Each enjoys the film first-personally; each is also empathically aware of the other experiencing the film, and each is aware of herself as experienced by the other. But for a genuine "we," these forms of other awareness must affect the quality of the individual experiences. The intentionality here is neither an aggregate of, nor reduced to, individual consciousness, but rather is an "interlocking" of first- and second-person experience "where the individuals only have the experience they have in virtue of their reciprocal relation to each other" (Zahavi 2014b, 245). In other words, Jane and Mary's own individual experience of the film encompasses/includes awareness of the other watching the film. For example, Jane does not see through Mary's eyes. Yet, the quality of watching "together" is different from watching alone. Here, her first-person experience is colored by *Mary's* experience of watching the movie. So also, mutatis mutandis, with Mary. According to Zahavi, the special reciprocity arises because being a "you" for the other implies that both Jane and Mary are implicitly aware of themselves "in the accusative, as attended to or addressed by the other" (247). Thus, the resulting consciousness is an affective reciprocity of mutual interpenetration whereby a first-personal experience is "colored by," "co-regulated," or "constitutively bound" with (245) experiences of themselves as being second persons for another. This is a "first-person plural"—a consciousness that incorporates perspectives not directly available to any single subject. Once again, my interactions with a second person include my awareness of her as looking on the world from her own "foreign" first-person lens, and consequently encompass an awareness of *myself* from that alien perspective.

My purpose here is not to engage with details of the in-house phenomenological literature on this point. Rather, the purpose is to see how we-intentionality can motivate care ethics to go beyond addressing vulnerability needs and engage with precarities. Zahavi himself, in emphasizing we-ness as a kind of sharing—enjoying the film together in the example above—goes on to caution that "not only can there be cases of intense you–me interaction, such as strong verbal disagreements or arguments, where there is not yet (or no longer) a we present, but even in more conciliatory situations, paying too much attention to the other might disrupt the shared perspective" (2014b, 249). But keeping this warning in mind, the intentional structure of the "shared" perspective may well be hospitable to situations when Jane, for instance, loved the film but Mary did not: it is possible that the affective intersubjectivity of we-ness—the pleasure of watching together—can persist despite dissimilarity in the hedonic content of the individual experiences involved. In fact, sometimes the pleasure in the joint project of watching together is enriched by the individuals not agreeing in their assessment of the film.

I suggest that caring is politically transformative if its empathic moment triggers such entangled intersubjectivity. In a paper co-authored with Elizabeth Spelman, Lugones has bemoaned the gap between the "you" and the "we." She notes there: "When I say 'we,' I am referring to Hispanas. I am accustomed to use the 'we' in this way" (1999, 17). But she then adds, "When I say 'you' I mean not the non-Hispanic but the white/Anglo women that I address" (17) and continues sadly to articulate the reasons for her "complaint-full discourse" with white/Anglo women where "we and you do not speak the same language" (17). The "you" and "we" here clearly are kept apart. Taking a leap, I wonder whether the connections between "Me, You, *and We*" spelled out in Zahavi's (2014b) chapter with that name (emphasis mine), might be able to negotiate the schism between a "we" and "you" that bothers Lugones—the impossible dichotomy of the radical other being either assimilated into or silenced by the privileged perspective. Our concern is whether the intentional structure of a subject-to-subject relation between two "yous" in cross-racial and cross-cultural empathy, a "we' in tension, can produce politically robust changes in institutional structures and policy that are respectful of differences between cultural groups noted so forcefully by Lugones. The next section attempts to address this challenge.

We-Intentionality of Solidarity

When the heart of empathic encounters consists in the caregiver's experience of the cared for as a "you," then transnational caring opens up space for a cultural other to have emotions contrary to those of the (differently situated) privileged caregivers, many of which the caregivers are unable to feel themselves and may even include the cared for's desire *not* to be empathized with. Cross-border empathic caring, freed of the constraint of "feeling what the other feels" or "identifying" with the other, is therefore exempt from the impossible task of experiencing what it is like to have been colonized or racially oppressed when one has not gone through these oppressions. Transitioning from a direct grasp of what the other feels (which, remember, is not to feel those feelings oneself) to the more complex structure of *we-ness* brings in interesting consequences. Importantly, it shifts the focus away from empathy as an individual skill of knowing others to a relation of (possible) *emotional dissonance*. The "interlocking" of the experiences of those involved in the cross-cultural encounter creates an affective terrain *in between* the empathizer and the empathized where a whole range of emotions can be presented. Cynicism, rage, bitterness, irony, sarcasm (in "adult" transnational cared fors, for example) are now held together with the volunteer caregiver's love and compassion, with no requirement for either to *feel with* the other. In this way, empathic moments become a space of affective tension rather than of cozy identifications.

Such re-situating of empathy is relevant for the analysis of caring itself as well as for understanding precarity. To begin with the former, traditional care theory[4] has spoken of the different stages of (1) "caring about" (making the particularized cared for important), (2) "caring for" (empathically grasping the inner world of the cared for), (3) "taking care" (working for the interests of the cared for), and (4) "reciprocity" (the cared for registering the efforts of the caregiver). It is interesting that the "reciprocity condition" (Noddings 1984), even in its early articulations, never implied that the cared for had to "care" for the caregiver in return or even accept her care. Rather, the idea of reciprocity was to allow the cared for to register her independent point of view and criticisms of the efforts of the caregiver, thus making care relational and not an individual excellence of the one caring. The entanglement of empathy with Zahavian we-intentionality has the advantage of showing how such reciprocity of care, or (4) above, follows naturally from (2) above. In other words, the very intersubjectivity of an empathic "caring for" involving the "special reciprocity" of a Zahavian we-intentionality ensures that caring itself stays relational. The cared for's possible counter-narratives are not erased but come to the forefront in the we-ness between her and the caregiver. The relationality of caring is thus not ad hoc but inbuilt in the very beginnings of the process that makes the cared for important by empathically reaching out to her. But of course, we need to go further to show how the relationally sustained archive of contrary feelings initiated by empathy helps mitigate precarities both nationally and internationally. Two trajectories need to be pursued here.

First, emotions in this in-between space are no longer merely personal, psychological proclivities of the protagonists involved but rather become indicative of their different locations and histories. Thus, emotional dissonance becomes the field of opposed pulls and pushes of structural positions. The disaffections expressed by the postcolonial cared for in the "relation" of caring are non-discursive signifiers of horrible histories, sometimes even without the subject having a clear picture of what the injustice was. As Carolyn Pedwell (2013) puts it, affective intersubjectivity of empathic care scrambles historical linearity and "presents" the *past* to those who either have not lived through it or no longer have the discursive means to engage with it. For instance, when the cultural other's rage or cynicism is "interlocked" with perspectives of privileged caregivers, abusive power relations that have decimated entire regions are brought to the surface, but without requiring that the caregiver experience those horrors herself or even without demanding that the cared for articulate them in language. These ugly histories are epistemically tracked on the emotional register of the once colonized, and we-intentionality makes visible the political reality that dominant discourses push into oblivion. Privileged tourist volunteers, of course, do not (and cannot) experience the past in the same way as the transnational recipients of their humanitarian efforts do. Yet, they can now "witness" those experiences through a we-ness with their cared fors. When face-to-face encounters morph into a consciousness reflecting multiple "yous," the resulting we-intentionality becomes rich with footprints of multiple perspectives on history. The "present" bleeds outside itself both temporally and spatially, and so the current needs of the cared for get located structurally, both horizontally, across nations, and vertically, across times. This is important because there can be no redress without a thick and nuanced understanding of the problems to be fixed. We-intentionality thereby gives political depth to "needs" that an ethics of care responds to by rearticulating them as socio-historically embedded.

However, merely understanding precarity—a thick grasp of the way structural conditions and power augment vulnerability—does not amount to their redressal. For the step from interpersonal structures of consciousness to actual institutional transformations in policy, we dig deeper into the triadic relation between the caregiver, the transnational cared for, and her world. The privileged volunteer tourist who grasps history *in* (though not "through") the eyes of the postcolonial cared for ends up confronting a construction of herself as *culpable.* Current privileges of the (volunteer tourist) caregiver trade on contentious pasts and make her complicit according to the perspective of those on the receiving end of that history. Of course, the caregiver is not involved agentially in the oppression, and more importantly this need not be her own self-appraisal. But the "dissonance" in these constructions of herself (by herself and by the cared for) can be disturbing and an important deconstructive moment. As marking an unjust past, negative emotions of the transnational cared for become protests and demands for justice. Through registering these emotions *and* encountering herself as complicit in the oppression they signal, the caregiver can begin to see herself as blameworthy too. This is a step toward a commitment to redress the wrongs and the owning of a responsibility to do so. Through such a dynamic, the privileged caregiver can become motivated to bring change—a motivation that can be (for different reasons) as strong as the colonial subject's wish for justice. In this way, through different affective pathways, the caregiver and cared for in transnational contexts converge on the importance of initiating progressive social agendas. This is the basis of solidarity or "potential political alliances," which, as Chandra Mohanty says, are determined by "common context of struggles against specific exploitative structures and systems" (2003, 49).

Solidarity here is not a product of identity, unity, or identification (Gould 2007). It allows for material and affective differences and yet is a joint commitment for political transformation. However, dispositions to act for more justice in the lives of others always raise questions about the origin of those dispositions, particularly when they undermine the privilege of the subject. How do tourist volunteers come to acquire the second-order motivation to be committed to social change, particularly when those changes might disadvantage themselves while advantaging the transnational cared fors? The answer, once again, lies in the fact that we-ness can be a first-person plural. Consider our earlier apolitical example first: Jane and Mary enjoy the film together because each is aware of the other's experience of the film and of *being experienced by the other as watching the film.* In parallel fashion, the caring "togetherness" of the volunteer and her cultural other is an awareness that holds together (1) the volunteer caregiver's own response to the situation that NGOs address, (2) her awareness of the cared for's affectively different response to it, and (3) a reciprocal awareness where the caregiver and the cared for are each aware of the other's awareness of themselves. This means that the volunteer caregiver grasps that the transnational other finds the world unjust and considers her (the volunteer) complicit in the injustice. But since the togetherness is reciprocal, she is also aware that her cared for knows that she (the volunteer caregiver) is aware that she stands indicted. After all, the volunteer tourist is aware of herself "in the accusative" and as "attended to" by the other. Because of this, the privileged caregiver cannot hide behind forms of *willful ignorance.* She stands exposed in the eyes of the other, knowing that the other knows that she knows the charges of complicity against her. This dynamic becomes an invitation for her to engage with the reasons for the indictment which, in turn, leads to exploring her power and privilege. The self-reflexivity induced in the privileged caregiver by affective we-ness is a critical stance. This finally leads to (4)—the caregiver endorsing the moral-affective legitimacy of the claims of the cared for. In this way, we-intentionality can be *self-transformative* of the caregiver by inducing a motivational redirection to bring about justice. It makes empathic encounters between the North and South more than simple and uncomplicated interpersonal relations of "loving" an exotic other.

Some words of caution are in order here. First, a dissonant construction of oneself by the colonial cared for can be emotionally negotiated in different ways. Defensiveness, dismissiveness, and turning a blind eye to affective complaints remain possible outcomes, as much as the paternalist compassion seen in the subjects of Mostafanezhad's fieldwork. Self-transformation based on a critical awareness of history (amounting to changes in what we feel motivated to do) is just one possible reaction to affective dissonance. According to Zahavi, empathy itself is a *continuum* and signifies different grades of intersubjectivity. When it leads to we-intentionality, it presents affective dissonance but cannot guarantee solidarity as the response to it. This notwithstanding, note that the birth of care lies in the moment of valuing or making the cared for *important*—a "caring about" her. Given such a normative grounding, it is likely that in the context of care, the point of view of the cared for will be considered important. Caregivers come around to engage constructively with disaffections expressed in we-intentionality with the cared for because she *cares* for them. Thus, the emergence of a political solidarity is quite plausible, even though not certain within the framework of empathic care.

Second, a shared commitment for institutional change is not necessarily a shared vision of what that change should be. Blueprints for going forward differ, particularly across social divides. The hopes of a populace damaged by a past are different from the hopes of those who have not been similarly victimized. In the collective reimagining of social transformation, it is important to countenance this difference. Thus, empathy alone cannot yield consensus on the details of, say, immigration policy, debt forgiveness, or tax treaties and all the varied policy changes geared to alleviating precarities. Discursive dialogues are necessary to determine *what* changes to pursue.

The intersubjectivity of empathy scrambles linearity but, in keeping the past alive, alerts us to the possibility of alternative imaginings and hopes of the future emerging from these different histories. Imagination comes in here not as tool to construct what the other feels but rather as a political skill to negotiate between these different visions of a just society.

But of course, even this makes a big assumption: that the once colonized are also committed to "acting together" with the ex-colonizer. That might not be the case. Political solidarity therefore must also include reciprocity from the side of the care for *on the level of action.* Affective intersubjectivity might fall short of ensuring this, even though (as we have argued) it can motivate privileged caregivers to build political alliances. As noted, however, receptivity to the different voices and stakeholders in empathic we-intentionality can be a form of critical listening. Such listening may go some way toward building trust of disadvantaged cared fors and nudge them into wanting to cooperate more substantially. Thus, the affective field sustained by empathic care could create the epistemological and affective conditions for a joint commitment to change and an ongoing collective thinking about what shape that might take.

In conclusion, let us return to Tronto's optimism that "*if we take the care perspective seriously,* it requires us to change the terms of the discussion" (2017, 37; emphasis mine) and move away from neoliberal agendas that exacerbate precarity. The problem lies in the conditional clause. *Can* we take the message of care "seriously" when we are in the grips of a very different neoliberal framing narrative? We see the failure to do so in the volunteer tourists of Mostafanezhad's fieldwork. The problem, in Tronto's own words, is that "from within a world in which everything becomes commodified, how is such a change (to the world of care) possible?" (2017, 37). In answer, Tronto turns to the "double movement" in the history of capitalism, wherein the valorization of the free market has always gone hand in hand with forces that look out for the social protection of labor. She puts her hopes on these latter forces to bring about the switch. But in doing so, Tronto distinguishes care as a "*political* ideal" about democratic allocation of responsibilities for vulnerability and the "daily work of care" (33). However, the attempt in this chapter has been to show that this daily care work involving empathy can bootstrap itself into motivating institutional changes that are required by the "new political idea." Tronto's alternative to neoliberalism is the notion of "caring with" or a sustainable pattern of "an ongoing cycle of care" that can continue to meet caring needs and "produce the virtues of trust and solidarity" (32). I have argued that quotidian care work involving a reconstructed notion of empathy can undergird the collective work of a "caring with." Empathic intersubjectivity is capacious enough to encompass the political dimensions of affective togetherness and help care expand its reach.

Ultimately, caring is not just work. An underlying affective intersubjectivity is a desired and valued aspect of care. The argument here dips into this latter dimension of care to make it sensitive to precarities and the social changes that respond to it. Of course, one needs to be careful because the insidious forces of neoliberal*ization* filter into this subterranean affective terrain. The shattered innocence of the volunteer tourist's desire to fix things for transnational others through her sheer choice to connect with them emotionally is a case in point. However, there is hope, since the very pervasiveness of neoliberalism conceived as a process moves it away from a "pure" form. "Conjunctural" or "local" formations of neoliberalism invoke the metaphor of situated struggle. Its reproduction and situational (re)constitution are "marked by friction, contradictions, and endemically uneven geographical development, volatile hybridity being its condition of existence" (Peck and Theodore 2019, 260). The argument here mines the tensions within the "conflicted 'insides'" of the constituted neoliberal moment of volunteer tourism to reclaim care redemption. The refashioning of empathy by neoliberalism in its takeover of volunteer tourism is loose and partial. This holds out the hope that a deeper and phenomenologically inspired experience of this affective moment would disrupt its neoliberal construction.

To sum up, the relation between vulnerability and precarity makes need fulfillment complex. Particular bodies "live" their vulnerabilities differently according to their political contexts. When responding to vulnerability, a caring relation has to be mindful of contingent causes that augment a "human" suffering. The complex intersubjectivity of empathic care across borders can motivate caregivers to look beyond vulnerability and engage with precarity. Thus, transnational North–South immersive experiences, despite dangers of them slipping into the status quo, do contain seeds of solidarity for transformative social change. But such political transformation is always a struggle—the struggle against framing ideologies and struggles with inbuilt dissonances within empathic intersubjectivity. The continued playing out of this struggle is also the process of caring.[5] It is not despite these differences and contentious relations between transnational subjects but *because* of them that empathy can engage with precarity. Paradoxically, then, empathy—the signifier of the "closeness" of caring—becomes a means of engaging with a "politics of difference."

Notes

I am grateful to Sharon Rowe, Eva Kittay, and Arindam Chakrabarti for comments on an earlier incarnation of the argument here. A version of this chapter was presented at the Annual CERC Conference on "Care Ethics and Precarity" held in Portland, Oregon, 2018. I have benefitted from comments from the audience there. I am especially thankful to the editors, Maurice Hamington and Michael Flower, for their very helpful feedback.

1. The deployment of "rights" within a perspective of care can be tricky. Kittay herself deals with the complexity and meaning of such a right (Kittay 2008). Furthermore, concentration on "rights" can easily become linked to the *choice* to do care work. But this kind of freedom can draw attention away from care as a "responsibility." Of course, Kittay's argument is subtle in showing how a "right" to care leads us to a social responsibility to care. See also Allison Weir (2008).

2. Bonnie Mann in conversation worried justifiably about using Dan Zahavi's apolitical analysis of empathy for care ethics. However, my point is to show that care can bootstrap itself into a political impulse by beginning with this neutral construal of empathy.

3. Emotion in care functions both as a way of coming to "know" another as well as a motivation to respond to what is known. See Hamington (2017, 266).

4. I have used Nel Noddings' (1984) terminology here. However, different care theorists use different language and parse these conditions differently. For a systemization of these different articulations of the conditions of care, see also Dalmiya (2016).

5. Of course, more work is needed to extend solidarity emerging from face-to-face immersive experiences to relations between distant members of groups and anonymous forms of we-intentionality. What we have here is just a first step in a direction that also opens up rethinking the institutional restructuring of volunteer tourism itself to nurture this complicated form of empathy.

Works Cited

Chabot Davis, Kimberly. 2014. *Beyond the White Negro: Empathy and Anti-Racist Reading.* Urbana: University of Illinois Press.

Dalmiya, Vrinda. 2016. *Caring to Know: Comparative Care Ethics, Feminist Epistemology, and the Mahābhārata.* New Delhi: Oxford University Press.

Ferrarese, Estelle. 2016. "Vulnerability: A Concept with Which to Undo the World as It Is?" *Critical Horizons* 17 (2): 149–59.

Gould, Carol. 2007. "Transnational Solidarities." *Journal of Social Philosophy* 38 (1): 148–64.

Hamington, Maurice. 2012. "Care Ethics and Corporeal Inquiry in Patient Relations." *The International Journal of Feminist Approaches to Bioethics* 5 (1): 52–69.

Hamington, Maurice. 2015. "Care Ethics and Engaging Intersectional Differences through the Body." *Critical Philosophy of Race* 3 (1): 79–100.

Hamington, Maurice. 2017. "Empathy and Care Ethics." In *Routledge Handbook of Philosophy of Empathy*, edited by Heidi Maibom, 264–74. Oxon, UK: Routledge.

Illouz, Eva. 2007. *Cold Intimacies: The Making of Emotional Capitalism*. Boston: Polity.

Jolie, Angelina. 2003. *Notes from My Travels*. New York: Pocketbooks.

Kittay, Eva Feder. 1999. *Love's Labor: Essay on Women, Equality, and Dependency*. New York: Routledge.

Kittay, Eva Feder. 2008. "The Global Heart Transplant and Caring across National Boundaries." *Southern Journal of Philosophy* XLVI:138–65.

Kittay, Eva Feder. 2009. "The Unique Harm of Migrant Care Work: Realizing a Global Right to Care." *Philosophical Topics* 37 (1): 53–73.

Kittay, Eva Feder, Bruce Jennings, and Angela A. Wasunna. 2005. "Dependency, Difference, and the Global Ethic of Longterm Care." *Journal of Political Philosophy* 13 (4): 443–69.

Lugones, Maria C. 1989. "Playfulness, 'World'-Travelling, and Loving Perception." In *Women, Knowledge, and Reality: Explorations in Feminist Philosophy*, edited by Ann Garry and Marilyn Pearsall, 275–90. Boston: Unwin Hyman.

Lugones, Maria C., and Elizabeth V. Spelman. 1999. "Have We Got a Theory for You! Feminist Theory, Cultural Imperialism and the Demand for 'The Woman's Voice.'" In *Women and Values: Readings in Recent Feminist Philosophy*, edited by Marilyn Pearsall, 14–24. London: Wadsworth.

Meyers, Diana Teitjens. 1994. *Subjection and Subjectivity*. London: Routledge.

Mohanty, Chandra Talpade. 2003. *Feminism without Borders: Decolonizing Theory, Practicing Solidarity*. Durham, N.C.: Duke University Press.

Mostafanezhad, Mary. 2013. "'Getting in Touch with Your Inner Angelina': Celebrity Humanitarianism and the Cultural Politics of Gendered Generosity in Volunteer Tourism." *Third World Quarterly* 34 (3): 485–99.

Mostafanezhad, Mary. 2014. "Volunteer Tourism and the Popular Humanitarian Gaze." *Geoforum* 54:111–18.

Noddings, Nel. 1984. *Caring: A Feminine Approach to Ethics and Moral Education*. Berkeley: University of California Press.

Peck, Jamie, and Nick Theodore. 2019. "Still Neoliberalism?" *The South Atlantic Quarterly* 118 (2): 245–65.

Pedwell, Carolyn. 2012a. "Economies of Empathy: Obama, Neo-liberalism, and Social Justice." *Society and Space* 30:280–97.

Pedwell, Carolyn. 2012b. "Affective (Self) Transformations: Empathy, Neo-liberalism and International Development." *Feminist Theory* 13 (2): 163–79.

Pedwell, Carolyn. 2013. "Affect at the Margins: Alternatives Empathies in a Small Place." *Emotion, Space, and Society* 8:18–26.

Prinz, Jesse. 2011. "Against Empathy." *Southern Journal of Philosophy* 49, Spindel Supplement: 214–33.

Raghuram, Parvati. 2016. "Locating Care Ethics beyond the Global North." *ACME: An International Journal for Critical Geographies* 15 (3): 511–33.

Slote, Michael. 2007. *The Ethics of Care and Empathy*. London: Routledge.
Tronto, Joan. 2013. *Caring Democracy: Markets, Equality, and Justice*. New York: New York University Press.
Tronto, Joan. 2017. "There Is an Alternative: *Homines Curans* and the Limits of Neoliberalism." *International Journal of Care and Caring* 1 (1): 27–43.
van Dijke, Jolanda, Inge van Nistelrooij, Pien Bos, and Joachim Duyndam. 2019. "Care Ethics: An Ethics of Empathy?" *Nursing Ethics* 26 (5): 1282–91.
Weir, Allison. 2005. "The Global Universal Caregiver: Imagining Women's Liberation in the New Millennium." *Constellations* 12 (3): 308–30.
Weir, Allison. 2008. "Global Care Chains: Freedom, Responsibility and Solidarity." *Southern Journal of Philosophy* XLVI:166–75.
Zahavi, Dan. 2014a. "Empathy and Other-Directed Intentionality." *Topoi* 33:129–42.
Zahavi, Dan. 2014b. "You, Me, We." In *Self and Other: Exploring Subjectivity, Empathy and Shame*, 241–50. Oxford: Oxford University Press.
Zahavi. Dan. 2015. "Self and Other: From Pure Ego to Co-constituted We." *Continental Philosophy Review* 48 (2): 143–60.
Zahavi, Dan, and Phillippe Rochate. 2015. "Empathy =/= Sharing: Perspectives from Phenomenology and Developmental Psychology." *Consciousness and Cognition* 36:543–53.

CHAPTER 4

Precariousness, Precarity, Precariat, Precarization, and Social Redundancy

A Substantiated Map for the Ethics of Care

ANDRIES BAART

Although the concept of precarity ranges well beyond the Netherlands—in fact, it has become a worldwide phenomenon—I start with an excellent example from that country. It illustrates one of the phenomena that we will elaborate on in a global context.

During the elections for the Lower House of the Dutch Parliament in 2016, the social-democratic party (*Partij van de Arbeid* [PvdA] or Labor Party) suffered a spectacular defeat. Its presence was reduced from 38 out of 150 members to only 9. This was unexpected and unprecedented in the long history of the party. Although there are reasons and conditions specific to the Netherlands that contributed to this steep decline, nearly all European social-democratic parties are on a rapid retreat, and right-wing populists are on the rise and taking over in one country after another (Wodak, KhosraviNik, and Mral 2013; Wodak and Krzyżanowski 2017). Like the Democrats in the United States, these big losers are desperately looking for adequate and satisfactory solutions to the problem. If they maintain their traditional political message using traditional language, they risk becoming obsolete. If they cooperate with neoliberal parties, as the Dutch PvdA has done, they lose their identity in the eyes of the electorate and are punished for it. And if they bend to the wishes of the people, they are likely to end up with populists and hate preachers. For the most part, the social democrats have rejected the last option on moral grounds. Throughout Europe (and beyond), we are currently witnessing these social-democratic parties trying to reinvent themselves, which is far from easy (Törnquist and Harriss 2016; Mouffe 2018; Mudge 2018).

In the Netherlands, the PvdA has, with the help of social-democratic communication experts, chosen to summarize its message as "certainty." This is intended to convey a unique selling point compared to the other parties and to chime with the main concerns of the electorate. The message is: if you are uncertain about your pension, the affordability of health care, and the fate of your parents suffering from Alzheimer's, vote Labor (PvdA); if you doubt whether there will be sufficient, fairly paid, and safe jobs, vote Labor; if you doubt whether your children will have access to a decent education without taking out crippling study loans or whether there will be affordable housing, vote Labor; if you suffer from the poor prospects of our environment and resources and if you worry that water, electricity, and public transport are not guaranteed due to the functioning of the market and because they are in foreign hands, vote Labor. The basic idea is clear and seemingly relevant: we know your concerns, we care about you, and we will abolish a system that undermines our confidence in one another and in our future. We know that you are suffering from terrifying uncertainty in all crucial domains of life, today even more than yesterday. And that it is predominantly caused, propelled, and prolonged by capitalistic regimes that affect the labor market, health care, education, and other crucial domains. Just one simple message, a symbol of traditional left-wing concerns, solidarity and care, but without explicitly voicing it.

I mention this attempt by the Dutch because, in my opinion, it is trying to address a big and urgent problem in the background: the widespread, all-penetrating, late-modern variety of precarity that is frightening everyone, from the poor to well-paid managers in the financial sector and middle-class white-collar workers to the proverbial hermit in isolated parts of the world, from robust youngsters to pensioners, and from the Global North to the Global South. Precarity pertains to much more than poverty, unemployment, bad housing, or unhealthy working conditions. Fundamentally, it is about pervasive uncertainty: you do not have any idea whether you will be able to survive until tomorrow; you cannot be sure whether there is a future at all, let alone whether there is somebody who cares about it. (For an excellent and broadly oriented overview of around four hundred publications on precarity, see Betti [2018].) Because precarity is closely linked to global economics, the phenomenon is not restricted to poor regions of the world but also pertains, in an adapted form, to wealthy countries, including the United States, the European Union, and the major emerging national economies of the BRICS (Brazil, Russia, India, China, and South Africa).

This chapter sets out to map the phenomenon of precarity in its complexity and ramifications and will explore its relation to care and caring. The superficial impression that precarity and care are the flipsides of the same coin will be reinforced and specified. The ethics of care is, in its actual form, mostly political-ethically orientated, and from that perspective, precarity is highly relevant: it may be interpreted as a key word of system-induced, late-modern neediness to which care should be an adequate response. I will sketch the credibility of this proposition.

In the first section, the central concepts of precarity and precariousness are explored and compared according to leading authors in the field. I will conclude by presenting my own enriched description of precarity. From a static understanding, we move to the second section: the more dynamic interpretation (precarization), the indispensable phenomenological extension (the *experience of* social redundancy), and intervention-oriented interest (the struggle against precarization). One of the conclusions will be that precarization is an extremely ambiguous and ambivalent phenomenon, which erases all illusions about the blessings that care and caring bestow, wherever such naivety might exist.

Precarity and Precariousness

Precarity as Job Insecurity (Pierre Bourdieu)

One of the early theorists on (the late-modern condition of) precarity is the French sociologist Bourdieu (Bourdieu 1998a, 1998b; Masquelier 2018). His challenging analysis of precarity deliberately reconceptualizes it as a *labor condition* with relatively new but disruptive characteristics. The driving mechanism behind it has been identified as the contemporary era of neoliberalism. Neoliberalism is reforming labor conditions permanently according to the requirements of the global market for flexibility, and by doing so, it is eroding the guarantee of full-time employment. Bourdieu (1998b, 83) has linked precarity (*précarité*) to job insecurity. Focusing largely on postindustrial societies of the Global North, Bourdieu declared that precarity "is now everywhere," referring to rising unemployment and the introduction of flexible employment relations in the jobs that remained.

Those who have followed Bourdieu's approach also view precarity primarily as a labor condition (see, e.g., Castel 2003; Kalleberg 2011, 2018; Ross 2009; Vosko 2010). From this perspective, precarity refers to precarious work, characterized by job insecurity, temporary or part-time employment, a lack of social benefits, and low wages.

Precarity as Social Disintegration by New Labor Conditions (Robert Castel)

Robert Castel (2003, 2009) attempts to deal with various forms of poverty, and he too introduces the concept of precarity. What do the long-term unemployed poor have in common? They express, according to Castel, a particular mode of dissociation from the social bond called "disaffiliation." This is a condition of misery that differs radically from that of poverty in the strict sense, being interpreted as a state whose forms may be described in terms of lack (lack of earnings, housing, medical care, education, power, participation, or respect). Situations of destitution constitute an effect at the point where two vectors meet: one the axis of integration/non-integration through work; the other an axis of integration/non-integration in social relations (into a social and family network). The resulting model of four "zones" of social life—vulnerability, integration, disaffiliation, and assistance (Figure 4.1)—serves as a reference grid against which we can interpret contemporary social circumstances and the rise of social vulnerability. Each of these may be interpreted as a zone of (more or less) precarity.

So, in Castel's view, the widespread current insecurity stems largely from the growing erosion of protective regulation, implemented from the nineteenth century onwards in order to create, at least in Northern Europe, a stable, safe, and fair situation for workers. These laws were intended to give them the right to work, well-regulated recovery time, extended social protection, and, for instance, indemnity against social risks, all implemented by the welfare state. This system is disintegrating, and the result is new zones of precarity associated with forms of poverty and disintegration.

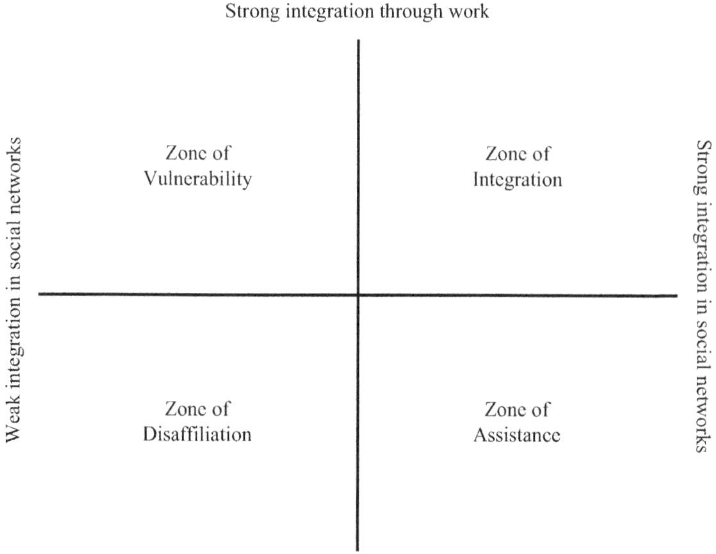

FIGURE 4.1. Castel's model of the four zones of integration and precarity.

Marchart (2013, 24) has adapted the zone concept on the basis of new insights, resulting in two additional schemes. In the first (Figure 4.2), the idea of "zones of precarity" is embedded in a bigger picture in which the zones are situated between society and class.

In the second model (Marchart 2013, 21), the idea of zones is revised and differentiated (inspired by Dörre 2005, 60). Here, four zones are reduced to three, and within each of these, differentiations are made and the "residents" of the zone allocated names according to their characteristics, for example "the secured ones" or "the dependent ones" (Figure 4.3). The picture comes gradually into sharper focus and is more closely related to empirical data.

Precarity as a Dangerous Class of Laborers (Guy Standing)

At first glance, Guy Standing's *The Precariat: The New Dangerous Class* (2011) would appear to continue in a similar vein, with its urgent tone of concern about the rise of job insecurity in the twenty-first

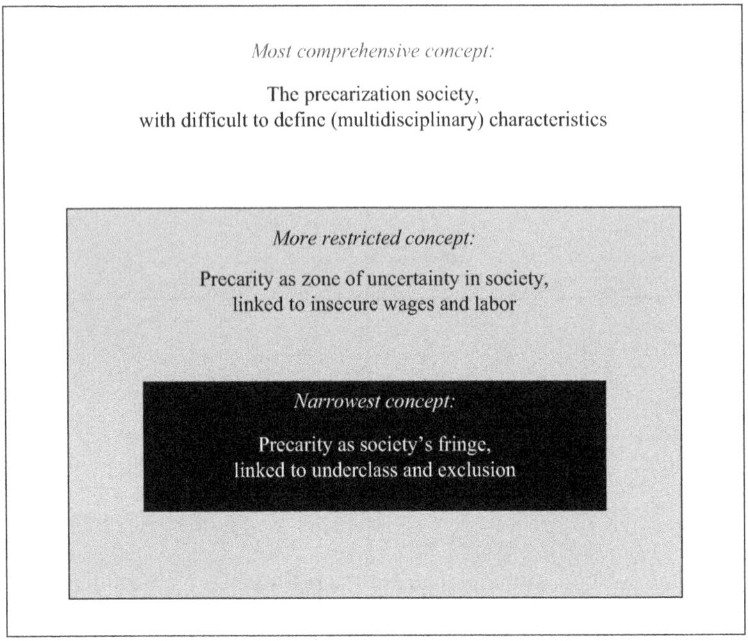

Most comprehensive concept:

The precarization society,
with difficult to define (multidisciplinary) characteristics

More restricted concept:

Precarity as zone of uncertainty in society,
linked to insecure wages and labor

Narrowest concept:

Precarity as society's fringe,
linked to underclass and exclusion

FIGURE 4.2. Marchart's model of the embedded zones of precarity (translated by the author).

century. Yet, the title alone suggests that the conversation has shifted from precarity as a labor condition to precarious workers as a socio-economic category or class. Standing uses precariat as a neologism formed by combining precarious with proletariat.

Several scholars have critiqued this class-based approach to precarity. Standing's rather apocalyptic depiction of the precariat as a potentially explosive force, fueled by anger and anomie, certainly revives Marx's description of the *Lumpenproletariat* as "social scum."

According to Standing, who is one of the leading thinkers about the precariat, precarity is best understood as a conceptualization in keeping with Marxist class theory (text quoted from or based on Hookes and Butler-Hookes 2016; spelling adapted):

> In the middle decades of the 20th century, capital, the trades unions and labor and social democratic parties all agreed to create a society and a welfare state oriented to laborism, based on a proletarianized

Zone	Integration Potentials of Wage Labor
Zone of integration	1a. Secured integration *(the secured ones)*
	1b. Atypical integration *(the self-managers)*
	1c. Uncertain integration *(the uncertain ones)*
	1d. Endangered integration *(the threatened by downturn ones)*
Zone of precarity	2a. Precarious occupation as chance / temporary integration *(the ones with hope)*
	2b. Precarious occupation as lasting arrangement *(the realists)*
	2c. Neutralized precariat *(the satisfied ones)*
Zone of disconnection	3a. Surmountable exclusion *(the ones eager for change)*
	3b. Controlled exclusion / arranged integration *(the dependent ones)*

FIGURE 4.3. Zones of precarity according to Marchart (2013, 21; translated from German by the author).

> majority, oriented to stable labor, with benefits linked to labor. For the proletarian, the main objective was better, "decent" labor, not escape from labor. The class structure corresponding to that system was relatively easy to describe, with a bourgeoisie—employers, managers and salaried professional employees—confronting a proletariat that between them formed the spine of society.

From the 1980s onward, neo-Keynesian economics was replaced by neoliberalism, which meant: privatizing every aspect of the public sphere; re-regulating the market in favor of large corporations; intensifying marketization of public goods (education, electricity, education, etc.); awarding huge state subsidies to large corporations and banks too big to fail; holding down wages and creating indebtedness to maintain consumption by the working class; commodifying education and creating students' debt to tame their tendency to political engagement; and intensifying and normalizing neoliberal discourse (Hookes and Butler-Hookes 2016). These are, in Standing's view (2011, 26–58), the conditions that triggered the formation of the precariat. In Standing (2014a and 2014b), he addressed the question: who is the precariat? Characteristic of the precariat are flexible or zero-hours labor contracts, temporary jobs, and working as casuals, part-timers, or intermittently for labor brokers or employment agencies. More crucially, those in the precariat have no secure occupational identity, no occupational narrative they can apply to their lives, and no occupational pride or honor. They find they have to do a lot of work for labor relative to the job itself, such as preparation that does not count as paid work. This is also the first working class in history that, as a norm, is expected to have attained a level of education that is higher than that required for the work they are expected to do or find. They must rely largely on income from wages, without additional benefits such as pensions, paid holidays, retrenchment benefits, and medical cover. They live on the edge of unsustainable debt and in chronic economic uncertainty. They are losing rights previously taken for granted by full citizens. Instead, they are denizens who inhabit a locale without civil, cultural, political, social, and economic rights, de facto and de jure (Hookes and Butler-Hookes 2016).

According to Standing (2011, 59vv), this precariat consists of women, youth (urban nomads), the elderly, ethnic minorities, the disabled, the criminalized (precariat from behind bars), and even the well-educated. These under-employed (ex-)students (Antonucci, Hamilton, and Roberts 2014; Hookes and Butler-Hookes 2016; Standing 2014b) have been attracted to Bernie Sanders in the United States and Jeremy Corbyn in the UK, as well as to Podemos in Spain and SYRIZA in Greece. Many graduates are heavily in debt from their student days. For a transformation to occur, the precariat must triumph in three overlapping R struggles (Standing 2014b): *recognition*, which it is rapidly achieving; *representation* in all agencies and institutions; and *redistribution*.

Precarity as No Longer an Exception but the Norm (Oliver Marchart)

Marchart (2013) is a deeply engaged researcher of contemporary social protests and their demands. He investigates their democratic and political implications and works toward a social theory of conflict and its contingencies. In so doing, he is broadening the concept of precarity in a decisive way. For Marchart to understand precarity as a *political* concept, it is necessary to go beyond economistic approaches that tend to regard social conditions as determined solely by the mode of production. Marchart introduces the most important economic and sociological theories of precarization and demonstrates that precarity has seized society as a whole. We simply and undeniably live in a society of precarity in which Fordism is an exception and tough precarity the norm (Neilson and Rossiter 2008). Modern society in all its aspects is characterized by various forms of invasive instability. And it surely has not been only since the financial crisis that matters related to working and living conditions have proved themselves to be precarious. Marchart (2013, 9–27) distinguishes narrow and broad concepts of precarity. In public debate, precarity is for the most part equated narrowly with poverty and seen as a "zone of disaffiliation" (Castel 2003), which threatens social coherence. A broad notion of precarity views it as a condition that interweaves society in its entirety and affects people across all social strata. Struggle about the extension of the concept is in fact a struggle about recognition of the phenomenon.

Precarity as Unprotectedly Embedded Precariousness (Judith Butler)

Judith Butler (2004, 2009), in contrast to these common conceptualizations of precariousness (not precarity!), understands it as a generalized condition of human life. The social nature of human existence means that we are dependent on and vulnerable to others. We are vulnerable both because we might, and normally will, lose the very people with whom we have formed (precious) relationships, and because we are exposed to others, which comes with the risk of violence, humiliation, domination, and so on. This inevitable precariousness, as Butler sees it, is about a common human vulnerability—one that is inherent in life itself and is a matter of fact: neither wrong nor good, not induced by societal or market conditions nor avoidable by smart interventions. But, as we will see, it makes a difference in what kind of condition this precariousness is situated. The meaning of my precariousness in a violent environment turns out not to be identical to my precariousness in a caring and attentive community. Butler argues against the desire to escape as quickly as possible from vulnerability and suffering, often through acts of violence committed in the name of security, prevention, and the common good. Instead, she suggests that staying with our precariousness and accepting it as a fact of life allows us to see, recognize, and appreciate the precariousness of others. And, Butler adds, it is in this recognition that an ethical encounter becomes possible. Hence, she also extends the meaning of precarity beyond labor. Thus, precarity, I conclude, is a specific kind of ontological vulnerability that constitutes a sensitive risk, on the one hand, and an ethical impetus, on the other.

Precarity as a Concept of the Global North to Be Reinvented by the Global South (Kathleen Millar)

My writing this chapter from South Africa prompts an observation. The disappointment or even the nostalgia so often attached to the discourse of precarity stems from what many have critiqued as its northern focus, rooted in the structures and benefits of well-developed welfare states. Hence, precarity appears new and exceptional only from the perspective of Western Europe and other highly industrialized countries, in which the Fordist–Keynesian social contract was most prevalent in the years following the Second World War.

By contrast, for most workers in the Global South, precarity has arguably always been the norm, even if it has not been called by this name (Millar 2017). The millions of rural-to-urban migrants who flocked to cities in Latin America or to the outskirts of the big cities in South Africa, constructing their homes and informal settlements in the urban periphery and performing unsecured work, if they could find it, could certainly have been described as precarious. The same could be said for the continually growing numbers of street vendors, domestic workers, day laborers, recyclers, and other unwaged workers who try to earn a living in the informal economy. Insecurity, dependency, poverty, and disenfranchized are the key words here.

Moreover, from a feminist and gendered point of view, not limited to the Global South, one should include here the even more precarious lives of women, susceptible to sexual and economic exploitation and abuse, disease (AIDS), domestic violence, neglect, and without rights, education, recognition, independence, and so on. Precarity develops not along the Global North–South but in the huge majority of cases along the gender axis.

Precarity: My Working Definition (Andries Baart)

Having explored all these approaches, we try to formulate some conclusions. At the least, it may be concluded that precarity is the subject of complex, long-lasting, learned, nuanced, and activist discussions. Whereas one might be inclined to think about precarity in esthetic, voluntary, or religious and exalted terms, the literature does not support that view and places urgent, burning issues on the agenda. Precarity is internally connected to injustice, an endangered life, and public neglect or the lack of care and rightful attentiveness. There is no position in the literature that is not contested. For me, as a care ethicist, precarity is a helpful, highly essential, and appealing concept if we understand it broadly and in association with a few other familiar concepts. When care and social support are related to poor, jobless, marginalized, and excluded people, then "precarity" seems instead to be a more appropriate, better, and powerful concept. This is how I understand precarity:

1. Precarity is condition of chronic insecure life, dominated by various uncertainties, deeply affecting one's life—physically, socially, and economically as well as psychologically and existentially.
2. Precarity is characterized by the deprivation of fundamental rights, honorable positions, political recognition, effective citizenship, or even affective attention—in short, a deplorable living condition. These rights, positions, and so on are often within reach, and in many cases were available and achieved but then passed them by.
3. Powerlessness is often an aspect of precarity: the insecure living conditions make the precarious ones even more vulnerable to and dependent on forces beyond their control. In most cases, they live the life of the poorest (poverty more broadly defined, see below).
4. Precarity is thus no accidental event but a system(at)ically induced condition with political profit for a happy few, often called "elite": unnecessary, avoidable, contestable.
5. Precarity is a concept of critical political theory, morally laden and oriented toward (improving) social practices of survival and living (including labor).

Precarization and Social Redundancy

Although precarity is a powerful and promising concept for understanding and analyzing modern neediness and adequate caring or helping responses, there are nevertheless valid reasons to extend the concept with a more phenomenological perspective. I will do that by explaining the usefulness/indispensability of the idea of "social redundancy" in the context of precarity. It has been developed in my *Theory of Presence* (Baart 2001, 318vv), and over the years, it has become even more relevant than in its original context of (an alternative conceptualization of) poverty. First, I will present the bigger picture ("map"), into which I believe precarity and the experience social redundancy fit. Then, I will explain the concept of "the experience of social redundancy," compare it with precarity, and illustrate its usefulness for the political ethics of care.

Mapping the Concepts

Structure

Let us begin by explaining the structure of the map (Figure 4.4). In my view, the concepts of precariousness, precarity, precarization, and social redundancy are part of a bigger (theoretical and normative) picture and will be situated in that encompassing framework (the map). These three concepts may be used at/linked to different levels: the descriptive/explorative, the analytic/theoretical, and the interventionistic/responsive discourse. They form the backbone or structure of the map. The map has three levels. The top, level A, illustrates analysis and theoretical reflection in answer to the question about the causes and meaning of the power and impact of late-modern modernization (A1). In the middle, level B, is the descriptive level, investigating and addressing the question of the phenomenon being focused on. Finally, level C, the bottom level, presents possible interventions and responses to the issue of precarity, trying to find out which remedies are available and helpful in (C1) the modern welfare state to alleviate the powers and impact of late modernization.

The map represents, as will be explained, a kind of a balance between powers of A1 and C1. In the middle (B), we sketch the life of the precarious ones *as it is lived and experienced,* thus how it presents itself to the one who has to live it. In essence, this description is predominantly phenomenological. Certain forces exert pressure on that life (from level A, arrow A2 down): these are the powers of late modernization (conceptualized in accordance with Giddens, Beck and Lash 2017) imposing a neoliberal regime, the discipline of the market, highly complex differentiations in the life world, and so on. These powers are counterbalanced (level C, arrow C2 up) by the welfare state's compensatory powers, which offer shelter, education, income, help, support, discipline, and so in attempting to alleviate the brutality of the late modernization and ensuring that people are able and ready to participate in that regime.

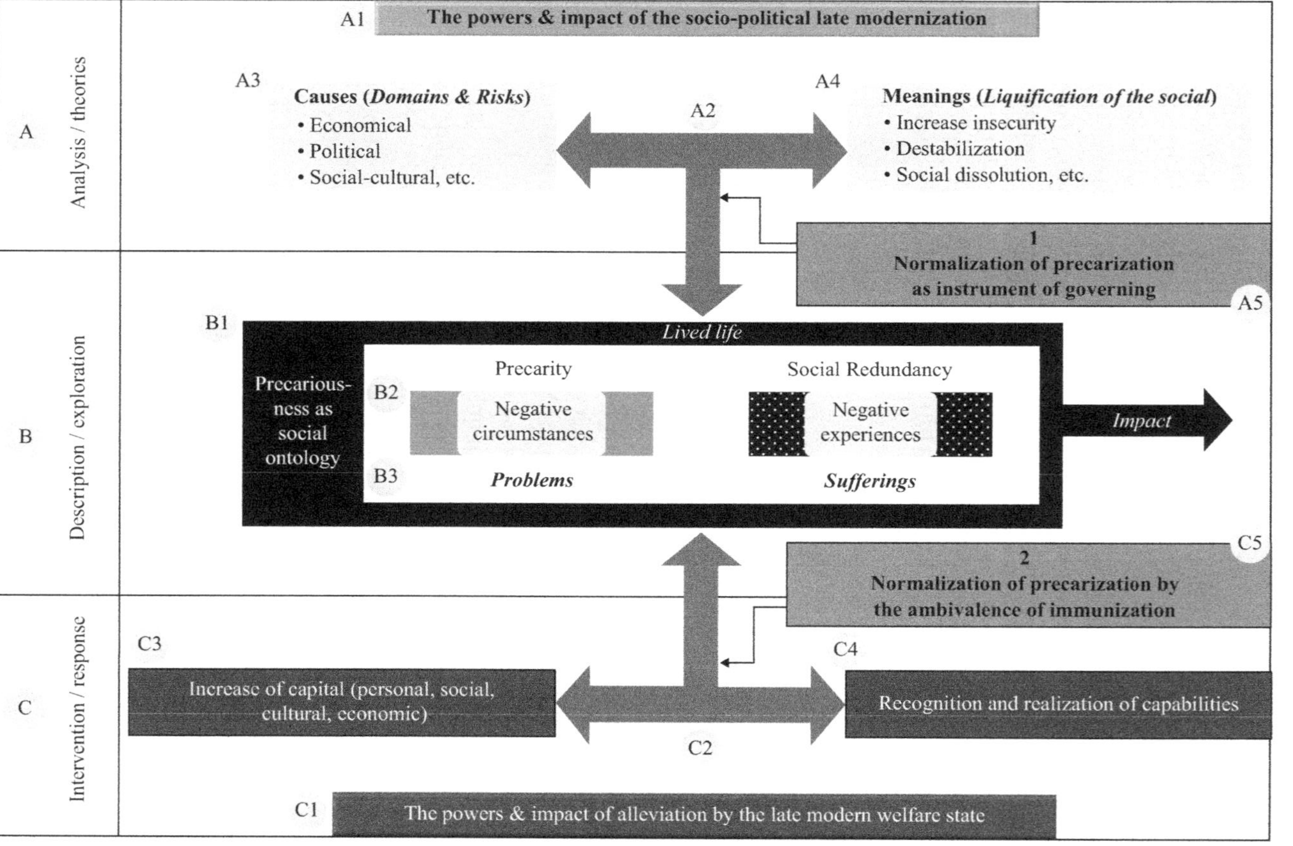

FIGURE 4.4. Overview of relevant concepts relating to precarity.

The map will be explained in the following steps. I begin with the middle level, where the central issue is situated, as explained earlier in this chapter: the lived life in precarity. Then, I turn to the top level, sketching the late-modern powers impacting on that lived live: they will be referred to as "(primary) precarization." Thereafter, I go to the bottom level and outline the powers that offer compensation for the pressure of late modernity: they turn out to be ambivalent and are called "(secondary) precarization." So, two opposite powers are putting pressure on the middle level, and both are, albeit in a different and ambivalent way, also causing "precarization." Finally, I will return to the middle level and have a closer look at how these powers apply in lived life.

Middle Level

In the center of the map (B), the overall framing (concept) is precariousness, in line with Isabel Lorey (2015, quoting Judith Butler) and criticizing Castel and Marchart. The black box (B1) represents precariousness, conceived as the ordinary, inevitable human vulnerability (with which is nothing wrong) in social arrangements: in family structures, cultures, a tough labor market, a school system, and so on, thus as a concept fitting into Butler's social ontology. Vulnerability per se does not exist: it is always embedded in something else and mostly in what we may call social arrangement. These arrangements heavily influence whether vulnerability becomes an unbearable burden or a joy (such as loving someone). I call this *inescapably embedded vulnerability "precariousness."* Rooted in precariousness are (B2) precarity and the experience of social redundancy, both being in a specific way the negative side of precariousness. Below, I will return to the center of the map.

Top Level

Here, theories that explain the downward pressure on the lived life are identified. These in turn are differentiated into theories about (A3, left) the causes and mechanisms and (A4, right) theories about the meaning of late modernization. The dichotomy of cause versus meaning is classical and parallels a positivistic and a hermeneutic approach to modernity. The two together feed into arrow A2 (down).

A quick look at the theoretical perspectives on the causes of the late-modern living condition may be helpful (A3). Figure 4.5 illustrates this. The overview of "destabilizing processes" (column 2) is categorized in

Domain	*Main destabilizing processes (A3)*	*At risk (A3)*
Economic	• Neoliberalization, flexibilization of the labor market • Globalization • Bank / monetary crisis	• Labor (opportunity, stability) • Social security, value of pensions, rents, etc. • Leisure time and family time
Political (geo-)	• Conflicts, civil wars • Transnational integrations (upscaling) • Populism / migration / autocratic regimes	• Democracy, civil participation, critical public sphere, transparency • Justice, rules of law and decency • Safety, peace, just order
Social	• Inequality / discrimination • Poverty, marginalization, exclusion • Individualization and ideal of self-reliance	• Equality • Solidarity • Wellbeing
Cultural	• Modernization • Secularization • Cosmopolitanism	• Traditions / Identity • Familiarity • Moral consensus
Technical	• Accelerated developments • Waste of natural resources • Amoral regulation of innovations	• Colonization of life world • Human scale • Controllability
Physical	• Climate change / pollution • Exhausting natural resources • Welfare diseases	• Sustainability • Food and water • Health

FIGURE 4.5. Causes of late-modern insecurity, categorized in domains and goods at risk, illustrating A3 in Figure 4.4.

six domains (column 1) and inspired by and selected from various sources (reports of the World Economic Forum and the Royal Geographical Society; the book by Hite and Seitz 2016). Column 3 lists what is in fact at risk when those destabilizing processes occur. Figure 4.5 indicates the enormous powers pressing on the lived life. The conclusion could be that we live in an extremely insecure world or "risk society" (Beck 1992, 1999) due to many diverse factors but predominantly caused by the economic (capitalistic) logic. Nevertheless, we should keep in mind that late-modern insecurity is global and has many faces; the same applies to precarity.

In Figure 4.4 (A4), we are still on the theoretical level and inquire into what it means to live in such a world: what is the experience of insecurity, destabilization, and social dissolution? I am strongly inclined to answer as Zigmunt Bauman did in his eight books on social fluidity (the most important being *Liquid Modernity* [2000], *Liquid Life* [2005], and *Liquid Times: Living in an Age of Uncertainty* [2007]). Everything becomes liquid: our contracts and expectations, our marriages and friendships, our social ties and our identities, our rootedness in time and place, our ideas about right and wrong, our culture and nation, and even our lives and bodies. Liquification means that all of these are turning into a shapeless, barely controllable mass tending to constant and relentless change. There is never one fixed or reliable certainty: one must work for it (certainty as a personal task and merit), and even then, it will not last. The modern world turns as long as nothing is fixed. Everything should be fluid—that is the tacit message. It is not a choice but nowadays a simple matter of fact. But apart from the much-contested Bauman, there is other insightful literature on "social insecurity" (Wacquant 2009; Vrooman 2016), "permanent reflectivity" (Beck, Bonss, and Lau 2003, and, in the tradition of Schelsky *Dauerreflektion*), large-scale losses (Rachwal 2017) or the fragmentation of communities, solidarity, and togetherness (Juul 2010).

These causes and meanings lead to the so-called normalization of the precarization (A5, right). I refer to Lorey (2015) and would describe this process as the constant, broadly accepted, culturally supported, penetrating, and self-extending (autopoietic) production of precarity (=precarization) with no other purpose than to govern. Precarization in this view is an effective and welcome mechanism (of the elites) to discipline and domesticate people. Here, we have the first form of precarization.

Bottom Level

In our late-modern society, these powerful forces are, at least partially, compensated for. That is the mechanism explained at the bottom of Figure 4.4 (for the development of the welfare state, see Baldwin 1990; Rothstein 1998; Larsen 2006; Hemerijck 2013; Bergqvist, Åberg Yngwe and Lundberg 2013; Offe 2014; Aravacik 2018). This compensation is sometimes motivated by genuine compassion or by obvious self-interest. It is in the interest of those who govern, run businesses, or wish to live a comfortable and carefree life that the people they need are healthy enough, qualified, keep on consuming (cars, TV sets, and smartphones), and are able to travel, discipline themselves ("behave"), and respect property. As I have said, this compensation need not be driven by cynical reasons, but regardless of the actual motivation for it, the people involved believe they are receiving medical care, education, clean water, professional help, grants or subsidies, a community center, jobs, or affordable transport. This kind of compensation(s) is mainly provided by the welfare state (including all kinds of nongovernmental organizations [NGOs]), but it is elucidating to be more precise. In C3 of Figure 4.4, the interventionistic frame is "capital" (in the tradition of Bourdieu and his successors): the welfare state provides the means to survive that could be interpreted as capital.

In their analysis of precarity and how to fight it, some authors chose to focus on resources, especially various forms of capital. Their leading question becomes: which (forms of) capital do you need in order to be able to overcome precarity? They are drawing on Pierre Bourdieu (1986), a French sociologist, who has developed his ideas on capital in close connection to others. His starting point is that with economic capital, precarious people can move ahead in our society. But, he states, there is also social and cultural capital that can be converted to economic capital. This basic scheme has been criticized, amended, and extended by many others (Boelhouwer, Gijsberts, and Vrooman 2014, 281–320; Omlo 2016). Looking at various modern sources, I present an overview of the forms of capital in the next section, relevant to this explanation of precarity and precarization. In this view, augmentation of these four kinds of capital is in essence what the welfare state, NGOs, or informal organizations have to offer the precarious ones when they provide care, social welfare, education, shelter, training programs, and support. It is up to the receiver to decide on what (jobs, leisure, quality of life, self-fulfillment) they want to spend the capital. But essentially, these forms of capital are responses to precarity and provide an opportunity to survive, or at least not perish.

Four Forms of Capital and Their Meanings

1. Economic Capital (Sometimes Called Financial Capital)

   Property, material assets, or gifts and favors to produce or buy what is needed for one's livelihood.

   - Money, property, shares, means of production (such as tools, equipment, etc.).
   - Subsidies, grants, pension, public (social) benefits, such as housing benefits and social assistance, school bursaries.
   - Free medical care, free public transport, free schoolbooks, free job training, and so on.

The profit of this kind of capital helps one to progress in society and to create better chances to survive and overcome some forms of insecurity.

2. Social Capital

   Supporting connections or official or unofficial assistance from people or groups.

   - Social networks and involvement, grounded in mutuality, trust, and cooperation by which power, strength, talents, and so on come together in favor of the common good.
   - Professional networks in favor of more personal goods: being part of those networks and being seen and cared for by professionals.

   Some add:

   - Societal capital, being in interest groups, pressure groups, client self-organizations, neighborhood alliances, advocates, lobbyists, and so on.

     The basic idea is that to be in (various) relations with (various) others is very helpful for survival, and those networks represent a kind of capital, sometimes even compensating for the lack of financial capital.

3. Cultural Capital

   Education, knowledge, and intellectual abilities that help one to get ahead.

   - Embodied: during socialization gradually acquired knowledge from traditional and cultural sources.
   - Objective: possession of artworks with a financial and symbolic meaning.
   - Institutional: formal confirmation of one's knowledge and skills.
   - Recognized competences, feeling valued in society and in the labor market, and so on.

   Some add:

   - Knowing (or having at one's disposal) alternative narratives, stimulating ideals, new identity models, better interpretations, more adequate explanations, and so on.

- Possessing ICT skills and knowledge to improve one's lifestyle.

  These cultural means (knowledge, education, alternative identity models, and alternative ideals) supply the means and the possibility to escape "fate," traditional limitations, and restrictions.

4. Personal Capital

   This is about "natural" assets that may function as capital useful, for instance for finding, obtaining, and keeping paid work.

   - Some call it personal capital, meaning physical and mental health and physical attraction.

     The basic idea is that if you can work hard, if you are a star soccer player, if you can dance and sing, or if you are beautiful, you have capital with which you could survive because there is work for you and people want you and will pay for your talents.
   - Others call it psychological capital, meaning you have resilience, self-esteem, and self-confidence and are resilient, psychologically sound, and so on. In this case difficult circumstances and challenges will not defeat you.

We now look at C4 in the bottom level, on the right. Since Sen put forward his extended, much discussed, and highly appreciated theory on capabilities, we have understood that it is not enough to have "capital" and other "resources" but that it is essential to have the freedom to utilize them, to cash in on opportunities, and to manage their risks (Sen 1985, 1992, 1993, 1999, 2004). Resources such as the different forms of capital do not have an intrinsic value. Instead, their value is instrumental and derives from the opportunity they offer people of a good life, that is, according to Sen, *to do and to be what they have reason to value,* which is not the same thing as an objectively determined list of needs to fulfill (contra Nussbaum 2011). It is not the opportunities that count but rather the actual possibility of converting these "chances" into "desired realities." Eminent poverty researchers such as Sabina Alkire (working in the tradition of Sen and drawing on precarity concepts) will always determine empirically which goods, *preferred by the local people,* are *realized* (Alkire 2005, 2016; Alkire, Jindra, Robles, and Vaz 2017). In those achieved goods, one finds the criteria of "less poverty" and "less precarity" *in the perspective of what locals have reason to value.* An example, a report in *New Scientist* (Le Page 2018), illustrates this: "Handing out free or subsidized mosquito nets is one of the most effective ways to tackle malaria. However, there have been anecdotal reports of people using the nets for fishing, rather than for protection while asleep." One senses the irritation: those stupid people do not know how to use their equipment ("economic capital") and ignore the goods that should be realized with its help. The cited article ends as follows: "However, sometimes people don't use the nets as intended simply because they don't have a piece of string, she [researcher] says. And part of the answer could be educating local communities and working with them to promote sustainable livelihoods." According to the capability approach, however, they use their freedom to convert opportunities and resources into "doings and beings" they have reason to value.

The theories about the so-called capability approach are complex and subtle (for discussion, see: Robeyns 2003, 2005, 2006; Brighouse and Robeyns 2010; Comim, Qizilbash, and Alkire 2008; Claassen 2014). From the point of view of the ethics of care, the capability approach is both very helpful and at the same time contested. Its critics hold it to be naïve about freedom of choice, the public realm, and the exploitative nature of capitalism. The same, mutatis mutandis, may be said of Bourdieu's capital theories: they do not slot easily into a care-ethical frame of thinking. Nevertheless, one may conclude that both theories adequately address the powers of a neoliberal regime (A) in a late-modern setting because they respond in a similar discourse as neoliberal way of thinking: in terms of capital, utilizing opportunities, converting chances into a better life, and so on.

In summary, to counterbalance the massive impact of late-modern powers successfully, which cause insecurity, precarity, instability, and so on, it is not enough to enhance a broad variety of people's capital; it is also essential that these resources be freely used to realize goods people have reason to value as closely relevant to their own views of a good life. To state it more bluntly, unused resources are no resources at all, unrealized opportunities are no opportunities at all. Hence, I have linked capital (C3) to capabilities (C4) as the input of the compensating power (C2).

But there is a problem with this compensating mechanism because it is not superseded above the late-modern condition and by consequence it is characterized by the same conditions that it tries to eliminate and compensate for—this critique of the welfare state is as old as the welfare state itself. Nevertheless, it is important to repeat it. Here, we have the second form of precarization (C5): the normalization of precarization as supported or (re)produced by the praxis and discourse of the welfare state and other "caring entities." See the well-trodden arguments: welfare keeps people poor, dependent, unmotivated, without self-confidence, and above all helpless because it offers incentives for learned helplessness, victimization, and armchair feelings of injustice—others should take care of you (see the impressive compendium of Leibfried and Mau 2008, vol. III; see also De Koster, Achterberg, and van der Waal 2012; Murray 2016). Some refer to the iatrogenic effect: made sick by the medical regime, stupid by the school, obese by the food business, and disinformed by the public (news) media. I think this picture is too general and somewhat exaggerated, but more importantly it does not offer the most relevant access to understanding this kind of precarization. I mention two better approaches (see also Lorey 2015, 41–61, arguing with and contra Castel).

First, from a formal perspective, the programs of organizations providing care, help, support, and so on are subject to the same rationality as the neoliberal market, new public management, and performance management. It means that one has to perform outstandingly or perish, prove constantly ("permanent transparency") that expected outcomes have been achieved, and compete incessantly for the next grant or subsidy. The prospect of continued employment is deliberately kept uncertain as a kind of incentive (you have to merit it), and risk is discouraged (so helpless, complex, unreliable, unbiddable employees are eliminated easily because caring about them is risky). In fighting the destructive powers and impact of the late modernity (A), one is reproducing them.

Second, what these (care) providers and help suppliers have to offer is always ambivalent. Yes, it helps, alleviates, and compensates, but at the same time it is reproducing in its goals and functioning the neoliberal regime it tries to "immunize" (Leibfried and Mau 2008, vol. II). This precarization introduces new uncertainties, ambivalence, and ambiguities (Bauman 1991). I have illustrated this kind of ambiguity (Baart 2017), and here I give three examples. (1) The late-modern ideal of "taking care of oneself" and being self-reliant means, on the one hand. "emancipation" and "diminishing paternalism" and, on the other, "dismantling solidarity" and the introduction of new forms of "privileged carelessness." These are mutually interdependent. (2) Stimulating the civil society, mutual engagement, and volunteering mean, on the one hand, empowering people and, on the other, creating a spare army of free labor forces whereby professionals become too expensive ("unaffordable"), too critical, or self-regulating. (3) Promoting neighborhood teams and communities that care means, on the one hand, the return to grassroots, basic participation, the life worlds, and the voice of the least, the last, and the lost, but it also means the legitimization of severe austerity and cuts in grants and costs and the withdrawal of professional help. This ambiguity is characteristic of this kind of precarization (C5), in this case by forces that claim to counterbalance the primary forces of precarization (A5).

Middle Level

Let us return to the middle level in Figure 4.4. In the black rectangle of ontological precariousness (Lived Life), two concrete shapes of it are drawn: "Precarity" and "Social Redundancy" (the experience of being socially redundant). Both may be seen as (B2) the negative effect of permanent precarization (A5 and C5). Note that in essence, precarity and social redundancy are the same, with one difference: "precarity" as a concept results from an *outsider's perspective* and refers objectively to a "social problem" or negative circumstances, whereas "the experience of being socially redundant" is a characterization *from within* and not about an "objective problem" but rather about (negatively) experiencing a reality, and more precisely, it is about "suffering" (from a rude reality). It is essential to have both perspectives on precarization in the same conceptualization, a more or less positivistic as well as a phenomenological one. In my *Theory of Presence* (Baart 2001, 318vv), I analyze the concept of "social redundancy" in detail. In Figure 4.6, both perspectives are compared so that it is easy to see how they complement each other. We are analyzing a complex phenomenon, and the complexity, depicted in Figure 4.6, should be respected and not radically reduced. The description or conceptualization of "precarity" in terms of a social problem, whether complex or not, is nevertheless limiting: the problem is also a kind of suffering. The distant, analytic register of describing precarity as a social problem creates an undesirable

	Characterization	
	The problem of precarity	The experience of social redundancy
Description	Being unsettled or doubtful; being dependent on chance; lacking in predictability, job security, material or psychological welfare	The constant feeling of being useless in the view of others, a burden to others, better not to exist.
Kind	Objective concept	Experiential concept
Generated	Analytically developed	Phenomenologically developed
Object	What is the problem of a specific class (the precariat)	How people suffer from not being valued
Question	How external conditions affect social class' life; narrowly (labor market) or broadly interpreted (all factors of endangerment)	How their lived life shows itself to those who are involved
Orientation	System	Life world
Point of view	From the outside	From within
Transferability	Generalized	Essentialistic
Interpretation	Traits of a category or position	Relational (others don't care / social indifference). Those others are sometimes conceptualized as the 'elite'
Main domain	(Mainly) economically labeled: this is the order of our economy	Politically labeled: this is the order of our society
Point	Main message: adjust to the modern labor market and its logic (in other domains)	Main (felt) message: without you, we would be better off
Main deficit	Lack of stability and certainty, endangered and dependent on (good or bad) luck.	Lack of recognition, not taken seriously, undervalued and underestimated

FIGURE 4.6. Precarity and the experience of being socially redundant compared.

one-sidedness, a way of holding off. A complementary political phenomenological view is more than welcome, and that is "the experience of social redundancy." We need both (Waldenfels 2011). But that is not the common practice in our field. In fact, I suggest amending the standard description(s) and that this correction should be empirically and politically informed.

Being trapped in the feeling of social redundancy is also suffocatingly depicted in many modern movies, novels, and diaries (see, e.g., Bardan 2013; Lawn 2017; Botha 2014; Henesy 2016; Elliott 2013; Giorgi 2013). I refer particularly to the merciless novels of the French author Édouard Louis (2018, 2019), recently translated into English.

From many studies, including some care-ethical studies, we know that negative experiences (feeling socially redundant and not recognized by the elite) provide fertile soil for both right- and left-wing populism: that is the impact (Figure 4.4, right arrow, B1). Here, political carelessness and social indifference, as a lack of adequate response to the processes of precarization, are exacerbating the situation. We may observe that everywhere, from Trump's United States to Erdogan's Turkey, Duerte's Philippines, Orbán's Hungary, and Bolsonaro's Brazil. Because I am interested in the impact (populism) and in the arrangements of the welfare state, this critical analysis is essential: the so-called remedies partially reproduce the problem (permanent precarization and the normalization of that precarization).

So, in my view, we need, beside precarity, the concept and the phenomenological or creative representations of the experience of social redundancy. The concept de-abstracts the issue and makes clear what is really at stake. It indicates a rupture in the usual (political/welfare) discourses about the precarious and embodies an appeal—it is an appealing concept in line with care and caring. Moreover, it installs in outsiders a critical memory. No longer can they say "we didn't know" and "we prefer to live in our little bubbles."

Discussion

The ethics of care is fundamentally both scholarly and practically committed to the phenomena of precariousness, precarity, and precarization. It is not always clear what care ethicists are talking about when they reflect on this cluster. To be of assistance, I have sketched a map of the key concepts involved and have intentionally drawn few distinctions.

1. The map is constructed around four discrete key concepts—precariousness, precarity, the experience of social redundancy, and precarization—and traces their mutual relations. In my opinion, "social redundancy" as a political phenomenological concept may not be excluded from the picture.

2. The map contains both static (precarity) and dynamic (precarization) concepts and is filled in with both analytic (problems, causes, capital) and phenomenological interpretations (suffering, meanings, and capabilities). This complementary structure should produce a complete and nuanced picture.
3. The map distinguishes between the ontological discourse (precariousness) and the empirical discourse (precarity as circumstances and experiences) and attempts to bridge the difference in a meaningful way.
4. The map is based on the literature that interprets these concepts *broadly:* more than poverty and job insecurity and above all linked to conditions of late modernity. In these interpretations, precarity, precarization, and social redundancy are negatively loaded and associated with suffering, lack of recognition, and the liquification of the existence.
5. The map is based on two balancing powers: precarization as an intended instrument of governing "the people," on the one hand, and, on the other, the powers of care and caring, help, and other offers by the welfare state that immunize, soften, or prevent the damage caused by that process. We have shown that those counterbalancing and compensatory powers also reproduce the process of precarization in many respects. They are deeply ambiguous and ambivalent.

It is against this background that we, as care ethicists, have to make our case: the justified place of care and caring in a late-modern context.

Works Cited

Alkire, Sabina. 2005. *Valuing Freedoms.* Oxford: Oxford University Press.

Alkire, Sabina. 2016. *Measures of Human Development: Key Concepts and Properties.* Oxford Poverty and Human Development Initiative (OPHI), University of Oxford, Working Paper No. 107.

Alkire, Sabina, Christoph Jindra, Gisela Robles-Aguilar, and Ana Vaz. 2017. *Multidimensional Poverty Reduction among Countries in Sub-Saharan Africa.* Oxford Poverty and Human Development Initiative (OPHI), University of Oxford, Working Paper No. 112.

Antonucci, Lorenza, Myra Hamilton, and Steven Roberts. 2014. *Young People and Social Policy in Europe Dealing with Risk, Inequality and Precarity in Times of Crisis.* London: Palgrave Macmillan.

Aravacik, Esra Dundar. 2018. "Social Policy and the Welfare State." In *Public Economics and Finance,* edited by Bernur Açıkgöz. London: Intech Open. http://dx.doi.org/10.5772/intechopen.82372.

Baart, Andries. 2001. *Een theorie van presentie* [A Theory of Presence], 3rd ed. Utrecht, the Netherlands: Lemma.

Baart, Andries. 2017. *The Many Faces of Neoliberalism.* Amsterdam: Free University. Key note on June 15, 2017, by Andries Baart, at the presentation of the book Biebericher, Thomas. 2017. *Onvermoed en onvermijdelijk. De vele gezichten van het neoliberalisme.* [Unexpected and Inevitable: The Many Faces of Neoliberalism]. Nijmegen, the Netherlands: Valkhof Pers.

Baldwin, Peter. 1990. *The Politics of Social Solidarity. Class Bases of the European Welfare State 1875–1975.* Cambridge: Cambridge University Press.

Bardan, Alice. 2013. "The New European Cinema of Precarity: A Transnational Perspective." In *Work in Cinema,* edited by Ewa Mazierska, 69–90. New York: Palgrave Macmillan.

Bauman, Zygmunt. 1991. *Modernity and Ambivalence.* Oxford: Polity.

Bauman, Zygmunt. 2000. *Liquid Modernity.* Cambridge: Polity.

Bauman, Zygmunt. 2005. *Liquid Life.* Cambridge: Polity.

Bauman, Zygmunt. 2007. *Liquid Times: Living in an Age of Uncertainty.* Cambridge: Polity.

Beck, Ulrich. 1992. *Risk Society: Towards a New Modernity.* London: Sage.

Beck, Ulrich. 1999. *World Risk Society.* Cambridge: Polity.

Beck, Ulrich, Anthony Giddens, and Scott Lash. 1994. *Reflexive Modernization. Politics, Tradition and Aesthetics in the Modern Social Order.* Palo Alto, Calif.: Stanford University Press.

Beck, Ulrich, Wolfgang Bonss, and Christoph Lau. 2003. "The Theory of Reflexive Modernisation: Problematic, Hypotheses and Research Programme." *Theory, Culture and Society* 20 (2): 1–33.

Bergqvist, Kersti, Monica Åberg Yngwe, and Olle Lundberg. 2013. "Understanding the Role of Welfare State Characteristics for Health and Inequalities—An Analytical Review." *BMC Public Health* 13:1234. https://doi.org/10.1186/1471-2458-13-1234.

Betti, Eloisa. 2018. "Historicizing Precarious Work: Forty Years of Research in the Social Sciences and Humanities." *International Review of Social History* 63 (2): 273–319.

Boelhouwer, Jeroen, Mérove Gijsberts, and Cok Vrooman. 2014. "Nederland in meervoud" [The Netherlands in Plural. In *Verschil in Nederland* [Difference in the Netherlands], edited by Cok Vrooman, Mérove Gijsberts, and Jeroen Boelhouwer. Sociaal en Cultureel Rapport 2014, 281–320. The Hague, the Netherlands: Sociaal en Cultureel Planbureau.

Botha, Marc. 2014. "Precarious Present, Fragile Futures: Literature and Uncertainty in the Early Twenty-First Century." *English Academy Review* 31 (2): 1–19. https://doi.org/10.1080/10131752.2014.965411.

Bourdieu, Pierre. 1986. "The Forms of Capital." In *Handbook of Theory and Research for the Sociology of Education,* edited by John G. Richardson, 241–58. New York: Greenwood Press.

Bourdieu, Pierre. 1998a. *Acts of Resistence: Against the Tyranny of the Market.* New York: New Press.

Bourdieu, Pierre. 1998b. "La precarité est aujourd'hui partout." *Les Inrockuptibles* 145 (April): 14–15; also in: Pierre Bourdieu. 1998. *Contre-feux. Propos pour servir à la résistance contre l'invasion neo-liberale,* 95–101. Paris: Liber—Raison d'Agir.

Brighouse, Harry, and Ingrid Robeyns, eds. 2010. *Measuring Justice: Primary Goods and Capabilities.* Cambridge: Cambridge University Press.

Butler, Judith. 2004. *Precarious Life: The Powers of Mourning and Violence.* New York: Verso Books.

Butler, Judith. 2009. *Frames of War. When Is Life Grievable?* New York: Verso Books.

Castel, Robert. 2003. *L'Insécurité sociale: qu'est-ce qu'être protégé?* Paris: Éd. du Seuil.

Castel, Robert. 2009. *La montée des incertitudes: Travail, protections, statut de l'individu.* Paris: Ed. du Seuil.

Claassen, Rutger. 2014. "Capability Paternalism." *Economics and Philosophy* 30: 57–73. https://doi.org/10.1017/S0266267114000042.

Comim, Flavio, Mozaffar Qizilbash, and Sabina Alkire, eds. 2008. *The Capability Approach. Concepts, Measures and Applications.* Cambridge: Cambridge University Press.

De Koster, Willem, Peter Achterberg, and Jeroen van der Waal. 2012. "The New Right and the Welfare State: The Electoral Relevance of Welfare Chauvinism and Welfare Populism in the Netherlands." *International Political Science Review* 34 (1): 3–20.

Dörre, Klaus. 2005. "Prekarisierung contra Flexicurity. Unsichere Beschäftigungsverhältnisse als arbeitspolitische Herausforderung." In *Flexicurity. Die Suche nach Sicherheit in der Flexibilität,* edited by Martin Kronauer, and Gudrun Linne, 53–72. Berlin: Edition Sigma.

Elliott, Jane. 2013. "Suffering Agency: Imagining Neoliberal Personhood in North America and Britain." In *Genres of Neoliberalism,* edited by Jane Elliott, and Gillian Harkins, thematic issue of *Social Text* 31, no. 2 (Summer 2013): 83–101.

Giorgi, Gabriel. 2013. "Improper Selves: Cultures of Precarity." In *Genres of Neoliberalism,* edited by Jane Elliott, and Gillian Harkins, thematic issue of *Social Text* 31, no. 2 (Summer 2013): 69–81.

Hemerijck, Anton. 2013. *Changing Welfare States.* Oxford: Oxford University Press.

Henesy, Megan Louise. 2016. "Novels of Precarity: Neoliberal Counternarratives in Contemporary British Women's Fiction." PhD diss., University of Southampton.

Hite, Kristen A., and John L. Seitz. 2016. *Global Issues: An Introduction.* Malden, Mass.: John Wiley.

Hookes, David, and Johanna Butler-Hookes. 2016. "To Save the Planet." http://pcwww.liv.ac.uk/~dhookes/IWFA.pptx.

Juul, Søren. 2010. "Solidarity and Social Cohesion in Late Modernity: A Question of Recognition, Justice and Judgement in Situation." *European Journal of Social Theory* 13 (2): 253–69.

Kalleberg, Arne L. 2011. *Good Jobs, Bad Jobs: The Rise of Polarized and Precarious Employment Systems in the United States, 1970s to 2000s.* New York: Russell Sage Foundation.

Kalleberg, Arne L. 2018. *Precarious Lives: Job Insecurity and Well-Being in Rich Democracies.* Cambridge: Polity.

Larsen, Christian Albrekt. 2006. *The Institutional Logic of Welfare Attitudes: How Welfare Regimes Influence Public Support.* Aldershot, UK: Ashgate.

Lawn, Jennifer. 2017. "Precarity: A Short Literary History, from Colonial Slum to Cosmopolitan Precariat." *Interventions* 19 (7): 1026–40. https://doi.org/10.1080/1369801X.2017.1401944.

Leibfried, Stephan, and Steffen Mau, eds. 2008. *Welfare States: Construction, Deconstruction, Reconstruction.* Cheltenham, UK: Edward Elgar Publishing; especially Volume III: "Legitimation, Achievement and Integration," Part II-V.

Le Page, Michael. 2018. "People Are Using Mosquito Nets for Fishing and That's a Bad Idea." *New Scientist*, January 31, 2018. https://www.newscientist.com/article/2222873-people-are-using-mosquito-nets-for-fishing-and-it-works-too-well/.

Lorey, Isabel. 2015. *State of Insecurity. Government of the Precarious.* Foreword by Judith Butler. Translated by Aileen Derieg. London: Verso Books. First published as *Die Regierung der Prekären* (2012).

Louis, Édouard. 2018. *The End of Eddy: A Novel.* Translated by Michael Lucey. London: Picador. First published as *En finir avec Eddy Bellegueule* (2014).

Louis, Édouard. 2019. *Who Killed My Father.* Translated by Lorin Stein. New York: New Directions. First published as *Qui a tué mon père* (2018).

Marchart, Oliver. 2013. *Die Prekarisierungsgesellschaft. Prekäre Proteste. Politik und Ökonomie im Zeichen der Prekarisierung.* Bielefeld, Germany: Transcript Verlag. http://www.oapen.org/download?type=document&docid=579941.

Masquelier, Charles. 2018. "Bourdieu, Foucault and the Politics of Precarity." *Distinktion: Journal of Social Theory* 20 (2): 135–55. https://doi.org/10.1080/1600910X.2018.1549999.

Millar, Kathleen. 2017. "Toward a Critical Politics of Precarity." *Sociology Compass* 11 (6): e12483. https://doi.org/10.1111/soc4.12483.

Mouffe, Chantal. 2018. *For a Left Populism.* London: Verso Books.

Mudge, Stephanie. 2018. *Leftism Reinvented: Western Parties from Socialism to Neoliberalism.* Cambridge, Mass.: Harvard University Press.

Murray, Charles. 2016. *In Our Hands: A Plan to Replace the Welfare State.* Washington, D.C.: AEI Press.

Neilson, Brett, and Ned Rossiter. 2008. "Precarity as a Political Concept, or Fordism as Exception." *Theory, Culture and Society* 25 (7–8): 51–72. https://doi.org/10.1177/0263276408097796.

Nussbaum, Martha. 2011. *Creating Capabilities: The Human Development Approach.* Harvard, Mass.: Harvard University Press.

Offe, Claus. 2014. *Europe Entrapped.* Cambridge: Polity.

Omlo, Jurriaan. 2016. *De aanpak van armoede.* [Solving Poverty]. Utrecht, the Netherlands: Movisie.

Rachwal, Tadeusz. 2017. *Precarity and Loss: On Certain and Uncertain Properties of Life and Work.* Wiesbaden, Germany: Springer.

Robeyns, Ingrid. 2003. "Sen's Capability Approach and Gender Inequality: Selecting Relevant Capabilities." *Feminist Economics* 9 (2–3): 61–92. https://doi.org/10.1080/1354570022000078024.

Robeyns, Ingrid. 2005. "The Capability Approach: A Theoretical Survey." *Journal of Human Development* 6 (1): 93–117. https://doi.org/10.1080/146498805200034266.

Robeyns, Ingrid. 2006. "The Capability Approach in Practice." *Journal of Political Philosophy* 14 (3): 351–76. https://doi.org/10.1111/j.1467-9760.2006.00263.x.

Ross, Andrew. 2009. *Nice Work if You Can Get It: Life and Labor in Precarious Times*. New York: New York University Press.

Rothstein, Bo. 1998. *Just Institutions Matter: The Moral and Political Logic of the Universal Welfare State*. Cambridge: Cambridge University Press.

Royal Geographical Society. n.d. "The 21st Century Challenges." Accessed October 21, 2018. https://21stcenturychallenges.org/challenges.

Sen, Amartya. 1985. *Commodities and Capabilities*. Amsterdam: North-Holland.

Sen, Amartya. 1992. *Inequality Re-examined*. Oxford: Clarendon Press.

Sen, Amartya. 1993. "Capability and Well-being." In *The Quality of Life*, edited by Martha Nussbaum and Amartya Sen, 30–53. Oxford: Clarendon Press.

Sen, Amartya. 1999. *Development as Freedom*. Oxford: Oxford University Press.

Sen, Amartya. 2004. "Capabilities, Lists, and Public Reason: Continuing the Conversation." *Feminist Economics* 10 (3): 77–80. https://doi.org/10.1080/1354570042000315163

Standing, Guy. 2011. *The Precariat: The New Dangerous Class*. London: Bloomsbury Academic.

Standing, Guy. 2014a. *A Precariat Charter: From Denizens to Citizens*. London: Bloomsbury Academic.

Standing, Guy. 2014b. "The Precariat." *Contexts* 13 (4): 10–12. https://doi.org/10.1177/1536504214558209

Törnquist, Olle, and John Harriss, eds. 2016. *Reinventing Social Democratic Development. Insights from Indian and Scandinavian Comparisons*. Studies in Asian Topics Series, No. 58. Copenhagen: Nordic Institute of Asian Studies, NIAS Press.

Vosko, Leah F. 2010. *Managing the Margins: Gender, Citizenship, and the International Regulation of Precarious Employment*. Oxford: Oxford University Press.

Vrooman, Cok. 2016. *Taking Part in Uncertainty. The Significance of Labour Market and Income Protection Reforms for Social Segmentation and Citizens' Discontent*. The Hague: The Netherlands Institute for Social Research.

Wacquant, Loïc. 2009. *Punishing the Poor: The Neoliberal Government of Social Insecurity*. Translated from French *Punir les pauvres*, 2004. Durham, N.C.: Duke University Press.

Waldenfels, Bernhard. 2011. *Phenomenology of the Alien. Basic Concepts*. Evanston, Ill.: Northwestern University Press.

Wodak, Ruth, Majid KhosraviNik, and Brigitte Mral, eds. 2013. *Right-Wing Populism in Europe: Politics and Discourse*. London: Bloomsbury Academic.

Wodak, Ruth, and Michal Krzyżanowski. 2017. "Right-Wing Populism in Europe and USA. Contesting Politics and Discourse beyond 'Orbanism' and 'Trumpism.'" *Journal of Language and Politics* 16 (4): 471–84. https://doi.org/10.1075/jlp.17042.krz.

World Economic Forum. 2019. "The Global Risks Report 2019, 14th Edition." http://www3.weforum.org/docs/WEF_Global_Risks_Report_2019.pdf.

CHAPTER 5

Global Vulnerability

Why Take Care of Future Generations?

ELENA PULCINI

A Global Challenge

Today, there is broad consensus on the idea that globalization, or rather what I prefer to call the global age, is characterized not only by a time–space compression but also by the interdependence of events and lives. The thesis that I will try to argue is that this time–space compression *objectively* produces an extension of the figure of the other and more precisely of the "significant other" (Mead [1934] 2015) as, to use the expression of Martha Nussbaum (2001), both the other distant in space and the other distant in time enter our "circle of concern." Due to the erosion of territorial boundaries and the speed of communications, information technology and uniformity produced by the market, and above all global challenges, the world seems to be getting smaller and smaller, potentially altering our perception of the distance of countries, places, and people.

This objective change, however, does not automatically translate into a *subjective* and ethical response, that is, the recognition of an obligation toward the distant other. The problem has also been posed, as we shall see, by some theorists of the ethics of care in the perspective of emancipating the latter from its "parochial" boundaries, namely from its purely intimate and private dimension (Tronto 2013; Held 2006; Robinson 1997). Undoubtedly, a first answer to this problem, also in the case of distant relationships, is to base the obligation on the recognition, by both parties, of the relationship's value (Collins 2015). In my opinion, however, this is not enough, epecially in the case of the other distant in time. Indeed, why should human beings take action for people to whom they are not bound by an emotional or professional relationship or a direct generational link? Why should we care about their needs and take their fate to heart? Do we have any kind of obligation toward them? It comes as no surprise that this difficulty in dealing with the problem of future generations is one of the most impervious challenges of our time, which has given rise, as we will see later, to what has been called the "motivation problem" (Partridge 1981; Birnbacher 2009).

It is important to emphasize that the question of motivational alienation had already emerged in twentieth-century philosophy. Günther Anders (1956) and Hans Jonas (1985) found the disturbing effects of the pathological drift of the modern subject and his unlimited hubris in the face of the emergence of two unprecedented global challenges: the nuclear threat and the ecological crisis. It is unclear whether this drift leads to the delirium of omnipotence of the *homo faber*, made possible by the dizzying development of technology, or whether it manifests itself in the acquisitive craving of the *homo oeconomicus*, fed by the capitalist development model (Pulcini 2012).

And these challenges or "global risks," to use the term of Ulrich Beck (1992)—such as climate warming and the erosion of resources, loss of biodiversity and foolish use of commons, the hole in the ozone layer and soil depletion, as well as the threat of global nuclear conflict and nuclear waste disposal—expose humankind to a condition of global vulnerability, jeopardizing if not the lives of future generations at least their right to a life worth living. Moreover, this condition of vulnerability inevitably leads to a condition of precariousness, understood in this case as a profound and objective uncertainty over the future—an uncertainty so severe as even to contemplate the possibility that there will be no future.

We are therefore faced with the paradox of a human action whose unlimited power seems at the same time to turn on its head into the possibility of self-destruction. The causes of all this can only be hinted at here, summarized as the assertion of a development model that progressively degenerates into a predatory and speculative capitalism, in turn supported and legitimized, especially since the second half of the twentieth century, by the neoliberal vision of the world. A vision—or we could also say an ideology—that, indifferent to purposes other than profit, sanctions the hegemony of economics and justifies its logic of pervading and colonizing every aspect of life, through the apparently neutral claim that TINA: There Is No Alternative.[1]

The awareness of the problem on the part of theoretical reflection has, for some decades now, resulted in a normative concern about the strategies to adopt, starting from some more or less shared watchwords, such as sustainable development and recognition of the rights of future generations, reduction of the emissions responsible for global warming and a fair distribution of burdens, awareness of the limits of natural resources, and the guarantee of fair access to common goods for all, aimed at affirming the need for "intergenerational responsibility." It is a concern that seems to be increasingly the object of broad consensus, as shown, among other possible authoritative examples, by the heartfelt appeal of Pope Francis's (2015) encyclical *Laudato sì*. In short, we can legitimately maintain that the current prevailing attitude is what Giuliano Pontara (1995) called the "thesis of (full) responsibility."

However, the scenario is more complex and problematic than it seems, owing not only to the variety and multiplicity of often conflicting responses but also to the difficulty that every normative approach visibly meets in dealing with this problem and the radical nature of the challenge posed to the traditional paradigms.[2] In this regard, it is enough to recall some of the most frequent objections put forward even by those who neverthless appear determined to look for solutions: first, the possible conflict between the interests of future individuals and those of the current, contemporary people, both deputized as the legitimate recipients of moral obligation; second, the impossibility of knowing what the effects of our actions will actually be, given the speed of technological development and its ability to remain up-to-date with the emergence of new obstacles; and last, the speciousness of privileging a given choice A (e.g., saving resources) over another possible choice B (wasting resources). Indeed, in this case, we encounter what Derek Parfit (1984) called the "non-identity problem," that is, the fact that individuals who will exist in the future if the first choice is made would still be different from those who would have existed had the second choice been made, which would end up relieving the present generation of responsibility toward the future generations.

We are therefore looking at an unprecedented and epochal problem, which today represents perhaps the greatest challenge for philosophical sociopolitical reflection,[3] in particular for the paradigm of justice, which has dealt with this problem but has not been able to find satisfactory answers. Indeed, all of the major theories of justice—Rawls and new liberalism, utilitarianism, and communitarianism—have hit a wall or failed outright to justify the obligation toward the future generations by proposing the same abstract and rationalistic assumptions that, at this level too, the ethics of care has always reproached it for (Gilligan 1982).

In brief, Rawls goes so far as to hypothesize that the subjects of the agreement on the principles of justice are no longer individuals who are solely concerned with satisfying their own interests but rather heads of families motivated by concern, which can be considered "natural enough," for the well-being of their children and grandchildren. But this does not solve the problem of the successive generations. Utilitarianism extends the right to happiness to the future generations—the conquest of happiness is a universal value, which makes the time factor irrelevant (Sumner 1978)—but it comes up against the difficulty of defining what future generations will consider as well-being, as we do not know what their tastes, needs, or preferences will be. The communitarian approach, which, in my opinion, is the most convincing, connects the obligation toward the future generations to our belonging to a transgenerational community (De-Shalit 1995). This, as I said, can be favored by the unprecedented condition produced by the global age—by the urgency of the challenges and the interdependence of the events and the lives that unite humankind in what Beck has called a "risk community" or a "community of destiny." Neverthless, this approach does not solve the problem of the subjective perception of belonging to an intergenerational community.

The impasse of the theory of justice, which is further confirmed in the maybe not ineffective but barely feasible proposed solutions and policies, has caused some authors to sustain the necessity to found a moral dimension, in turn based on a new global awareness, a reawakening of the conscience of individuals as capable of thinking and recognizing themselves as one humanity, and members of an intergenerational community.

While I agree with this approach, I think, however, it requires a fundamental question to be asked: what kind of subjectivity do we need for this purpose? The first problem is in fact the inadequacy of the consolidated mainstream paradigm of the modern subject: that of the *homo oeconomicus* and rational choice, of a sovereign and self-referential subject, concerned solely with pursuing his own interest and, since the twentieth century, obtusely shortsighted about the future—a figure, as already mentioned, who is evidently at the basis of the genesis of capitalism as well as its pathological drifts. The inadequacy of this paradigm requires us to rethink the subject in the sense of being up to the new challenges and being able to take responsibility toward future generations.

In this regard, we can recall two exemplary and radically diverse answers:

1. Hans Jonas and the duty to respond to the call of the vulnerable other. Since the twentieth century, Jonas has argued that the destructiveness that produced the ecological crisis—which can be traced back to the limitlessness of the *homo faber*'s hubris and his unlimited power—can only be countered by a subject able to take charge of the future, as she feels the duty to answer the silent but cogent call of the other distant in time, of future generations whose vulnerability works as a provocation, an imperative that forces us to take care of them.[4]
2. The ethics of virtue and the empathetic subject (Jamieson 2003, 2008). According to the ethics of virtue that disputes the unilaterally egoistic vision of the paradigm of rational choice, we need a virtuous character that is able to live up to our globalized and interconnected world—a character, as Dale Jamieson (2007) specifies, endowed with those "green virtues" (such as humility, temperance, and caution) that confirm our willingness to commit ourselves to the defense of the planet and to change our way of life concretely for a sustainable future.

Although both of these powerful proposals allude to the need to rethink the subject in relational terms (Pulcini 2013, 9–14), two objections can be raised: (1) neither gives a fully satisfactory answer to the problem of motivations, and (2) the first indeed suffers from a deontological-metaphysical excess, the second from the lack of a contextual vision. In short, Jonas's limit lies in his presupposing a subject capable of welcoming the other's appeal out of pure duty and altruism—a subject that he fails to justify fully, oscillating as he does between affective-intellectualistic motivations (the heuristic of fear) and metaphysical motivations (we have the duty to be responsible toward future lives because being is better than nothingness; see Pulcini 2013). And the limit of the ethics of virtue is that it is too demanding and not universalistic enough. To take just one significant example, a person who is ethically very sensitive to the suffering of the other distant in space (such as migrants) can remain completely indifferent to the fate of future generations toward whom he can very easily implement defense mechanisms such as denial and self-deception.

Sources of Motivation: Vulnerability, Debt, Reciprocity

The answer to the shortcomings of these proposals lies in that relational ontology that finds one of its richest theorizations in the ethics of care.

In this regard, there are those who, like Christopher Groves, rightly stress that the same internal logic of care makes it open to the future: "the structure of care is irreducibly temporal and concerned with the futurity of concrete situations, and these situations are by no means limited to face-to-face encounters. . . . Care is thus a way of conceiving of human self-concern as inherently futural, as bound up with the potential things have for making my projects turn out well or badly" (2009, 24). While undoubtedly an acceptable statement, regarding the intrinsic possibility of the extension of care, it does not, however, fully respond to the "motivation problem," that is, the need to explain why, despite the assumption of a relational ontology, we do not take care of the world and, on the psycho-anthropological level, which resources the subject can presently draw from to engage in an ethic for the future.

I propose summarizing these resources in three notions—vulnerability, debt, and reciprocity—which we can recognize as the sources of the motivations for taking care of the future generations, as long as we give these notions a new meaning reflecting a more radical vision of the subject. In other words, if understood in the new sense that I will now try to explain, these three notions can become the foundation of an ethics of care that can respond to the precarious condition of the world and the uncertainty of the future more effectively than other ethical approaches.

But first it is necessary to make two clarifications concerning the link between vulnerability and precariousness. While taking into account the multiple meanings that the two concepts assume according to the context, it seems to me undeniable that the first always alludes to a vulnus (Valadier 2011), to a wound that, as we will see better, is ontological, constitutive of the human being (Weil [1948] 2002) and the whole living world, as well as containing the very idea of openness, and exposure to otherness. The second, precariousness, instead indicates a contingent, but not necessarily transitory, situation that can occur as a possible consequence of this vulnus—a consequence that in the case of future generations consists, as I mentioned before, in the precariousness of the very existence of humankind and in the possible loss of the future.

Vulnerability as a Vulnerability of the Subject

We have seen, with Jonas, a first sense of vulnerability understood primarily as vulnerability of *the other* and recognized as a motive for responsibility. The urgency and radical nature of the challenges that threaten the future of the entire living world can only be countered by responding to the call that reaches us from the other distant in time. And it is a call from which one cannot escape because it indeed comes from another vulnerable subject, from a fragile, imperfect, and transient "object," as Jonas calls it, probably emphasizing the "passive" state of future generations,[5] whose fragility and imperfection have the power to bind us and demand our attention:

> Yet just this far from "perfect" object, entirely contingent in its facticity, perceived precisely in its perishability, indigence, and insecurity, must have the power to move me through its sheer existence (not through special qualities) to place my person at its service, free of all appetite for appropriation. (Jonas 1985, 87)

The strength of the other's vulnerability is equal to that which causes parents to take care of the newborn, whose "breath alone" requires us to take charge of its life, becoming "the timeless archetype" of responsibility and care. It is this same meaning of vulnerability as vulnerability *of the other* that has been emphasized by Paul Ricoeur. In a perspective similar to that of Hans Jonas, Paul Ricoeur affirms that the "fragile," that is to say "what is perishing by natural weakness and what is threatened by the blows of historical violence," is what has the power to awaken our feeling, to provoke our pain and our indignation, our concern in the face of something we "perceive as deplorable, unsustainable, inadmissible, unjustifiable" (Ricoeur 1994, own translation), and that consequently requires our care. There is no responsibility, in other words, except when we feel we are made responsible by someone who, due to her fragility, trusts in our help and asks us to take charge of her destiny.

There is, however, a second meaning of vulnerability that tends to shift the point of view from the object to the subject, seeing the vulnerability of the latter as the motivational source of the ethical relationship with the other. It is a theme that stretches from the philosophies of otherness (Ricoeur and Lévinas) up to contemporary feminist reflection (from Nussbaum to Butler) and that allows us to identify the sources of the responsible/virtuous subject not in an abstract ethical imperative or in an altruistic sentiment inspired by the other's vulnerability, nor even in a virtuous character whose roots remain partly obscure, but rather in the same subject's perception of her own vulnerability and in the recognition of her own dependence and interdependence.[6]

In short, only a subject that recognizes her own vulnerability as a value can welcome the call that comes from the other. In this sense, suffice it to evoke the perspective of Emmanuel Lévinas (1991), whose affirmation of the primacy of otherness, which assumes even more radical tones, is, however, equivalent to presupposing a subject dismissed from his claims of sovereignty, expropriated from his own foundations—a subject that is formed starting from the ethical rupture of the absoluteness of identity and his hubris. Because it is in the very moment in which she accepts the responsibility that the subject herself is constituted as such—not as that representative figure of modernity, which is the Cartesian subject, autonomous, sovereign, and master of himself, but as a relational subject, aware of the condition of mutual dependence and interdependence that characterizes humankind.

This is a crucial theme, dwelt on by many voices of contemporary feminist thought, albeit from different perspectives, yet united in their critique of the modern and liberal concept of the independent and rational subject and their enhancement of dependence and vulnerability. This is the case in particular of Eva Kittay and Judith Butler. In her *Love's Labor,* Kittay (1999) starts from these premises for her critique of John Rawls's (1971) *A Theory of Justice.* Founded on the assumption of free and equal individuals, Rawls's just society excludes all those who do not fit this picture from the social contract, and those resources (care, in the first place) that dependent subjects need (because of illness, childhood, or old age) from the list of primary goods. A complete and convincing theory of justice therefore requires a more inclusive concept of equality, capable of accounting for dependence and vulnerability.[7]

Judith Butler, instead, places the emphasis on the figure of the subject and his potential ethical qualities and, in so doing, chooses to embark on an intense imaginary dialogue with Lévinas, with whom she indeed shares what she calls the "necessary grief" for the death of the subject—not of the subject tout court but of the sovereign subject who is his own master.[8] It is a mourning that opens the possibility of thinking a different structure of the Self—a Self aware of her constitutive dependence, of the bond that inextricably links her to another in a relationship of mutual interdependence. In other words, the Self is constituted starting from an original "intrusion" by the other—an intrusion that inaugurates the subject at the same time that she (the other) expropriates him (the subject) of his own identity, in which she violates him, decentralizing and wounding him,[9] delivering him to a vulnerable condition. Butler returns to this concept, which is also shared by a large part of the feminist thought on this subject, several times.[10] In her reflection, however, which probes its multiple facets (ontological, ethical, and social), the vulnerability (of the Self) assumes a strong ethical depth as it becomes the presupposition of responsibility. Vulnerability is a primary, original condition, so much so that we can recognize it as the very sign of the human, of the constitutive and unavoidable fragility of the human condition. It is something that we cannot avoid, something that "one cannot will away without ceasing to be human" (Butler 2004, xiv), and whose origins cannot be traced because it is coeval with the very origin of life and precedes the formation of the subject himself.[11] Recognizing one's own vulnerability therefore means recovering the truth of the intrinsic social nature of the human condition, which makes us all dependent on each other, exposed to the risk of the relationship, united by a mutual and indissoluble bond that connects our lives. This, Butler says, "does not dispute the fact of my autonomy, but it does qualify that claim through recourse to the fundamental sociality of embodied life, the ways in which we are, from the start and by virtue of being a bodily being, already given over, beyond ourselves, implicated in lives that are not our own" (28). Vulnerability is therefore a resource—an "extraordinary resource" that the Self must grasp and exploit to recover her relational nature and the sense of her being in the world.[12] It is an ethical resource, and it is where the very source of responsibility lies because it is precisely in being exposed to the other and in the "failure" of his sovereign position that the subject finds the sources in order to act responsibly.

I would like to add, however, that vulnerability—and precariousness, as its non-transitory consequence in a world subject to radical challenges—is, can be, a resource as long as we grasp it and know how to exploit its fertile relational potential. This objective, which is anything but automatic, requires the clear awareness of our condition, the ability to free it from a secular process of repression due to the development of the modern paradigm of subjectivity. In other words, it requires a subject aware of her own vulnerability. In order to be perceived and recognized, vulnerability must then become experience—experience of failure, loss, suffering, or even of one's own fragility and precariousness. These are obviously anything but unusual experiences because they are inscribed in our very DNA, which the global age can withdraw from repression in the face of challenges that evoke the specter of our powerlessness. This means giving the opportunity to re-access the awareness of vulnerability, as well as transforming it into shared experiences on a planetary level, promoting the whole of humankind as a new subject of collective action and enhancing vulnerability as an opportunity for community and mutual interdependence. "But where the danger is, also grows the saving power"—the words of Friedrich Hölderlin (quoted by Heidegger [1977] in *The Question Concerning Technology*)—seem to take on a prophetic flavor today. Suffice it to consider the global risk par excellence, in other words climate change and its devastating effects. If it is true that we are threatened by the risk of destruction of the living world produced by ourselves, it is also true that there lurks the chance to bring to light that ontological bond, betrayed by history and society, which consecrates us as subjects in a relationship, tied to each other by a common destiny.

Debt as a Positive Condition

The perception, and the experience of our vulnerability therefore make us sensitive to the other's vulnerability and empathically open to taking care of him. But this is not enough, in my opinion, to motivate us to take up responsibility toward future generations. Instead, this requires a further form of awareness concerning the fact that we are ourselves responsible for the risks to which human lives and the survival of humankind are exposed and, consequently, debtors to those who will come after us. The same neologism, "Anthropocene," coined to describe the transition to the new era in which we currently live, tends to emphasize the enormous and prevalent impact that human action has on nature and the environment today (Crutzen 2006; Pellegrino and Di Paola 2018). It is in fact due to our unlimited (primarily technological) power that, for the first time in history, the risk of self-destruction of humanity is no longer just an apocalyptic fantasy but a real threat.

Hence, we are called upon as debtors to repair the damage we have inflicted on the world and future generations. And this means that we are obliged, here and now, to take care of the future, since care is also, as Tronto points out, a reparation of the world.[13] This was undoubtedly one of the most effective intuitions of Hans Jonas, who identified the fundamental "novelty" of the global age in the connection between power and responsibility (and care as the practical side of responsibility[14]): "Here, everything is new," Jonas says in *The Imperative of Responsibility,* "and doesn't resemble what was until now. What man can do and what man must do as the consequence of the irresistible practice of his might, this has never been experienced before. Yet, our wisdom concerning the right behavior has been designed by our experience" (1985, 7). Because as a *homo faber* who has perverted into a "finally unbound Prometheus," we have the power today to endanger the future of the whole living world. It is our unlimited power to make decisions today that will gravely affect the lives of future generations, making us consequently indebted to them. It is this power that ensures that, unlike our position with respect to the past generations, the future ones do have rights and, as Annette Baier among others sustains, these can legitimately be claimed "against us":

> It is possible that we stand to future generations in a relation in which no previous generation has stood to us; so that, although we have no rights against past generations, future generations do have rights against us. . . . Our knowledge and our power are significantly different even from our grandparents' generation, and might be thought to give rise to new moral relationships and obligations. (1981, 176)

In short, our unlimited power has created a situation in which the rights of future generations correspond to our condition of debt and obligation toward them. Recognizing ourselves as debtors is the necessary premise to respond to the other's appeal without waiting for an immediate and symmetrical counterpart. In other words, it is to put ourselves in a donative perspective and accept the asymmetry of the gift.[15]

It is not by chance that the idea of debt is reproposed by scholars attentive to the theme of the gift in a positive sense. It is put forward as the ontological state of dependence and mutual bond on which to reestablish the community dimension eroded or broken by the immune vocation of modernity and modern individualism. From Marion to Esposito, from Ricoeur to Godbout, the notion of debt tends to enhance the condition of dependence and constraint that is common to human beings, as they belong to a network of reciprocity in which everyone is always at the same time, donor and donee.[16] It is on this view that Paul Ricoeur bases not only the critique of the *homo oeconomicus* paradigm and the modern sovereign subject, but also the critique of the (Rawlsian) theory of justice. It is recognizing ourselves as being in a condition of debt that allows us to give rise to "an economy of the gift," that is, to go beyond justice even, which follows the "logic of equivalence" and of symmetrical reciprocity, to enter the "logic of superabundance," which is asymmetrical and not bound to the immediate and symmetrical response of the other.[17] Once again, all this can find further strength in the global age due, as I am trying to suggest, to our power and its harmful effects on the other distant in time.

The gift therefore should not be understood as a gesture of pure altruism but in fact, as theorized in particular by Marcel Mauss

(1966), as a structure of reciprocity or rather of that particular form of reciprocity that the contemporary theorists of the Maussian gift call "extended" or "generalized" reciprocity (Godbout and Caillé 1998), in which what matters is not the "mutual benefit" understood as the realization of pure individual interest, but rather the creation of a bond and the reaffirmation of the intrinsic value of the social bond (see Pulcini 2012, 161 ff.).

And this is precisely, as we shall now see, the form of reciprocity that we can presuppose in the relationship with future generations.

Extended Reciprocity

A constitutive concept of every subject's relational vision, reciprocity is a fundamental term of the ethic of care that also underlines its desirable asymmetry, especially in the case of a particularly vulnerable care receiver. Indeed is care not, so to speak, the form par excellence of gratuitousness and gift? Nevertheless, the "generalized" reciprocity in which the very essence of the gift is expressed is more complex in its undoubtedly paradoxical aspects. It implies not only the disposition to give "more" than the other, but also implies the delay in time, and the possibility of giving back, not to the one from whom the gift was received but also to someone *else.* In this case, this means that the act of giving does not come from a direct motivation toward the recipient, but rather from the subject's awareness of her own vulnerability and of her being in debt. However, as already noted, being in debt loses any negative value to, on the contrary, take on the connotation, as Godbout says, of a "positive mutual debt": "One could assert that the state of indebtedness is introduced when he who receives, instead of rendering, gives in his turn" (1994, 210, own translation).

It is therefore a debt that we do not feel the need to settle. On the contrary, we wish to remain in this debt, as it testifies to the enhancement of our constitutive dependence and establishes a circle of reciprocity based on that essential component of the social bond, which is *trust,* giving rise to a spatially and temporally ramifying meshwork of responsibility and care in the face of our increasing global precarity.[18]

Now, it is interesting to recall that Marcel Mauss himself, with precocious intuition, had thought this form of reciprocity to be the one that can found the relationship between generations and the gift to future generations. In an essay following *The Gift*, Mauss ([1931] 1969) distinguishes two forms of reciprocity: the first, which is direct, symmetrical, and dual; the second, which is instead temporally delayed and indirect, as it implies the presence of a third party in the dynamics of the gift. It is what he specifically calls "indirect alternative reciprocity" (by virtue of which B returns to C what he has received from A, and C in turn will give D what he has received from B, thus inaugurating a chain that extends to infinity over time), and therefore it seems to be perfectly suited to describing intergenerational responsibility, as it pushes the link between generations far beyond direct family/parental proximity. It is a paradoxical reciprocity, according to Marcel Hénaff (2010, 84), which, however, as Mauss reminds us, commonly occurs when we transmit, mostly unintentionally, knowledge and beliefs, customs and values to those who will follow us in an even remote future.

What is important to point out here is that, nowadays, Mauss's intuition in the context of the gift paradigm allows us in the first place to conceive of a third form of responsibility, which is neither reciprocal in the sense of a symmetrical exchange nor purely one-sided in the Jonasian sense, re-proposed among others by Groves,[19] but rather inspired by the subject's awareness of her own vulnerability. Second, it can provide a valid motivational context and a plausible justification for some theories of intergenerational justice that, albeit from different perspectives and without any evident reference to Mauss, propose the idea of an indirect reciprocity. This non-systematic and nonuniform set of theories is united by the idea that from time to time each generation feels the obligation to transmit what it has received from previous generations to the future ones, according to a descending chain of reciprocal indirect obligations.[20] The most interesting aspect is that in some authors, not suspected of any intentional convergence with the gift paradigm, there emerges a contestation of possessive individualism and the invitation to think of ourselves not as the owners but as the custodians of what we have received. "We all inherit a social order, a cultural tradition, air and water," sustains, for example, Annette Baier, "not as private heirs of private will-makers but as members of a continuous community. . . . We inherit them not as sole beneficiaries but as persons able to share and pass on such goods to an indefinite run of future generations" (1981, 73).[21]

Motivations to Care

Starting from this perspective, we can say that what drives us to take responsibility for future generations is not, nor can it be, a direct motivation (whether this is the pursuit of one's own interest, a personal and emotional bond, or a reaction to suffering), but rather "indirect motivations," namely, those motivations that produce a certain good or value as a collateral effect (Birnbacher 2009). These might be, as I suggested, the recognition of one's own vulnerability, the awareness of sharing a condition of mutual debt as members of a global community, or the perception of the risks and potentially irreversible damages produced by our power. They are motivations that imply, to use the words of Ernest Partridge, a Self capable of transcending herself, of going beyond selfish and interested motivations and therefore capable of a self-transcending concern toward future generations—a Self, in other words, capable of care for the future.

This possibility of self-transcendence was already implicit in that ancient moral paradox according to which the most satisfying life is achieved when we are able to transcend ourselves. But, in the global age, it is all the more nurtured by the desire to break out of the narrow borders of a Self who is building his own prison and own destruction. As Partridge maintains, a self-transcending concern toward future generations is not only possible but also "healthy" for the Self's realization. Coming out of ourselves to take care of the other and the world is not an act of pure altruism or sacrifice but rather what follows from the capacity to recognize ourselves as links in an intergenerational chain confirming the value of relationships beyond the space–time dimension and hope for a better world. In other words, the indirect motivations have nothing to do with a banal altruism, but rather with the recognition of our own condition of interdependence and the flourishing of the Self.

This might suggest that this kind of motivation cannot be inspired or fueled by emotions or empathic feelings. We are in fact accustomed to thinking that empathy and emotions, which is where, it goes without saying, the main motivational resource resides, presuppose the proximity of the other or at least his existence. Hence, it once again becomes inevitable to ask: what feelings can we have toward someone we cannot see, cannot touch, and who does not yet exist?

While this is not the place to tackle the complexity of this theme,[22] I would like to show that emotions do not always or necessarily presuppose the presence and physicality of the other.

In the first place, it seems legitimate to assume the possibility of expanding the "circles of empathy"—as already affirmed by the ethics of sympathy of David Hume and Adam Smith, and recently reproposed by authors such as Peter Singer (2011)[23]—while extending it today to the new "significant other" represented by future generations. Second, starting from the awareness of vulnerability and interdependence, it is possible, as Günther Anders had already suggested, to reawaken and expand the imagination in order to prefigure the future and activate empathic passions. Third, I would like to point out that empathic passions are not only those positive passions such as love for the the other or compassion for the sufferer, which presuppose the concrete existence of the other, but also those traditionally considered "negative," such as shame and guilt for our voracious and destructive actions, or fear, in the sense of the fear of losing what has value for us.

What is undoubted is that the ethics of responsibility cannot work without this emotional dimension unless it wants to limit itself to a pure abstract and duty-based principle. And this also means that responsibility should be translated into the concrete commitment and affective disposition that characterizes care,[24] understood, in its precise etymological meaning, as concern and solicitude. This obviously requires the idea of care to emancipate itself from a pure relationship of proximity. Vulnerability of the self, positive debt, extended reciprocity, and expanded empathy form the set of conditions that inspire care toward the other distant in time. They constitute the basis of a possible extension of the idea of care[25] and its emancipation from a pure relationship of proximity, allowing it, as I suggested at the beginning, to go beyond a dimension of "parochialism" (Robinson 1997) potentially to extend beyond the narrow confines of proximity, as long as the other distant in time becomes significant for us, and finally to become an ethic for the global age, an ethic for the future.

It is therefore right to argue, following Maurice Hamington, that unlike traditional ethics (Kantian, utilitarian), the ethics of care contains concern for future generations and the idea of sustainability regarding the environment in its very ontology:[26] "A care ethics is also much less likely to struggle conceptually with the problem of having moral obligations to future people and beings. . . . The practice of caring involves caring for future generations, and in so doing, dependency relations are established that bring with them normative obligations" (Hamington and Sander-Staudt 2011, xi). It is also true, however, that this requires an effort of imagination that can awaken empathic passions, and a permanent determination on the part of the responsible subject to engage in care. In other words, care of the future requires the capacity to transform attention toward the other[27] into a constant and structural endowment—to be activated, paradoxically, even in the absence of the other.

Finally, as we know, according to many care theorists, care is also a *practice* (Tronto 1995; Held 2006; Kittay 1999), which in this case assumes a particular connotation, consisting not only of decisive public battles (such as the struggle for access to common goods or the political denunciation of environmental disasters) but also of small, everyday gestures such as not wasting water, recycling, or defending a green area in a neighborhood. Indeed, we cannot speak of care except as a daily commitment, although in the case of the other, distant in time, care can only be preventive, that is, to be effective, it should start before potentially irreversible and irreparable events happen, which can compromise the very future of humankind and the living world—events produced, as we have seen, by the pathological distortions of modernity and the hegemonic model of the *homo oeconomicus*, plagued by blindness toward the meaning and purpose of his action.

In other words, care can become the revolutionary value to counter the challenges threatening humanity and the living world and to build an ethic of the future. It can become, I would suggest, an actual "form of life," that is, a set of social practices that shape the Self's vital relationships with the natural, cultural, and intersubjective world.[28] As a form of life, care has the concrete and symbolic power to generate a new and different vision of the world and the commitment necessary to achieve it—a worldview that is intrinsically ethical and can therefore effectively counteract the hegemony and ideological power of neoliberalism, denying its inevitability, freeing new values, and opening new perspectives of coexistence.

It therefore translates, together with the change of optics and a change of paradigm, into the activation of practices, attitudes, and purposes alternative to the existent ones: contrasting the hybris of the *homo oeconomicus* with the dependence and fragility of the human condition; blind, unlimited, meaningless, and purposeless action with an awareness of the limit; and indifference with concern and attention for the fate of the other and the world. It gives life to a new ethics, which—emphasizing vulnerability and interdependence, attention to the other, and conservation of the world—seems to be a privileged point of view on which to base the criticism of the existing and the hegemonic form of life: namely, the capitalist and utilitarian way of living that exalts unlimited individualism, acquisitive passions, and instrumental reason, which is no longer able to give effective answers to the problems that emerge in the current sociocultural context.

The strength of the ethics of care lies in it sinking its roots not in normative precepts or deontological imperatives but indeed in a form of life, in material and symbolic forms of organizing one's life and one's world. As Sandra Laugier (2015, 233) pointed out,[29] the peculiarity of the ethics of care is that it pursues not so much what is right as what is important. It allows us to recognize what appears to be anything but evident to the common conscience, as it has the power to direct "our attention to the ordinary, to what we are unable to see, though it is right before our eyes" (226). It is the concrete manifestation of a sensitivity and attention, as Iris Murdoch (222) would say, to the details, to the ordinary and the particular(s), which allows what is generally overlooked to be revealed and be given importance: that is to say that microcosm of needs, expectations, and bonds that we tend to forget and devalue, to relegate to an area of opacity and invisibility, despite the fact that they form the daily fabric of everyone's life, the living material of our very existence. "Care is everywhere," Laugier (226) says again, acknowledging it the pervasiveness of a form of life, "and it is such a pervasive part of the human form of life that it is never seen for what it is: a range of activities by which we organize our world so that we can live in it as well as possible"[30]—above all, because it results, I would like to reiterate, in a daily commitment,[31] in practices characterized by continuity, constancy, and an ontological status of permanence. While, on the one hand, these qualities belong to all the dimensions of care, they appear even more constitutive and indispensable for the care of the other distant in time. In this case, the care loses any character of contingency and episodicity, which, despite everything, may characterize the other forms of are,[32] to become a permanent attitude based on a certain vision of the world and on the will to engage, even in the absence of the other, in everyday practices that can promise the other and the world survival and a life worth living. The daily commitment that we are able to offer today is, in other words, the only proof of our determination to take care of the world and future generations, the only confirmation of our desire to keep a promise—all the more appreciable insofar as we know well that, in this case, we will not be exposed to any sanction or blame that could directly affect us. In other words, there is no doubt that care for future generations is exemplary of care as a form of life, since it requires an immanent criticism of the dominant forms of life, a radical change of mentality, the adoption of alternative practices and behaviors starting from a daily commitment—in short, a different way of thinking of the world and being in the world that inspires our action by transforming its deepest underlying motivations in order to achieve a better future.

Notes

1. For one of the most effective definitions of the complex and variegated concept of "neoliberalism" (on which, see Peck and Theodore 2019), see Wendy Brown (2018): "Neoliberalism is semiotically loose, but designates something very specific. It represents a distinctive kind of valorization and liberation of capital. It makes oeconomics the model of everything . . . [including] the *economization* of democracy." https://tocqueville21.com/interviews/wendy-brown-not-neoliberal-today/.
2. On the complexity of this debate, see Menga (2016).
3. Dale Jamieson clearly underlines the unprecedented difficulties intrinsic to the moral challenges of our time "most of what typically accompanies this core [of the moral problems] has disappeared . . . : it is difficult to identify the agents, or causal nexus that obtains between them; thus it is difficult to assign responsibility, blame, and so forth" (2007, 476).
4. "But still, a silent plea for sparing its integrity seems to issue from the threatened plenitude of the living world" (Jonas 1985, 8).
5. "The ontology has changed. Ours is not that of eternity, but of time" (Jonas 1985, 125).
6. On the positive concept of vulnerability, see Valadier (2011).
7. "The present work is intended to clear the way for an understanding of equality that is compatible with dependency concerns, that understands not only the demands of fairness but the demands of connection . . . . Equality is an ideal of justice—its domain is rarely understood to include the values and virtues of care" (Kittay 1999, 18).
8. "But this death, if it is a death, is only the death of a certain kind of subject, one that was never possible to begin with, the death of a fantasy of impossible

mastery, and so a loss of what one never had. In other words, it is a necessary grief" (Butler 2005, 65).

9. "For both, though, the primat or impress of the Other is primary, inaugurative, and there is no formation of a 'me' outside of this originally passive impingement" (Butler 2005, 97).

10. For a critical reflection on the feminist debate around this topic, see Casalini (2016, 30–48).

11. "That we are impinged upon primarily and against our will is the sign of a vulnerability and a beholdeness that we cannot will away" (Butler 2005, 100; see also Butler 2004, 45).

12. "To foreclose that vulnerability, to banish it, to make ourselves secure at the expense of every other human consideration is to eradicate one of the most important human resources from which we must take our bearings and find our way" (Butler 2004, 30).

13. Tronto defines care as "a species activity that includes everything that we do to maintain, continue, and repair our 'world' so that we can live in it as well as possible" (Tronto 1993, 103).

14. Indeed, Jonas (1985, ch 4, § VII) sees care, understood as parental care for the newborn, as the timeless archetype of all responsibility.

15. On the topic of the gift as a critical paradigm in modern individualism, please see Pulcini (2012, ch. 5).

16. See Marion (2002), Godbout (1994), and Ricoeur (1995, 32–33); in a deconstructive perspective, which tends to emphasize the gift (munus)–debt nexus (see also Esposito 2010).

17. According to Ricoeur (1994, 31), in the best of cases, Rawls's model of distributive justice draws a society in which "the feeling of reciprocal dependency . . . is yet subordinate to that of reciprocal disinterest." As Ricoeur continues, it is not that this model is totally lacking the idea of reciprocity, "but the juxtaposition of interests prevents the idea of justice from rising to the level of real recognition and a solidarity in which everyone feels *in debt* toward everyone else" (own translation). On the distinction between justice (equivalence) and gift/agape (asymmetry), see also the important analyses of Jean Luc Boltanski (2012).

18. On the importance of trust in the social bond, emphasized by all Maussian gift theorists, see, among others, Giddens (1990) and Hollis (1998).

19. "What is required is a recognition of responsibility that consisently carries through the intuition of Hans Jonas that future-oriented responsibility, particularly in contemporary societies, is primarily non-reciprocal" (Groves 2009, 22).

20. Not by chance also defined as "descending reciprocity" (Gosseries 2008).

21. See also Pope Francis in his Encyclical *Laudato si'*, "The world we have received also belongs to those who will follow us" (2015, 118). And even more radically, the native American saying recalled by Gosseries (2008, 62), "We do not inherit the Earth from our Ancestors, we borrow it from our children."

22. I dealt amply with this topic in Pulcini (2013, 2016).

23. On the possibility of extending empathy in the global age, see also Rifkin (2009).

24. "Caring is not simply a cerebral concern, or a character trait, but the concern of living, active humans engaged in the processes of everyday living. Care is both a practice and a disposition (Tronto 1993, 104).

25. There is still little and very much secondary attention by care theorists to this topic. I will limit myself to mentioning Held (2006), Robinson (1997), and Tronto (2013).

26. "Care ethics is concerned about sustainability because much of care is focused on mantaining life and this includes being responsible for the well-being of future generations" (Hamington and Sander-Staudt 2011, xi).

27. Here, I mean "attention" in the sense of Simone Weil ([1942] 1982), that is, as the "purest form of generosity."

28. With the words of Rahel Jaeggi, forms of life are "forms of human coexistence shaped by culture, to 'orders of human coexistence' that includes an 'ensemble of practices and orientations' but also their institutional manifestations and materializations" (2018, 14).

29. On the context of the Wittgesteinian philosophy of lifeforms see Laugier (2015, 234–35): "At the center of care is our ability for (our disposition to) moral expression, which, as Cavell and Charles Taylor have shown in various ways, is rooted in ordinary human and other lifeforms, in the (Wittgensteinian) sense of a simultaneously natural and social aggregate of forms of expression and connection to others. It is the form of life that determines the ethical structure of expression, and this expression, conversely, reworks life and gives it form."

30. See also Laugier and Paperman (2006) and Laugier, Paperman, and Moliner (2009).

31. Mortari speaks explicitly of a "daily ethic of care" (2015, 218).

32. We can only give care out of love so long as the love lasts; we can be caregivers, in the sense of welfare providers, only for some periods or stages of life.

Works Cited

Anders, Günther. 1956. *Die Antiquiertheit des Menschen.* Munich: C. H. Beck.

Baier, Annette. 1981. "The Rights of Past and Future Persons." In *Responsibilities to Future Generations. Environmental Ethics,* edited by Ernest Partridge, 171–83. Buffalo, N.Y.: Prometheus Books.

Beck, Ulrich. 1992. *Risk Society: Towards a New Modernity.* Translated by Mark Ritter. London: Sage.

Birnbacher, Dieter. 2009. "What Motivates Us to Care for the (Distant) Future?" In *Intergenerational Justice,* edited by Axel Gosseries and Lukas H. Meyer, 273–300. Oxford: Oxford University Press.

Boltanski, Jean Luc. 2012. "Agape: An Introduction to the States of Peace." In *Love and Justice as Competences: Three Essays on the Sociology of Action.* Translated by Catherine Porter. Cambridge: Polity.

Brown,Wendy. 2018. "Who Is Not a Neoliberal Today?" *Tocqueville21,* January 18, 2018. https://tocqueville21.com/interviews/wendy-brown-not-neoliberal-today/.

Butler, Judith. 2004. *Precarious Life: The Power of Mourning and Violence.* London: Verso Books.

Butler, Judith. 2005. *Giving an Account of Oneself.* New York: Fordham University Press.

Casalini, Brunella. 2016. "Politics, Justice and the Vulnerable Subject." *Gênero & Direito* 3:30–48.

Collins, Stephanie. 2015. *The Core of Care Ethics*. Basingstoke, UK: Palgrave Macmillan.

Crutzen, Paul J. 2006. "The Anthropocene." In *Earth System Science in the Anthropocene: Emerging Issues and Problems*, edited by Eckart Ehlers and Thomas Krafft, 13–18.. Berlin: Springer.

De-Shalit, Avishai. 1995. *Why Posterity Matters. Environmental Policies and Future Generations*. London: Routledge.

Esposito, Roberto. 2010. *Communitas: The Origin and Destiny of Community*. Translated by Timothy Campbell. Stanford, Calif.: Stanford University Press.

Giddens, Anthony. 1990. *The Consequences of Modernity*. Cambridge: Polity.

Gilligan, Carol. 1982. *In a Different Voice*. Cambridge, Mass.: Harvard University Press.

Godbout, Jacques. 1994. "L'état d'endettement mutuel." *Revue du MAUSS* 4: 205–19.

Godbout, Jacques, and Alain Caillé. 1998. *The World of the Gift*. Montreal, Canada: McGill-Queens University Press.

Gosseries, Axel. 2008. "Theories of Intergenerational Justice: A Synopsis." *Survey and Perspectives Integrating Environment and Society* 1 (1): 61–71.

Groves, Christopher. 2009. "Future Ethics: Risk, Care and Non-reciprocal Responsibility." *Journal of Global Ethics* 5 (1): 17–31.

Hamington, Maurice, and Maureen Sander-Staudt, eds. 2011. *Applying Care Ethics to Business*. Dordrecht, the Netherlands: Springer.

Heidegger, Martin. 1977. *The Question Concerning Technology and Other Essays*. Translated and introduction by William Lovitt. New York: Harper and Row.

Held, Virginia. 2006. *The Ethics of Care: Personal, Political and Global*. Oxford: Oxford University Press.

Hénaff, Marcel. 2010. "Mauss et l'invention de la réciprocité." *Revue du MAUSS* 2 (36): 71–86.

Hollis, Martin. 1998. *Trust within Reason*. Cambridge: Cambridge University Press.

Jaeggi, Rahel. 2018. *Critique of Forms of Life*. Translated by Ciaran Cronin. Cambridge, Mass.: Belknap Press.

Jamieson, Dale. 2003. "Ethics, Public Policies and Global Warming." In *Morality's Progress*, 282–95. Oxford: Oxford University Press.

Jamieson, Dale. 2007. "The Moral and Political Challenges of Climate Change." In *Creating a Climate for Change*, edited by Susanne C. Moser and Lisa Dilling, 475–82. Cambridge: Cambridge University Press.

Jamieson, Dale. 2008. *Ethics and Environment*. Cambridge: Cambridge University Press.

Jonas, Hans. 1985. *The Imperative of Responsibility: In Search of an Ethics for the Technological Age*. Chicago: University of Chicago Press.

Kittay, Eva Feder. 1999. *Love's Labor: Essays in Women, Equality and Dependency*. New York: Routledge.

Laugier, Sandra. 2015. "The Ethics of Care as a Politics of the Ordinary." *New Literary History: A Journal of Theory and Interpretation* 46 (2): 217–40.

Laugier, Sandra, and Patricia Paperman. 2006. *Le souci des autres—éthique et politique du care*. Paris: Éditions de l'EHESS.

Laugier, Sandra, Patricia Paperman, and Pascale Moliner. 2009. *Qu'est-ce que le care?* Paris: Payot.

Lévinas, Emmanuel. 1991. *Otherwise Than Being or Beyond Essence*. Dordrecht, the Netherlands: Springer.

Marion, Jean-Luc. 2002. *Being Given: Toward a Phenomenology of Givenness*. Translated by Jeffrey L. Kosky. Stanford, Calif.: Stanford University Press.

Mauss, Marcel. 1966. *The Gift*. London: Cohen & West.

Mauss, Marcel. (1931) 1969. "La cohésion sociale dans les sociétés polysegmentaires." In *Oeuvres*, vol. 3:11–27. Paris: Minuit.

Mead, George Herbert. (1934) 2015. *Mind, Self, and Society*. Edited by Charles W. Morris. Chicago: University of Chicago Press.

Menga, Ferdinando. 2016. *Lo scandalo del futuro. Per una giustizia intergenerazionale*. Rome: Edizioni di Storia e Letteratura.

Mortari, Luigina. 2015. *Filosofia della cura*. Milan: Cortina.

Nussbaum, Martha. 2001. *Upheavals of Thought. The Intelligence of Emotions*. Cambridge: Cambridge University Press.

Parfit, Derek. 1984. *Reasons and Persons*. Oxford: Oxford University Press.

Partridge, Ernest. 1981. "Why Care about the Future?" In *Responsibility to Future Generations. Environmental Ethics*, edited by Ernest Partridge, 203–20. Buffalo, N.Y.: Prometheus Books.

Peck, Jamie, and Nick Theodore. 2019. "Still Neoliberalism?" *The South Atlantic Quarterly* 118 (2): 245–65.

Pellegrino, Gianfranco, and Marcello Di Paola. 2018. *Nell'Anthropocene*. Rome: DeriveApprodi.

Pontara, Giuliano. 1995. *Etica e generazioni future*. Rome-Bari: Laterza.

Pope Francis. 2015. *Encyclical Letter Laudato si' of the Holy Father Francis: On Care for Our Common Home*. London: Catholic Truth Society.

Pulcini, Elena. 2012. *The Individual without Passions*. Translated by Karen Whittle. Lanham, Md.: Lexington Books.

Pulcini, Elena. 2013. *Care of the World. Fear, Responsibility and Justice in the Global Age*. Translated by Karen Whittle. Dordrecht, the Netherlands: Springer.

Pulcini, Elena. 2016. "What Emotions Motivate Care?" *Emotion Review* 9 (1): 64–71.

Rawls, John. 1971. *A Theory of Justice*. Cambridge, Mass.: Harvard University Press.

Ricoeur, Paul. 1994. *Persona, comunità e istituzioni. Dialettica tra giustizia e amore*, edited by A. Danese. Fiesole, Italy: ECP.

Ricoeur, Paul. 1995. "Love and Justice." In *Philosophy and Social Criticism* 21 (5/6): 23–28.

Rifkin, Jeremy. 2009. *The Empathic Civilization*. New York: Penguin Books.

Robinson, Fiona. 1997. "Globalizing Care: Ethics, Feminist Theory, and International Relations." *Alternatives: Global, Local, Political* 22 (1): 113–33.

Singer, Peter. 2011. *The Expanding Circle. Ethics, Evolution, and Moral Progress*. Princeton, N.J.: Princeton University Press.

Sumner, L.Wayne. 1978. "Classical Utilitarianism and the Problem of Population Policy." In *Obligations to Future Generations*, edited by Richard I. Sikora and Brian Barry, 91–111. Philadelphia, Pa.: Temple University Press.

Tronto, Joan. 1993. *Moral Boundaries*. London: Routledge.

Tronto, Joan. 2013. *Caring Democracy: Markets, Equality and Justice*. New York: New York University Press.

Valadier, Paul. 2011. "Apologie de la vulnerabilité." *Etudes* 414 (2): 199–210.

Weil, Simone. (1942) 1982. "Lettre à Joë Bousquet." In *Correspondance*, edited by Simone Weil and Joë Bousquet. Lausanne, Switzerland: Editions l'Age d'Homme.

Weil, Simone. (1948) 2002. *Gravity and Grace*. London: Routlege.

CHAPTER 6

Care

The Primacy of Being

LUIGINA MORTARI

To Care for Life

In the field of human experience, some things are essential and indispensable. Nonetheless, it is often true that this very essentiality, though evident in daily life, may escape one's notice and its ontological significance paradoxically remain unperceived (Heidegger 1962, 69). The phenomenon of care gives crucial proof of this. Care is fundamental in life, even if for a long time Western culture has largely overlooked its significance in human life (Hamington 2004, 1).

The unequivocal result of a systematic phenomenological analysis of experience is that care is so essential and indispensable because life cannot flourish without it. Human beings have an undeniable need to care: to care for themselves and receive care from others, and to care for others and to care for things, animate or inanimate, material or spiritual. This is why "all people want to be cared for" and "the world would be a better place if we all cared more for one another" (Noddings 2002, 11). Goodness is vital just as is the defense against our suffering; care is the compulsory response to these needs.

When we consider birth, our coming into the world, we imagine light that opens on to being. Consequently, we could affirm that coming into being is like coming into light, a state of being enlightened. It is care that enlightens the entity that is the human being. Because of this, care is the essential ontological trait of being-there or, in other words, it is the structure of the being of being-there (Heidegger 1992,

252). Indeed, being-there takes on its own existence by caring for itself. The relating to existence by caring-for represents an existential that possesses the trait of necessity because, from the beginning to the end of a human being's life, she has to care for herself, for others and for things. Given that the human being is delivered into life through the practice of care, we may say that "each one of us is what s/he pursues and cares for" (Heidegger 1988, 159).

The affirmation that we become what we care for and that the ways of caring shape our being means that if we care for certain relationships, our being will be structured from the elements that derive from these relationships, whether they are beneficial or harmful. If we care for certain ideas, the structure of our thought will be shaped by this care. In other words, our mental experience will rely on the ideas that we have cultivated and will suffer the lack of those we have neglected. If we take care of things, enjoying them and relating to them will structure our existence. If we care for certain people, whatever happens in the relational exchange with the other will become part of ourselves. Care, in fact, could be defined as a *fabric of being.*

Care is required by the quality of our being-there, which once it enters our lifetime "is already encumbered with the excess of itself" (Lévinas 2001, 15). Solidity is a quality that is opposed to lightness, and a human being cannot live like a puff of wind. From the very beginning, when, at birth, his body is touched by light, he has to take up a heavy burden: the duty of taking care of his life, "the care that a being takes for its endurance and conservation" (Lévinas 2001, 10).[1]

Even in the most perfect of worlds, where the horrors of war or starvation have been eliminated and where everybody has enough to sustain their life, there will always be a need for care. In some phases of life, a state of fragility and vulnerability makes us especially dependent on others—during childhood, for instance, or when we are ill. In other phases, such as adulthood, even if we have some degree of autonomy and self-sufficiency, without the caring help for others, we cannot cultivate and express our potentiality-for-being, nor can we find comfort for our pain. Care is ontologically essential; it protects life and helps make existence possible. Good care keeps one's being steeped in goodness, and it is this goodness that gives shape to the generative basis of our being and that structures the layer of being keeping us securely among things and among others. Practicing care is therefore putting ourselves in touch with the heart of life.

The Ancient Knowledge of Care

Knowledge of the primacy of care first comes to light in the ancient myth of Cronos. This myth, which is narrated by Plato[2] (*Statesman,* 269a–75e), recounts that there had once been a happy time for the human race—a time when the gods cared for humankind. There was no brutality, war, or any internal dissent; the gods tended human beings and took care of them. Human beings had an abundance of fruit from the trees and many other plants, which grew not through cultivation but because the Earth sent them up of its own accord. This was the existence of those living in the time of Cronos; he even took care of the rotation of the whole universe (271d 4).

But this condition of bliss, during which human beings were the objects of divine care, was of finite temporal duration, and when the period of time was completed and the movement of the cosmos reached its due measure, the gods withdrew to an observation point outside the movement of the world (272e), and all the gods in turn abandoned the areas entrusted to their care. Thus, it happened that the motion of the universe no longer knew the first order with which it moved, and human beings found themselves abandoned, without divine care, "left without care of gods"[3] (274b 6). Once care from the gods ceased to be available to human beings, they had to live their lives depending on their own resources and care for themselves by themselves (274d), observing an indispensable requirement for teaching and education (274c). The myth of Cronos enunciates an ontological thesis on the human condition. It theorizes that the condition in which human beings are born and live is one where they are asked to "take care for themselves by themselves" (274d 11–13).

A fundamental theory of the primacy of care is to be found in the works of Plato. In the *Phaedrus,* it says that care is an essential characteristic not only of mortal men but also of the gods. Indeed, it maintains that Zeus carries out his divine task of "putting all things in order and caring for them" (Plato, *Phaedrus,* 246e). In Book VII of the *Republic,* Socrates explains to Glaucon that those philosophers who have acquired, through scaling the heights of knowledge, a right vision of the beautiful, the just and the good, and are consequently capable of governing a city, should self-evidently be obliged to "care for and guard" the other citizens (520a). In the *Laches,* Lysimachus opens the dialogue by affirming that it is the duty of adults to care for the young and that the term "care" means taking on the responsibility of their education so that they become excellent practitioners of the art of living (179a–d). In the *Alcibiades I,* Socrates explains that in order to learn the art of living, first you must learn to care for yourself. Later, theorizing about care finds its place in Latin philosophy, most specifically in Seneca, a proponent of Stoicism, where in his work *Letters to Lucilius,* he explains that because our life consists of time, the worst thing we can do is neglect to care for the time of our life.

After the expert theorizing on care in Greek and Latin culture, the subject was long neglected by philosophy. Only during the last century has it returned to the center of philosophical debate in the works of thinkers such as Heidegger and Lévinas. After this, the work of Carol Gilligan, who initiated the discussion on the difference between the ethics of care and the ethics of justice, has been of seminal importance. Starting from these original considerations, today the debate on care is passionate; it is examined in connection with many different areas of contemporary life (education, health, social services, ethics, politics, management, etc.), but what is missing is a rigorous theorization on the primacy of ontological care. The need to delineate an analytics of care finds its inception here.

At this point, an eidetic problem manifests itself. In order to address the issue of a theorization of care, we need to know what is meant by care. So, we begin by formulating an initial definition of care and then go on to develop a theoretical hypothesis that will lead to a salient and rigorous conceptualization. A simple, straightforward definition of care, deriving from the phenomenology of everyday life, is the following: *to care for* is to take something or someone to heart, to worry about, to be concerned, to devote oneself to something.

To formulate a stringent theory starting from this simple and essential definition, it is necessary to answer the following question: Why is care essential?

Why Is Care Essential?

In order to establish solidly the thesis that considers care as essential to existence, we must delineate a phenomenology of the ontological qualities of the human condition. Only after examining the concept of care in regard to human ontology is it possible to evince the fact that care stands in a relationship of necessity regarding these qualities. Care is essential because we suffer from a radical ontological weakness. We are both fragile and vulnerable.

Before entering this descriptive reasoning, it is necessary to specify that to search for the ontological qualities of the human condition common to both males and females is not contrary to the feminist view that considers it fundamental to evidence the differences between male and female. What feminists rightly challenge are male-conceived cultural frameworks that have been successfully defined as the standard model of humanity as a whole; what feminists assert by contrast is the right to difference (Groenhout 2004, 8–9). But while defining standards is a question of value (i.e., a normative action), describing the essence of the human condition is a descriptive process that searches for what is common to each human being. By following the phenomenological method that asks us to describe only what appears, the results make it evident that human life is fragile and vulnerable, since it inescapably depends on other human beings as well as on the context where they live (Groenhout 2004, 10).

Fragility

When the mind thinks of the divine as the opposite of the human, the former is perceived as a fully completed and perfect form, since nothing divine needs further development. Any finite entity, on the other hand, is an imperfect and limited presence. It is substance without form, it becomes with time, and its becoming is stimulated by the compulsion to search for form. We are not meant to exist in reality in a pure and simple way. We cannot be at one with the world as migrating birds are at one with the flight paths they have always followed and who seem to have always inhabited the horizon. We carry within us a fracture with the world's order, and because we are lacking this order, we are called upon to search for a meaningful balance to maintain us in a right relationship with reality.

We are beings lacking control over existence, as we do not decide our birth but discover ourselves already to be in the world, and once there, we belong to the flowing of time. We are in a constant state of need; we are not finite, complete, autonomous, or self-sufficient in our being. This ontological state of lack of control over experience is proved by the fact that we are always desiring a fullness of the reality of life that we can never grasp. Since we are made of material and spiritual substance, we constantly need to procure things to nurture and preserve the being of our body and our soul.

We are lacking in the sense that each of us is an entity without the power to pass from nothingness to being, and in our essence, we are something that can be, and within this "can," there is all the risk of not coming into being. Our ontological essence is "having the possibility of *being*" (Stein 2002, 34) in the sense that we have a disposition toward being. Having the quality of being possible does not mean not being but rather being the potentiality to become, and that becoming is the passage from "being possible" to "being present." I find myself as already given in the life and discover myself as an inconsistent entity. I am a fragile being, since I do not exist by myself, I am nothing by myself, in every moment I am facing the void, and I must receive being as a gift moment after moment, over and over again (55).

The entity we are does not possess its own being but rather is given it from elsewhere. The lack of being may be perceived in our enigmatic origin and in our end, in the emptiness of our past, in the impossibility of calling into being everything that is striving to become. We are dependent beings, depending on where we come from, on the world we are living in, and where we are testing our being. So, it is legitimate to state that an essential quality of the human condition is its fragility, which lies in not having sovereignty over its being. Our being is insubstantial, "limited in its transience from moment to moment and thus exposed to the possibility of nothingness" (Stein 2002, 58).

Our ontological fragility is evinced by the fact that we are born without a form for our being and with the duty to forge this form in the course of time, without it being clear what we are supposed to do to give good shape to our becoming and its unpredictable possibilities. In this sense, we are essentially a problem for ourselves.

The matter of life is time, and from the moment we come into life, we start losing time. If only what is present is real, then our being—trapped between not-being-anymore and not-being-yet—suffers from a profound fragility. Notwithstanding the fact that we can cope with fragility by using our reason, the quality of our condition makes us very similar to other living beings. Semonides reminds us that "As leaves on the trees is the lot / of men" (frag. 29, in Waterfield, 2000). It is this ontological weakness that makes us beings who are destined to question our being-there constantly.

We feel this exposure to nothingness profoundly. We start to feel it at the moment we become aware of the finiteness of our being-there, of the fact that death annihilates life. Death looms over being-there simply because being-there is a becoming with a limited duration and with no sovereignty over this becoming. When we think within the shape of self-reflection, we discover ourselves to be inconsistent, and this inconsistency is manifested by the fact that, even if we do not plan it, even if it is not within the frame of our desiring, at any moment life can disappear. The possibility of no longer existing, which puts an end to being-there, is a constant that accompanies the entire span of being in the world. It is this ominous, ever-present feeling of vanishing from being-there that is the root cause of anguish—the anguish of an unpredictable and inevitable disappearance into nothingness.

However, this void is not only the phenomenon that nullifies life—death, which takes life away forever—but also the void that eliminates valuable things, such as the ties of friendship and love, leaving us without anything that makes life worth living. And it is that very feeling of the possibility of losing what we value, without the power of keeping these things within existence, that engenders a sense of our fragility.

Vulnerability

The first natural feeling that a human being perceives is that she is alone: a single specific entity. We feel that we can "exchange everything . . . except existing" (Lévinas 1987, 42), that this has nothing to do with anybody other than the existent himself. In this sense, each one of us is "a monad and a solitude" (52). We are alone, faced with our responsibility for the existential scheme, faced with the demand to give a fully human meaning to our time, faced with pain when it suffocates the soul like fog in autumn. When we have to cope with the most important things in life, when we are required to make crucial decisions, we are often inexpressibly alone. The art of existing has to deal with this irremediable solitude, so that while co-existing with others in the world, we can at least pencil in traces of meaning, insofar as we manage to give voice to our singularity, our originality.

The evidence of my solitude is the work of my consciousness. But my consciousness, which is mine and mine only, finds its generative matrix in the plurality of being-there; it is, in fact, the emerging form of the silent dialogue of the soul with itself that reproduces in our innermost being the dialogue that each of us engages in with others. In point of fact, we are made by the colloquy with the others. It is an indisputable phenomenological given that life is not a solipsistic event, since it is always closely connected with the lives of others. For the human being, existence is always co-existence, as no-one is capable of fully realizing the project of existing by themseves. In the *Nicomachean Ethics,* Aristotle (1999) defines the human being as a naturally political entity, that is, someone who sojourns with many others who give life to the city.

We are lacking being, and for this very reason, we feel an intense need to relate to whoever, like us, has an ontological need of the other. This compulsive relationality explains the phenomenon of the intense attachment of the baby to whoever takes care of it (Bowlby 1969). Since at the beginning of life ontological weakness is at its highest, the attachment of the baby to its mother is a vital need. And if, with time, this need fades and a sort of precarious autonomy takes shape, the search for meaningful relationships, different and of varying intensity though they may be, accompanies the becoming of each of us. This happens because relating to others is an ontological structure of being-there: to exist is always to co-exist. Relational substantiality is something totally inescapable because even when the entity that we are withdraws into an intra-subjective space—the space where the mind dialogues with itself—the relationship with others goes on, since even when we are alone, our thoughts maintain the relationship with the thoughts we formulated with others, and the emotions that move our hearts are threads that keep us connected. This is the relational substance of being-there or, to say it with Rilke, we are within a network of relationships, we are not like flowers that live only for one season, because our feeling comes from far away: it is like sap that is fed not only by present relationships but also from past ones, which, even if forgotten, structure the vital background of being.

Ontological concepts are fundamental and because of this are included among the structural elements of a paradigm of thought. We can verify how non-relational ontology contaminates many types of discourse, including the ethical and the political. The shortcoming of Western political thought is that of having founded itself on a conception of the human being as an independent, autonomous, and self-sufficient individual. Preconfigured thus, it overlooks the condition of dependence on others that characterizes significant phases of each of our lives, and that is a lasting condition for many. Theories of equality are based on the idea of a citizen who, being an individual, a single entity, possesses certain rights. In this way, Paul Ricoeur, when he discusses care during his reinterpretation of the object of ethical discourse, considers the subject in a traditional manner, forgetting that each person inevitably contains his never-accomplished autonomy and will always be dependent on others. Ricoeur also affirms that the person is a being able to act on reasoned initiative and from choice in order to establish and attain a hierarchy of goals. The other (autrui) is imagined as "the one who can say 'I,' just as I can, and, like me, may consider himself an agent, an author and responsible for his acts" (Ricoeur 2007, 36).

Eva Kittay (1999, 23), on the other hand, bases her thought on relational ontology and disputes political thought as being founded on a non-relational vision of human life. With the affirmation "I too am a child's mother" because "everyone is some mother's child," she reminds us that we all come from a relationship, and because of this, we are undeniably relational beings. Consequently, equality is invoked not just as something that refers to us as individuals but also as a characteristic we share with another person. Assuming relationality as a primary ontological category leads us to a political vision that is "connection based" rather than "individual based" (Kittay 1999, 28).

And so, whatever exists, from the moment it does exist, coexists (Nancy 1996). It could be posited that it is the "with" that makes being, rather than something that is added to being. Relating to the other is so intimate and significant that when we lose someone, it feels as if a part of us has gone with them. We are not simply "surrounded" (Lévinas 1987, 42) by beings and by things with whom/which we would be free to decide whether to relate, but we are profoundly relational, since the morphogenetic matrix of the being of each of us is shaped by vital energy deriving from the network of relations within the space where we become, which space it contributes to structuring through its action. The ontology of relationality becomes then the horizon in the light of which we should interpret our being-there with others in the world.

But if other people, things, and the world nurture our existence, at the same time, they condition us; they may be a source of well-being but also of harm. Our present companion may sweeten this instant of our life with a caress or may, with a word, wound our innermost soul. The other may help to widen our horizons but may also restrict our freedom. Things may be available for building a good life, but at the same time, they define the boundaries of the world's habitability. Nature nurtures us but may also provoke catastrophes. We are conditioned beings because everything we come into contact with immediately becomes a condition of our existence (Arendt 1958, 9). Our conditioned quality of existence is at the root of our vulnerability.

But at the same time, the relational structure of being-there, our reciprocal conditioning, makes care extremely necessary: just as we need care from other people, so they need it from us. When we act with care for ourselves and for others, our being is obeying what reality deems necessary. And it is by obeying reality that we human beings bring to fruition the essence of humanity.

The Essence of Care

Care That Preserves Life

Our ontological weakness makes us needy. Life is constantly lacking some specific component essential to its continuation: if it has to do without this, it ends. The first problem is to procure what is necessary to nourish life. The constant urgency to procure things for ourselves represents an ineluctable necessity. Being thrown into this world means dealing with the permanent task of coping with life. This leads to the ontological burden of caring for life. In the first place, the care for life manifests itself as a search for things that nourish and preserve the life cycle. Care is essentially care about the being of being-there, and the particular being-there that manifests itself as care is "being toward something" (Heidegger 1992, 312–13).

In Ancient Greek, the word *mérimna* defines care as the action of providing everything necessary to preserve life. Care as *mérimna* is the way of being that epitomizes the answer to *ormé* as discussed by the

Stoic philosophers or, in other words, the tendency to persist in being—an inevitable inclination, since we are all designed to live (Kant 1996). Being-there is constantly expected to face the threats of a world that tests our capacity of staying in the here and now and deals with this through the way of being of provision that is in itself care (Heidegger 1992, 254).

The term *mérimna* recurs frequently in the Gospel and describes the concern of dealing with life, safeguarding the possibility of the continuation of being-there and having always and forever to procure things in order to go on existing. The acquisition of things is not in point of fact the degraded form of activity it is considered to be by overly fastidious philosophies, such as those fostering the illusion of a being uplifted from the material aspect of existence (Lévinas 1987, 59). Our care for things so we may satisfy our needs in the world is not a debased level of life in comparison to another more metaphysical plane of existence, but it is the way of being that belongs to us, that coincides with us, because we are embodied entities that live in the world. The care for things is our care for life.

Care to save life from its weakness is inevitable, and it is increased exponentially by the anxiety that affects our spirit when faced with our ontological fragility. Our lack of sovereignty over life engenders apprehension and fear, which can lead us to a frantic seeking of things with the illusion that acquisition allows us to find a shelter for our fragility. It is this very craving, however, that ends up consuming life itself. In the parable of the birds, Jesus invites us not to trouble ourselves too much about life and to consider the birds in the sky (Matt. 6,25), since excessive concern for things and attachment to material riches suffocate the *logos* or, in other words, the direction of the sense of experience (Matt. 13,22). In inviting us not to care too much about material things, the Gospel uses the term *mérimna*. Concern for life, which is necessary to protect the continuation of being, can be transformed into excess, into a form of relentless perseverance in collecting what might be useful, and this excess that causes anxiety can be interpreted as a consequence of the anguished realization of our condition of lacking, needy beings.

A blessed life is perceived as "sine angore curae," as life without the anguish of care (Saint Augustine 2001, 55, 17)—a necessary condition that helps us to find the happy medium in caring. The awareness of being needy and unable to find a permanent defense against our want is transformed into a feeling of impotence that, if it is allowed to proliferate in our souls, can cause us to act compulsively in an attempt to quiet our sense of lack and to fill our life with an excess of things that make us feel anchored. For this reason, even though the following poetic fragment is referring specifically to her love life, we perceive as universal Sappho's prayer: "vex not my soul with agonies and anguish" (1, frag. 1; *Poeti greci* 2011), and in this case, anguish translates as the term *mérimna.* And we can add, nurture it in the hope of finding the right balance of care.

Care That Makes Being Flourish

Caring for life, however, does not only mean providing things to maintain life the way it is. The simple fact that every human being comes to life lacking some form of being-there means that his duty is to find the very best possible shape of his own existence. The fact that we are always lacking is a gateway toward possible becoming, toward being called to transcend and seek further forms of being. Besides having to find things to preserve life, every human being has the obligation to care for existence so that she can become her own potentiality-for-being. Care, in point of fact, may be understood as caring for one's possibilities (Heidegger 1962, 216).

The consequence of our ontological fragility is that we are never capable of being-there in a pure and simple way. On the contrary, we are called upon, once and for all, to do our duty of becoming our potentiality-for-being by responding positively to the obligation to transform the quality of life and make it into the best possible experience of being-there. The human being is not a fixed point in the becoming of being; it is neither finished nor complete. Rather, it is a nucleus of being-in-the-possibilities in continual transformation, driven constantly toward and beyond the way it exists. It is a self in search of its own shape, and because of that, it is forced to depart from what it is, to overtake itself. The essence of being-there lies within this lack of shape of being that compels constant transcendence. To take upon ourselves the duty of transcendence means *to care for the span of life.* The *proprium* of the human condition is to accept its own transcendence (Zambrano 1950) because its living nucleus is a potentiality that needs to overcome what already exists and to look toward further horizons. Our own transcendence means that our being is always what it has to be, and it is called upon to become everything that it is not yet but that it could be.

We may therefore affirm that there is a kind of care that needs to work to provide things that nurture and preserve life and another kind that should be envisioned as a search for evidence-based conditions that allow for transcendence—a going beyond what is already taken for granted in order to create new kinds of being-there. This is how I interpret the "double sense" that Heidegger confers on care: as providing and as dedication (Heidegger 1992, 303). Among the studies discussing care, there is a prevalent, not to say almost exclusive, attention for care as an answer to the need to find out what is indispensable for survival—what Bubeck (2002, 161) defines as the work necessary to maintain and reproduce, disregarding the idea that it is just as necessary to devote ourselves to the search for the best quality of life possible while permitting the realization of various possibilities proper to being. There is a need for care in order to awake souls and make them greater not only to make men more efficient in action (Cicero 1991, I, 12) but also to fulfil better that adventure, which is their own life.

For example, good maternal care does not consist only in satisfying the needs that are expressed and externalized by the baby, but also in offering those experiences that stimulate its being to grow and to flourish in all its ontological dimensions. A good teacher not only organizes learning activities as presented in the syllabus but also tries to anticipate the needs of each student in order to offer that experience that nurtures the cognitive, ethical, aesthetic, social, and spiritual potential of every one of them. A caring nurse not only provides competent therapy but also takes the time to put the patient in the condition of regaining his or her autonomy, and to feel consoled by this, as soon as possible.

Favoring the potential to transcend what we are or what we think we are in order to open ourselves to ulterior things is proper to the essence of the soul, which Heraclitus (Waterfield 2000) said possesses a *logos* that makes it grow (frag. 14)—a fruitful and seminal *logos* that provides the being with seeds of possibilities and with the necessary energy to make it flourish. The soul that follows its *logos* is always in search of its best shape. This potential toward the recondite can give rise to fear and a propensity to retreat, without the realization that useless struggle is a waste of time. On the other hand, when the soul listens to its desire for transcendence and persists in the search for that source of knowledge that helps in finding the right way of living, then "it is the wisest and the best" (Heraclitus, frag. 14). For the very reason that the human being lacks form, our being is in continuous potential becoming, and during the process of transcending, it takes on a shape of sorts, even if this shape is always provisional and ahead of itself. If care is essentially care of being-there, and being-there implies the possibility of being, then care, insofar as it is the care of being-there, has the potential to realize the possible in its best forms—those that we feel realize existence in its good sense.

To be bound to the care that responds to the necessity of transcendence means that we cannot dwell in the ways of being-there most appropriate to us because we have not been granted the quietness of simply being-there. Care is an ontological action, necessary because human life is uncertain and incomplete. This being of mine, which I find prolonged moment by moment, never comes in a complete shape nor is it ever possessed by me, but rather needs the work of living that is necessary to give it shape. The work of living is incessant because "the being of the ego is alive only from moment to moment. It cannot be quiescent because it is restlessly in flight. It thus never attains true self-possession" (Stein 2002, 54). It is alive, gifted with vital strength, with potentialities that are waiting to be actualized, but at the same time, it is vulnerable and fragile: it has to go on working to preserve its life and to sustain its existence.

In order to care for oneself, it is not enough to accept the burden of transcendence, of the search for forms that go beyond the existing situation, but we must also take care of what is happening within our own being quite apart from any intentional investigation. The condition of the human subject is characterized by the fact that any action toward its own being intended to give it a shape, even if it is unsuccessful in what it set out to do, ends up by being effective in giving it some shape all the same. This pliability of being makes constant vigilance necessary regarding the ways of our own becoming. In this sense, the duty of existing does not include the quality of lightness, and always imposes a presence that is extremely attentive and intensely responsible.

Being born without shape and with the onus to find one, the human being is therefore called upon to care for itself. To care for ourselves in order to look for a better kind of potential self means to search for a horizon that radiates significance. Caring for ourselves is a tiring job. It interweaves the threads of being-there, but without ever completely accomplishing the realization of its pattern, because the human being finds it impossible to connect to her being everything that he considers essential to the planning of a good life. From the beginning of his life he is bound to the duty of giving a shape to his own individual way of existing without having any control over the steps of his own development. We take care of ourselves in order to cope with the fragility and vulnerability of the human condition, without being able to reduce our individual fragility and vulnerability, either in our body or in our soul.

"Among other things, care means being out for something" (Heidegger 1992, 308). In this action, our being-there tends toward something that does not yet exist, and for this reason, we can say that care is the answer to the condition of being on our own path toward something, toward the actualization of some of our potentialities. Caring for the self means not only finding what is necessary to live, to guarantee our own life span and preserve it, but also how to build a living space in which we can fully realize our own potentiality-for-being.

The lack of a full and entire being that characterizes human life represents at the same time openness toward further and not preestablished possibilities of existence. Our state of being is actually that of finding ourselves always open to possible ways of being regarding the how and why of our present being. Existing means answering the appeal to embody the possibilities of being-there. This embodiment of one's own potentiality-of-being requires care. To care for life therefore means committing to the duty of actualizing the possible in such a way as to implement the way of being that enhances all that is best in the individual so that life may be worth living.

We are always running the risk of a fragmented life—one that is divided into periods of time without a central focus, periods with no connection between one another. The soul feels the need to find a center—a living heart from which it can draw the necessary energy to walk with joy in time. Caring for existence is about making life a living whole.

As a nonfinite entity, the human being is called to transcendence, and this call to realize our own potentiality-for-being by transforming possibility into reality never ceases. If transcendence is something that the human being must be subjected to, undertaking the care for our own existence is accepting the call to transcendence, to move beyond the possible, and to enact it into reality. Seizing the possibility of existing and projecting our own way of being-there to facilitate the actualization of the possible means to stay in the world with a project. Being in the world with a project of our own is an existential, a way of existing. This way of existing, which consists in taking upon oneself the onus of giving a good shape to our own becoming, is not to be understood technically as a "managerial" approach to the possibilities of existing because planning is an integral part of a being that has been thrown into life and is therefore immediately conscious of being unable to control what happens during her becoming. This type of awareness manifests itself through emotion (anguish, fear, apprehension, etc.) that constantly reveals to our consciousness the weakness of every project.

Having care for existence as a project for the actualization of our own possible being, and therefore as an opening to transcendence, finds its most radical expression in the dialogues of Plato, where we find Socrates engaged in theorizing the primacy of care for ourselves intended as care of the soul. In *Laches,* Lysimachus begins the dialogue by affirming that adults have the duty to care for young people, and this care means that the former has to take upon themselves the responsibility of the education of the young and teach them to excel in the art of living (179a–d). In the *Alcibiades I,* Socrates explains that in order to learn the art of existing—that which constitutes the meaning of life itself—we have to learn how to care for ourselves. We find the same concept in the *Apology,* where Socrates, while setting forth the original meaning of educational practice, affirms that it is the duty of every educator to stimulate the other to "care for himself" (*Apology,* 36c), and he explains that the essence of care for oneself consists in caring for our own soul so that it acquires the best shape possible (*Apology,* 30b). Education is therefore a procedure of care, and he-who-cares promotes at the same time in the other the ability of caring for himself, since the self corresponds to the soul (*First Alcibiades,* 130e). Thus, caring for ourselves means caring for our soul (*First Alcibiades,* 132c). Given the fact that in the Platonic perspective the soul is the most valuable of things, in the dialogues where he discusses the sense of care, Socrates talks about care for the soul (*First Alcibiades,* 132c), and while talking about this type of care, he uses the term *epimeleia. Epimeleia* means care that nurtures the being in order to make it flourish. It is not an answer to the urgent demand for survival, to the inexorable obligation to endure, but responds to the desire of transcendence, to the need of horizons of meaning toward which to actualize our own being as a potentiality-of-being.[4] Caring for oneself in order to be able to plan our own time meaningfully signifies allowing our being to be born into existence. Since everyone's existence always takes place within a political sphere, Plato uses the word *epimeleia* for the art of successful government, and he actually talks about "caring for the city" (Plato, *Republic,* VI, 770b).

In the Gospel of John (3,5), the possibility of a birth "from water and from breath" is declared. Only those who are capable of this birth may attain the true reality that is heaven. If we ignore the purely religious interpretation of this passage from the New Testament, we could postulate that birth from water and from air might indicate the possibility of being born in the soul—one capable of helping us find a way to be-there with fluidity and lightness, one that does not let the burden of consciousness or the difficulties of existence prevail. Water washes away, it flows, and air allows us to breathe. We are all born from flesh (John 3,6), and our being remains flesh throughout our lifetime, but precisely because we are able to think and to feel, and through our thoughts and our affective life we experience something else, we can be born to the other, to another sort of breath of life, unburdened by the feeling of emptiness caused by the work of life. But as we are social beings, this possibility can only be disclosed to us by others, by those who know how to take care.

We would all love to live a good life. The Gospel is also called the text of joy because our soul thirsts for joy. Life, however, rarely spares us from difficulties, moments of more or less intense pain and anguish. The burden of anguish can be borne, or it can break down all resistance, destroy every foundation. If we have experienced a type of care that has given our soul vital energy, we are then able to face anguish without being overcome. The newborn who is held in arms that not only carry its body but also its mind has experienced a calm source of energy that nourishes being; the child who finds a teacher who supports it with his or her presence, who accepts it as it is and with trust leads it to other possible forms of its own thinking and feeling, can move forward without being alienated by anguish.

Suffering can exhaust our soul to the point that we can see no way out: care is like a light diffused over the soul, letting us discover a crack through which we can catch a glimpse of something else. This is not the cold light of knowledge or *logos matematicos* but rather the warm light of seminal reason, the *logos spermatikos* of the Stoics—a spiritual breath that warms time and fertilizes life with the seeds of possibility. The absence of care, on the other hand, makes us weaker, more fragile, more vulnerable to pain. Taking care is taking away the burden of suffering, as far as it is possible to do so, lifting up the sufferer from his lonely thoughts and emotions and together finding the right pace for the walk through time.

Care That Heals the Injuries of Being-There

Another type of care is necessary. It is the care that mends the being in moments of extreme vulnerability and fragility, when the body or the soul becomes ill: it is care as *therapy.* Therapy is the care required to reduce pain in the body or in the mind.[5] Our body is an extremely vulnerable entity because it may suddenly stop working properly, and when this happens, we experience physical suffering. For this very reason, "the art of medicine cares for the interests of the body" (Plato, *Republic,* I, 241e). Therapy is a perpetual necessity: in the poet Menander's words, "pain and life belong to one another" (Plutarch 1878, 186).

It is a question not only of bodily pain but also of soul suffering: we find ourselves immersed in bodily pain as if by chance, from the outside, whereas as far as the pain of the soul is concerned, it is something that arises from the deepest part of our inner life. Episodes of temporary pain accompany our daily life while allowing the usual routine of existence to carry on, but there is also a kind of pain, continuous or intermittent, that absorbs vital energy and grinds the soul down in a way that seems to strip the very flesh from it.

Disease brings starkly to light all our dramatic ontological weakness—that of an entity that finds itself thrown into the world of life and has to continue its being-there without any control over the becoming that drags the potentiality-of-being through time. In the experience of illness, the feeling of the interruption, if not the shattering of the normal rhythm of life, reveals the weakness of the human condition.

My being-there exists, if only erratically, because it lacks power over the development of experience, and due to that, it feels pain in all its reality when it penetrates the flesh and when it runs rampant in the recesses of the soul. When we suffer, we feel the true impediment of our bondage to being-there. When the body is healthy and when the soul is well, the task of caring for our existence, difficult though it may be, makes it possible to perceive being as a gateway toward the possibility of positive development, opening to the world and growing toward our potentiality-for-being. When we feel well, we perceive our being as a vital center, able to produce forms of existence where the life force that fosters our becoming can materialize as meaningful experience, a necessary aid on life's adventurous path.

In order to inhibit the feeling of anguish, sometimes, for a few moments, our mind can disregard ontological inconsistency, although still sensing it in all its reality. But when our body sickens, when pain invades the soul, the instability of being is experienced in all its heaviness. Being-there is endured in the difficulty of finding oneself trapped in forms of becoming that have not been chosen and have proved to be unavoidable. We experience the impossibility of an ontological alternative, of backing away from being-there; we are aware of a deep-rooted passivity, and this awareness generates anguish. This anguish becomes bearable only if the extreme passivity we are subjected to is accepted and the soul knows how to cultivate the art of quiet resistance. What we have to find is not the supposed levity resulting from a lack of thought—that clear and calm simplicity of being-there that could be compared to the flight of a bee following in the air itineraries that have already been traced. This condition is not given to us because in our essence we are thinking beings. We should rather learn, in this case, the ability to accept what we are. Acceptance of our ontological quality, without resorting to fantasizing or ungrounded imagination, and the resulting gain of momentum necessary to reinterpret existence, requires work on the part of mind and heart that is an essential part of care for the self.

The condition of being ill makes the person feel that they are not only at the mercy of biological life, which follows its own rules, but also at the mercy of other people—those who have the power of decision on their behalf. Illness brings humble awareness regarding the small amount of control over our being-there that was gained with difficulty over time through both the noetic and practical acts, and in certain cases, the subject experiences the condition of being reduced to an object—not, however, simply to something inanimate rather but to an entity that is intensely sensitive, that feels the lightness of a smile and the sweetness of a caress but also the pain of an insult, the inexorable passage of time, and endures the diminishment that suffering produces in being.

A full life is a life that is experienced in every moment, in every action, even the most apparently meaningless. When things are going well, every moment is perceived as precious because any event, even the most insignificant, can open a path to unexpected existential destinations, where our being can be nourished by something quite new. A period of illness, on the contrary, radically changes the way of perceiving being-there. If in good times we aspire to the fullness of being-there, in difficult ones, we would like to be relieved from being: to feel a reduction of the life force, to find ourselves on the borders of our being, to reduce our sensitivity to reality. This type of experience happens not only in the case of a diseased body but also, if not always, when the spirit is unwell. If we accept that the essence of a human being is her/his spiritual activity, then when pain penetrates the soul's vulnerability, the subject feels threatened in her innermost being. When pain persists and seems as if it will never stop, as if it will never give us room to breathe or access to other ways of being, then, paradoxically, our one wish is to lower the level of that vital energy that keeps us in touch with the reality of our existence.

The substance of life is time. Life time flows into the present to make us feel as if we ourselves are actually happening, instant by instant. This feeling of happening as a succession of fleeting moments, even if it does not save us from experiencing the anguish of our inevitable extinction, can, however, shine out in its meaning, full of the pleasure of fragments of being, which, kept together by the world-building exercise of thought, give the happy sensation of consistency. When we are in pain, however, time changes its quality: it becomes mute, impenetrable, and moments that could be filled with the illumination of invention and meaning are no longer available. Time becomes something solid and relentless that oppresses the soul by robbing it of its very essence: the breath of life. The trickling away of time during positive moments is perceived with anguish because it reminds our consciousness of life's evanescence and therefore of the fading of any possibility of becoming our potentiality-for-being. But when we experience pain, especially pain caused by diseases that leave their mark, the inexorable passage of time can instead become something that we almost long for. We would actually be glad if existential possibilities disappeared as a consequence of time's transient nature, if this disappearance might become, indeed, the structural quality of the present. We crave the possibility of becoming other, of passing into another substance, less vulnerable and lighter. We would like to become a cherry tree, when at the end of flowering it loses its petals in the wind, to turn into one of its branches that can let pain go like the petals, so as to feel the suffering of our material being no longer.

When we are well, our mind distances itself from every negative image. Not only does it wish to continue being forever, without finitude, but it also craves the possibility of experiencing fullness of being, "a being capable of embracing the totality of the ego's contents in one changeless present instead of its having to witness the continually repeated disappearance of all these contents almost at the very moment they have ascended onto the stage of life" (Stein 2002, 56). On the contrary, when we experience pain, whatever imposes itself on the mind is far from our own wishes. We still want, probably even more than before, to exercise a control of sorts over our being-there, but no longer to implement the intensity of vital energy, rather to weaken, to numb our sensibility so that feeling vanishes completely and we escape pain and eliminate the suffering that consumes our vital force. In this situation, the inconsistency of being sensitive and to some extent mentally debilitated can almost be beneficial. In this sense, ascetic disciplines of diminishing, of clearing space in order to experience the essential, is an ethical activity, since it prepares us for some of the more difficult moments of existence, making us ready for the traversing of thorny paths.

There are philosophers who, through the use of sophistically honed metaphors, put into words emotions and thoughts that are part of ordinary life. This is the case of the Platonic image of the soul that would like to attain the ability of detaching itself from the ties of the body—an image representing the desire for an existence that is relieved from the burden of material life. In the *Phaedo,* Plato talks about the body as a prison, where the soul, the only noble part of the human being, finds itself confined. When the soul remains tied to the body and tries to satisfy its innate thirst for knowledge through exploiting the senses, it is destined to wander, "as if drunk," among irrelevant cognitive data, since the senses, as they keep the mind connected to the material world, allow reference only to secondary and conditional knowledge that reveals nothing essential. On the contrary, when the soul is free from the chains of the body and seeks only what is "pure, eternal, immortal" (Plato, *Phaedo,* 79d), it remains faithful to the quality of its essence that consists in searching for what is indispensable for a true life. The idea of a soul that frees itself from the burden of material life and, thus alleviated, can access another level of reality, one where nothing can trouble it, is not an absurd invention. It expresses the profoundly human desire to avoid a merging of the spiritual breath with the flesh when this flesh is suffering, the desire to feel the soul as free from the body when it is ill, and, more radically, to avoid material life when it is too exhausting.

When pain subjugates the body, suffering penetrates the tissues of the soul. At this point, the negative quality of inner life seems to eradicate the life force necessary to sustain a positive response to the striving toward transcendence. It is as if the material body consumes every drop of spiritual energy. At these times, we would like to feel the soul take flight (Plato, *Phaedrus,* 246c) and, in a wingbeat, free itself from the burden of material life to fly elsewhere, to soar into the blue sky, where only good things can find a dwelling and where it would experience "true reality without colour or shape, intangible" (Plato, *Phaedrus,* 247c) for the very reason that there is nothing connecting it to material life, nor causing it distress, leading it only to wisdom. The Platonic idea of "a pure and tender soul" (*Phaedrus,* 245a) that knows how to approach perfect and simple things, and to contemplate them "in a pure light" as the soul itself is pure (*Phaedrus,* 250c), expresses not only the desire for truth that everyone feels trembling in their minds, a compulsion that becomes stronger when life is more burdensome and more difficult, but also the desire for a different life, inaccessible to the upheaval of pain.

We tend to see in Platonic thought the root of the dualism between soul and body that then encumbered Western culture, permitting reductive approaches to every aspect of life. It is true that reasoning across separate universes is a risky simplification, since the quality of the real, where everything is interconnected, is betrayed in its integrity. However, the idea that the soul is something that can escape the material world should also be analyzed from another perspective. In reality, this vision represents the human aspiration to be able to live a life that is not threatened by possible injuries to being-there and that is not mingled with things that degenerate, lose their shape and order. Far from being a deceptive epistemological fantasy, the idea of a pure thought[6] that is not merged with the matter of the sensible world in which no form is permanent because of its constant development is the answer to a typically human desire to tap into a sure and certain source of ideas—a desire that for us, who are finite and fragile, may possibly evoke a different space from that in which we now find ourselves.

Reality, however, differs from our ideal. It is, in fact, the condition in which our body and soul are united, not perceived as distinct substances only bound together for a specific period but rather inextricably mingled with one another. If all phenomenological philosophy invites us to transcend the dualism of body and soul, Edith Stein goes beyond this. To do so, she does not suggest an associative logic that considers body and soul as united entities, as two separate substances that cohabit one next to the other. Instead, she invites us to consider being-there as one single entity composed of a body that subsists by means of its spiritual breath and of an incarnate soul. If we cease to consider body and soul as two separate entities, but rather conceive of the body as spiritual substance and the soul as corporeal substance, then our way of relating to the other necessarily changes. Taking care of a newborn means dealing with a body that feels the touch of its carer in a spiritual way. In the health-care field, to touch the body of a sick patient is identical to touching his or her soul: just as physical pain penetrates the soul, the soul's strength overflows into the body. Since the soul lives within the body, permeating every single atom of substance, actions we are subjected to through the body are also felt by the soul. Treating a baby without gentleness is an action that takes no thought for her soul. Prescribing therapy mechanically, without taking time to listen to the patient is an action that reduces him to an object. Handling the body of an elderly person without the requisite gentleness means abusing her intimate feelings. Any invasion of the other is not "only" carried out on the flesh of the body but goes deep into the flesh of the soul.

What the ancients used to know has been forgotten by modern medicine. Forgotten is the fact that body and soul are one and that chemical care has to be integrated with spiritual care. In the *Charmides* (155e), Plato explains that the remedy for a disease consists not only of organic medicine—herbs—but also of medicine made of *logoi,* in other words by good discourse. Both have to be used together. Socrates, addressing the young Charmides, explains that "one must not to attempt to cure the eyes without the head, or the head without the body, so neither ought you to attempt to cure the body without the soul" (*Charmides,* 156b and c). For a certain type of rational and reductive medicine, a patient is nothing but a body. He, on the contrary, is a person. He is not an unimportant, insensible substance but an incarnate soul or a spiritual body. This indivisibility of substance and spirit makes the human being a material structure that breathes in a spiritual way. A person feels the quality of corporeal life in the soul because our body has a spiritual substance. This spiritual life, diffused in the material structure, is sustained by bodily energy, and precisely because it is incarnate in the body, it shares its quality of life.

One type of pain is engendered in the flesh, and another comes from the soul, but rarely are they separate. When they occur, they are indivisible: one overflows into the other, contaminating the different levels of being. Spiritual pain, when it is not processed and therefore becomes unbearable, finds the body a perfect place in which to develop and manifest itself. Physical pain can overflow into the soul, sometimes a slowly spreading stream, at other times a flood that devastates everything in its path, to the point that the soul is no longer aware of itself but only of pain. Faced with pain, which ruthlessly exposes the mind to the vulnerability of being-there, the heart suffers all the impotence of the human condition.

The sick person, thinking of the experience she is undergoing, cannot help perceiving her being as if it had been engulfed by a profound darkness, whose *logos* remains indecipherable. With disease, the sense of life's precariousness becomes a terribly heavy weight, bringing sharply to light the fragility of human life. We would like a pure and simple existence and instead feel it shattered and randomly redistributed onto many different planes, tugged this way and that by burdensome thoughts and pierced by contrasting feelings. Planning, an essential quality of existence, has always to measure up to an unclearly defined becoming because of our constant conditioning by other things. However, during disease, the mere idea of forward thinking becomes painful because, while in the midst of suffering, the actual meaning of planning disappears.

When we experience good care in life, that care fills the soul with trust so that we are able to deal with pain without letting it overwhelm us. The absence of care, on the other hand, makes us weaker, more fragile, ready to be nullified by pain. The Gospel of Matthew, quoting Isaiah, states: "Himself took our infirmities and bore our sicknesses" (Matt. 8:17). There exists suffering that we feel we cannot bear alone. Only a god can bear it and lighten our load. Perhaps there is a disease of the soul that only the source of a transcendental energy can cure. We, however, live among others just as fragile as we are, but it is precisely these others who can help us to bear our burden without feeling that we will collapse. Being able to take care of the other is also this: being there when the other feels all the fatigue of the labor of life, being willing to share what we have in order to carry out the work on the tapestry of existence together, so that cold loneliness may not extinguish vital energy. There is no existence without self-care, but self-care needs the sustaining care of others. For this reason, care for others is a great and inalienable value. When care as therapy takes on the responsibility of the person in its entirety of mind and body, then it is not merely mending what was broken in the body but also caring for the entire being.

Therefore, the term "care," being charged as it is with different meanings, is polysemic. There exists one type of care necessary to go on living, another necessary to existence, so that it may tend toward transcendence and sustain the being-there of sense, and yet another that heals both the spiritual and the material being when body or soul are sick. The first one is care as work to preserve us as an entity, the second is the art of existing in order to make the being flourish, and the third is a sort of mending technique, a "sewing-up" of the wounds of being-there. The essence of care responds to an *ontological necessity,* which includes a *vital necessity,* that of continuing to be; an *ethical necessity,* that of being-there with sense; and a *therapeutic necessity,* that of repairing being-there.

On the basis of the ontological considerations developed above, we may affirm that the practice of care is implemented in three ways: by procuring things to preserve life, by fostering being through the cultivation of each person's potentiality, and by healing the wounds each person has sustained both in body and in spirit.

The Need for Another Political Vision

The discourse about care developed here has an ontological perspective, that is, a non-temporal one, since in order to theorize about care, it is primarily necessary to ground the need of care on an ontological basis. But care is a daily action that is practiced in a precise time, and our time is dominated by neoliberalism, that is, a vision that is in radical opposition to the ethics of care. Indeed, neoliberalism is a vision based on a laissez-faire economics, on a confidence in free markets as the most efficient allocation of resources, and on the emphasis on a minimal state intervention in economic and social affairs. Neoliberal policy emphasizes both the doctrine that "private" is superior to "public" and the primacy of individualism and freedom of choice. According to neoliberal vision, the welfare policy is targeted to hamper economic growth, to encourage unemployment and set poverty traps, and to be an unaffordable burden on economic growth (MacGregor 2005, 143).

This degraded political vision encourages ways of being that are completely extraneous to the logic of care. Indeed, we can see that neoliberal politics has dismantled public welfare resources and shifted responsibility for care onto the individual citizens (Ward 2015, 45). Neoliberalism has also polluted the ancient concept of self-care. According to Socrates, self-care is a transformative practice to cultivate the soul in order to prepare oneself to live a responsible political life (*First Alcibiades*), but in the neoliberal vision, self-care is reconceptualized to place responsibilities for health and welfare firmly in the individual citizens, thus obscuring the responsibility of the state to provide adequately for its citizens (46).

Since the values of neoliberalism are opposite to those that inspire the labor of care, care is devalued and underestimated with the consequences that caregivers become profoundly vulnerable, and when the caregiver is vulnerable, the recipients of care, already fragile since dependent on others, also become more vulnerable (West 2002, 89).

Care is an ethical practice that embodies ways of being inspired by virtues: respect for the other, responsibility, search for justice, generosity, courage, and so on. These virtues manifest themselves when the caring one assumes the way of being of the other as something worthy of regard, considers the needs of the other as central, puts the other at the center of attentiveness, has the courage to declare what is unjust, and acts in order to restore justice. Instead, neoliberalism encourages competition, self-assertion, indifference to the other, a kind of coldness of heart. While the essence of care is the logic of responsibility, neoliberalism sponsors an acquisitive way of living; while care requires availability to the other, neoliberalism brings out the egoism that the ancient Greek philosopher Plutarch called *philautia,* the love for oneself (Plutarch 1878, 471d), and *philautia* is the most dangerous enemy of politics.

If politics consists of the actions that aim to construct a world where all citizens can live a life worthy of being lived (Plato, *Apology;* Aristotle 1991), then neoliberalism is not politics but the negation of politics. Care is the labor of life, but in the context of neoliberalism, to care, the more natural and necessary labor, requires "heroic daily efforts" (Tronto 2015, VII). In a wrong political context, we need to make great efforts in order to find energy and time to dedicate ourselves to what is essential: to educate the children not only to learn technical competences but also wisdom for life; to spend time with our children in helping them to develop all their cognitive, affective, aesthetic, social, ethical, spiritual, and political potentialities; to ensure the safety of our loved ones (2); to provide a decent life for our elders who need affective and ethical recognition; to engage ourselves in the well-being of the community; to commit ourselves in political actions. But this dedication to care for life requires fighting against the consumption of time imposed by a neoliberal style of living that calls our attention to what is not essential for an authentic good life and consumes the time of life in unnecessary tasks associated with bureaucracies that are the servants of neoliberalism.

What can we do, and should we do, in order to construct a politics of care? What ought to be done to outline in any way and in any context the value of actions of care; to make political interventions in order to bring attention to the works of care; to make social discourses that criticize all that is connected with the free market and with an economy that destroys nature and at the same time makes the life of those who are more vulnerable still more fragile; to keep the word in a public context whenever a work of care is devalued or at risk. As Plato affirms, the truth is something that we do, and we fabric life with both gestures and words. And what we are called to do is both a politics of everyday and a Politics of state grounded on the value of care. Politics always searches for "bright and shining actions" (Plutarch 1878, 473f), but this aim is generally interpreted in a market and imperialistic framework. A good politics does not abandon this ideal but rather interprets it in the light of the ethics of care. To make bright and shining actions means to engage ourselves in all the daily situations in which we can give care to another and in which we should express our gratitude for those who care for people whenever it is necessary.

Notes

1. Feminist thinkers often consider it problematic to refer to those philosophers who do not have a feminist orientation. This is the case with Lévinas, but Groenhout (2004, 79) considers his account of ethics as too important for the theory of care to dismiss it and suggests that it is useful to examine his thought without being obliged to follow it in every aspect. The same viewpoint is also valid for other thinkers just like Heidegger who in 1927 theorized care as the structure of human existence. Like Groenhout, I think that care theory and care ethics could benefit from a rigorous reflection on different perspectives. What is important is to maintain a critical stance and remain faithful to the imperative suggested by the Spanish philosopher Maria Zambrano (1950), who fears a thought that remains trapped within the theory and invites us "to go into reality," that is, to subject each idea to an analysis of the lived experience.

2. The critical remark in the previous paragraph is not valid for a thinker such as Plato, who occupies an important role in this study. Certainly, from a feminist perspective on care, the Platonic philosophy exhibits many critical aspects, as for example the radical devaluation of the bodily life and a conception of philosophy as a dialogue only among men, but we cannot disregard the centrality of the concept of care in his thought. Indeed, Plato elaborates the concept of "care for oneself" and conceives it as a preparation for political responsibility; he defines education as care and politics as the practice of care for the community. Without forgetting that the theory of care has its roots in the feminist culture, we should maintain a rigorous dialogue with other perspectives on care, since the confrontation could fertilize new generative frameworks of thinking. Sharing the same perspective, we find Vrinda Dalmiya (2016), who constructs bridges between care and both virtue epistemology, which has an Aristotelian root, and the Sanskrit epic.

3. The translations from the original language of the ancient classic texts are made by the author.

4. The term transcendence is generally used to indicate something beyond the self, that is actually both the outside and the inside world that reveal themselves to the conscience, which is the sphere of immanence, since it is inseparable from the self. Here, instead, I use the term in the sense indicated by Zambrano (1950) as the ability of going further than what is given, a leaning out toward the ulterior.

5. To indicate therapeutic actions in Greek, we have two words: *therapy* and *iatreia*. The first word indicates an action that takes into consideration the person and his complexity, also including the spiritual dimension of experience. The second word specifically refers to the activity that is exercised by physicians to treat the diseases of the body. We can say that this distinction corresponds to the English words "disease" and "illness." The first term indicates the condition of breakdown of balance in the body; the second word indicates the subject's experience of her condition and consequently the elaboration process of the meaning of the disease. A caring action that perceives a condition of sickness only as "disease" is qualitatively different from one that considers it as an "illness." In the first case, we apply a cure; in the second, we apply care (Benner and Wruble 1989, XII).

6. It is probably not by chance that Plato uses the term *abatos* to indicate the quality of purity of the soul, as it also means inviolable, inaccessible, prohibited, sacred. Perhaps it was to remind us that this condition of the soul, which would make it unreachable by things that happen, is that of being inaccessible and forbidden to those who live on Earth. Curiously, the Greek term *batos*, from which derives the privative *abatos*, not only means "practicable" and "accessible" but also "bramble" and "thorn." Even if the platonic *abatos* does not have any relation to *batos* that indicates the bramble, it is easy to think that an *abatos* soul, far from earthly life, is that which knows no earthly thorns.

Works Cited

Arendt, Hannah. 1958. *The Human Condition*. Chicago: University of Chicago Press.

Aristotle. 1999. *Nicomachean Ethics*. 2nd ed. Indianapolis, Ind.: Hackett.

Benner, Patricia, and Judith Wrubel. 1989. *The Primacy of Caring*. Menlo Park, Calif.: Addison-Wesley.

Bowlby, John. 1969. *Attachment and Loss. Volume I: Attachment*. London: Hogarth Press.

Bubeck, Diemut Grace. 2002. "Justice and the Labor of Care." In *The Subject of Care: Feminist Perspectives on Dependency*, edited by Eva Feder Kittay and Ellen K. Feder, 160–85. Boston: Rowman & Littlefield.

Cicero. 1991. *On Duties*. Cambridge: Cambridge University Press.

Dalmiya, Vrinda. 2016. *Caring to Know: Comparative Care Ethics, Feminist Epistemology, and the Mahābhārata*. New Delhi: Oxford University Press.

Groenhout, Ruth E. 2004. *Connected Lives: Human Nature and an Ethics of Care*. Lanham, Md.: Rowman & Littlefield.

Hamington, Maurice. 2004. *Embodied Care*. Urbana: University of Illinois Press.

Heidegger, Martin. 1962. *Being and Time*. New York: Harper and Row. Originally published as *Sein und Zeit*. Tübingen, Germany: Niemeyer, 1927.

Heidegger, Martin. 1988. *The Basic Problems of Phenomenology.* Bloomington: Indiana University Press. Originally published as *Die Grundprobleme der Phänomenologie.* Frankfurt am Main, Germany: Vittorio Klostermann Verlag, 1975.

Heidegger, Martin. 1992. *History of the Concept of Time. Prolegomena.* Bloomington: Indiana University Press. Originally published as *Prolegomena zur Geschichte des Zeitbegriffs.* Frankfurt am Main, Germany: Vittorio Klostermann Verlag, 1979.

Kant, Immanuel. 1996. *The Metaphysics of Morals.* Cambridge: Cambridge University Press. Originally published as *Die Metaphysik der Sitten.* Königsberg: Nicolovius, 1797.

Kittay, Eva Feder. 1999. *Love's Labor: Essays on Women, Equality, and Dependency.* New York: Routledge.

Lévinas, Emmanuel. 1987. *Time and the Other.* Pittsburgh, Pa.: Duquesne University Press. Originally published as *Le Temps et l'Autre.* Paris: PUF, 1983.

Lévinas, Emmanuel. 2001. *Existence and Existents.* Pittsburgh, Pa.: Duquesne University Press. Originally published as *De l'existence à l'existant.* Paris: Vrin, 1947.

MacGregor, Susanne. 2005. "The Welfare State and Neoliberalism." In *Neoliberalism: A Critical Reader,* edited by Alfredo Saad-Filho and Deborah Johnstone, 142–48. London: Pluto Press.

Nancy, Jean-Luc. 1996. *Être singulier pluriel.* Paris: Galilée.

Noddings, Nel. 2002. *Starting at Home: Caring and Social Policy.* Berkeley: University of California Press.

Plato. 1997. *Complete Works.* Indianapolis, Ind.: Hackett Publishing Company.

Plutarch. 1878. "Of the Tranquillity of the Mind." In *Plutarch's Morals. Vol 1.* Boston: Little, Brown, and Company.

Poeti greci. 2011. *Da Omero al VI secolo dopo Cristo.* Milan: Baldini Castoldi Dalai.

Ricoeur, Paul. 2007. *Etica e morale.* Brescia, Italy: Morcelliana.

Saint Augustine. 2001. "*Letters 1-99. Vol. II/1,*" in *The Works of Saint Augustine.* Hyde Park, N.Y.: New City Press.

Stein, Edith. 2002. *Finite and Eternal Being: An Attempt at an Ascent to the Meaning of Being.* Washington, D.C.: ICS Publications. Originally published as *Endliches und Ewiges Sein: Versuch eines Aufstiegs zum Sinn des Seins.* Band II of *Edith Steins Werke.* Freiburg im Breisgau, Germany: Verlag Herder, 1949, 1986.

Tronto, Joan Claire. 2015. *Who Cares? How to Reshape a Democratic Politics.* San Bernardino, Calif.: Cornell University Press.

Ward, Lizzie. 2015. "Caring for Ourselves? Self-Care and Neoliberalism." In *Ethics of Care: Critical Advances in International Perspective,* edited by Marian Barnes, Tula Brannelly, Lizzie Ward, and Nicki Ward, 45–56. Bristol, UK: Policy Press.

Waterfield, Robin. 2000. *The First Philosophers: The Presocratics and Sophists.* Translated by Robin Waterfield. New York: Oxford University Press.

West, Robin. 2002. "The Right to Care." In *The Subject of Care,* edited by Eva Feder Kittay and Ellen Feder, 88–114. Boston: Rowman & Littlefield.

Zambrano, María. 1950. *Hacia un saber sobre el alma.* Buenos Aires, Argentina: Losada.

Zambrano, María. 2004. *I sogni e il tempo.* Bologna, Italy: Edizioni Pendragon. Originally published as *Los sueños y el tempo.* Madrid: Siruela, 1992.

CHAPTER 7

Deliberate Precarity?

On the Relation between Care Ethics, Voluntary Precarity, and Voluntary Simplicity

CARLO LEGET

In her book *State of Insecurity: Government of the Precarious,* Isabell Lorey (2015) distinguishes between three versions of precarity. In the first version, there is the existential dimension of "precarious life" as has become famous as by the book of the same title by Judith Butler (2004). It concerns the vulnerability of each human being, rooted in human corporeality and mortality, and related to care and reproduction. This version of precarity is familiar to care ethics, describing the human condition from a care-ethical perspective.

Second, Lorey continues, we find precarity as a political construction as old as the liberal-capitalist state in which insecure conditions of employment are unequally distributed among citizens. Precarity is then seen as a structural category—gendered, classed, and raced—by which relations of violence and inequality are instituted. Again, this view on precarity is more than familiar to care-ethical thinking.

The third version of precarity in which Lorey is interested can be called precarization as governmentality. In this version, the insecurity of citizens is deliberately sought for and instrumentalized in order to govern them. In this version of precarity, it is the government striving for individual self-regulation in order to produce and secure normality and to safeguard the productivity of the state. In neoliberalism, this has escalated into a rat race of self-optimization, flexibilization, and privatization of the risks of precarity.

The first of these versions of precarity is so characteristic of the human condition that it can be denied and neglected (as neoliberalism does) but not avoided, and therefore it has to be taken care of. The other two versions of precarity, however, are matters of injustice, and we should resist and even fight them actively.

Although Lorey's distinction between these three versions of precarity is helpful in its clarity, one might ask whether she does not overlook a fourth version of precarity that is connected with a deliberate choice for a specific way of life. Historically, for example, the phenomenon of a deliberately chosen precarious lifestyle has been characteristic of the life of monks in both the Eastern and Western world. In the West, mendicant friars such as the Dominicans and Franciscans have had a lifestyle based on voluntary poverty, dependency, and a marginal position in society, which is intrinsically related to a precarious life. But people outside of religious institutions also sometimes deliberately choose a precarious way of living, such as, for example, the French philosopher Simone Weil (1909–43).

Some readers might be inclined to object to the idea of a deliberately precarious lifestyle from the outset. I can think of three arguments. In the first place, one might say that there is nothing inherently good in precarity: it is lack of positive values such as security, safety, and justice. Striving for things that are not inherently good is perverse, and this kind of perversion should be avoided. Although I agree that searching for a precarious life as a goal in itself might be questioned, it does not exclude the possibility of searching for such a lifestyle as a means to an end. If the reasons behind deliberate precarity make sense, such a lifestyle as a whole might appear in a different light.

Second, knowing that so many people are struggling to survive and fighting against a situation of precarity, deliberate precarity might appear as a perverse and peculiar romanticization of precarity by privileged people who have the luxury to make a choice about it. In that sense, it is almost offensive to those who do not have a choice. Although such a romanticization would indeed seem to be an offense to those who struggle to survive, the deliberate choice for such a lifestyle because of a good end could also be considered as an example of "privileged responsibility," reversing the expression that Joan Tronto coined, on the precondition that this choice in one way or another is related to the struggle of those who do not have this choice.

Third, one might argue that if both objections formulated above are taken away, it is still not a very good idea to choose deliberately a lifestyle marked by precarity because it weakens and robs one of the position and power to fight against precarity and have impact in this area. Although I think that this objection makes some sense at first sight, it overlooks that there is a great variety of ways in which one can fight against precarity. Deliberate precarity may be chosen to live in solidarity with and being related to a specific precarious group, empowering them to fight themselves against poverty and injustice, and protesting against precarization with the authority of someone who knows firsthand what precarity is and what it does to people.

Therefore, although objections to deliberate precarity do make sense, there might also be grounds to explore what we can learn from people who embrace precarity voluntarily as a lifestyle. Let us take a closer look, then, at two historical examples and see what insights we might gain from them.

Deliberate Precarity in Thirteenth-Century Christianity

As in Northwestern Europe the feudal society and economy changed into a market and profit economy, from the eleventh century onward, more and more people moved to the cities, and a new kind of precarious life came into existence (van den Eijnden 1994). In the feudal era, poverty basically had a social meaning characterized by lack of power and influence. From the market economy onward, however, it meant being without money, food, and clothing. Whereas the former "poor people" living in rural areas would not die from lack of food in the first place, in the cities, more and more poverty meant the risk of dying from starvation.

This change in the economic situation resulted in a new way of considering wealth, especially the wealth of the Church. First, this reform took place in the monasteries, leading to a more austere life, as for example the Cistercian monks did in the footsteps of Bernard of Clairvaux. This, however, did not really change the richness and power of the medieval monasteries. Also, given the fact that in the cities a new class came into power (magistrates and rich merchants), a second movement of people said farewell to a lifestyle of luxury. In these so-called evangelical movements, a way of life imitating Christ was promoted, leading a lifestyle of poverty in solidarity with the poor.

Both the lives and aspirations of Dominic de Guzman (1170–221), founder of the Dominican Friars, and Francis of Assisi (1181/2–26), founder of the Franciscan order, can be placed in this movement. In this chapter, I want to focus on the work of a mendicant friar who is seen as one of the great philosophers and theologians of the scholastic period: Thomas Aquinas (1224/25–74). Aquinas himself lived a life of evangelical poverty, and he reportedly used any small piece of paper to formulate his thoughts on. Although one might question whether he really suffered from lack of food or a marginal position in society (the way he is usually depicted suggests otherwise), his theological writings give a deep insight into why he considered embracing a lifestyle of precarity making sense and even a gift of God.

Interpreting and understanding the work of Thomas Aquinas as I was trained to do, it is pivotal to start with the most fundamental and influential idea of his worldview: human beings are created to be united with God, in both this life and the hereafter, and God is most generous in offering guidance and opportunities to find the way to the mystery of love He is (Leget 1997). Leading an evangelical lifestyle of poverty, obedience, and chastity is one of the ways one might seek to be united with God.

The life that a mendicant monk such as Aquinas led could easily be misunderstood as a life motivated by self-interest, instrumentalizing the precarious situation of less fortunate fellow human beings in order to be rewarded by God. Such a "hermeneutics of suspicion" (Ricoeur), however, would foreclose any possible new insight into our subject. I would therefore rather follow a "hermeneutic of love," trying to understand Aquinas on his own terms, reconstructing what might be valuable in embracing precarity.

First, then, it is important to acknowledge that Aquinas distinguishes between voluntary and involuntary poverty. Poverty is not something that is to be pursued in itself, and the involuntary poor should be sustained and helped. Poverty as part of a freely chosen evangelical lifestyle, however, can be seen as a way of imitating the life of Christ—a life marked by precarity in a number of ways. Such a monastic lifestyle was not seen as something obligatory for all Christians. It was considered to be an option for those with a special vocation to devote one's life entirely to God.

Second, one might say that there is some instrumentality to deliberately choosing a precarious lifestyle because it is chosen for the sake of something else. The primary goal, however, was not to maximize one's chances to be rewarded with a ticket to heaven. In order to understand the logic of Aquinas's theology, one should see monastic life as a spiritual love affair. A love affair, in its best versions, is a free response to an offer. The greater the love, the more one wants to organize one's life around the loved one and give oneself in return to someone who does the same. Monastic life—leading a life of poverty, chastity, and poverty—can be seen as the ultimate effort to empty oneself of everything distracting from one's union with God. Moreover, the imitation of Christ can be considered as an imitation of a lifestyle that God himself chose to lead among human beings, Christ being the incarnation of God.

The example of mendicant friars in the Middle Ages shows that a precarious lifestyle can be deliberately chosen with specific goals in mind. In Aquinas's view, such a lifestyle expresses a concern to be connected with God. But what about the relation to one's fellow human beings? Could one not argue that in the end, this deliberate precarity still is a selfish enterprise, more connected with one's own spiritual well-being than with the transformation toward a society in which poverty is banned altogether?

The problem with such an interpretation is that it fails to understand the radically different orientation of Aquinas's theocentric worldview. In his premodern understanding of the world, the order of things pointed to an invisible core: the relationship with God. The right order of love is (1) to love God, (2) to love one's soul, (3) to love the soul of one's neighbor, and (4) to love one's body. Living the life of a mendicant friar is an expression and witness of this—an embodied act aimed at a spiritual transformation of the world. In Aquinas's case, his service to humankind was aimed at teaching theology and preaching the word of God. At the same time, mendicant friars were supposed to share their food with the poor.

Deliberate Precarity in the Twentieth Century

Aquinas's voluntary choice for a precarious lifestyle is an interesting contrast to our contemporary world marked by a neoliberal market economy. If confronts us with a dimension of voluntary precarity that may be called symbolic, as presenting an orientation in life that questions the power structure of the status quo. At the same time, one might question the transformative power of this deliberate precarity because, in Aquinas's work, the highly hierarchical political order of his time is rather taken for granted than questioned. A more contemporary example in which this transformative power is also taken into account is the life of the French philosopher Simone Weil.

Coming of age in France in the 1920s and 1930s, in her short life, Simone Weil made an important contribution to twentieth-century philosophy by a unique combination of philosophical reflection, mysticism, and political engagement, including a deliberate lifestyle of precarity (Maier 2013). In modern philosophy, Weil is often studied because of her reflection on attentiveness, and her thought also had great influence on care theory. Her influence, however, remained only partial on this topic seemingly because of reservation toward her excessive self-abnegation or neglect of the more practical and concrete ideas about politics and technology (Bourgault 2016).

Being confronted with the miserable socioeconomic conditions of the working class in France, she chose to lead the precarious life of automobile industry factory workers in order to understand their condition from firsthand experience to the point of physical and mental exhaustion (Maier 2013, 232). In Weil's view, understanding the precarity of the factory workers should be based on attentive listening as an embodied act because only by using all one's senses can one get an idea of the vulnerability of another person's situation. This situation is always constituted by political and institutional factors, as she discovered how the speed and technological management of the factory workers prevented them from having a meaningful relation with their work (Bourgault 2016, 329; Maier 2013, 233). As Maier concludes:

> While she recognizes the desperation that uprooted persons face, Weil's work invites us to recognize that the precariat's foremost challenge is not social, economic, or political but spiritual in nature and that the depth and existential peril of a rootless moment requires a saintliness characterized by extraordinary, perhaps superhuman, endurance. (230)

Both the precarious life of mendicant monks such as Thomas Aquinas and that of Simone Weil are ways of living that can be called forms of deliberate precarity. Both ways of living also have great congeniality to a care-ethical approach to the world in terms of responsibility, social engagement, a caring attitude, and a preference for those who are silenced. As such they are examples of a lifestyle that shines as a protest against the individualist market-driven lifestyle promoted by neoliberalism. Despite the many dissimilarities between both thinkers, and despite the fact that neither Thomas Aquinas nor Simone Weil would consider their deliberate precarious lifestyle as something to be adopted by everyone, they provoke a number of reflections on valuable qualities of a deliberate precarious lifestyle for care ethics.

In the first place, a deliberate precarious lifestyle may have a spiritual dimension in that it is a meaningful way of living for those who choose it, which connects them with a greater purpose and goal in life. It is self-transcending instead of self-absorbed or self-centered, opening up toward the well-being of fellow human beings. It aligns well with the practice of care as "everything that we do to maintain, continue, and repair our 'world' so that we can live in it as well as possible. That world includes our bodies, ourselves, and our environment, all of which we seek to interweave in a complex, life-sustaining web" (Tronto 1993, 103).

Second, deliberate precarity has an epistemological dimension, as it is a way of gaining embodied knowledge that otherwise would remain inaccessible. Acknowledging the fact that knowledge is multidimensional and rooted in our embodied experiences, this way of life opens up to the positions and perspectives of marginalized fellow human beings in a unique way. It can be seen as an embodied engagement, a lifestyle of listening to the oppressed and marginalized by sharing their physical, social, economic, and political situation, as Simone Weil sought by working in the automobile industry of her day (Bourgault 2016).

Third, such a lifestyle has an ethical–political dimension in that it expresses solidarity with precarious groups in society by sharing their situation, empowering their networks, and giving voice to their experiences on a political level. This dimension is both ethical and political at the same time in the sense that it connects one's personal engagement with the efforts to work toward a better society.

Fourth, a deliberate precarious lifestyle has a symbolic–expressive dimension by living and embodying values that are critical to mainstream culture. This symbolic–expressive dimension is of importance by communicating alternative values and questioning ways of living and doing that seem to be self-evident. Because those who live such a lifestyle practice what they preach, they have a communicative impact based on authenticity and a greater or lesser degree of self-sacrifice (van Nistelrooij 2014).

Fifth, deliberate precarity can be transformative by not only dreaming of a better world but also engaging in practices that contribute to it. Both Thomas Aquinas and Simone Weil were intellectuals who did not isolate themselves from or step out of the turmoil of their times. On the contrary, both were examples of a lifestyle combining active service with contemplative attentiveness. Deliberate precarity, just like care, can be seen as a social practice with transformative potential (Bourgault 2016).

Despite the value of the deliberate precarious lives that Aquinas and Weil lived, one cannot deny that the lives of both are inspiring exceptions rather than role models. Having grasped, however, both the congeniality to care ethics and the possible value of such a deliberate precarious lifestyle, one can ask whether there are contemporary examples that are an invitation to all people. Considering the broad range of grassroots movements aiming at social reform, perhaps the movement of voluntary simplicity comes closest to the deliberate precarity I am interested in. Not really connected to care theory or care ethics, to my knowledge, but sharing some of the same inspiration that we discovered in our previous examples, it seems worth taking a closer look at this movement.

In the rest of this chapter, I will first give a short account of what the voluntary simplicity movement is about. Subsequently, the movement will be placed in the broader picture of an analysis of contemporary society. Then I will reflect on the relation between voluntary simplicity and care ethics and conclude by formulating some questions for care ethics.

Voluntary Simplicity in the Twenty-First Century

The movement of people returning to the simple life—growing their own vegetables, returning to the country, and so on—is a social phenomenon going on for decades in the Western world. In a paper published in 1977, Duane Elgin and Arnold Mitchell describe this movement as one toward voluntary simplicity—a phrase they borrowed from the American social philosopher Richard Gregg, who coined the term in his essay *The Value of Voluntary Simplicity,* published in 1936 (Elgin and Mitchell 1977). Although the name denotes a social movement that is expressed in many forms, Elgin and Mitchell identify what they call a skeletal list of underlying values that are shared: material simplicity (a non-consumerist lifestyle), human scale in working and living environments (against anonymity, incomprehensibility, and artificiality), self-determination at the grassroots level and less dependency on the private and public sector, ecological awareness (social responsibility and global citizenship), and personal growth (both psychologically and spiritually)[1]—or, in the words of Simone de Beauvoir, "Life is occupied in both perpetuating itself and in surpassing itself; if all it does is maintain itself, then living is only not dying" (Elgin and Mitchell 1977, 9).

Next to sketching the shared values of voluntary simplicity, the paper by Elgin and Mitchell is also helpful in understanding what voluntary simplicity is not. In the first place, voluntary simplicity is not a (more or less romantic and naïve) "back-to-nature" movement. An urban existence is not incompatible with voluntary simplicity, and many initiatives and experiments relating to voluntary simplicity have been conducted by people living in big cities. Second, voluntary simplicity is not limited to the countermovement of the 1960s. Many people sharing this lifestyle are of age, and it is adopted by all generations. Third, voluntary simplicity should not be confounded with living in poverty. Living in poverty can be degrading and provides little opportunity to surpass oneself. Fourth, voluntary simplicity is not a panacea for social problems. It does not cure the global problems that we confront, but it may provide a basis from which societal responses might emerge. Fifth, it is not an idealist movement without resources: it is a movement shared by many creative and talented people. Sixth, it is not a movement that is confined to the United States, but rather, in many different forms, it is also present in, for example, many European nations. And finally, it is not a temporary hype but rather, as both the paper from 1977 and the origin of the term in 1936 show, a movement rooted in ideals that are shared by people over a long time in the Western world.[2]

Elgin and Mitchell wrote their paper in 1977, a few years before the rise of neoliberalism. Reading the paper more than forty years later, one cannot help but to be shocked by the topicality of the list of "contemporary societal problems" they identify as calling for a more simple way of life and the continuity of these problems after forty years of neoliberalism: the prospect of running out of cheaply available industrial raw materials, the process of energy shortages and the difficult transition to a much more energy-sufficient economy, the risk of polluting ourselves to death, climate change, the growing threat of terrorism, the vulnerability of highly complex and interdependent technology, the changing balance of global power, growing dissatisfaction with the output of our industrial society, challenge to the legitimacy of leaders of nearly all major institutions, loss of social purpose and direction coupled with individual alienation, excessive social bureaucracies and protests that we have become a overregulated society, domestic economic inequities, and more competition for a fixed or slowly growing pie.

Realizing that we are still struggling with basically many of the same problems can only make us modest with regard to the possibilities of social change and societal reform. The fact that both authors are optimistic in their paper with regard to the percentage of people who are sympathetic with the ideals for voluntary simplicity (according to polls from late 1975, no less than 92 percent of Americans were willing to eliminate annual model changes in automobiles, 92 percent were willing to forego meat for one day a week, and 73 percent were willing to prohibit the building of large houses with extra rooms that are seldom used), one can only struggle not to become cynical about the gap between good intentions and actual behavior—or rather, it is naïve to underestimate the powers (both internal and external to ourselves) that prevent us from solving the societal and cultural problems we wrestle with for decades. And as a matter of fact, neoliberalism has only made things worse, undermining the potential for that change that Elgin and Mitchell still were hopeful of.

The voluntary simplicity movement has been around for some decades now, and it has been studied from a number of disciplines, including sociology, political theory, law, economics, and marketing. Although in the writings in this movement the focus is rather on capitalist consumerism than on neoliberalism (a term hardly mentioned), the intrinsic connection between the two needs no further explanation. Samuel Alexander, based on empirical research among people leading a voluntary simple lifestyle, discerns six major obstacles that people identify as keeping them from a "simpler" lifestyle of restrained or reduced consumption: (1) suitable transport, (2) suitable employment, (3) insufficient product information, (4) resisting consumer temptations, (5) suitable social activities, and (6) suitable housing (Alexander 2015, 89–112). It shows that in trying to live such a lifestyle, one is directly confronted with the fact that it is running against what our consumer society expects of us or, as Alexander phrases it, "people in consumer societies are 'locked in' to high consumption, energy-intensive lifestyles" (Alexander 2015, 90)—hence the importance of political and economic change. How, then, should we see the voluntary simplicity movement: as a personal lifestyle or as a politically motivated social movement?

It seems that the voluntary simplicity movement is precisely at the intersection of these two classifications. For this reason, some scholars propose introducing the category of lifestyle movements that are characterized by the following: they promote individual and ongoing private action, understood as efforts toward social change, its adherents engaging in cultivating a morally coherent, personally meaningful identity. Moreover, these movements tend to be structurally diffuse yet with a degree of continuity and coherence, and they target cultural practices and codes (Haenfler, Johnson, and Jones 2012, 5). How, then, can we understand the rise and continuity of these movements in our time? What does it tell us about the culture we live in?

Voluntary Simplicity as a Sign of the Times

For more than two centuries, artists, philosophers, and sociologists, among others, have described a changing attitude of Western civilization toward the world. In 2016, the German sociologist Hartmut Rosa published a book, as the result of more than ten years of studying the acceleration of our time, in which he not only offers an analysis of the developments in modernity that have contributed to the many crises that our contemporary world is faced with, but also proposes a solution of how to deal with these crises in a constructive way. Although Rosa is no care ethicist and speaks of care only marginally, his analysis is insightful for care ethics and aligns well with many of the concerns of both the voluntary simplicity movement and care theorists (Rosa 2016, 2019; Bourgault 2016).

According to Rosa's analysis, in the last centuries, human beings have made great progress in mastering the world by making the world "available" (*verfügbar*) through a great number of scientific and technological developments. This process of making the world available, in Rosa's view, has four elements: making the world visible, accessible, controllable, and usable (2019, 21–24). As a result of this, in some parts of the globe, there is more prosperity and better public health combined with a greater life expectancy and higher economic standards than ever before in history.

Because of the process of increasing prosperity in some parts of the world, a high price is paid by people living in other parts of the world. These people are exploited by large structures of injustice and precarization. At the same time, the planet's natural resources are used and wasted up to the degree that the damage done to our planet is beyond repair, demanding our attention in the form we call the climate crisis (Klein 2015, 2019). During all this, however, something fundamental seems to have happened with our relationship to the world. Built on an imperative of escalation of a growth orienting society, the economic system is not able to stabilize itself unless it invests in continuous (economic) growth, (technical) acceleration, and (cultural) innovation. These imperatives, however, enforce the dominance of a reifying relationship to the world in which even our leisure time is commodified and exploited. As a result of this, the world has gradually been turned into a world that does not "speak" to us anymore but rather is seen as dead material that can be made "available" and used to whatever we think is necessary. The world has turned into a "mute" world.

Rosa's analysis is not new, building on familiar analyses we already find in the idea of alienation as described by Karl Marx and in Simone Weil's experience of the alienating effect of acceleration in the French factories of the 1930s. What his analysis helps us to see, however, is how neoliberalism, with all its perverse effects on caring relationships, is the wrong answer to a deeper and more fundamental problem. It is the wrong answer because it sustains the process of acceleration that turns the world that we live in into a "mute" world: a great heap of dead and meaningless raw material. This process of acceleration is the great cage in which we are all trapped. In Rosa's view, the very definition of modernity is precisely this trap of dynamic stabilization. Our situation can be compared to trying to maintain our economic position by running up to a staircase that continuously accelerates—a situation as hopeless as it is exhausting. The numbers of people who suffer from depression and burnout are a sad sign of the effect of all this on our mental health.

Rosa's proposal to deal with this situation is to search for an alternative relationship to the world. In his book, he calls this relationship one of "resonance" as opposed to the phenomenon of alienation. Resonance is marked by four elements: (1) an opening up to the world so that the world may speak, for which he uses the outward oriented concept of e→motion; (2) the element of being touched by the world that speaks, which he tries to articulate by the concept of af←fect; (3) a transformative element by which both I myself and the world change forever; and (4) an element of unavailability or inaccessibility (*Unverfügbarkeit*). This last element refers to the fact that resonance is not a new trick to "fix" the world but rather is inspired by the philosophical tradition of phenomenological thinking.

In his work, Rosa discusses a number of what he calls "axes" of resonance that he classifies as horizontal axes (family, friendship, politics), diagonal axes (relating to objects, work, schools, sports, and consumption), and vertical axes (religion, nature, art, history). It is not hard to recognize the simplicity movement as being related to a number of these axes. By developing a new relationship to material goods, living environments, the economic system, and our ecological environment and by investing in human relationships and personal growth, the voluntary simplicity movement can be seen as a movement investing in restoring an alienating relationship to the world by developing a more resonant relationship with the world. But what about care ethics? Can care ethics also be seen as a contribution to a more resonant relationship to the world? Can Rosa's theory help to see the connections and differences between voluntary simplicity and care ethics?

The Relation between the Voluntary Simplicity Movement and Care Ethics

Reading about the voluntary simplicity movement, the concept of care is hardly mentioned or reflected on. At first sight, the movement seems to focus on our relation to consumer goods rather than our relation to our fellow human beings. Reconsidering Elgin and Mitchell's list of skeletal values, however, all values can be seen as expressing a more caring relationship toward material goods, one's social network, our natural resources, and one's own psychological and spiritual well-being. In fact, considered from a care-ethics perspective, it is surprising that the concept of care is so much lacking in the writings of this movement. But is that a problem, and if so, for whom?

Perhaps this is not so much a problem as a missed opportunity, just as the fact that Hartmut Rosa's writings on acceleration and resonance lack a reflection on the importance of care in the world he is envisioning. In my view, the idea of deliberate precarity may function as a lens that enables us to see (1) the congeniality of care ethics and voluntary simplicity to the benefit of both; (2) the fact that both ask for an embodied personal engagement that has impact on our identity and values; and (3) the transformative and political dimension of both deliberate precarity and voluntary simplicity as ways of resisting neoliberalism. I will make my argument in five steps, building on Rosa's analysis and elaborating on the five valuable characteristics of voluntary precarity taken from Thomas Aquinas and Simone Weil.

First, the idea of voluntary precarity can make us see that both care ethics and voluntary simplicity have a spiritual dimension in the sense of decentering our life goals from neoliberalist individualism toward practices of a meaningful life for both ourselves and the world we live in. A more caring relationship to the world we live in is the key to both ways of looking at the world and being in the world: beginning with an attitude of engaged and embodied attentive listening, both lifestyles take responsibility and take care by engaging in caring practices. Moreover, both are in resonance (Rosa) with what or whom they care for and do so from an inner motivation and drive.

Second, voluntary simplicity has an epistemological quality of making space and time: a space and time to listen, to be aware, to be sensitive, and to step out of the consumerist and accelerated market driven neoliberalist economy that turns the world into a "mute" world in which eventually we ourselves are being exploited. Here, elements of our analysis of the voluntary precarity of Thomas Aquinas (emptying oneself, following the response to a call) and Simone Weil (emptying oneself for attentive listening and sharing the fate of the precarious) next to the analysis of Harmut Rosa (being in resonance again) are joint toward a epistemology of caring: attentiveness opens up to caring practices, caring about leads to caring for, and voluntary simplicity is caring about the quality of life, the future of humanity and other life forms, and caring for a better world.

Third, voluntary simplicity and care ethics have a joint ethical and a political dimension resisting neoliberalism that cannot be separated—or, as care ethicist Sophie Bourgault (2013) put it, if we want to reform a greed-driven economy, we need both state reform and character reform (moderation). Just as in care ethics the ethical and the political cannot be separated, in voluntary simplicity, we are dealing with an ethical lifestyle of caring about the world we live in, with a political agenda and ambition.

Fourth, voluntary simplicity has a symbolic–expressive dimension: it engages in practices that are contrary to what the consumerist market economy expects from us, as Samuel Alexander has described based on his empirical research among people belonging to this movement. A lifestyle of voluntary simplicity expresses another way of caring for the world we live in by practices that are symbolic representations of the more caring and just society that is strived for. By riding the waves of the self-marketing pressure of our neoliberalist culture in a clever way, this symbolic–expressive dimension can even be used to resist neoliberalism on its own terms.

Fifth, by engaging in these embodied and attentive practices, voluntary simplicity is a transformative lifestyle contributing to a better world—a more caring world. Leading a life of voluntary simplicity is living a caring life, up to the smaller and greater sacrifices that are intrinsically linked with living a life of attentiveness and responsibility. That brings us to our final concluding remarks.

In this contribution, I have explored the idea of a deliberate precarious lifestyle as a fourth approach to precarity, next to the three versions Isabell Lorey distinguishes. I distilled some valuable elements of such this lifestyle by considering the voluntary precarious lifestyle of Thomas Aquinas and Simone Weil. Because the lifestyles of both were never meant to be adopted by the majority of citizens, I confronted valuable elements of their embodied practices with the voluntary simplicity movement as coming close to a contemporary version of such a lifestyle. I concluded that the voluntary simplicity movement indeed incorporates many elements of a spiritual, epistemological, ethical–political, symbolic–expressive, and transformative nature. What conclusions and recommendations can be drawn from this with the development of care ethics in mind?

The fact that lifestyles of deliberate precarity never have been and never will be mainstream should not prevent us from studying them and asking ourselves what we can learn from them. It would be an unproductive and unjust way of silencing these lifestyles, as they may give us food for thought on the nature of care in more everyday situations.

Moreover, care ethics might learn from the spiritual and transformative dimensions of deliberate precarity. As we have seen in the example of voluntary simplicity, people are attracted to change their lifestyle by the promise of a more resonant and meaningful relation to the world around them. Care theory might work with this observation as an important motor for political change.

On the other hand, care theory has something to offer the simplicity movement as well. The problems that humanity is facing in the twenty-first century are so manifold that care theory might play an important role in connecting the various movements that are congenial to it and help understanding how they are all rooted in a more caring way of dealing with the world we live in as a way of resisting neoliberalism and transforming our world into a life-sustaining web in which precarization no longer has a place.

Notes

1. For the problem of defining the voluntary simplicity movement, see Johnston and Burton (2003).
2. For a more recent discussion of the same objections, see Alexander (2011).

Works Cited

Alexander, Samuel. 2011. "Property beyond Growth: Toward a Politics of Voluntary Simplicity." PhD diss., University of Melbourne.

Alexander, Samuel. 2015. *Prosperous Descent: Crisis as Opportunity in an Age of Limits*. Melbourne, Australia: Simplicity Institute.

Bourgault, Sophie. 2013. "Prolegomena to a Rehabilitation of Platonic Moderation." *Dissensus—Revue de philosophie politique de l'ULg* 5 (Mai): 122–43.

Bourgault, Sophie. 2016. "Attentive Listening and Care in a Neoliberal Era: Weilian Insights for Hurried Times." *Etica Politica* 18:311–37.

Butler, Judith. 2004. *Precarious Life: The Power of Mourning and Violence.* London: Verso Books.Elgin, Duane, and Arnold Mitchell. 1977. "Voluntary Simplicity." *Co-evolution Quarterly* (Summer).

Haenfler, Ross, Brett Johnson, and Ellis Jones. 2012. "Lifestyle Movements: Exploring the Intersection of Lifestyle and Social Movements." *Social Movement Studies* 11 (1): 1–20.

Johnston, Timothy C., and Jay B. Burton. 2003. "Voluntary Simplicity: Definitions and Dimensions." *Academy of Marketing Studies Journal* 7 (1): 19–36.

Klein, Naomi. 2015. *This Changes Everything: Capitalism vs. the Climate.* New York: Simon and Schuster.

Klein, Naomi. 2019. *On Fire: The Burning Case for a Green New Deal.* London: Allen Lane.

Leget, Carlo. 1997. *Living with God: Thomas Aquinas on the Relation between Life on Earth and "Life" after Death.* Leuven, Belgium: Peeters.

Lorey, Isabell. 2015. *State of Insecurity: Government of the Precarious.* London: Verso Books

Maier, Craig T. 2013. "Attentive Waiting in an Uprooted Age: Simone Weil's Response in an Age of Precarity." *Review of Communication* 13 (3): 225–42.

Rosa, Hartmut. 2016. *Resonanz: Eine Soziologie der Weltbeziehung.* Berlin: Suhrkamp.

Rosa, Hartmut. 2019. *Unverfügbarkeit.* Vienna: Residenz Verlag.

Tronto, Joan C. 1993. *Moral Boundaries: An Ethic of Care.* New York: Routledge.

van den Eijnden, Jan G. J. 1994. *Poverty on the Way to God: Thomas Aquinas on Evangelical Poverty.* Leuven, Belgium: Peeters.

van Nistelrooij, Inge. 2014. *Sacrifice: A Care-Ethical Reappraisal of Sacrifice and Self-Sacrifice.* Leuven, Belgium: Peeters.

CHAPTER 8

Precarious Political Ontologies and the Ethics of Care

MAGGIE FITZGERALD

The work of care ethicists such as Sara Ruddick (1989), Joan Tronto (1993), and Fiona Robinson (1999) has laid substantial groundwork in terms of working toward an ethics of care that is both critical and political. Care ethics in this tradition has sought to grapple with political questions surrounding institutions (e.g., FitzGerald 2020; Stensöta 2010; Tronto 2010; Urban 2019), democracy (e.g., Sevenhuijsen 1998; Tronto 2013), and the potential of care as a global ethic (e.g., Held 2006; Robinson 2013).

Alongside but not yet explored in depth by the care ethics literature is a growing literature on multiple ways of being in and seeing the world—described by the language of the pluriverse (e.g., de la Cadena 2015; Mignolo 2013)—which highlights diverse ways of being in the world and draws attention to the political processes through which different ontologies come into contact, conflict, and in many ways co-constitute each other. While ontology is most commonly understood as the assumptions and framings through which we understand the world and conditions of being, ontology in this literature is better captured by Mario Blaser's (2009, 877) concept "political ontologies," which focuses on the practices through which "ontologies perform themselves into worlds." That is, political ontologies are not preexisting framings of the conditions of being or claims about the world; instead, they are performative and constituted in/through the interactions of humans and nature across varying contexts and times. More simply, political ontologies consist of the ongoing, shifting, dynamic, and (de)stabilizing practices and relations that bring worlds into existence.

This understanding of ontology also implicitly suggests a multiplicity of ontologies globally: as enacted and practiced, ontologies must be multiple, as different sets of relations and practices bring different ontologies into existence. At the same time, however, these different ontologies are not separate units—the relations that constitute a world do not end at that world, given our shared material existence. Instead, the concept of political ontology points to multiple worlds or a pluriverse—a matrix of entangled ontologies that are connected through relations of power (Mignolo 2013). In this way, the pluriverse is more than one but less than many (de la Cadena 2015). It is an acknowledgement that while we reside in the same present, our worlds can be very different. These differences are not reducible to each other, nor do they preclude ontological interactions. Instead, these differences, and the notion of the pluriverse, demand that we dwell in the entanglement between worlds and pay attention to the ways in which the enactment of certain worlds are prevented or disparaged through these entanglements.

This idea of multiple political ontologies, I believe, presents a more expansive political landscape compared to traditional or mainstream notions of the global. In particular, the notion of multiple political ontologies does not simply ground the political in competing interests, viewpoints, or goals within a single world but rather locates politics as the very processes through which a multitude of worlds conflict, shape each other in often contradictory and complex ways, and create the very boundaries and configurations of the social order. The purpose of this chapter is to begin to explore how care ethics might allow us to understand better the nature of political ontologies and their specific locations within the pluriversal matrix. This, I believe, is an important first step for rethinking ethical deliberation in the context of the pluriverse. More specifically, this chapter argues that the ethics of care, with its focus on relationality and vulnerability, can better orient us to contemplate the pluriverse. This reorientation may prove fruitful for beginning to think through further how the ethics of care can help us navigate real and pressing dilemmas that arise as worlds interact and conflict.

To this end, this chapter proceeds as follows. First, I describe more fully the political landscape of the pluriverse by mobilizing a distinction between politics and the political, whereby the political in the pluriverse can be understood as the very processes that bring worlds into existence and define the social order. To help illustrate, I also introduce a case study of a conflict between two political ontologies: the Māori world and the neoliberal modern world of the New Zealand government. This conflict revolves around the protection of the Whanganui River, and I return to this case study throughout the argument. Next, I turn to the task of demonstrating how the ethics of care, with its emphasis on mutual vulnerability, provides a useful orientation from which to understand the nature of political ontologies. Specifically, given the relationality between worlds, I draw upon care ethics to make the ontological claim that all political ontologies are themselves inherently vulnerable. At the same time, however, I mobilize a conceptual distinction between vulnerability and precarity in order to highlight the processes and the material relations of power (such as ongoing processes of neoliberalization) that shape the configuration of the pluriverse and render certain political ontologies *more* vulnerable—that is, precarious—than others. This provides a useful framework for contemplating the pluriverse because the ontological assumption of vulnerability allows us to focus on the simultaneous contingency of all ontologies, and thus points to the possibility of new pluriversal configurations. At the same time, the lens of precarity attunes us to the ways in which material relations of power also affect the configuration of worlds, often with the effect of marginalizing certain worlds and stabilizing others. Together, these two lenses of vulnerability and precarity, I suggest, foreground the interplay between stability and instability that is central to the configuration of the pluriverse, and better orients a critical political ethics of care to understand the nature of political ontologies and the ethical issues that arise as these ontologies evolve and conflict.

Politics, the Political, and the Case of the Whanganui River

The idea of the pluriverse, I contend, presents a more robust political landscape than mainstream conceptualizations of the global that are premised on competing paradigms within a single world. The work of Jenny Edkins (1999) and her distinction between politics and the political is useful for understanding this landscape. In contrast to "politics," which can be understood as the political reality as is already described and acknowledged,

> "the political" has to do with the establishment of that very social order which sets out a particular, historically specific account of what counts as politics and defines other areas of social life as *not* politics. (2, emphasis in original)

In other words, for Edkins, the political represents the moment of movement in which the social order is reconfigured and shifted, revealing the limits of its boundaries. In the pluriverse, worlds or political ontologies are connected through relations of power. The differentials in these power relations situate certain worlds "above" and "below" others, resulting in a configuration of political ontologies that may be thought of as a social order (albeit one that is contingent, fluid, and shifting). When this relational web of ontologies is arranged as a hierarchy of domination, certain worlds exist outside of politics; they are rendered invisible or incomprehensible by the logic of the dominant world. At the same time, when these relations of power shift and the marginalized worlds illuminate, and perhaps even reconfigure, the boundaries of the dominant world, there is a political moment that may redefine the order itself and, in so doing, redefine what counts as politics. In this way, the pluriverse, I argue, is always already operating at the level of the political.

An example will help to illustrate this. In March 2017, the local Māori tribe of Whanganui in the North Island of New Zealand won recognition for the Whanganui River as their ancestor, meaning that the river must be treated as a living entity. The river was granted this recognition, and the same legal rights as a human being, after 140 years of struggle by the Māori people. Under this new status, the New Zealand legal system sees no differentiation between harming the tribe and harming the river "because they are one and the same" (Roy 2017).

This case, I suggest, is an example of a conflict between two worlds.[1] On the one hand, the New Zealand government—constituted by the modern world, which in its current neoliberal manifestation is premised on thick individualism, private property, and a clear distinction between humans and nature—constructs the river as property. On the other hand, the Māori tribe knows the river as an ancestor and still-living kin. This understanding is key to the enactment of the Māori's relational ontology, which is devoid of the human/nature and living/nonliving binaries that constitute the modern world (Povinelli 2016). However, under the current configuration of the pluriverse, whereby the neoliberal modern world dominates and marks the boundaries of "legitimate" politics, the Māori world was rendered unintelligible for more than 140 years. The river was not viewed by the state as kin, or as a living entity, but rather was treated as property. Indeed, even the Māori's own view of the river as kin was not acknowledged by the state. As a result, the reproduction of the Māori people's world was undermined, as the river was both treated in a way that violated the logic of their world and denied a subject status that was key to their broader political ontology.

The 140-year struggle to recognize the river as a living entity, then, is an example of the political as defined by Edkins. In this case, the Māori fought to bring into relationship two incommensurable logics: their own understanding of the river as kin and the view of nature as property that in part constitutes modernity. In so doing, the Māori made visible that which was invisible, namely, their relationship with the river, and more fundamentally, the world that this relationship in part enacts. Importantly, in bringing together these two incommensurable logics, equivocation was not overcome. The New Zealand government does not see the river as a human in a literal sense, nor do the Māori fully embody the legal human rights framework that facilitated this recognition. Rather, in bringing together these two logics, a tentative reconfiguration of the social order was achieved, one in which "the contradiction of two worlds in a single world" (Rancière 1999, 27) is foregrounded. This is the political landscape that I am attempting to reckon with from an ethics of care perspective.

Care Ethics, Mutual Vulnerability, and Precarity

The literature on the ethics of care can be traced back to psychological theory (Gilligan 1982) and feminist philosophy (Noddings 1984; Ruddick 1989), which identified an approach to moral reasoning based on the relational self and the enhancement and preservation of specific relationships. As Carol Gilligan (1982) argues, this relational approach or "voice" differed from the rationalist voice that dominates moral philosophy and psychology, and which conceives of morality as the impartial application of rules and principles to abstracted ethical dilemmas (Hutchings 2010, 28–29). The relational voice, on the other hand, constructs moral problems "as a problem of responsibility in relationships" (Gilligan 1982, 73). As a result, moral selves emerge through relations of responsibility and care for particular others (Robinson 1999), and morality is understood as practices—present in and a feature of almost everything we do (Urban Walker 1998)—and specifically the practices that unfold in and through our relations with others (Robinson 2011).

Consequently, the ethics of care involves a different conceptualization of moral agents, who are now understood to be mutually dependent and vulnerable beings constituted by social, political, and economic relations, as opposed to autonomous and independent (neo) liberal subjects (e.g., Kittay 2002; Kittay, Jennings, and Wasunna 2005; Hekman 1995). Because we are embedded in and constituted by complex relations of power, the ethics of care not only suggests that moral thinking and moral practices must pay attention to the political, social, and economic contexts (e.g., Hankivsky 2004; Tronto 2013) that shape morality, but actually rejects a separation between morality and politics (Tronto 1993). Further, given that sociopolitical and economic contexts are multiple, and that moral agents are constituted by their unique context, the ethics of care also suggests a multiplicity of relational moral selves. Indeed, subsequent work on the ethics of care built on this "discovery" of a different voice to highlight the heterogeneity of moral subjects and, correspondingly, a multiplicity of moral voices/epistemologies/theories (Hekman 1995, 30). In so doing, the ethics of care also uncovers and resists hierarchies of power that render certain moral voices as "less" than others.

For this reason, the ethics of care, starting from a relational ontology of mutual vulnerability, is a political ethic. It challenges the hierarchy of moral voices that legitimizes rationalist approaches to ethics while rendering other moral epistemologies as incomprehensible or less developed. Simply put, care ethics "challenge[s] the logics of the present order" (Hoppania and Vaittinen 2015, 78) and thus operates at the level of the political.

Notably, the idea of ontological precarity has also gained currency in recent years (Millar 2017). Despite the fact that the word "precarity" does not appear in her collection of essays, this idea is most often traced back to Judith Butler's book *Precarious Life* (2004). As Kathleen Millar (2017) argues, this book and the growing literature that has picked up on the idea of "precarious lives" mobilize precarity as a term to capture the inherent vulnerability of our being that stems from our relational ontology. Accordingly, I suggest that the notion of precarious life à la Butler parallels the social ontological assumption underpinning the ethics of care: we are all mutually vulnerable, constituted in and by our relations.

Lastly, it is worth noting that this conceptualization of precarity differs from the precarious literature that focuses on recent changes in the economic relations of production resulting from neoliberal processes (e.g., Bourdieu 1998; Fudge and Owens 2006; Kalleberg 2009; Millar 2017; Standing 2014; Vosko 2006). In particular, these neoliberal processes have brought about "a distinctive kind of valorization and liberation of capital" (Brown 2018) premised upon a robust individualism that endorses the myth of self-sufficiency so as to justify the dismantling of social and collective safety nets. Although this body of work has made important contributions in terms of understanding the ways in which labor is (re)shaped by these neoliberal processes, it has also been critiqued for how the focus on precarious labor relations (re)produces a nostalgia for a better time, when labor relations were apparently "secure" and "stable" (Barchiesi 2012a, 2012b; Neilson and Rossiter 2008). The concept of precariousness in this literature does little to challenge the centrality of wage labor and the ways in which wage labor is constitutive of the neoliberal modern world. It thus engages in a critical way with politics, but fails to offer a fully fledged critique at the level of the political.

From Vulnerability to Precarity

While the emphasis on mutual vulnerability in the ethics of care literature, or ontological precarity in the "precarious lives" literature, operates at the level of the political—and, as I show below, can thus be usefully applied to the context of the pluriverse—this emphasis can also lead to some conceptual muddiness. Kelly Oliver (2015), for example, argues that conceiving of ethics as premised on shared vulnerability is limited because it does not provide us with much guidance on how to recognize and foreground the ways in which social and political conditions and relations of power render some more vulnerable than others. Put differently, in the ontological claim that all subjects are vulnerable, it can become easy to conflate this basic ontological premise with the ways in which the uneven distribution of material relations of power shape lived experiences of vulnerability. Similarly, Brett Neilson and Ned Rossiter (2005) criticize Butler's (2004) discussion of precarious life for failing to provide tools to analyze the uneven distribution of basic (ontological) human vulnerability. To help overcome this limitation, and to provide greater conceptual clarity, I wish to put forth a conceptual distinction between vulnerability and precarity, whereby precarity is *intensified* vulnerability resulting from unequal distributions of power that render certain subjects more vulnerable than others. In this way, vulnerability is a necessary but not sufficient condition for precarity.

This distinction, I suggest, is particularly useful in the context of the pluriverse, where we are faced with the significant task of understanding how and why certain political ontologies are marginalized in the social order. It is here that I think the ethics of care, when combined with the distinction between vulnerability and precariousness,[2] can make a contribution. As care ethics emphasizes, all subjects are vulnerable. This ontological claim, I believe, can be applied to political ontologies more broadly, given that worlds are (re)produced by relations and given the connections between worlds. By foregrounding the mutual vulnerability of all worlds, care ethics reminds us that political ontologies, as well as the hierarchy of political ontologies, are contingent. The relations between political ontologies are necessarily unstable, open to change, and vulnerable. Further, in foregrounding the contingency of the hierarchy, a care ethics lens also opens space for a critique of the current configuration of the pluriversal matrix: if all political ontologies are inherently vulnerable, why do we give credence to some and not others? Why are certain political ontologies relegated to the margins of the global political economy, currently dominated by neoliberal modernity?

Although this opening is an important first step, I contend that we also need a lens of precarity[3] to answer these questions and to investigate the practices and relations of power that render certain political ontologies more vulnerable—that is, precarious—than others.

Therefore, the distinction I put forth here between vulnerability and precarity is meant to bolster both the literature on the pluriverse and the ethics of care in a mutually constitutive way. A critical and political ethics of care can help us contemplate and better understand the political landscape that is the pluriverse by orienting us to pay attention to the ways in which vulnerable worlds are not equally vulnerable due to unevenly distributed relations of power. At the same time, the distinction between vulnerable and precarious political ontologies facilitates a more robust political ethics of care by foregrounding not only vulnerabilities at the interpersonal or material level but also the ways in which vulnerabilities—and relations of power shaping these vulnerabilities into precarity—operate at the ontological level, shaping subjectivities and even worlds. The next section turns to a more robust discussion of what I mean by precarity and demonstrates the analytical usefulness of precarity in this context.

Expanding Precarity through Political Ontologies

Even though Guy Standing's (2014) conceptualization of precarity focuses on wage labor—and thereby offers us a criticism of politics instead of the political, as argued above—I suggest that his articulation of three dimensions of precarious work nonetheless provides a fruitful starting point to think about the configuration of the pluriverse, given its materialist focus on the relation between precarity and the means of production. First, Standing (2014, 969) argues that precarity is marked by particular relations of production. Those involved in precarious work have insecure labor, are in and out of jobs, and must continually contend with a sense of insecurity. Second, precarity is marked by distinctive relations of distribution. The flexibility of the wage in precarious work, and the instability of economic resources, "means that [members of the precariat] have chronic income insecurity, experiencing volatile earnings and chronic economic uncertainty" (970). Finally, for Standing, precarity also involves particular relations to the state, characterized by a lack of citizen rights (971), including the right to a secure economic, social, cultural, political, and civil existence.

These three dimensions of precarious labor, I suggest, can be usefully applied to the pluriverse, as they point to a broader understanding of precarity when reconsidered at the level of political ontology. That is, if we rethink this articulation of precarity at the level of being-in-the-world (as opposed to focusing on labor relations), we can see that a precarious existence is characterized by unstable subjectivities, unequal and insecure material well-being, and denigrated political potentiality.

My decision to draw upon Standing's notion of precarity, despite the aforementioned critique of his concept as engaging only with politics, is therefore purposeful. Precarity, as developed here, is meant to capture the ways in which certain political ontologies are rendered *more* vulnerable in the global political economy, currently dominated by neoliberal modernity. Thus, on the one hand, this analysis operates at the level of ontology and the enactment of worlds. On the other hand, this analysis also operates at the level of the global political economy, as it is concerned with the ways in which material and ideational relations of power shape the configuration of worlds in the pluriverse. Retaining Standing's (2014) understanding of precarity, rooted in material relations of work and steeped in a critique of neoliberal economic restructuring, while rethinking it at a more fundamental ontological level, facilitates both of these tasks: this expanded understanding of precarity captures the relationship "between precarity as a socio-economic condition and precarity as an ontological experience" (Millar 2014, 35; see also Millar 2017). That is, the understanding of precarity developed and mobilized here is meant to link the study of the global political economy with questions of subjectivity, existence, and experience.

To demonstrate, consider Standing's first dimension: the precariousness of relations of production. If we begin with the concept of political ontologies, I argue that the idea of precarious relations of production, as described by Standing, can be expanded to include not just the relations of material production but also the relations through which worlds are produced. Certain political ontologies face greater instability than others. The existence of these worlds relies upon practices that are marginalized by relations of power and knowledge that legitimize some acts, relations, and knowledges while rendering others "outside" what is acceptable or reasonable politically (Blaser 2016). For instance, as Cristina Rojas (2016) illustrates, the political ontological division between the modern and non-modern renders some things thinkable and others unthinkable (that a river could be living kin, for instance). The relations of power that shape the modern/non-modern binary create limits to what is considered valid, to which practices and ways of being are legitimate. These limits point to the precariousness of the production of (certain) worlds.

The idea of precarious relations of distribution can similarly be expanded to refer to the uneven distribution of resources across worlds. This includes material resources, which, due to colonialism, primitive accumulation (e.g., Federici 2004), and ongoing dispossession of land, have been unevenly and violently redistributed across worlds. Importantly, however, from a political ontological perspective, the relations of distribution must also refer to the distribution of more intangible resources, such as political power, and the dignity of having one's epistemic and ontological stance seen as valid. In other words, political potentiality is also unevenly distributed across worlds, as some political ontologies are able to mark the boundaries of "legitimate" politics (i.e., reflect, produce, and/or reproduce a given social order), rendering the politics of other political ontologies invisible (de Sousa Santos 2007).

Finally, precarious relations to the state, when confined to a discussion of precarious labor, are linked to the Western idea that citizenship and citizen rights should be (or are) tied primarily to employment and market relations. Social safety nets, membership in political collectivities, and access to political and economic rights are deeply connected to employment status and participation in the labor market in a variety of ways (Esping-Andersen 1985). However, if instead of limiting the concept of precarity to labor we begin with the idea of political ontologies, we can move to a broader analysis of the ways in which citizen rights, and the relation between people and the state, are shaped far beyond the relations of production. Rather, members of certain political ontological groups are denied rights simply because of their ontologies.[4]

To help illustrate this broadened notion of precariousness, consider the example of the Whanganui River introduced previously. Using the lens of precarious political ontologies, the three dimensions of precariousness just discussed can be located in the Māori's struggle to protect Whanganui. First, throughout the struggle to gain meaningful recognition of the Whanganui River as still-living kin, the Māori's political ontology experienced precarity in terms of the relations of production necessary to produce their world. The river, as co-constitutive of the tribe, is necessary for the (re)production and resilience of the Māori's world. Without protection for Whanganui, the relations of production necessary to (re)produce their world were rendered precarious.[5] Indeed, preventing harm to Whanganui was the Māori's motivation for initiating and sustaining a 140-year struggle with the New Zealand state. The Māori's political ontology also faced precariousness vis-à-vis the relations of distribution, as their relation to Whanganui was not validated[6] by the logic of modernity or the government constituted by this logic. The distribution of who (and what) was seen as a legitimate political agent and issue was uneven, such that the Māori's political ontology faced instability as a valid political standpoint. In other words, the distribution of authority across these two worlds was uneven, with the Māori's political ontology receiving "less" legitimacy as a world within the pluriversal matrix, currently dominated by modernity. Finally, the Māori's political ontology was also characterized by a precarious relation to the state. For the Māori, Whanganui is an ancestor and still-living kin, and the state's 140-year long refusal to acknowledge this further marginalized the Māori's world by denying certain agents (such as Whanganui) the rights that the Māori ontology deems appropriate.

Putting the Pieces Together: Vulnerable Relations and the Power of Precarity

Thus far, this chapter has made several conceptual moves. First, drawing upon the ethics of care, this chapter asserts that political ontologies are vulnerable. This is an ontological claim about the nature of the worlds that comprise the pluriverse, stemming from their relationality. Political ontologies, as previously described, are not independent units but rather more than one (unique worlds) but less than many (always already connected). Second, this chapter develops a distinction between this understanding of vulnerability, as a basic ontological premise, and precarity, which, I suggest, can be understood in the context of the pluriverse as *intensified* ontological vulnerability. Put differently, precarity refers to the ways in which the (re)production of certain worlds are rendered more insecure and unstable as a result of the uneven distribution of material and ideational power in the global political economy, currently dominated by neoliberal modernity. Together, this framework, as I now show, opens up analytical space for the study of political ontologies. In particular, I suggest that this framework allows for a more robust analysis of the *simultaneous* stability and instability of the relations between political ontologies, and helps us foreground the unknowable potentiality of the relations that comprise the pluriverse.

First, the assertion that all political ontologies are vulnerable emphasizes that the pluriverse is not a static assemblage. Rather, worlds co-constitute each other, albeit in complex ways, and this contentious, unequal, and fluid entwinement means that worlds are always susceptible to change. The assertion that all political ontologies are vulnerable highlights the relatedness of these worlds, and the ways in which political ontologies are performative and require ongoing processes of legitimation and enactment. Second, the idea of precarious political ontologies allows us to foreground the dynamics that effect the enactment of worlds so that we can pay closer attention to the relations of power that allow certain political ontologies to be enacted more easily than others.

For example, Elizabeth Povinelli (2011) demonstrates how the political ontology of which the sovereign state is a central figure (what I have here called neoliberal modernity) is built on the back of a political ontology of "the prior," the worlds of the indigenous as filtered through the modern lens. As Povinelli explains, the prior, as a political ontology, only comes into being when the modern political ontology comes into being. Indigeneity and the sovereign state—and the political ontologies of which these concepts are a part—were (re)constructed together. The modern (and its corresponding system of governance) could only be delineated by simultaneously marking the "premodern" or prior; these political ontologies—the binary of the modern and premodern—only make sense relationally. If there was no premodern, there could be no modern, and vice versa. At the same time, however, this process of mutual construction was not equal; the prior (as in premodern) was constructed so as to be governed by the modern (Povinelli 2011, 24).

Povinelli's discussion here points to a significant analytical challenge related to the study of political ontologies: how do we explain and understand "the persistence of the occupying ontologies" (Escobar 2016, 21) without treating this persistence as given? How do we understand the current configuration of political ontologies without reifying this configuration? It is here that I think the concepts of vulnerable political ontologies and precarious political ontologies can make a contribution. The ontological claim that all worlds are vulnerable reminds us that even seemingly "stable" political ontologies are dependent and insecure, and that a reconfiguration of the political is always already possible. In other words, the very concept of vulnerable political ontologies renders current configurations of power "unstable." The precarious lens developed here extends this by further foregrounding the reality that the precarity of the subverted ontologies is directly linked to the stability of the occupying ontologies, therefore pointing to the precarity of the occupying ontologies as well. The precarity of one world, due to the mutual dependency and vulnerability of all worlds, always renders other worlds, including those that are dominant, as at least potentially precarious as well. In this way, the idea of precarious political ontologies allows us to focus on the ways in which unevenly distributed material and ideational relations of power render certain worlds precarious while also locating power in that very precarity.

Returning once again to the example of the Māori and their struggle to protect the Whanganui River, one can see the power of precarity at work. As the previous section demonstrated, the configuration of the pluriverse, dominated by neoliberal modernity, involves a distribution of power that renders the Māori's political ontology precarious. At the same time, however, I contend that the precarity of the Māori's world also renders the neoliberal modern world of the New Zealand state precarious, thereby illuminating the mutual vulnerability of the two worlds. That is, while in this example the Māori world faced (and perhaps continues to face) a more onerous struggle for legitimacy than the neoliberal modern world, neoliberal modernity was (and continues to be) fundamentally challenged by the very existence of the Māori world. In this way, a focus on precarious political ontologies not only helps uncover the particularities of the ways in which certain worlds are marginalized in the current order, but also keeps the relationality between political ontologies at the fore of our analyses.

In other words, precarity, as developed here, highlights those worlds at the margins of the global political economy, specifically those that have been excluded, purposefully reshaped, devalued, and even erased, while also equally emphasizing that even apparently "stable" or "hegemonic" worlds are vulnerable and unstable, dependent upon marginalized worlds, and susceptible to falling precarious themselves. This second point is important, for just as Tiina Vaittinen (2015) has located political power in vulnerable bodies that exert pressure on the state, a focus on the precarity of worlds also locates power in precarity: those worlds that are precarious, and therefore to some extent not subsumed wholly by the dominant political ontology, wield a particular type of power—one that illuminates the limits of the dominant or occupying ontology and, in so doing, poses a challenge to the logic of said ontology.

Thus, the idea of vulnerable and precarious political ontologies, by reminding us of the interplay between the stability and instability of different worlds, provides analytic space not only to explore the (unequal) relations between worlds (i.e., the relations that allow some worlds to be enacted more easily than others), but also to foster meaningful dialogue on what Isabelle Stengers calls the "cosmos": "the unknown constituted by these multiple, divergent worlds and . . . the articulations of which the[se worlds may] eventually be capable" (2005, 995). Vulnerability, as an analytical tool, has the potential to highlight the mutual instability of all worlds, while precarity, in the context of political ontologies, foregrounds those worlds at the margins of the political order. These same worlds, in part because of their marginality, have the power to expose and challenge the limits and logic of dominant worlds. They remind us that there are in fact ways of being and knowing that exceed "the pervasive political rationality of neoliberalism" (Peck and Theodore 2019, 256) that shapes the global political economy so fundamentally today. In so doing, precarious political ontologies foreground the unknowable potentiality of vulnerable worlds that may emerge as political ontologies conflict and remind us that the "reality principles" (Brown 2018) generated by neoliberal relations of power are not, and need not be perceived as, the only principles by which to live. More simply, in continually pointing to the limits of the neoliberal modern world order, these precarious political ontologies, as well as unknown worlds yet to come, have the potential to "fracture"

(Rojas 2016) current systems of power and their homogenizing tendencies. By allowing us to focus on this potentiality, the concepts of vulnerability and precarity provide a useful starting point from which to contemplate the political landscape that is the pluriverse from a care ethics perspective so as to help us begin to move toward new configurations in which a multitude of worlds can flourish.

Notes

1. Some may suggest that this is simply a conflict between cultures as opposed to a conflict between worlds. However, the concept of the pluriverse, and of multiple worlds, is in part a response to the tendency to devalue certain ways of being as simply "beliefs," "traditions," or "culture," while other ways of being are viewed (often implicitly) as "true" or inherently valid. In naming the Māori world a world, and describing this conflict as a conflict between worlds, I am giving "full ontological weight" (Holbraad, Pedersen, and Viveiros de Castro 2014) to the practices and relations that constitute their way of being and knowing. Although it is beyond the breadth of this chapter to develop this more fully, I believe that giving this ontological weight to non-Western ways of being is a necessary step toward decolonization and toward destabilizing the hierarchies of power that render some ways of being as "true" and others as less legitimate. Such destabilization is a key political task for the pluriversal literature.

2. Some scholars employ a distinction between precarity and precariousness (e.g., Butler 2011; Kittay 2018). Here, I use these terms interchangeably.

3. Again, precarity here is now meant to denote "intensified" vulnerability or the specifically unequal distribution of vulnerability.

4. Importantly, when I use words such as "citizen," "rights," and even the "state," I am not attempting to assert that other worlds would also use these words or concepts to articulate their desired forms of social and political life. For instance, certain political ontologies may not have a conceptualization of the state or may reject the state as the ideal form of social and political structuring all together. Similarly, when I say members of certain worlds are denied rights, I am not asserting that they necessarily want rights in the thick, liberal sense. Rather, I am using these words—constitutive of my world, which I call neoliberal modernity—as empty signifiers, meant to indicate, albeit imperfectly, whatever conceptualization of the good life is inherent to different political ontologies. This imperfect use of words reflects the fact that I am, to some extent, bounded by the limits of the discourse of my own world, and acknowledges that translation between worlds is never "one to one" (e.g., de la Cadena 2015; Strathern 2004).

5. To reiterate, what is of significance for this example is that the Māori world requires certain relations for it to be (re)enacted through time–space. Their world is constituted by/with their relationship with Whanganui. Thus, it is the very fact that the relationship is threatened (i.e., Whanganui was not protected, and therefore the relationship was rendered precarious) and, equally importantly, that the terms of the

relationship (i.e., whether Whanganui is acknowledged as living kin as opposed to property) are reframed by another world that is of moral salience. To frame the conflict as a problem because threatening Whanganui means that a certain practice, ceremony, or tradition cannot be conducted would reduce the significance of this relationality and is too instrumental of a reading of the ways in which worlds are practiced, enacted, and (re)produced.

6. In particular, the relationship is either ignored all together (and Whanganui is framed as property as opposed to still-living kin), or it is reduced to a "belief" or "tradition," as opposed to given ontological status as an actually existing part of the Māori world. See also footnote 1 for more on this distinction.

Works Cited

Barchiesi, Franco. 2012a. "Liberation Of, Through, or From Work? Postcolonial Africa and the Problem of 'Job Creation' in the Global Crisis." *Interface: A Journal For and about Social Movements* 4 (2): 230–53.

Barchiesi, Franco. 2012b. "Precarity as Capture: A Conceptual Reconstruction and Critique of the Worker-Slave Analogy." *UniNomade*. http://www.uninomade.org/precarity-as-capture/.

Blaser, Mario. 2009. "Political Ontology: Cultural Studies without 'Cultures'?" *Cultural Studies* 23 (5–6): 873–96.

Blaser, Mario. 2016. "Is Another Cosmopolitics Possible?" *Cultural Anthropology* 31 (4): 545–70.

Bourdieu, Pierre. 1998. *Acts of Resistance: Against the Tyranny of the Market*. New York: New Press.

Brown, Wendy. 2018. "Who is Not Neoliberal Today?" *Tocqueville* 21, January 18. https://tocqueville21.com/interviews/wendy-brown-not-neoliberal-today/.

Butler, Judith. 2004. *Precarious Life*. London: Verso Books.

Butler, Judith. 2011. "For and Against Precarity." *Tidal: Occupy Theory, Occupy Strategy* 1:12–13.

de la Cadena, Marisol. 2015. *Earth Beings: Ecologies of Practice across Andean Worlds*. Durham, N.C.: Duke University Press.

de Sousa Santos, Boaventura. 2007. "Beyond Abyssal Thinking: From Global Lines to Ecologies of Knowledges." *Review* XXX (1): 45–89.

Edkins, Jenny. 1999. *Poststructuralism and International Relations: Bringing the Political Back In*. London: Lynne Rienner.

Escobar, Arturo. 2016. "Thinking-Feeling with the Earth: Territorial Struggles and the Ontological Dimension of the Epistemologies of the South." *Revista de Antropología Iberoamericana* 11 (1): 11–32.

Esping-Anderson, Gøsta. 1985. "Power and Distributional Regimes." *Politics and Society* 14 (2): 223–56.

Federici, Silvia. 2004. *Caliban and the Witch: Women, the Body and Primitive Accumulation*. Brooklyn, N.Y.: Autonomedia.

FitzGerald, Maggie. 2020. "Reimagining Government with the Ethics of Care: A Department of Care." *Ethics and Social Welfare* 14 (3): 248–65.

Fudge, Judy, and Rosemary Owens. 2006. *Precarious Work, Women, and the New Economy.* Portland, Ore.: Hart Publishing.

Gilligan, Carol. 1982. *In a Different Voice.* Cambridge, Mass.: Harvard University Press.

Hankivsky, Olena. 2004. *Social Policy and the Ethic of Care.* Vancouver, Canada: UBC Press.

Hekman, Susan. 1995. *Moral Voices, Moral Selves: Carol Gilligan and Feminist Moral Theory.* University Park: Pennsylvania State University Press.

Held, Virginia. 2006. *The Ethics of Care: Personal, Political, and Global.* Oxford: Oxford University Press.

Holbraad, Martin, Morton Axel Pedersen, and Eduardo Viveiros de Castro. 2014. "The Politics of Ontology: Anthropological Positions." *Cultural Anthropology,* January 13. https://culanth.org/fieldsights/462-the-.

Hoppania, Hanna-Kaisa, and Tiina Vaittinen. 2015. "A Household Full of Bodies: Neoliberalism, Care and 'the Political.'" *Global Society* 29 (1): 70–88.

Hutchings, Kimberly. 2010. *Global Ethics: An Introduction.* Cambridge: Polity.

Kalleberg, Arne L. 2009. "Precarious Work, Insecure Workers: Employment Relations in Transition." *American Sociological Review* 74:1–22.

Kittay, Eva Feder. 2002. "When Caring Is Just and Justice Is Caring: Justice and Mental Retardation." In *The Subject of Care: Feminist Perspectives on Dependency,* edited by Eva Feder Kittay and Ellen K. Feder, 257–76. London: Rowman & Littlefield.

Kittay, Eva Feder. 2018. "Precariousness, Precarity, and Disability." Keynote address at the Care Ethics Research Consortium Inaugural Conference, Portland, Oregon, September 27–28.

Kittay, Eva Feder, Bruce Jennings, and Angela A. Wasunna. 2005. "Dependency, Difference and the Global Ethic of Longterm Care." *The Journal of Political Philosophy* 13 (4): 443–69.

Mignolo, Walter. 2013. "On Pluriversality." http://waltermignolo.com/on-pluriversality/.

Millar, Kathleen. 2014. "The Precarious Present: Wageless Labor and Disrupted Life in Rio de Janeiro, Brazil." *Cultural Anthropology* 29 (1): 32–53.

Millar, Kathleen. 2017. "Toward a Critical Politics of Precarity." *Sociology Compass* 11: e12483.

Neilson, Brett, and Ned Rossiter. 2005. "From Precarity to Precariousness and Back Again: Labour, Life and Unstable Networks." *The Fibreculture Journal* 5: n.p.

Neilson, Brett, and Ned Rossiter. 2008. "Precarity as a Political Concept, or, Fordism as Exception." *Theory, Culture and Society* 25 (7–8): 51–72.

Noddings, Nel. 1984. *Caring: A Feminine Approach to Ethics and Moral Education.* Berkeley: University of California Press.

Oliver, Kelly. 2015. "Witnessing, Recognition, and Response Ethics." *Philosophy and Rhetoric* 48 (4): 473–94.

Peck, Jamie, and Nik Theodore. 2019. "Still Neoliberalism?" *The South Atlantic Quarterly* 118 (2): 245–65.

Povinelli, Elizabeth A. 2011. "The Governance of the Prior." *Interventions* 13 (1): 13–30.

Povinelli, Elizabeth A. 2016. *Geontologies: A Requiem to Late Liberalism*. Durham, N.C.: Duke University Press.

Rancière, Jacques. 1999. *Dis-agreement: Politics and Philosophy*. Translated by Julie Rose. Minneapolis: University of Minnesota Press.

Robinson, Fiona. 1999. *Globalizing Care: Ethics, Feminist Theory, and International Relations*. Boulder, Colo.: Westview Press.

Robinson, Fiona. 2011. "Stop Talking and Listen: Discourse Ethics and Feminist Care Ethics in International Political Theory." *Millennium: Journal of International Studies* 39 (3): 845–60.

Robinson, Fiona. 2013. "Global Care Ethics: Beyond Distribution, Beyond Justice." *Journal of Global Ethics* 9 (2): 131–43.

Rojas, Cristina. 2016. "Contesting the Colonial Logics of the International: Toward a Relational Politics for the Pluriverse." *International Political Sociology* 10 (4): 369–82.

Roy, Eleanor Ainge. 2017. "New Zealand River Granted Same Legal Rights as Human Being." *The Guardian*, March 16. https://www.theguardian.com/world/2017/mar/16/new-zealand-river-granted-same-legal-rights-as-human-being.

Ruddick, Sara. 1989. *Maternal Thinking: Towards a Politics of Peace*. Boston: Beacon Press.

Sevenhuijsen, Selma. 1998. *Citizenship and the Ethics of Care Feminist Considerations on Justice, Morality, and Politics*. London: Routledge.

Standing, Guy. 2014. "Understanding the Precariat through Labour and Work." *Development and Change* 45 (5): 963–80.

Stengers, Isabelle. 2005. "A Cosmopolitical Proposal." In *Making Things Public: Atmospheres of Democracy*, edited by B. Latour and P. Weibel, 994–1003. Cambridge, Mass.: MIT Press.

Stensöta, Helena. 2010. "The Conditions of Care: Reframing the Debate about Public Sector Ethics." *Public Administration Review* 70:295–303.

Strathern, Marilyn. 2004. *Partial Connections*. Lanham, Md.: AltaMira Press.

Tronto, Joan. 1993. *Moral Boundaries: A Political Argument for an Ethic of Care*. New York: Routledge.

Tronto, Joan. 2010. "Creating Caring Institutions: Politics, Plurality, and Purpose." *Ethics and Social Welfare* 4 (2): 158–71.

Tronto, Joan. 2013. *Caring Democracy: Markets, Equality, and Justice*. New York: New York University Press.

Urban, Petr. 2019. "The Moral Life of Public Institutions: A Care Ethical Perspective." Paper presented at the University of Ottawa, Ottawa, Canada, February 21.

Urban Walker, Margaret. 1998. *Moral Understandings: A Feminist Study in Ethics*. New York: Routledge.

Vaittinen, Tiina. 2015. "The Power of the Vulnerable Body." *International Feminist Journal of Politics* 17 (1): 100–118.

Vosko, Leah F., ed. 2006. *Precarious Employment: Understanding Labour Market Insecurity in Canada*. Montreal, Canada: McGill-Queen's University Press.

CHAPTER 9

Care Ethics and the Precarious Self

A Politics of Eros in a Neoliberal Age

SACHA GHANDEHARIAN

Care Contra Neoliberalism

In a 2017 article, Joan Tronto proposes that an effective critique of neoliberalism as a set of politico-economic structures, practices, and ideologies begins with a common understanding of persons "as *homines curans* (caring people)" (27). As Tronto writes, "Neoliberalism reveals itself to be an ideology in the face of an ethic of care" (37). Indeed, there has been much written on both the way neoliberalism has shaped "the organisation of the resources and relations of care" (Hoppania and Vaittinen 2015, 77) and how a return to the relational ontology that underpins the ethics of care, as a moral and political theory, implies a thoroughgoing critique of those very social, political, and economic structures and ideologies (e.g., Casalini 2018; Hoppania and Vaittinen 2015; Robinson 2010, 2015; Tronto 2017). A relational ontology foregrounds *relationship* as the most significant topic for moral consideration as opposed to an atomistic ontology that privileges a view of subjects as autonomous agents. This chapter contributes to this conversation by investigating the capacity for care ethics to resist, and/or serve as an antidote to, neoliberalism. It does so with a particular focus on the question of *subjectivity* in light of the notion of *precarity*. I argue that a more robust theory of subjectivity, with precarity at its center, will aid the ethics of care in serving as a theoretical starting point from which to resist the forces of neoliberalism.

Specifically, I argue that the notion of *precarity* is central to understanding the logic of subjectivity and intersubjective relations. In other words, our experience of our own selfhood, as well as our relationships with other *selves,* is shaped by our vulnerability and dependence relative to those other selves. The central claim of this chapter is that eros (or desire) can serve as a conceptual bridge that connects the notions of care and precarity, thus aiding in the constitution of a more robust notion of subjectivity and intersubjective relations reflective of the relational ontology that underpins the ethics of care as a moral and political theory (Dingler 2015; Hollway 2006; Robinson 2010, 2011, 2015). I propose to start with a very broad, commonsense understanding of desire, which will then be fleshed out more fully in the body of the chapter. A close reading of the relationship between care and eros will thus broaden our understanding of the relational and ethical self and its inescapable precariousness. This reading constitutes a critique of the ways in which neoliberal ideology has shaped dominant conceptualizations of the self as well as the self–other relation. I argue that this investigation of the self–other relation, which seeks to uncover the relationship between care, precarity, and eros, is significant vis-à-vis discussions of whether the notion of care, broadly conceived, can serve as an antidote to neoliberalism.

My proposed conceptualization of subjectivity is centered on one key premise: *to be a subject means to be a body in relation to other bodies, with these relationships being implicated and influenced by relations of power, both material and symbolic.* For example, hierarchies of power can exist in relation to material inequalities, as well as in the (non)recognition of certain identities. Such a view of subjectivity is one that is founded on, as well as foregrounds, an underlying *precariousness* (broadly conceived) as the condition of possibility for embodied selfhood and intersubjective relations (see Bourgault 2014; Butler [2004] 2006; Ettlinger 2007; Millar 2017). By utilizing the notion of eros as explicated by Luce Irigaray (2002) and Byung-Chul Han (2017a), and engaging with Kelly Oliver's (2002, 2004, 2015) conceptualization of "the relationship between dependence and subjectivity" (2002, 324) as connoting a "structure of witnessing," this chapter develops a particular understanding of precarity. Specifically, precarity as developed here refers to an *unguardedness* that grounds relations among human selves (see Petherbridge 2016, 591). When combined with eros, conceived as an ethical energy permeating said relations and which can direct our attention toward precarious others, this understanding emphasizes that the journey toward otherness is itself a precarious one. In other words, we are always precarious relative to the other, given our mutual vulnerability and dependency. In addition, as will be argued in the body of the chapter, the journey to meet the other always presupposes a certain level of precarity. By demonstrating the interplay between precarity and eros, this analysis thereby seeks simultaneously to build upon the theory of subjectivity inherent within care ethics, while also bolstering the ethics of care's effectiveness as an antidote to neoliberalism. By antidote to neoliberalism, I mean a theoretical orientation through which we can effectively critique both the ideology of neoliberalism and the practices and institutions that are co-constitutive with said ideology. Indeed, as Catrin Dingler posits, "The experience of care escapes total reification and enables the possibility of transformed human relationships" (2015, 213). Relations of care are sites that foreground the fluidity of context within human relationships, as well as the particularity of the individuals involved in said relations. Care thus "escapes total reification" in the sense that it demonstrates that human relations can never be reduced to a singular, or static, model of the subject and social relations (e.g., liberal individualism).

The Ethics of Care

The ethics of care is grounded on the simple premise "that human relatedness and the practices that support it shape us in profound ways" (Deveaux 1995, 115). Specifically, it is the practices of care within those relationships that, for care ethicists, are the most important (and traditionally overlooked) subject for moral consideration. Therefore, it is not the abstract and universal rules of a disembodied rationality that grounds moral behavior but rather the everyday (embodied) experiences of responsibilities in contextually specific relationships with others (Deveaux 1995). In this sense, social life can be characterized by a shared "interdependence" on care. To varying degrees over time, all individuals will in some way require care, in addition to responding to the needs of others (Robinson 2011, 4; Tronto 1993, 162).

Furthermore, these others, from the perspective of the ethics of care, are always "concrete" as opposed to "generalized" others, meaning that the various particulars of an individual's identity and broad socioeconomic context are morally salient, rather than extraneous, features of any "moral situation" (Benhabib 1985). Indeed, for care ethicists, *politics* and *ethics* are co-constitutive (Tronto 1993). Fiona Robinson emphasizes the *political* nature of care when she writes:

> Vulnerability and dependence, moreover, are features of all human subjects as well as many social groupings at some point; levels of vulnerability, and the implication of vulnerability are, in part, a reflection of existing power relations in the context of relationships. (2010, 142)

It is crucial, therefore, to consider *care* as a central aspect of human life that transcends all social boundaries, extending from intimate familial relations (Chodorow 1978; Noddings 2002; Ruddick 1989) all the way up to domestic (Bourgault 2017; Hankivsky 2004; Tronto 2010, 2013) and international (Held 2006; Robinson 1999; Tronto 2012) political institutions. This recognition—that the phenomenon of care is inherently a social and political phenomenon—means that we can observe relations of care, at both micro and macro levels, through a similar lens. It is helpful here to consider Tronto's suggestion that we evaluate care relations in light of a set of "phases":

> By describing four phases of care—*caring about,* i.e. recognizing a need for care; *caring for,* i.e. taking responsibility to meet that need; *care giving,* i.e. the actual physical work of providing care; and, finally, *care receiving,* i.e. the evaluation of how well the care provided had met the caring need—we have highlighted many points where conflict, power relations, inconsistencies, and competing purposes and divergent ideas about good care could affect care processes. (2010, 160)

This section has sought to provide a clearer picture of how relations and practices of care permeate all facets of the human experience. This picture encourages a moral orientation attentive to mutual vulnerability and dependence as that which characterizes a relational social ontology. With this understanding of the ethics of care and a relational ontology, we can now turn to the question of *precarity.*

Precarity and Care

In order to uncover the role that precarity plays within this picture of society and politics as animated by the central phenomenon of care, it is helpful to begin by returning to Carol Gilligan's *In a Different Voice* and, in particular, to one of the central discoveries made in the text, which is that in "illuminating life as a web rather than a succession of relationships, women portray autonomy rather than attachment as the illusory and dangerous quest" ([1982] 1993, 48). While this is certainly reflective of the kind of relational ontology that the ethics of care is largely premised upon, it is interesting and instructive for the phenomenology of precarity that I wish to present in this chapter to think about the particular choice of words used in the text. In Gilligan's observation, it is striving for autonomy that is described as a "dangerous quest." While I am certainly not suggesting that Gilligan and the substantial amount of work she inspired in any way discounts the relations of power that are implicated in the webs or networks of care that take place—ranging from interpersonal relations of care to "global care chains" (see Milligan and Wiles 2010, 742)—I do argue that it is helpful, as a starting point in thinking about the relation of care and precarity, to begin with the assumption that the reality of our shared interdependency and mutual vulnerability involves us in a "dangerous quest" from the very beginning, even when the reality and importance of human "attachment" is foregrounded. One of the strengths of the ethics of care is a recognition of this shared interdependency and vulnerability, which is acknowledged without necessarily attributing a "positive" or "negative" judgment to it (see Petherbridge 2016, 591). The picture of precarity that I wish to draw is one that acknowledges the "dangerous quest" of human attachment, without seeing said danger as necessarily "good" or "bad." At this point, it is helpful to link this preliminary description of care and precarity with Judith Butler's observance in *Precarious Life* of "a more general conception of the human . . . one in which we are, from the start, given over to the other, one in which we are, from the start, even prior to individuation itself and, by virtue of bodily requirements, given over to some set of primary others" ([2004] 2006, 31).

If we begin with the acknowledgment that we are fundamentally involved in relations of shared interdependency and attachment and that this condition is a "dangerous quest," we are left with the question of how to venture forward along this journey. Gilligan offers an interpretation of the point of view of Amy, one of the participants in her study, as an example of how to move forward: "Her world is a world of relationships and psychological truths where an awareness of the connection between people gives rise to a recognition of responsibility for one another, a perception of the need for response" ([1982] 1993, 30). Amy acknowledges the reality of shared interdependency, mutual vulnerability, and a broader relational ontology. She concludes that the realization of this fact imparts responsibility and motivates response. The way to move forward is thus to reorient our thinking toward the specific contexts of particular *relationships* and the ways in which those relationships attend to the need to give, and receive, care.

Thus, I argue that the central question for the ethics of care, as a moral and political theory, is *how* we should respond to the particularity of the other. Once shared interdependency and mutual vulnerability is recognized, how do we move forward while staying true to the realization that morality is about particular, context dependent practices, and not universal principles or rules? How can we best critique the structures and values of neoliberalism, which continuously reinforce an atomistic social ontology and rigid market logic? As Brunella Casalini observes:

> The neoliberal world is one that produces insecurity and, at the same time, *calls on every individual to take care of his or her vulnerability and precarity and to achieve resilience*, that is, a capacity to endure periodic, inevitable moments of crisis while remaining ever capable of springing back after each setback. (2018, 2, emphasis added)

I argue that by turning to Irigaray (2002) and Han (2017a) on the topic of eros, care ethicists are better able to theorize what motivates us to respond to human need, as well as how such a response should be undertaken, in a way that stays true to our mutual vulnerability and precarity, as well as inherently undermining neoliberalism as a set of sociopolitical values and practices. In other words, the concept of eros facilitates a more robust theory of subjectivity—from an ethics of care perspective—in addition to serving as a critique of neoliberalism. Irigaray (2002) and Han (2017a) both theorize eros and the intersubjective encounter in a way that simultaneously recognizes precarity as the ontological ground of human subjects and intersubjectivity, as well as the answer to the question of how to move forward in responding.

The notion of eros that I develop in reading Irigaray (2002) and Han (2017a) alongside each other suggests that the way to move forward in responding to the other, who we recognize as vulnerable/precarious, is to bring to the forefront our own precarity. Reading the ethics of care alongside the above theory of eros leads us to the conclusion that the ethical intersubjective encounter, understood within a broader relational ontology, requires us to *meet precarity with precarity.* This *meeting precarity with precarity* is simultaneously premised upon, and reinforces, a rejection of neoliberal norms and expectations. In order to develop this argument, I now turn to Irigaray's reinterpretation of "philosophy" as meaning a "wisdom of love" as opposed to "the love of wisdom" (1).

Eros, Precarity, and Care

Irigaray critiques the history of Western philosophy and, by extension, moral philosophy in much the same way as the ethics of care. For Irigaray, Western philosophy is characterized by

> a logic that formalizes the real by removing it from concrete experience. . . . Objectivity is thus not one and, moreover, the sensible and feelings have their objectivity and are worthy of being thought. Besides, they must be thought so that one can communicate with the other recognized as other. (2002, 2, 8)

For Irigaray, a "wisdom of love" must begin with a focus on "a listening to the other" (15), which avoids a "dialogue [that] is limited to a complicity in the same saying" (35), and rather acknowledges "the irreducibility of the other" (36). For Irigaray, leaving behind the Western logos (rationality) requires that we develop a new language, this time inspired by eros. This language is what she calls "loving speech" (57). This new linguistic order is meant to reflect a more relational ontology and a "subjectivity [which] is essentially relational. Whoever is capable of providing in oneself a place not only for the other but for the relation with the other is human" (80). It is not only that the relation with the other is what is most characteristically human, but more so that identity itself "is elaborated in relation-with, each one giving to the other and receiving from the other what is necessary for becoming" (93). Irigaray's goal here is a simple one: to advocate for a form of dialogue that fosters acceptance and receptivity to "difference" as opposed to privileging and enforcing "sameness" (155–57).

Our shared interdependency and mutual vulnerability therefore situate us as not only materially precarious in the presence of the other but ideationally as well. Our very being, as subjects, depends on a becoming "between-two" (Irigaray 2002, 16). This point becomes especially crucial for the upcoming discussion of Oliver's (2002, 2004, 2015) analysis of the importance of "address and response" within the "structure of subjectivity." What is useful about Irigaray's "wisdom of love" is the way in which it clears the ground for a new "grammar of thinking" (2002, 91) that is conducive to the relational ontology of an ethics of care. Furthermore, such a "grammar of thinking" recognizes both the importance of our concrete relations with others, as well as the ways in which said relations can be influenced by the symbolic power of a language (*logocentrism*) that reflects sociohistorical material relations of power.

Having said that, meeting the other with a disposition of "loving speech" or, we could say, with a form of receptiveness that is ungoverned by any preexisting moral code or symbolic order necessitates what we can think of as a form of *self-inflicted precarity.* It is here that Han's (2017a) theorization of eros becomes relevant to the effort to read the ethics of care alongside Irigaray's (2002) notion of love. As Han (2017a) writes of the erotic experience (which we should not frame as exclusively, or necessarily, sexual),[1] "The Other, whom I desire and who fascinates me, is *placeless.* He or she is removed from the language of sameness" (1–2). Furthermore:

> It [eros] sets into motion freely willed *self-renunciation,* freely willed *self-evacuation.* A singular process of *weakening* lays hold of the subject of love—which, however, is accompanied by a feeling of strength. This feeling is not the *achievement* of the One, but the *gift of the Other.* (3)

The above demonstrates the relationship between care, precarity, and eros that I wish to draw out in this chapter by reading Han alongside Irigaray and the broader ethics of care literature. Eros is that which draws us "toward the Other" (Han 2017a, 3); it is the name for how the other "fascinates" us. In terms that are more familiar to the literature on care, eros is that which motivates us to turn our *attention* to the vulnerability of the other and to recognize their need for care. As Simone Weil writes in *Gravity and Grace*, "Attention is bound up with desire. Not with the will but with desire" (2002, 118; see also Bourgault 2014).[2] At the same time as eros acts as that which initiates our attentiveness toward the other and their underlying vulnerability and/or precarity, it also instructs us as to how to receive and proceed in the face of the other and their precarity. Eros requires us to be receptive and responsive to the other, and this requires us to recognize and enhance our own precarity in what Han describes as a kind of "capacity for death." As Han goes on to write, "Although one dies in the Other, this death is followed by a return to oneself" (23).

In order to be truly attentive, receptive, and responsive to otherness, we therefore need to recognize and foreground our own precarity. As Han (2017a) writes, "A successful relationship with the Other finds expression as a kind of *failure*." However, this is not wholly passive but rather is a kind "of *being able not to be able*" (11). For Han, "eros" is situated as a kind of active force or "power." Yet, it is one that initiates a form of "powerlessness and unconsciousness . . . instead of affirming myself, I lose myself in (or for) the Other, who then rights me again" (24). This notion of eros is in some sense the ethical energy underlying non-domineering forms of care, as it focuses attention on the contextual specificity of the other. Indeed, I argue that a concept of eros helps us to theorize fully an ethics of care (and an understanding of subjectivity under care ethics) that is non-domineering or non-dominating. Dingler alludes to this notion of *openness-in-reception* in her investigation of subjectivity and the ethics of care when she writes:

> Caring practice shows that the subjectivities of both are constituted and altered in an open and unpredictable way. So the particular experience of care helps us understand that the concept of relational subjectivity can only be realized in ongoing practice, in which difference is expressed and negotiated always anew. (2015, 214)

Eros therefore becomes the bridge between care and precarity in a dual sense. First, it is the force or energy that directs attention toward the other and their precarity. Second, it is the power that enables reception of and response to the other's precarity through an acceptance and cultivation of our own precarity. A relational ontology therefore necessitates that subjects *meet precarity with precarity.* Further, I suggest that we can understand this relation of precarity as being primarily facilitated by eros as opposed to logos. As Han puts it, "without eros, logos is deteriorating into data-driven calculation, which is incapable of reckoning the event, the incalculable" (2017a, 43). It therefore seems that what we are in need of amidst the rampant individualism found in our neoliberal context is a "wisdom of love" (Irigaray 2002).[3]

In order to explore the relationship between eros, care, and precarity further as situated within a broader social and political realm, understood as being characterized by a relational ontology and intersubjective encounters, it is helpful to turn to Oliver's notion of subjectivity as a "witnessing structure" (2002, 326). For Oliver, and by way of Hegel, subjectivity itself is dependent upon "relations to the world and others" and, consequently, "an ethical obligation lies at the heart of subjectivity itself" (325). The "structure of witnessing" is characterized "as the possibility of address and response" (325). Subjectivity continuously relies on "the ability to address others and be addressed by them" as well as "the ability to respond to others and oneself" (326). Furthermore:

> Responsibility . . . has the double sense of opening up the ability to response . . . and ethically obligating subjects to respond by virtue of their very subjectivity itself. Response-ability is the founding possibility of subjectivity and its most fundamental obligation. (327)

Oliver and the notion of "witnessing subjectivity" is an important addition to my argument in this chapter for two reasons. First, the "structure of witnessing" conceives of intersubjective encounters as taking place within an "environment" in which we are situated in relation to others as a result of "the circulation of energies" (330); these "affective" energies bind us and impart on us "ethical obligation." For Oliver, "The response-ability inherent in the material world becomes an ethical responsibility in the world of human subjectivity" (330). This both provides a broader framework and structure for thinking about eros as one such energy that characterizes intersubjective encounters *within* a broader sociopolitical context *and* helps us see how recognizing the material precarity of otherness requires the manifestation of a responsive ethical precarity. Oliver, in line with the other thinkers who have been analyzed thus far, characterizes such attention to the way our "energy" affects "other people" as a "loving attention" (330). Furthermore, "Subjectivity itself is dependent upon the circulation of energy sustained through the process of witnessing. Witnessing is the heart of the circulation of energy that connects us, and obligates us, to each other" (331).

The second reason Oliver's (2002) notion of "witnessing" is crucial is connected to the first and centers around Oliver's distinction between "subject position" and "subjectivity," where the former is constitutive of "politics" and the latter "ethics" (2015, 483). This insight is crucial in the sense that it recognizes that intersubjective encounters always take place within a context of power relations between subjects embedded and shaped by their particular context. Such an approach "brings together the historical context and finite situation of particular subjects, on the one hand, with the witnessing structure that makes subjectivity an infinite open system of response, on the other" (482). It is important to note that for Oliver, this is a constant "tension" that is constitutive of the subject, and neither are positions to be overcome or subsumed by the other; politics and ethics are always co-constitutive (2004, 80–81). Eros as a "circulating energy," I argue, can draw our attention to the other's "subject position," that is, their precarity, but then since the structure of eros (as developed in this chapter) is to *meet precarity with precarity,* the other is not reduced or defined by their "subject position." Instead, the ethical encounter constituted by eros holds out the possibility for novelty. In this sense, love can be thought of as an "event" (Han 2017a, 45–46), which admits of "an ontology of relationality and interdependence that accepts the existence of vulnerability without reifying particular individuals, groups or states as 'victims' or 'guardians'" (Robinson 2010, 132).

A further synthesis between Oliver's notion of "witnessing subjectivity" and Han's (2015) conceptualization of "burnout society" offers a fruitful way of understanding the structure of neoliberal (global) capitalism, the agents within it, and the relations between those agents (or subjects) and the structures within which they find themselves. Such a synthesis reveals the ways in which the "burnout society" can be characterized as one in which "subject position" becomes the predominant form in which self and other understand their being in the world and the encounters that constitute said world. Such an understanding not only comes to hinder relations of care, ranging from the personal to institutional level, but also hampers the possibility of social agency and critique, as guided by eros and a critical political ethics of care.

A Politics of Eros in a Neoliberal Age

In *The Burnout Society*, Han offers the following diagnosis of the contemporary subject, as situated within neoliberal society, which is key to the argument being put forth in this chapter:

> The late-modern achievement-subject is subject to no one. . . . It positivizes itself; indeed, it liberates itself into a *project*. However, the change from subject to project does not make power or violence disappear. . . . This development is closely connected to capitalist relations of production. Starting at a certain level of production, auto-exploitation is significantly more efficient and brings much greater returns . . . than allo-exploitation, because the feeling of freedom attends it. Achievement society is the society of self-exploitation. The achievement-subject exploits itself until it burns out. In the process, it develops auto-aggression that often enough escalates into the violence of self-destruction. (2015, 46–47)

The "achievement-subject" in Han's framework is a subject overshadowed by what Oliver calls "our subject position"—"constituted in our social interactions and our positions within our culture and context" (2004, 81). The "burnout society" and the "achievement-subject," as co-constitutive phenomena, hinder the originary dimension of subjectivity as "address and response."

More specifically, contemporary subjects find their "subject position"—described by Han (2015) as a condition of "burnout"—as one determined by the structures of neoliberal (global) capitalism, where "the subject breaks down under the compulsion to perform and produce accomplishments over and over" (Han 2017a, 23). As a result, individuals under the conditions of neoliberal capitalism are increasingly better understood as being "projects" as opposed to "subjects," and this distinction/shift is of crucial importance for the argument put forth in this chapter, since it entails that "as the entrepreneur of its own self, the neoliberal subject has no capacity for relationships with others that might be *free of purpose*" (Han 2017b, 2; see also Weidner 2009). When one speaks of the rabid individualism of contemporary neoliberal society, it is not that we are more and more isolated in a literal sense, but rather that more and more of our relations with others are becoming *purposeful* and/or purpose laden. It is in this sense that subjectivity, in "burnout society," has been overshadowed and/or overtaken by "subject position"—as "projects" fueled by purpose and achievement under the conditions of neoliberal capital. This subject-as-project is hindered from *meeting precarity with precarity.*

Within the "burnout society," practices of care have thus been affected by the pressures of "achievement." As Casalini observes, "neoliberalism . . . necessitates an instrumental approach to care, which renders genuine self-care and care of others virtually impossible, at least for most persons" (2018, 2). Hanna-Kaisa Hoppania and Tiina Vaittinen, echoing Han, argue further that "the commodification of care or its measurable exchange are not ends in themselves. Rather, they are necessary to the extent that they feed into the neoliberal project of governing life in terms of enterprise" (2015, 81). To put it simply, the relations of care upon which human beings are mutually dependent suffer when subjects become "projects" under neoliberal capitalism.[4]

We should recall here that Oliver describes subjectivity as having two dimensions: on the one hand, there is "subjectivity" as "the structure of address and response" (2004, 79), and on the other, there is "subject position." The goal of such a differentiation is to "attempt to navigate between the extremes of conceiving of the subject either as the foundation for action apart from social circumstance on the one hand, or as the simple effect of social context on the other" (2004, 80–81). This theory of subjectivity therefore attempts to provide an answer to the agent–structure problem (see Bieler and Morton 2001). However, as is demonstrated by Han's assessment of contemporary neoliberal society, the crisis we face is one in which subjectivity *itself* is being hollowed out and replaced by "subject position." Theoretically, agent and structure are best seen as mutually constitutive forces. However, a critique of contemporary society reveals the way in which the theoretical problem of agent–structure has manifested concretely in contemporary society as one in which the balance has been shifted toward the extreme of structure as "subject position" and experienced in the form of "projects" and "achievement." This shift has important consequences vis-à-vis the force or energy of eros and its ability to help us navigate the self-other relation within contemporary society as constituted by the discourses and practices of neoliberalism.

If the goal is to "politicize . . . the subject à la subject position and insist . . . on a fundamental ethical obligation at the heart of subjectivity itself thereby bringing together the political and ethical dimensions of subjectivity" (Oliver 2004, 81), then one must proceed to a critique of how the overdetermination of "subject position" vis-à-vis intersubjective relations is one of the predominant features of contemporary neoliberal society and global capitalism. Through both Han and Oliver, we see how the relationship with the Other is being undermined by the mechanisms of neoliberal capital and its emphasis on individualism and efficiency. For Oliver (2004), a sense of self depends on "the ability to address," and "respond to," "oneself," which is co-constitutive with "the ability to address," and "respond to," "others," as well as be "addressed," "and responded to," by those same "others" (83). Therefore, there is a crucial link between the ways in which we engage with others and how we are able to engage with ourselves. In other words, "If the possibility of address is undermined or annihilated, then subjectivity is also undermined or annihilated." Furthermore, "the inner witness is where subject position and subjectivity meet," and hence our "agency" can be negatively impacted if the intersubjective relations that we "internalize" are characterized by forms of injustice and/or exclusion (Oliver 2004, 83). The addition of Han's (2015) "burnout society" to this framework demonstrates the positive side of this undermining of subjectivity. When our "ability to address," and "respond to," others is dominated by purpose and achievement, our "inner witness" equally views itself entirely in the light of purpose and achievement. As such, the subject loses not only its ability to engage in undetermined intersubjective encounters but also its critical potentiality, its feeling of agency apart from overarching systemic constraints.

Han (2017a) and Oliver (2015) offer similar paths in the resuscitation of the power of subjectivity. These paths can be characterized as starting with a return to *precarity* as an inherent feature of intersubjective encounters and, furthermore, as a necessary feature of social critique. A return to the radical openness of the "address and response" "structure of subjectivity" means that we must "dwell in the space of the incalculable, a space without moral rules or laws" (Oliver 2015, 487). This is obviously a precarious space, since one (theoretically) cannot depend on preconceived notions of self, other, or the rules that should govern an encounter. Instead, this "space" requires us to "respond to each individual and each situation anew according to its singularity" (489) and "our embodied relationality" (490). In this sense, we are dependent on, and vulnerable to, the other for the formation of our subjectivity, as well as in the intersubjective encounters that are the continuing foundations of said subjectivity as an ethical practice (Oliver 2002).

This mutual vulnerability in the face of otherness is obfuscated when "[t]he Other . . . is entirely subject to the teleology of use, to economic calculation and evaluation" (Han 2018, 68). The flipside of seeing others through this lens of "projects" and "achievement" is that the self comes to see its own vulnerability as a failure, as something to remedy. This not only participates in placing limitations on one's own sense of agency, but also depoliticizes intersubjective encounters by obfuscating their creative potentiality, that is, the ways in which such encounters can be the source and/or manifestation of a different way of being (see Gibson-Graham 2006). As Han (2018) writes:

> Listening has a political dimension. It is an act, an active participation in the existence of Others, in their suffering too. It is what joins and connects people to form a community in the first place. Today, we hear a great deal, but are increasingly losing the ability to listen to Others and give an ear to their language, their suffering. Today, everyone is somehow on their own with themselves, with their suffering, with their fears. Suffering is privatized and individualized. Thus it becomes an object of a therapy that tampers with the I, with its psyche. Everyone is ashamed and simply blames themselves for their weakness and inadequacy. No connection is established between my suffering and your suffering. Thus the *sociality of suffering* is overlooked. (75)

The above points us to the ways in which eros can be conceived as an energy that animates politics. Eros as a *meeting precarity with precarity* allows for a language, or grammar, of listening that is more in tune with the disposition of attentiveness explicated within the political ethics of care literature. Such a reconceptualization of the self–other relation, in a way that attempts to mirror a vision of society as constituted by a relational ontology, can also serve as an effective critique and reevaluation of politics *as such* in our neoliberal times. Han echoes this sentiment when he writes that "political action occurs in a sphere that intersects with eros on manifold levels. Eros can be transformed politically. . . . Political action is mutual desire for another way of living" (2017a, 44). He goes on to write: "Eros manifests itself as the revolutionary yearning for an entirely different way of loving and another kind of society" (46). This kind of political potentiality, facilitated by eros as a *meeting precarity with precarity,* is ever present in the care relation, since, as Hoppania and Vaittinen observe, the "neoliberal order" can never fully commodify the care relation. Therefore, "in the context of the prevailing neoliberal discourse, care provides a constant opening of the political" (2015, 71). Care, as a political potentiality, "refers to the latent forces of disruption that are imbued in the corporeal character of care relations that challenge the logics of the present order" (77–78).

The synthesis put forth in this chapter has suggested that eros can be conceived as a bridge between care and precarity in a dual sense. First, it is the force or energy that directs "loving attention" toward the other and their precarity as made explicit in their "subject position." Second, it is the power that enables reception of and response to the other's precarity through an acceptance and cultivation of our own precarity as a precondition for intersubjective encounters. That is, we are dependent upon the "address and response" of the other as the other is dependent upon ours. Lastly, the relation between self and other initiated and guided by eros is that which can lead to political openness and change. Precarity as a "*being able not to be able*" is a condition that counters the demands of "achievement, performance, and ability" in our neoliberal age (Han 2017a, 11). Furthermore, these moments inspired and/or animated by eros are constitutive of the practices of care enacted in response to and in line with the self's underlying and overarching precarity.

By demonstrating the interplay between care, precarity, and eros, this analysis has sought simultaneously to build upon the theory of subjectivity inherent within care ethics and, in doing so, bolster the ethics of care's effectiveness as an antidote to our neoliberal times.

Notes

This research was generously funded by a Social Sciences and Humanities Research Council of Canada Doctoral Award (752-2018-1785). I would like to thank the editors, Maurice Hamington and Michael Flower, sincerely for their careful readings and extremely valuable feedback on multiple drafts of this chapter. I would also like to thank Fiona Robinson for the numerous discussions and helpful comments, which greatly improved the chapter. Thank you too to Maggie FitzGerald for the helpful conversations. Finally, I would like to thank the organizers of The Care Ethics Research Consortium Inaugural Conference (2018) for the opportunity to present and receive feedback on an early version of this chapter.

1. For a broader discussion of how the erotic has traditionally been reduced to the sexual act, as well as how it can be reclaimed within a broader feminist politics, see Audre Lorde's "Uses of the Erotic: The Erotic as Power" in *Sister Outsider* ([1984] 2007).

2. Simone Weil has been fruitfully read alongside the ethics of care (see especially Bourgault 2014). The scope of this chapter does not allow for a more thorough investigation of Weil, whose notion of attention is significantly guided by her Platonism. The quote from Weil included in this chapter is helpful in communicating the relationship between care and eros that I wish to put forth in this chapter. However, it is important to note that there is a broader and more complex philosophical (and spiritual) context at play in Weil's work that prevents a simple insertion of her thought into the care ethics literature. I thank Sophie Bourgault for her helpful comments on this subject.

3. The use of eros, or love, in this chapter has a clear affinity with broader efforts in moral philosophy—and the ethics of care—which strive to revalue the role of emotion and/or sentiment in the study of ethics. This revaluation is in response to dominant traditions in Western philosophy that privilege impartial rationality. It is beyond the scope of this chapter to engage in a robust analysis of such efforts. However, it should be noted that my use of these concepts (eros and love) seeks to situate them as those ethical energies that initially turn our attentiveness toward the other or orient us to receive the other. Thus, it is perhaps most useful to see eros/love as used here as precursors, or the "inciting incident," which can then be followed by more substantive emotional states or instances of empathy, as opposed to thinking of eros as emotional states or instances of empathy as such.

4. An important part of the analysis here is that it is not only a critique of relations of care that are formally commodified within a neoliberal market economy. Within a neoliberal society, more intimate, and/or familial, practices and relations of care equally become constrained and shaped by neoliberal expectations of efficiency and achievement.

Works Cited

Benhabib, Seyla. 1985. "The Generalized and the Concrete Other: The Kohlberg–Gilligan Controversy and Feminist Theory." *Praxis International* 5 (4): 402–24.

Bieler, Andreas, and Adam David Morton. 2001. "The Gordian Knot of Agency-Structure in International Relations: A Neo-Gramscian Perspective." *European Journal of International Relations* 7 (1): 5–35.

Bourgault, Sophie. 2014. "Beyond the Saint and the Red Virgin: Simone Weil as Feminist Theorist of Care." *Frontiers: A Journal of Women Studies* 35 (2): 1–27.

Bourgault, Sophie. 2017. "Prolegomena to a Caring Bureaucracy." *European Journal of Women's Studies* 24 (3): 202–17.

Butler, Judith. (2004) 2006. *Precarious Life: The Powers of Mourning and Violence.* New York: Verso.

Casalini, Brunella. 2018. "Care of the Self and Subjectivity in Precarious Neoliberal Societies." Presented at the Care Ethics Research Consortium Inaugural Conference, Portland, Oregon, 27–28 September 2018. https://ethicsofcare.org/wp-content/uploads/2019/04/BC-IA.pdf.

Chodorow, Nancy. 1978. *The Reproduction of Mothering: Psychoanalysis and the Sociology of Gender.* Berkeley: University of California Press.

Deveaux, Monique. 1995. "Shifting Paradigms: Theorizing Care and Justice in Political Theory." *Hypatia* 10 (2): 115–19.

Dingler, Catrin. 2015. "Disenchanted Subjects? On the Experience of Subjectivity in Care Relations." *Ethics and Social Welfare* 9 (2): 209–15.

Ettlinger, Nancy. 2007. "Precarity Unbound." *Alternatives* 32 (3): 319–40.

Gibson-Graham, J. K. 2006. *A Postcapitalist Politics.* Minneapolis: University of Minnesota Press.

Gilligan, Carol. (1982) 1993. *In a Different Voice: Psychological Theory and Women's Development.* Cambridge, Mass.: Harvard University Press.

Han, Byung-Chul. 2015. *The Burnout Society.* Translated by Erik Butler. Stanford, Calif.: Stanford University Press.

Han, Byung-Chul. 2017a. *The Agony of Eros.* Translated by Erik Butler. Cambridge, Mass.: MIT Press.

Han, Byung-Chul. 2017b. *Psychopolitics: Neoliberalism and New Technologies of Power.* Translated by Erik Butler. New York: Verso.

Han, Byung-Chul. 2018. *The Expulsion of the Other: Society, Perception and Communication Today.* Translated by Wieland Hoban. Medford, Ore.: Polity Press.

Hankivsky, Olena. 2004. *Social Policy and the Ethic of Care.* Vancouver: UBC Press.

Held, Virginia. 2006. *The Ethics of Care: Personal, Political, and Global.* New York: Oxford University Press.

Hollway, Wendy. 2006. *The Capacity to Care: Gender and Ethical Subjectivity.* New York: Routledge.

Hoppania, Hanna-Kaisa, and Tiina Vaittinen. 2015. "A Household Full of Bodies: Neoliberalism, Care and 'the Political.'" *Global Society* 29 (1): 70–88.

Irigaray, Luce. 2002. *The Way of Love.* Translated by Heidi Bostic and Stephen Pluháček. New York: Continuum.

Lorde, Audre. (1984) 2007. *Sister Outsider: Essays and Speeches.* Berkeley, Calif.: Crossing Press.

Millar, Kathleen M. 2017. "Toward a Critical Politics of Precarity." *Sociology Compass* 11 (6): 1–11. https://doi.org/10.1111/soc4.12483.

Milligan, Christine, and Janine Wiles. 2010. "Landscapes of Care." *Progress in Human Geography* 34 (6): 736–54.

Noddings, Nel. 2002. *Starting at Home: Caring and Social Policy.* Berkeley: University of California Press.

Oliver, Kelly. 2002. "Subjectivity as Responsivity: The Ethical Implications of Dependency." In *The Subject of Care: Feminist Perspectives on Dependency,* edited by Eva Feder Kittay and Ellen K. Feder, 322–33. Lanham, Md.: Rowman & Littlefield.

Oliver, Kelly. 2004. "Witnessing and Testimony." *Parallax* 10 (1): 78–87.

Oliver, Kelly. 2015. "Witnessing, Recognition, and Response Ethics." *Philosophy and Rhetoric* 48 (4): 473–93.

Petherbridge, Danielle. 2016. "What's Critical about Vulnerability? Rethinking Interdependence, Recognition, and Power." *Hypatia* 31 (3): 589–604.

Robinson, Fiona. 1999. *Globalizing Care: Ethics, Feminist Theory, and International Relations.* Boulder, Colo.: Westview Press.

Robinson, Fiona. 2010. "After Liberalism in World Politics? Towards an International Political Theory of Care." *Ethics and Social Welfare* 4 (2): 130–44.

Robinson, Fiona. 2011. *The Ethics of Care: A Feminist Approach to Human Security.* Philadelphia, Pa.: Temple University Press.

Robinson, Fiona. 2015. "Care Ethics, Political Theory, and the Future of Feminism." In *Care Ethics and Political Theory,* edited by Daniel Engster and Maurice Hamington, 293–311. Oxford: Oxford University Press.

Ruddick, Sara. 1989. *Maternal Thinking: Toward a Politics of Peace.* Boston: Beacon Press.

Tronto, Joan C. 1993. *Moral Boundaries: A Political Argument for an Ethic of Care.* New York: Routledge.

Tronto, Joan C. 2010. "Creating Caring Institutions: Politics, Plurality, and Purpose." *Ethics and Social Welfare* 4 (2): 158–71.

Tronto, Joan C. 2012. "Partiality Based on Relational Responsibilities: Another Approach to Global Ethics." *Ethics and Social Welfare* 6 (3): 303–16.

Tronto, Joan C. 2013. *Caring Democracy: Markets, Equality, and Justice.* New York: New York University Press.

Tronto, Joan C. 2017. "There Is an Alternative: *Homines Curans* and the Limits of Neoliberalism." *International Journal of Care and Caring* 1 (1): 27–43.

Weidner, Jason R. 2009. "Governmentality, Capitalism, and Subjectivity." *Global Society* 23 (4): 387–411.

Weil, Simone. 2002. *Gravity and Grace.* Translated by Emma Crawford and Mario von der Ruhr. New York: Routledge.

CHAPTER 10

Resisting Neoliberalism

A Feminist New Materialist Ethics of Care to Respond to Precarious World(s)

EMILIE DIONNE

Across critical humanities scholarship, it is no longer regarded as controversial that neoliberal politics and precarity go hand in hand. Their relation is now recognized as deeply entangled, even as co-constitutive, and thus as hardly separable. Precarity is worrisome in part because of its embodied and material effects, which are real, tangible, and irreversible. These effects are also not "going anywhere" but are here to stay; and most worrisome perhaps, these effects are manifold, that is, they can—and do—take multiple forms or meanings. Informed by feminist new materialism (FNM) and feminist theory, this chapter proposes to work with a new dynamic and agential conception of matter to enable another course of *mattering* of "precarious matters"—one that is more ethical and livable.[1] I argue that this work can vitally enrich care ethics, as it aims to respond to increasing, exacerbating, and globalized precarity. More boldly, I propose to do this work by working *with* matter, which is deemed agential, that is, a possible participant-in-action.

FNM's Dynamic Ontology

FNM's work on new developments in the natural sciences (e.g., physics, biology, geology, environmental studies) reveals an ontology of matter that is constantly in the process of being made rather than given (i.e., already determined).[2] In this ontology, the making of matter is intimately tied to knowledge practices. This is the case because knowledge practices operate by intervening in the "mattering process."

Matter is *always mattering* rather than simply "materializing," meaning that the material enactment or configuration contains and conveys discursive signification and is value laden. According to FNM, this is the case because processes of materialization involve intricately processes of sense making. They argue but also show concretely through their work with and on the natural sciences that (material) matter and meaning become together; they acquire "determinacy" (configuration, in Barad's words [2007, 104–10, 118, 127, 140–41; 2003, 814–15, 829–30]) together. Hence, meaning and matter are always connected, and matter as meaning exists only in context, that is, as intimately tied to a context and to all concomitant "things" that also are tied to (i.e., have emerged in) this context (e.g., other material objects such as scientific devices of observation or measurement but also practices of knowledge or concepts). Outside or without context, matter cannot be scientifically known because it is indeterminate—ontologically indeterminate. Actually, it is indeterminacy itself (Barad 2007, 104–10, 118, 138).

As mentioned, matter (like meaning) does acquire something akin to "determinacy," but this achievement is ultimately temporary, irreversible, but nonetheless mattering. Ontologically, matter remains open and dynamic, but any achievement, any enactment whereby matter acquires temporary and situated "determinacy," leave traces on matter that mark matter irrevocably but do not determine it. The traces cannot be erased, and they also are "alive" in the sense that they too will take part in processes of mattering to come (i.e., future entanglements, future configurations). Yet, there is an important sense that "becoming" is future oriented only and is why the "how" of materiality mattering matters so much to FNM. Traces bear the marks of past enactments, as a memory that is much alive, and get involved. The past thus never sits still—a process that Barad identifies as *re-member-ing.*

For FNM, the "matter of matter" still ought to matter (i.e., be valued and be considered by) to knowers because of "how" matter *matters* (i.e., how it materializes and to which meanings it is tied).[3] The processes of mattering are not innocent "matters" (pun intended). They are future oriented and inform future courses of mattering. Knowers are intimately implicated in how matters matter. Knowing necessarily involves accountability and responsibility on the part of knowers, despite the fact that one cannot know in advance all of the consequences to which a particular scientific enactment can lead or how it will inform future trajectories of mattering of matter (Barad 2007, 37). This is why knowledge practices must be conducted with care, even requiring the adoption of an agential-material ethic of care, as FNM argue.

This is also why FNM so vehemently insist that knowers be involved in ethics and ontology, even when they do not account for it; knowledge practices proceed *ontologically*, that is, by ways of making concrete (i.e., mattering) enactments, all "matters" (meaning and materiality; meaning, as will we see, is always "enfolded" with the material) are marked forever. These traces that will not go anywhere, however, are not over-determined; they can *matter* differently, but the only outcome that is impossible is their complete erasure or disappearance. These traces, in other words, are also dynamic, open; made of "ontologically dynamic matter." They too will participate in the processes that will inform future courses of mattering of any matter.

Responding to Precarity with a Feminist New Materialist Care Ethics: A Proposal

These new insights on matter provide a critical point for the argument of this chapter: materiality can *matter* otherwise (materially, discursively, and as material–discursive entanglement), and precarity, and its manifold material effects, may be responded to otherwise, notably in ways that activate or participate in a new trajectory of mattering (i.e., of material and discursive transformation in the future). Of course, neither discursive nor material matters that currently exist can become just about anything in the future. A close attention to new developments in ontology is warranted—specifically ones that mobilize the contribution of feminist and care ethics scholarship. In the era of manifold precarity (cf. Butler 2006, 2009, 2012; Tsing 2015), FNM's responses to precarity can support care ethics in the work of addressing neoliberal precarity, and participate in the work of healing, alleviating, or transforming precarity and its multifarious effects on people's lives.

Informed by these approaches, this chapter shows the relevance and contribution of FNM and feminist posthumanist ethics to care ethics. Care ethics would benefit from incorporating contributions from feminist engagements with the sciences in trying to respond to the multifaceted issue of precarity, which is exacerbated by neoliberalism, specifically by considering what is called the "ontological turn" in science (cf. Alaimo and Hekman 2008; Barad 2007; Haraway 2016, 2017; Tsing 2015; Tsing et al. 2017). Through this contribution, I propose to offer concrete conceptual tools to supplement and support current ethics of care to address the issue of precarity in neoliberal times/and make matter *matter* otherwise following the FNM ethics of *response-ability* (Haraway 2008, 2017).

To this effect, the objective of this chapter is threefold. First, I present key concepts and the philosophy of FNM about matter as dynamic, relational, and agential. In part 1, I focus on the contribution of feminist theoretical physicist Karen Barad—specifically her concepts *of* agential matter, agential realism, *and* intra-action. Part 2 tackles the issue of precarity by proposing a conceptualization of it. To do so, I rely on the work of Judith Butler (2006, 2009, 2012), and I integrate Isabell Lorey's (2009, 2011, 2015) contribution with her concept of governmental precarization. I complete this part with two illustrations of how neoliberalism brings about the emergence of an ontology of precarity, thus becoming embodied and configuring a "corporeality" (corporeal and reality) that participates ontologically, that is, in the making of *more* precarity, and a precarious ontology, whereby matter *matters* precariously. In the third and final section, I revisit FNM's contributions to offer concrete, practical tools to operationalize the "mattering otherwise" of this precarious ontology. I focus on the contribution of Elizabeth A. Wilson (2004, 2008, 2015), feminist biologist, and her approach of organic empathy. I conclude this chapter with a condensed operational definition of a FNM-improved ethic of care for everyday practice.

FNM: Karen Barad's Agential Realism

Barad, prominent figure of what has come to be called the "feminist new materialism," developed the groundbreaking ethico-onto-epistemological approach of agential realism. In this section, I offer a quick dive into Barad's rich conceptual apparatus and ontology because it provides us with the foundation of a new materialist care ethics whereby "precarious matters" can be made to *matter* otherwise, both materially and discursively, in the future, as well as to explore how one can work *with* matter, that is, with materiality or with the nonhuman, or also with concepts or words, which are also discursive–material entanglements, and which participate, as is well known since Foucault, to the "materialization" of material matters.

Barad's "agential realist" approach lays out a dynamic, open, always in-the-making, and indeterminate concept of matter. She engages quantum physics to claim that matter *matters* in ways that have ontological, epistemological, political, and ethical effects, and that it ought to matter to any knower how matter *matters,* that is, how it is made, specifically, as a material–discursive entanglement tied to a context of emergence and tied to manifold relations, that is, with other "things/entanglements." Furthermore, this "mattering" intimately involves knowledge practices, which are ontological processes in this dynamic ontology (i.e., they concomitantly make the "matters" they hope to study, to know). Emphasizing the materiality of matter is about insisting on the importance of this new ontological insight, notably the irreversibility of *mattering* practices, of which knowledge practices are part. The sciences proceed to know matter by ways of acting, of making enactments, of intervening. They thus participate in configuring matter, which is ontologically indeterminate. A second important contribution of Barad is that, contra representationalism, matter is not inert, passive, or raw, therefore lending itself to just about any representationalist attempt, passively. Matter too participates in knowledge practices; in scientific encounters, matter is enticed, triggered, to partake (Barad 2007, 161–68). This, of course, complicates the knowledge endeavor on both ontological and epistemological levels. Third, applying the works of theoretical quantum physicist Niels Bohr, philosopher of the sciences Ian Hacking, and poststructuralist thinkers such as Michel Foucault, Judith Butler, and Jacques Derrida, Barad argues and shows that matter is *performative* (Barad 2007, 46–50, 150–51). Let us examine each of these contributions in further detail.

In this new ontology, matter is ontologically indeterminate, that is, always in-the-making rather than having a fixed entity that would remain stable (the same) regardless of time or space (Barad 2007, 137, 140–41, 149–53). Additionally, matter is an entanglement of discursive and material components, a complex pattern of material–discursive entanglements (Barad 2007, ch. 4). This is true of the "object of observation"—Barad's term for what was formerly called the "object" of a scientific inquiry—as well as of the instruments of knowledge, which include concepts as much as material devices, such as a microscope; and with "knowers" and an ensemble of other practices, bodies, objects, or concepts (to give examples), we have "agencies of observation," which were formerly called "subjects" of knowledge (Barad 2007, 114–15). These are also material–discursive entanglements. Everything is in actuality a material–discursive entanglement, but this does not mean that anything is consequently equal or equivalent or that the distribution between materiality and the discursive is the same or equivalent in any entanglement. Barad's point is rather that any material or discursive object is tied to a context of emergence, that is, it is part of its "identity," a.k.a. what is/was traditionally understood as the "identity" (or "essence") of a thing. Moreover, the material and the discursive are always mutually involved, entangled. Finally, neither "exists" as what they are (i.e., what can be known) without consideration for the *spacetimemattering* phenomena from which they originate.[4]

Hence, any material or discursive object encompasses material or discursive elements or relationships. For example, the microscope is a device that is located in a given point in the space–time–*matter* continuum and irrevocably tied to its context, which encompasses considerations for culture, politics, gender, race, nationalism, and so forth. It does and cannot exist as it is outside of this continuum, and to know well what the microscope is and what it does, one must consider its context of emergence and its manifold relations with the other "things" within this context, materially and discursively (Barad 2007, 51):

> [Hacking] argues . . . that experimentation should be understood as a complex practice in its own right. Take the example of microscopy. In Hacking's account, "seeing" atoms or other entities with the aid of a microscope is not a matter of simply looking . . . but an achievement that requires a complex set of practices to accomplish.

As matter materializes (i.e., emerges in the real and forms the real, as agential), it does so in entanglements with meaning (i.e., discursive elements). And the reverse is also true: words, meaning, or concepts emerge in entanglement with matter (material matter). To know, in this "picture," means to account for entanglements and situations.

As noted earlier, matter does not exist as a fixed entity, but it does acquire something akin to one—a configuration entangling the material and the discursive, located in a situation and a space–time–matter*ing* (recall that matter is always dynamic, ontologically), a temporary achievement solely. Put otherwise, a temporarily stabilized "matter-as-mattering" is an enactment that leaves marks on matter-as-mattering, therein informing/influencing its future possible (and impossible, a.k.a. virtualized) trajectory of materialization. Irrevocably intricate to the context of its emergence (i.e., *of* it, actually) and caught in manifold relations, matter is configured. And perhaps more striking is that none of these "objects," these "matters," precede the others. In other words, one could not say that one "object" (i.e., objects of observation) was already constituted as this, that is, with a given identity, and subsequently encountered another object, that is, the agency/ies of observation, and that an interaction took place that transformed them both. This relates to Barad's new concept of *intra*-action, which I will discuss further below.

From this perspective on matter, one can start to see why Barad conceives of matter as performative. In *Bodies That Matter*, Butler describes matter as a "process of materialization" that is a process "that sediments [itself] over time, that crystallizes itself" (1993, 9). On this conception, Butler shows the inherent material effects of discursive practices and the need to be ethically attentive when uttering and reproducing discourse. This is because of "citationality," the process whereby individuals "take on" discourses that they perform with their body, that they embody. It is this way and through ongoing repetitions and iterations that matter sediments itself—in this case, human bodies (Butler 1993, 9). For Butler, therefore, discourses are active and intervening and ontology-making practices.

Barad is inspired by this conception but also concerned that Butler's conception of matter provides no space for the agency, dynamism, or ontological openness of matter. Drawing from Bohr's work in quantum physics, specifically his principle of indeterminacy,[5] Barad shows concrete examples from theoretical physics that demonstrate that matter itself contributes to Butler's conception of matter as a process and to its citationality and performativity. Matter gets "marked" through practices of knowledge, which influence how matter can *matter* in the future but without determining it, fixing it, or sedimenting it forever.

The double-slit experiment in physics provides a good illustration of Bohr's indeterminacy principle and Barad's concept of matter as performative:

> From the perspective of classical mechanics, the two-slit experiment evidences a stark distinction between particle and wave behaviors. When particles are aimed at the partition with the double slits, we find that most of the particles land on the detection screen directly opposite each of the two openings in the partition . . . , with a smaller number scattering off to either side. . . . Waves, on the other hand, exhibit a very different pattern. . . . When waves impinge on a barrier with two openings, they spread out as they emerge from each of the slits. (Barad 2007, 101–2)

The waves make a diffraction pattern due to their interference with one another:

> What happens if we perform this experiment using electrons? The surprising . . . result is that electrons, tiny particles of matter, produce a diffraction pattern! (Barad 2007, 102)

Barad explains that this only happens when we fire multiple electrons through the slits, but if we fire only one electron, the pattern on the screen displays the results for a particle:

> But here's the rub: we collect the data for each event, and look at the overall pattern after a large number of electrons has gone through, and . . . [we observe a] interference pattern [diffraction]. (Barad 2007, 102)

She continues with Bohr's findings:

> Bohr argued that if we were to perform a two-slit experiment with a which-path device (which can be used to determine which slit each electron goes through . . .), we would find that the interference pattern is destroyed. That is, if a measurement is made that identifies the electron as a particle, as is the case when we use a which-path detector, then the result will be a particle pattern, not the wave pattern that results when the original unmodified two-slit apparatus is used. (Barad 2007, 104)

For Bohr, the measurement participates in the determination of matter, in context. Without the measurement, matter is and remains indeterminate. The measurement is part of the apparatus through which "the real" is made. It has an ontological effect.

Earlier, I mentioned Barad's concept of intra-action, which she puts forth against the notion of interaction. Barad's dynamic and agential ontology and her conception of matter as indeterminacy show that matter does acquire configurations (knowable scientifically). Reckon that matter acquires configuration notably through scientific endeavors. Here we have it: matter never stays still but rather enfolds constantly. This is its "essence," which is to have none, ontologically, or rather to gain "one" but only in strict conditions (i.e., within a localized situation of temporary interiority called a *phenomenon*, defined below). Matter also acquires configuration but only as a temporary achievement, temporarily and contextually. Ultimately, matter remains open and dynamic but only as a future-oriented endeavor. Enactments, as Barad and other new feminist new materialists insist, *matter* discursively and materially. They leave marks that affect the ongoing *mattering* process that is matter. Hence, despite its "inherent indeterminacy," the materiality of matter still ought to matter to knowers because their practices are never detached from the *mattering* process but rather constitutive of, participating in, and entangled with the process itself. Moreover, the traces left on matter are themselves "lively," agential. This of course complicates this ontology, the ability to know, as well as the responsibilities inherent in doing so.

Careful examination of how scientific practices operate and how knowing is possible, given Barad's conception of matter, needs clarification. It is important because it will inform how a FNM ethic of care must account for its participation in activating other trajectories of mattering of precarity. Hence, how does "knowing work"? And how is it an ontology-making endeavor or even a project? First, I mentioned that Barad abandons the concepts of "subject" and "object" where each stands in putative opposition to and independent of one another. Instead, she proposes the concepts of "agencies of observation" and "object of observation," two concepts that account for their situatedness within a *phenomenon*, that is, a temporary situation of stability and interiority within a larger ontology of indeterminacy, as well as their mutual and irrevocably entanglement, intra-action, which is constitutive of them both and mutually entangling to one another. I have already touched briefly on "agencies of observation" as no longer pertaining solely to a "(human) knower." Agencies of observation encompass nonhuman elements, material and discursive ones, such as instruments of measures (e.g., the microscope) or concepts. Nonhuman elements can also refer to culture, race, gender, politics, or history, which are part of the background, the situation, of any human knower (cf. Haraway 1991, ch. 9). Agencies and objects of observation, contra formerly subjects and objects, are two material–discursive entanglements, that is, they are inherently and always dynamically entangled and co-constituted. They are also context bound, partial, temporary, dynamic, open, and complex entanglements of meaning and matter; they are irrevocably tied to their context of creation, of emergence; finally, they do not exist as they are here and now identically outside this context or in another context, that is, another "space–time–*mattering*" (Barad 2007, 179–81; see also endnote #3).

Agencies of observation include nonhuman elements, notably race, class, gender, culture, history, economy, or politics (i.e., nationalism, militarism, etc.). To make all this a bit clearer, consider the following example. Barad uses the Stern–Gerlach experiment, a demonstration of space quantization, to illustrate how "knowing" materializes as a singular phenomenon where agencies of observation *and* objects of observation materialize and matter at once, apart together, and how the knower materializes/matters as a singular phenomenon (Barad 2007, 179, 394; 2014; see also endnote #3). In this example, Barad explains how Stern, a leading scientist for the experiment, smoked a particular brand of cheap cigars. As it turned out, the specific composition of the type of cigar he smoked is what allowed him and his fellow scientists to witness a particular result; it made a scientific result materialize. Barad identifies the factors influencing Stern's choice of cigar: the manner of his embodiment, his gender, his nationality, and his economic class all played a role. Here is how she describes the situation:

> Stern held the plates in his hands and studied them at a distance close enough so that the plates could absorb the fumes of Stern's sulfuric breath, turning the faint, nearly invisible, silver traces into jet black

> silver sulfide traces. . . . The reproducibility of the experiment depends on the cigar's presence. Not any old cigar will do: the high sulfur content of a cheap cigar is crucial. Class, nationalism, gender, and the politics of nationalism, among other variables, are all part of this apparatus (which is not to say that all relevant factors figure in the same way or with the same weight). (2007, 165)

This example shows that it is out of particular configurations of contextually bound factors that a singular scientific result materializes and that the nonhuman is materially and discursively informed (i.e., the matter of the cigar intertwines material and discursive elements such as gender, race, class, nationalism, or politics). Without this mix of both spatial and historical features, the scientific result would not have been observed; it would have neither materialized nor mattered. Agencies of observation understood in this way suggest that the knower inherits her milieu; she is indebted to these entanglements when engaging in the enactment of the agential separation that makes a phenomenon matter and she *matters* out of it, that is, she is *of* them including materially. In sum, agencies of observation are complex entanglements, fully enmeshed in the *phenomena* that materialize in intra-action.

Equipped with this conceptual apparatus, I now turn to the topic of precarity. I present my conceptualization of it, which thinkers inform it, and the material–discursive effects of precarity, specifically its embodied performative effects. And then I ask how FNM helps us to entice other courses of *mattering* of precarity.

The Precarious Times of Neoliberalism: Theorizing Neoliberal Precarity

The implications that come out of Barad's and new materialist works are manifold. This section starts with an overview of my conceptualization of precarity, working with Butler's dual conceptualization of "the precarious" (Butler 2006, 2009), Isabell Lorey's notion of "governmental precarization" (2011; cf. 2015), and illustrative cases from Lorey and Lisa Parks (2009), who both tackle the *mattering* effects of precarity on human bodies and subjectivity, albeit in different ways. In both cases, the readers will hear echoes of Butler's concept of performativity and Foucault's work on biogovernmentality.

In *Frames of War* (2009) and "Precarious Life" (2012), Butler initiates philosophical reflections on the precarious—a concept that is twofold: precariousness and precarity. Precariousness, she explains, speaks to the ontological vulnerability that characterizes living entities. This vulnerability stems in part from their organic status. Living entities can be harmed or become ill; they die. For Butler, there is more. It is specifically the inherent sociality of living beings that renders them ontologically precarious. Living beings need relationships with others to become, to grow, to be part of the world, and to dwell in it. Life depends and thrives on sociality. For Butler, precariousness as ontological is to be understood within an ontology that is immanent, that is, always in-the-making, context bound, and relational.[6]

Butler's concept of precarity complicates the story whereby lives can be apprehended as "precarious," that is, as the result of situated social, cultural, and historical considerations whereby some forms of precariousness are amplified and other attenuated. For example, specific and situated sociocultural norms participate in an ordering and a distribution of precariousness, that is, whereby some forms of precariousness will be recognized as precarious by the dominant or hegemonic groups in given communities or in society, and consequently apprehended and responded to as such by the powers that be. Other forms of precariousness, however, fail to be recognized as precariousness and therefore to entice ethical responses or attention from others. They are not seen as precariousness by socially agreed-upon norms, which means that social provisions such as institutions of care or compensations and benefits (e.g., social nets, benefits or programs, care organizations) capable of alleviating these forms of precariousness are not put to the task for these lives or in these situations.

For Butler, precarity is more accurately understood as a hegemonic institution of what counts/is legitimized as "precariousness." These practices establish what forms of precariousness ought to be considered "universal" to all humans as opposed to those specific to a particular subgroup or individual. In the latter case, the individual is usually deemed accountable and responsible for her situation and its deleterious effects; the state or society is not responsible to address, prevent, or redress. This ordering practice is of course exacerbated by neoliberalism, where the figure of the responsible and self-sovereign individual dominates. This practice also contributes to the intensification and exacerbation of the precariousness of those whose forms of precariousness are not seen or are devalued; individuals are left with the burden of their situation resting solely on their shoulders. Precarity thus hierarchizes forms of precariousness, legitimizing some and denying others. It is through the institution of mechanisms meant to alleviate, respond to, prevent, or neutralize (some) precariousness (but not others) that precarity participates in creating precariousness.

To Butler's concepts of precariousness and precarity, Lorey adds another dimension: that of governmental precarization. Working with Foucault's concepts of biopower and governmentality, Lorey (2009, 2011, 2015) characterizes governmental precarization as a mode of governance that is unique to the "neoliberal times" of advanced capitalism. It refers to a process whereby a person participates in generating *more* precariousness for herself and others, and ontologically so: that is, by adhering to certain considerations regarding creative work and productivity, as well as selfhood (i.e., self-realization/creation), a person comes to adopt and to perform (i.e., to embody) particular behaviors and attitudes that in actuality exacerbate and create more precarity. Examples of such behaviors would be preferring part-time or contract work to permanent employment because you do not have to work from an office and at fixed hours, or opting for self-employment but without touching social benefits because one considers one has the flexibility of one's schedule and projects. Of course, it is not "precariousness" per se that individuals opting for such situations of employment desire, but rather the features that are perceived as constitutive of freedom of work, creative work, or self-productivity at work are intimately tied to precarity in neoliberal economies.

Through governmental precarization, one participates in the actualization of more precariousness for an increasing number of others, and differently so, meaning that differences of precariousness themselves proliferate differentially.[7] In neoliberal times too, as an author such as Rosalyn Diprose (2002) notably insists, the figure of the liberal-humanist self-sovereign, rational, able-bodied, and responsible "person" continues to dominate and inform the social and individual imaginaries of one given culture or society (Diprose 2002, ch. 9; see also Code 2006, introduction). People are increasingly individualized and held as the sole culprits of their situation, and their precariousness. As "capable" and "rational" individuals, it is demanded that they be able to make their own independent, enlightened, and rational choices. Through governmental precarization, a person is enticed to invite precariousness into her life—but also into that of others, and even *of* the world.[8] This is the case because she comes to see the precariousness that may come to befall her as her responsibility and will similarly see and apprehend the precariousness lived by or befalling others the same way, and hold them responsible for it.

Lorey (2011, 197–98) uses the example of cultural producers to illustrate this new process. Some cultural producers, such as researchers or creative workers, hold on to the idea that "creativity" requires a particular type of everyday freedom for it to happen. Yet, often the procedures that regiment "regular work" (i.e., permanent employment) prevent creativity and productivity to happen freely. Specifically, a standardized and structured organization of labor such as the nine-to-five workday, five days a week, with a fixed office, regulated times for break, statuary holidays, mandatory and limited days for vacations and sickness, and so forth are progressively viewed by cultural workers as hindering creativity. They will resort to situations of self-employment or part-time or contract work, which are perceived as more effective from the viewpoint of work productivity, but this is most often done at the expense of valuing or accounting for the other dimensions of a person's life—personal, emotional, familial, and so on:

> The common parameters of cultural producers, however, should be that they are well or even very well educated, between twenty-five and forty years-old, without children, and more or less intentionally in a precarious employment situation. They pursue temporary jobs, live from projects and pursue contract work from several clients at the same time, one right after the other, usually without sick pay, paid vacations, or unemployment compensation, and without any job security, thus with no or only minimal social protection. The forty-hour week is an illusion. Working time and free time have no clearly defined borders. Work and leisure can no longer be separated. In the non-paid time, they accumulate a great deal of knowledge, which is not paid for extra, but is naturally called for and used in the context of paid work, etc. (Lorey 2009, 197)

In her study, Lorey observed that many of the features that are seen as enabling creative work and productivity are also conditions that perpetuate a self-sovereign conception of the autonomous individual. Mobilizing Foucault's concept of "governmentality," she shows how cultural workers espouse (i.e., perform) increasingly an "entrepreneurial" conception of the self (see also Peters 2009; Standing 2014) whereby the person is conceived as individually responsible but also capable of making (crafting/sculpting) herself as self. Freedom and flexibility are thus here viewed as essential components to such self-making. But veiled in this narrative is the questionable, erroneous, conception of the "human person," which is neither stable (able-bodied) throughout time, nor universal, or independent of relationships and various supports (e.g., social, familial). Many feminists, care ethicists and critical disability thinkers have worked to show that this claim and conception of autonomy is a myth. Thinkers such as Carol Gilligan (1993, 2003), Joan C. Tronto (1993, 2013), Eva Feder Kittay (2013), Diprose (2002, 2011, 2013), Code (1987, 1991, 2006), and Catriona Mackenzie and Natalie Stoljar (2000) have produced powerful alternatives to conceptions of strict autonomy. For examples, see the concepts of relational autonomy (Mackenzie and Stoljar 2000), intercorporeal generosity (Diprose 2002), and the person as always a second person first (Code 1987, 1991).

For thinkers such as Lorey and Diprose, the endurance and pervasiveness of the neo/liberal figure of the sovereign self, autonomous, and rational person, coupled with the rise of the model of the entrepreneurial self, serve to ensure the continuous denial of the underlying complex and relational networks that sustain and enable this neo/liberal conception of autonomy. Moreover, as Diprose has pointed out, there are further denials: of corporeal gifts, such as care and reproductive labor, that is, of the economy of affects (cf. Gutierrez-Rodriguez 2014); of the value of certain forms of labor and people at the expense of others; and even of the ground upon which lives are lived (e.g., the appropriation of lands, such as those of Aboriginal communities; Diprose 2002, 146–47). Of course, maintaining the myth of the self-sovereign individual is neither easy nor automatic. It requires complex and ongoing processes, the description of which would exceed the space provided here.[9] But to make my position clear, consider the figure of the "entrepreneurial self" that drives so strongly the Western psyche. This is one clear example of how a process is a particular embodiment with its performative effects and is done at the expense of other modes of embodiment. I follow feminist thinkers, care ethicists, and feminist new materialists who argue that these unrealized "selves" would be more *response-able* and sustainable for living and dying in a shared and entangled world.[10] Fundamentally, what is ignored is the centrality of what care ethicists and feminist critical disabilities thinkers have well documented: the *transient nature* of the porous and dynamic "self" fully enmeshed in context.

As seen in Lorey's example, when precariousness and precarity *matter* and come to stay through the effects of governmental precarization, they also become a self-sustaining and new ontology-making process that becomes ingrained and incredibly difficult to change or counteract. As an ontology-making process, governmental precarity participates in making matter (and the world and reality) *matter* as precarious, that is, *as* precariousness inducing. Bodies and matter participate in this new ontology too; they perform it. To demonstrate this, I turn to the analysis of Lisa Park's (2009) of airport securitization following the 9/11 attacks on the World Trade Center.

In *Points of Departure: The Culture of US Airport Screening*, Parks (2009) describes some of the material and discursive transformations that took place in airports after 9/11. Airport security, she explains, literally exploded as an ontology-making process, whereby new bodies and practices not only came into being and populated the world but also came to stay. The design, implementation, endurance, and mutation of new techniques and objects (including human and nonhuman bodies) that went into supporting and creating airport surveillance (e.g., monitoring, security, and securitization) are multiple. First, consider how individuals had to be hired as agents and then trained; how this training had to be developed and refined, in intimate contact with its implementation (i.e., close contact with actual airport processes). New objects and techniques too (e.g., visual practices; the handling, interactions, and encounter of objects and bodies, notably humans) were designed, created, implemented, and systematically modified *intra-actively* with the flows of airport processes, for example visitors' circulation and behaviors, identification of potential and real threats and sources of in/security. New bodily capacity *and* incapacity too:

> The airport checkpoint has become a state-led exercise in hand–eye coordination where workers apply manual and ocular labour to minimise risks. In addition to physical injury, there must be profound

> ontological confusion at the checkpoint. . . . TSA workers sustain more injuries on the job than all other federal employees. In 2004 they were injured four times as often as construction workers and seven times as often as miners (Strohm, 2005 [Cited in text]). . . . Most common injuries are muscle and back strains due to heavy lifting, tendonitis, hernias and cuts and lacerations sustained while reaching into bags for sharp objects. (Parks 2009, 167)

Note how these encounters are intra-active rather than interactive: that is, they are made together ("together-apart," as Barad [2007, 2014] describes, the ontology-making process that is agential realism; see endnote #3). Co-constitutive, emerging together, and linked. There is also no "going back"; new objects and techniques are here to stay, although they will transform and evolve. But bodies and subjectivities are transformed by such introductions; new selves emerge, who are marked for specific (some and not other) trajectories of *mattering*. This is what Barad would call an "enfolding becoming" (Barad 2007, 502).[11]

For Parks, new airport security objects, techniques, skills, and processes translated into the irrevocably and irreversible material and discursive transformation of those involved with and in them such as the security agent who receives training and *intra-acts* with these new objects, that is, the instruments of surveillance as newly made "objects of observation." These individuals are being trained to identify and perceive insecurity, which means that they are intimately and ontologically involved in the production of in/security. These agents tackle newly seen and made objects, which are being identified (i.e., which *matter,* become seen) as sources of in/security primordially. Likewise, visitors are seen/observed as potential carriers of suspicious items or embodiers of suspicious behaviors. Think also of the interaction and intra-action that enfold for those who think and who tackle "objects of airport in/security," for example shoes that are considered as sources of contaminants, removed, handled, observed in new ways; human bodies that are "called upon" and regulated by curt and systematizing voices, pushed in lines, made "orderly"; injunctions reiterated to behave and create responsible travelers ("Do not lose sight of your belongings"). These are all new registries of emotions that are produced and put in circulation, thus producing a new and "here to stay" economy of affects (cf. Gutierrez-Rodriguez [2014] on this concept). Ultimately, from this mode of constant suspicion is activated a particular epistemic frame—and not others. Objects *matter* as "matters" and active sources/ creators of in/security. Finally, the "new" bodies and practices of airport security also participate in the *virtualization* of "others," that is, bodies, objects, or practices, but more precisely, given how each of these are actually entanglements of matter and meaning, always in the process of being made intra-actively, how they *matter* is significant (i.e., those that will not become "actual" or that have been virtualized; on the virtual and the virtualization of matter in agential realism, or rather the "void," see Barad 2007, 354; 2010, 254; see also Avery F. Gordon [2008] on "material ghosts").

With this example, one can see the material and *mattering* effects of *in/security* on matter and how it affects an agential reality, the ontological enfolding that is the real, that is a dynamic ontology (Barad 2007, 180–81).[12] The effects of "neoliberal times" are worrisome because they "precarize" bodies, create and exacerbate precariousness. Yet, the insights of FNM on matter as dynamic, open, ontologically indeterminate, and agential provide us tools to interact/intra-act differently with the various matters of a new ontology of the precarious, whereby we can respond ethically to precarity and bring about new ways and new trajectories of *mattering* precariousness, counteracting the effects of the emergence of this new ontology.

In the following section, I examine feminist new materialist Wilson's (2008, 2015) work in biology and her approach of *organic empathy* as one particularly inspiring and effective caring approach that can support the work of care ethicists. This approach provides one of the cornerstones for a feminist new materialist contribution of care ethics.

Organic Empathy and Precarious Matter as "Hurt" Matter

Wilson's work consists of a close feminist new materialist examination of recent developments in human biology, specifically the "gut" and metabolic processes, as well as psychophysical states and psychotherapeutic treatments that involve pharmaceutical drugs. Her analyses show that human biology increasingly reveals and adheres to an open and dynamic conception of biological function and matter. She provides varied examples of human biology's dynamic, relational, and agential "nature" and practical tools to work *with* matter, notably to trigger alternative courses of *mattering* of biological matter.

In "Organic Empathy: Feminism, Psychopharmaceuticals, and the Embodiment of Depression" (2008) and *Gut Feminism* (2015), Wilson explains that in the treatment of depression with psychotherapeutic treatments, drugs continue to be designed to "speak" solely to the brain. Similarly, the psychotherapeutic methods that accompany the usage of such drugs generally pay little attention to organic matter, or do so only in passing, as a somewhat passive vehicle whose responses are expected to be straightforward, unidimensional at best, and relatively stable, despite the fact that in order to reach the brain, a drug must circulate through an entire organic network:

> The synthesis of serotonin requires ongoing commerce between the brain and the gut and the cultural milieu. . . . Too narrow a focus on the brain as the sole biological source of psychological malady will obstruct the lines of connection that tie organ to organ and that underpin the biological possibility of recovery. (Wilson 2008, 384–85)

Wilson's research shows that little or no attention is paid to how the body is affected—and its own capacity to respond, its agency, is altered—by depressive moods and food disorders. This lack of attention, interest, and care, according to Wilson, can contribute to the failure or lack of positive responsiveness to a particular treatment, especially in cases where a food disorder is present. This is the case, Wilson (2015, 60–65) demonstrates, with regards to cases where food disorders intersect (or rather intra-act) with cases of depression. Indeed, even today, scientists largely continue to struggle and to disagree with regards to where the seat of depression truly lies when there is the presence of a food disorder. Is it in the brain or "in the gut"? Is it physiological or psychological? (Wilson 2004, 83–84; 2015, 15) As Wilson (2015, 84) points out, studies show that more often than not, when a food disorder is present, psychopharmaceutical treatments of depression rarely succeed. This, her FNM-informed research shows, is because there is a lack of attention on the body as viscera, a complex, indeterminate (in-the-making), and agential organic network composed of organic processes (rather than discrete, separate, and self-contained organs) that continually reshapes itself and does so irreversibly, with attention here paid to its material composition (matter): “the gut *is* an organ of mind: it ruminates, deliberates, comprehends” (Wilson 2015, 5). In the case of food disorders/depressive mood intra-action, Wilson’s study shows that there is no single (one, quantifiable) siege of the depressive mode (i.e., solely localizable in the brain). Rather, it appears the depressive mode installs itself throughout the body, in the viscera: “pharmacological data clearly indicate that antidepressants work with the whole body” (Wilson 2015, 103).

For Wilson, however, the issue goes beyond the mere ineffectiveness of drugs to treat depression. Drugs that focus solely on the brain, in a conversation with the brain, have various and multidimensional effects (e.g., corporeal and incorporeal) on the body/viscera. Yet, those fail to be seen or taken into account by the practitioners who focus only on the brain (Wilson 2008, 2015). Even if the drug’s effects on organs other than the brain are tangential, they nevertheless exist and *matter,* in an ongoing and an agential way, that is, future oriented, taking on “a life” of its own (Wilson 2015, 99). These effects are real enactments; they leave traces on matter-as-mattering that will (in)form matter’s becoming, akin to an ongoing mode of “re-*member*-ing” (Barad 2007, 394; see also Barad 2014; Dionne 2018, 2019).

For Wilson, to entice or “install” new processes within the body (e.g., damaged or impeded processes), organic matters and processes as viscera require unique forms of intra-active care, that is, of attention, of response. It is not enough that a drug circulates and reaches the brain. Organic processes are complex and spread across organs as dynamic networks; they constantly remake themselves, and therefore it is not solely the organs that should be targeted as the main “interlocutors.” The “picture” of human biology as “organ-ic” and “organism-ic” causes issues because it participates in the establishment of an epistemology and a concomitant *agnotology* (i.e., epistemology of ignorance) where depressive states are predominantly and perhaps exclusively seen through certain categories, medicalized, and thus preventing the apparition of other understandings. Wilson draws from Sándor Ferenczi’s notion of organic thought to highlight a more agential reality of organs and the body as viscera:

> Many feminist theorists seem to gesture toward a flat organic realm elsewhere as a way of securing a more valuable or dynamic account of politics closer to home. The organic—conceptually dull and politically

> dangerous—lurks at the periphery . . . , underwriting the claims about embodiment. . . .
>
> Ferenczi provides one way through this impasse. Under Ferenczi, biology is strange matter, proficient at the kinds of action (regressions, perversions, strangulations, condensations, displacements) usually attributed only to nobiological systems. This biology is not the flat . . . substrate seen in many feminist or neuro-humanities arguments. . . .
>
> Conversion hysteria . . . shows the dynamic character of all organic matter. (Wilson 2008, 58–59)

In Wilson's picture of the viscera, however, the brain never stands alone. Instead, the viscera works by way of "connections," as a network whereby the viscera exists/becomes within and across those connections, rather than as a system, in which discrete and separate entities (i.e., the organs) interact with one another (all the while retaining their putatively strict and impermeable boundaries): "we can . . . think about a broader network of alliances in which . . . the body (gut) has powerful effects on how the drug works and how mind is mobilized" (Wilson 2015, 99):

> Such notions of the brain as an autonomous, self-contained organ are common enough in both the scientific and popular imaginary. . . . The synthesis of serotonin requires ongoing commerce between the brain and the gut and the cultural milieu. . . .
>
> Too narrow a focus on the brain as the sole biological source of psychological malady will obstruct the lines of connection that tie organ to organ and that underpin the biological possibility of recovery. (2015, 384–85)

Working with an agential and affective conception of matter, Wilson suggests that there are other ways to interact (and intra-act) with the viscera affected by a depressive mood, whereby more positive and successful outcomes can arise. First, a drug-based psychotherapeutic treatment of depressive moods actually involves the whole body as viscera, with different organs and organic processes exhibiting different responses to drugs, even as they are aimed only at the brain (Wilson 2008, 58–59; 2015, 384–85). Intentional or not, the drug nonetheless engages with the viscera in a number of ways, but also, importantly, in some and not others, thus making "preconceptions." Such engagements affect a "new configuration" akin to an affective economy that entices specific and unique affective responses from different places (i.e., organic processes, networks) within the viscera (Wilson 2008, 379).

As a response, a more caring and careful one, Wilson proposes to embed an empathic approach in the psychopharmaceutical treatment of depression inspired by psychotherapy. Relationships are central to the therapeutic encounters. Specifically, relationships are conceived as connections or even bridges in the psychological state that operate as pathways or supporting strings. Therapeutic encounters are often going to reveal that a person who has experienced a traumatic event has established particular relationships with either objects or persons specifically in order to be able to survive their trauma. Such relationships or bridges, however, can be damaging or hurtful, that is, coping mechanisms that are unsustainable in the long run. New relationships or pathways must be established, but this cannot be done by simply severing the ultimately hurtful coping mechanisms. By treading carefully, creating a temporary relationship with a new object or the therapist, previous pathways can be healed (Wilson 2008, 385–90; 2015, ch. 3).

For Wilson, psychotherapy's ontology of relationships conceives of relationships as integral to becoming—living, dwelling, contributing, surviving. In this ontology of relationships, relations are considered the strong and secure bounds that are necessary for any person to become in the world, to respond, and to act. Using this psychotherapeutic conception of relationships, Wilson advocates for a partnership-like approach to organic matters. Such an approach, which deals with organic processes as agents, can entice more positive and agential responsiveness from organic matters and thus participate in the creation of an organic response-ability (i.e., an ethic/culture of the unique, differential response). Through psychotherapy, patients can strengthen their capacity to recreate positive and beneficial relationships and connections that will enable them to sustain themselves. But to do this, their capacity to have and create positive and beneficial connections must be healed or else such connections will not be sustainable in the long run. The same goes with organic matter for Wilson.

Organic empathy is modeled on approaches of psychotherapy, whereby broken or damaged pathways and connections within the psychological structure are repaired by temporarily creating new and supportive relationships that enable new pathways to be formed, that are strong and enduring. Behind this approach is the philosophy that relationships are necessary for a person to *be* a person—relationships are of various types and not necessarily uniquely with people or objects that are external to a person. Yet, without this patchwork of connections and relationships, a person is unsupported and unable to "weave" herself in the world and thus be and become (Wilson 2015, 119).

Wilson's approach cares for organic matters. The approach is about enticing and disposing the knower to adopt new noticing capacities, for example new corporeal availabilities toward matter and matter's dynamic and unique agential capacity. It is also about making matter interested in order to entice its participation and capacity to participate. Organic matters, if properly and uniquely disposed (invited, enticed, and cultivated), can be strong allies in curing depressive moods.[13]

A FNM Ethic of Care in Precarious Times

Throughout this article, I have engaged various feminist thinkers with the promise of crafting a FNM ethic of care that, in my view, offers a strong, effective, concrete, and feasible approach for care ethics to respond to precarity in neoliberal times. FNM offers as a unique contribution—a conception of material and discursive matter as dynamic, affective, indeterminate, and agential. Because there is no matter that exists "out there" as fixed, new ways of *mattering* of preoccupying material and discursive matters, such as precarity in neoliberal times, can emerge (i.e., can be enticed or co-made). Care ethics, in other words, is always and already participating in the ongoing enfolding, ontology-making project that is the world as agential realism. Yet, how it participates and responds is the relevant question. The materiality of matter matters and does so in different ways. Every past enactment exists and will stay, but it is not fixed; it does not sit still. Modes of responsibility will not be strict but rather partial and shared, a shared and distributed agency and responsibility.[14] More importantly (or troublesome perhaps), materiality and thus material enactments are lively and agential, meaning that they too participate in ongoing processes of mattering integral to this ongoing enfolding ontology.

Matters must be encountered with care and cared for. They must also be healed and recognized as damaged too in the context of a governmental precarization—healthy and sustainable pathways or relationships that enable a person to become, to weave herself in a world that is always in-the-making must be created. Wilson's organic empathy provides a model for how to start such work, to learn anew, to hear, to notice, to listen, and then to *work with*, respond to, and help in creating a capacity for others to respond as well.

The aim of this chapter was threefold. I first presented the ethico-onto-epistemological approach of Barad, agential realism, which provides the foundation to see matter as ontologically open and dynamic as well as agential. What is "material" is thus not fixed or determined, but rather it is irreversible. In other words, any enactment *does matter,* but how one understands materiality, in this dynamic and immanent ontology, is drastically altered. Any past enactment thus requires a response that cannot be ignored without consequence. She also shows us the agential role(s) that matter can play (and in multifaceted ways).

Part 2 tackled the issue of "precarity" by proposing a conceptualization that relies on the works of Butler and Lorey. Inspired by Butler's twofold concept of the "precarious" (precariousness and precarity), I explored Lorey's Foucauldian notion of governmental precarization. With this third component, I have shown how, in neoliberal times, we are shifting into an ontology of precarity, whereby precarity comes to matter, intensify, and exacerbate itself. This is of course a great source of worry for care ethicists and a growing target of preoccupation and action. I completed this contribution by proposing concrete tools to respond to precarity and enable new courses of *mattering* of precarious matters and this precarious ontology (e.g., organic empathy toward the multifaceted effects of neoliberalism and precarity, notably on the emergence of harmful modes of embodiment). With Wilson's organic empathy, we have seen how matters can be enticed as actants and healed, and with them, new courses of *mattering* of a dynamic ontology can start to enfold.

Matter understood agentially can help care ethicists attend with care to the effects of precarity in precarious neoliberal times. Care ethics is enriched by considering FNM's views of a world that is increasingly agential in light of its new, constantly increasingly, situation of shared, mutually entangled, and complexifying conditions of globalization, growing sickness, fragile ecological transformations, and the various insecurities that trouble us. Let us, in care ethics, open up the communities of partners and allies to the nonhuman that is matter *it*self.

Notes

1. Given that this chapter relies on the concept, rendered as the verb "to matter," that is, as in the form *mattering*, a preliminary explanation is in order. When I employ the word "to matter," I point to (at least) two definitions and usages of the term. First, according to the Oxford Dictionary, "matter" as a noun refers to physical substance that would be separate from mind or spirit or energy. Second, as a verb, "to matter" is defined as to convey that something is important or significant, influential.

2. Contributions that one can say provide a good overall sense of what FNM is are: Alaimo and Hekman (2008), Alaimo (2000, 2010, 2016), Barad (1996, 2003, 2007, 2010, 2011, 2012, 2014, 2017), de la Bellacasa (2011, 2017), Despret (2004, 2014, 2016), Giffney and Hird (2008), Haraway (2008, 2016, 2017), Hayward (2012, 2010a, 2010b), Hustak and Myers (2012), Myers (2012, 2015a, 2015b, 2017), Myers and Dumit (2011), Tsing (2015), and Wilson (2008, 2015). The history of FNM can also be traced (back) to feminist science studies, with foundational thinkers such as Sandra Harding (1986, 2016), Haraway (1988, 1991), and Strathern (2005).

3. I use italics when the verb "to matter" is used to encompass the entanglement of material and meaning-making processes.

4. Barad creates the neologism of *spacetimemattering* because her theory of agential realism "introduces an altogether different understanding of dynamics . . . [where] the . . . notions of causality, . . . agency, space, time, and matter, are all reworked" (Barad 2007, 179). She further argues that "intra-actions are the dynamics through which temporarily and spatiality are produced and iteratively reconfigured in the materialization of phenomena and the (re)making of the material-discursive boundaries and their constitutive exclusions" (179). Following this, we understand it is never sufficient to speak of a process of *mattering* whereby entities acquire (temporary) determinacy that allows actions and knowledge (as well as time and therefore history to happen); *mattering* processes—processes of bounded, internal, entangled "determinacy"—implicate space and time as well, thus also affecting their identity. "Matter is not situated in the world," she continues, "[it] is worlding in its materiality . . . Spatiality is intra-actively produced." So is time. "Space, time, and matter are mutually constituted through the dynamics of iterative intra-action" (181).

Phenomena, for Barad, is the concept she uses to speak of what is the "situation" from which an *object of observation* and *agencies of observation* acquire a certain configuration/temporary determinacy that allows them to be known but only insofar as their relationships/entanglements/intra-action is acknowledged. "Phenomena are ontologically primitive relations—relations without preexisting relata." They designate "particular instances of wholeness" where things are "together-apart (Barad 2007, 139, 118–21; see also 114–15, 127–28). She distinguishes it from how phenomenologists use it (see Barad 2007, 412n30).

"Together-apart" is the term she started using more consistently after 2012 that describes the result of the "agential cut/agential separation" whereby things are "split," separated from an ontological situation of *indeterminacy* but through the enactment of a single slice that produces two or more, and inherently links "entities" to one another: they are separated but linked by their common origin. On the concept of "together-apart," see Barad (2007, 179, 394). See also Barad (2014).

5. Barad extends Bohr's principle of *indeterminacy* to describe how reality is made. Yet, what is "made" requires a profound rethinking about the nature of identity, as relational, as entanglement. As part of his well-known disagreement with Werner Heisenberg's principle of *uncertainty* in knowing, Bohr argues that scientists are not so much confronted by the limits of their instruments when attempting to acquire knowledge about the world. Rather, they face matter that, without context, is ontologically indeterminate. With the help of Bohr's work, Barad explains that, ontologically speaking, matter/materiality can (and does) acquire determinacy, but this determinacy cannot be isolated from its context of emergence. Each configuration is irrevocably tied to other things, notably the apparatuses of knowledge that participate in the emergence of a given object. For Barad/Bohr, instruments of knowledge, such as measuring devices, become irrevocable parts of the "object" of knowledge's identity.

6. For a critical engagement of Butler's work on the "precarious," see Diprose (2011, 2013) and Ann V. Murphy (2011).

7. Forms of precariousness do not "speak" to one another and often do not compare or even "see" one another. Precariousness can be "all-encompassing," and especially so when complicated through the operations of "precarity," that is, the sociopolitical ordering of precariousness. It can "seize" fully the attention of a person, or rather, her corporeal affective configuration, rendering her thus unavailable affectively to other forms of precarious as precariousness.

Joan Tronto's *Care Ethics* considers that care is comprised of four sub-elements: (1) care as "*attentiveness,* a proclivity to become aware of need"; (2) care as "*responsibility,* a willingness to respond and take care of need"; (3) care as "*competence,* the skill of providing good and successful care"; and (4) care as "*responsiveness,* [the] consideration of the position of others as they see it and recognition of the potential for abuse in care" (Tronto 1993, 126–36). This chapter shows that all of these sub-elements are at stake in the onto-ethico-epistemology of FNM.

8. That is, a world that is lively, always transforming/becoming, in the process of being-made, and facing increased challenges with environmental disorders and precariousness. For examples, see Tsing et al. (2017) and Tsing (2015).

9. For examples, see the works of feminist thinkers such as Diprose (2002), Luce Irigaray (1974, 1983, 1984), as well as of feminist disability thinkers. Notably, see the edited volume of Kim Q. Hall (2011).

10. As examples, see concepts in critical disability studies, feminist disability studies, and feminist care ethics or bioethics such as complex personhood, relational selves, and social citizenship (cf. Bartlett and O'Connor 2010; Dionne 2019, 2013; Lanoix 2007; Mackenzie and Stoljar 2000; Nedelsky 2011).

11. "Becoming is not an unfolding in time but the inexhaustible dynamism of the enfolding of mattering" (Barad 2007, 180).

12. On the topic of an ontology of in/security or *securization,* readers are invited to see the respective works of Claudia Aradau (2004, 2011). See also Aradau and Van Munster (2007, 2011) and Mark Neocleous (2007).

13. The concept of "relationship" is also predominant in the work and practice of FNM. Relationships are tantamount notably because this is how anything becomes, that is, through intra-action, intra-actively. Consider the works of de la Bellacasa (2011, 2017). See also Marilyn Strathern's foundational work on *partial connections* that inform much of FNM, notably Donna Haraway's concept of *situated knowledges* (1991), and her most recent work in the Anthropocene (2008, 2016, 2017). The concept of relationship is also central in Diprose's feminist work (2002, 2011, 2013) and in feminist new materialist/anthropologist Anna L. Tsing (2015) who explores relationships between humans and organic nonhumans (e.g., mushrooms and other "environmental damaged" matters). See also Tsing et al. (2017).

14. See Jane Bennett (2010), Haraway (1991, 1997, 2016), and Tsing (2015) on these concepts.

Works Cited

Alaimo, Stacy. 2000. *Undomesticated Ground: Recasting Nature as Feminist Space.* Ithaca, N.Y.: Cornell University Press.

Alaimo, Stacy. 2010. *Bodily Natures: Science, Environment, and the Material Self.* Indianapolis: Indiana University Press.

Alaimo, Stacy. 2016. *Exposed: Environmental Politics and Pleasures in Posthuman Times.* Minneapolis: University of Minnesota Press.

Alaimo, Stacy, and Susan Hekman, eds. 2008. *Material Feminisms.* Indianapolis: Indiana University Press.

Aradau, Claudia. 2004. "Security and the Democratic Scene: Desecuritization and Emancipation." *Journal of International Relations and Development* 7 (4): 388–413.

Aradau, Claudia. 2011. "Security that Matters: Critical Infrastructure and Objects of Protection." *Security Dialogue* 41, no. 5: 491–514.

Aradau, Claudia, and Rens Van Munster. 2007. "Governing Terrorism through Risk: Taking Precautions, (Un)knowing the Future." *European Journal of International Relations* 13 (1): 89–115.

Aradau, Claudia, and Rens Van Munster. 2011. *Politics of Catastrophe: Genealogies of the Unknown.* New York: Routledge.

Barad, Karen. 1996. "Meeting the Universe Halfway: Realism and Social Constructivism without Contradiction." In *Feminism, Science, and the Philosophy of Science,* edited by Jack Nelson, 161–94. Dordrecht, the Netherlands: Springer Science & Business Media.

Barad, Karen. 2003. "Posthumanist Performativity: Toward an Understanding of How Matter Comes to Matter." *Signs: Journal of Women in Culture and Society* 28 (3): 801–31.

Barad, Karen. 2007. *Meeting the Universe Halfway: Quantum Physics and the Entanglement of Matter and Meaning.* Durham, N.C.: Duke University Press.

Barad, Karen. 2010. "Quantum Entanglements and Hauntological Relations of Inheritance: Dis/continuities, Spacetime Enfoldings, and Justice-to-come." *Derrida Today* 3 (2): 240–68.

Barad, Karen. 2011. "Nature's Queer Performativity." *Qui Parle: Critical Humanities and Social Sciences* 19 (2): 121–58.

Barad, Karen. 2012. "On Touching—The Inhuman that Therefore I Am." *Differences* 23 (3): 206–23.

Barad, Karen. 2014. "Diffracting Diffraction: Cutting Together-Apart." *Parallax* 20 (3): 168–87.

Barad, Karen. 2017. "Troubling Time/s and Ecologies of Nothingness: Re-turning, Re-membering, and Facing the Incalculable." *New Formations* 92 (92): 56–86.

Bartlett, Ruth, and Deborah O'Connor, eds. 2010. *Broadening the Dementia Debate: Towards Social Citizenship*. Bristol, UK: Policy Press.

Bennett, Jane. 2010. *Vibrant Matter: A Political Ecology of Things*. Durham, N.C.: Duke University Press.

Butler, Judith. 2003. *Bodies that Matter: On the Discursive Limits of Sex*. New York: Taylor & Francis.

Butler, Judith. 2006. *Precarious Life: The Powers of Mourning and Violence*. New York: Verso Books.

Butler, Judith. 2009. *Frames of War: When Is Life Grievable?* London: Verso Books.

Butler, Judith. 2012. "Precarious Life, Vulnerability, and the Ethics of Cohabitation." *Journal of Speculative Philosophy* 26 (2): 134–51.

Code, Lorraine. 1987. "Second Persons." *Canadian Journal of Philosophy* 17 (suppl. 1): 357–82.

Code, Lorraine. 1991. *What Can She Know? Feminist Theory and the Construction of Knowledge*. Ithaca, N.Y.: Cornell University Press.

Code, Lorraine. 2006. *Ecological Thinking: The Politics of Epistemic Location*. Oxford: Oxford University Press.

de La Bellacasa, Maria Puig. 2011. "Matters of Care in Technoscience: Assembling Neglected Things." Social Studies of Science 41 (1): 85–106.

de La Bellacasa, Maria Puig. 2017. *Matters of Care: Speculative Ethics in More than Human Worlds*. Minneapolis: University of Minnesota Press.

Despret, Vincianes. 2004. "The Body We Care For: Figures of Anthropo-Zoo-Genesis." *Body and Society* 10 (2–3): 111–34.

Despret, Vincianes. 2014. *Que diraient les animaux, si . . . on leur posait les bonnes questions?* Paris: La Découverte.

Despret, Vincianes. 2016. *Penser comme un rat*. Versailles, France: Éditions Quae.

Dionne, Émilie. 2013. "Thinking the Pluri-Person through Ironic Practices of Story-telling." PhD diss., York University.

Dionne, Émilie. 2018. "'Excitable Matter(s), Angry Matter(s): Ontologies-in-the-Making.' Joined Review of *Rendering Life Molecular: Models, Modelers, Excitable Matter*, by Natasha Myers (2017), and *Gut Feminism*, by Elizabeth A. Wilson (2015)." *Feminist Review* 120 (1): 152–56.

Dionne, Émilie. 2019. "The Pluri-Person: A Feminist New Materialist Figure for a Precarious World." *Symposium* 23 (2): 94–112.

Diprose, Rosalyn. 2002. *Corporeal Generosity: On Giving with Nietzsche, Merleau-Ponty, and Levinas*. New York: State University of New York Press.

Diprose, Rosalyn. 2011. "Building and Belonging amid the Plight of Dwelling." *Angelaki* 16 (4): 59–72.

Diprose, Rosalyn. 2013. "Corporeal Interdependence: From Vulnerability to Dwelling in Ethical Community." *SubStance* 42 (3): 185–204.

Giffney, Noreen, and Myra J. Hird, eds. 2008. *Queering the Non/Human*. Burlington, Vt.: Ashgate Publishing.

Gilligan, Carol. 1993. *In a Different Voice*. Boston: Harvard University Press.

Gilligan, Carol. 2003. *The Birth of Pleasure: A New Map of Love*. New York: Vintage.

Gordon, Avery F. 2008. *Ghostly Matters: Haunting and the Sociological Imagination*. Minneapolis: University of Minnesota Press.

Gutierrez-Rodriguez, Encarnacíon. 2014. "Domestic Work–Affective Labor: On Feminization and the Coloniality of Labor." *Women's Studies International Forum* 46:45–53.

Hall, Kim Q., ed. 2011. *Feminist Disability Studies*. Indianapolis: Indiana University Press.

Haraway, Donna J. 1988. "Situated Knowledges: The Science Question in Feminism and the Privilege of Partial Perspective." *Feminist Studies* 14 (3): 575–99.

Haraway, Donna J. 1991. *Simians, Cyborgs, and Women: The Reinvention of Nature*. New York: Routledge.

Haraway, Donna J. 1997. *Modest_witness@second millenium. Femaleman_meets_oncomouse*. New York: Routledge.

Haraway, Donna J. 2008. "Otherworldly Conversations, Terran Topics, Local Terms." In *Material Feminisms*, edited by Stacy Alaimo and Susan Hekman, 157–87. Indianapolis: Indiana University Press.

Haraway, Donna J. 2016. *Staying with the Trouble: Making Kin in the Chthulucene*. Durham, N.C.: Duke University Press.

Haraway, Donna J. 2017. "Anthropocene, Capitalocene, Plantationocene, Chthulucene: Making Kin." Multitudes 65 (4): 75–81.

Harding, Susan. 1986. *The Science Question in Feminism*. Ithaca, N.Y.: Cornell University Press.

Harding, Susan. 2016. *Whose Science? Whose Knowledge? Thinking from Women's Lives*. Ithaca, N.Y.: Cornell University Press.

Hayward, Eva. 2010a. "Fingeryeyes: Impressions of Cup Corals." *Cultural Anthropology* 25 (4): 577–99.

Hayward, Eva. 2010b. "Spider City Sex." *Women and Performance: A Journal of Feminist Theory* 20 (3): 225–51.

Hayward, Eva. 2012. "Sensational Jellyfish: Aquarium Affects and the Matter of Immersion." *Differences* 23 (3): 161–96.

Hustak, Carla, and Natasha Myers. 2012. "Involutionary Momentum: Affective Ecologies and the Sciences of Plant/Insect Encounters." *Differences* 23 (3): 74–118.

Irigaray, Luce. 1974. *Speculum de l'autre femme*. Paris: Les Éditions de Minuit.

Irigaray, Luce. 1983. *Ce sexe qui n'en est pas un*. Paris: Les Éditions de Minuit.

Irigaray, Luce. 1984. *Éthique de la différence sexuelle*. Paris: Les Éditions de Minuit.

Kittay, Eva Feder. 2013. *Love's Labor: Essays on Women, Equality and Dependency.* New York: Routledge.

Lanoix, Monique. 2007. "The Citizen in Question." *Hypatia* 22 (4): 113–29.

Latour, Bruno. 2004. "How to Talk about the Body? The Normative Dimension of Science Studies." *Body and Society* 10 (2–3): 205–29.

Lorey, Isabell. 2009. "Governmentality and Self-Precarization: On the Normalization of Cultural Producers." In *Art and Contemporary Critical Practice: Reinventing Institutional Critique*, edited by Gerald Raunig and Gene Ray, 187–202. London: may fly.

Lorey, Isabell. 2011. "Governmental Precarization." *Traversal Journal* 8:1–11.

Lorey, Isabell. 2015. *State of Insecurity: Government of the Precarious.* New York: Verso Books.

Mackenzie, Catriona, and Nathalie Stoljar, eds. 2000. *Relational Autonomy: Feminist Perspectives on Autonomy, Agency, and the Social Self.* Oxford: Oxford University Press.

Martin, Aryn, Natasha Myers, and Ana Viseu. 2015. "The Politics of Care in Technoscience." *Social Studies of Science* 45 (5): 625–41.

Murphy, Ann V. 2011. "Corporeal Vulnerability and the New Humanism." *Hypatia* 26 (3): 575–90.

Myers, Natasha. 2012. "Dance your PhD: Embodied Animations, Body Experiments, and the Affective Entanglements of Life Science Research." *Body and Society* 18 (1): 151–89.

Myers, Natasha. 2015a. *Rendering Life Molecular: Models, Modelers, and Excitable Matter.* Durham, N.C.: Duke University Press.

Myers, Natasha. 2015b. "Conversations on Plant Sensing." *Nature Culture* 3:35–66.

Myers, Natasha. 2017. "From the Anthropocene to the Planthroposcene: Designing Gardens for Plant/People Involution." *History and Anthropology* 28 (3): 297–301.

Myers, Natasha, and Joseph Dumit. 2011. "Haptic Creativity and the Mid-Embodiments of Experimental Life." In *A Companion to the Anthropology of the Body and Embodiment.* Vol. 22, edited by Frances E. Mascia-Lees, 239–61. Chichester, UK: Wiley-Blackwell.

Nedelsky, Jennifer. 2011. *Law's Relations: A Relational Theory of Self, Autonomy, and Law.* Oxford: Oxford University Press.

Neocleous, Mark. 2007. "Security, Liberty and the Myth of Balance: Towards a Critique of Security Politics." *Contemporary Political Theory* 6 (2): 131–49.

Parks, Lisa. 2009. "Points of Departure: The Culture of US Airport Screening." In *Deleuze and Law,* edited by Rosi Braidotti, Claire Colebrook, and Patrick Hanafin, 163–78. London: Palgrave Macmillan.

Peters, Michael. 2009. "Education, Enterprise Culture and the Entrepreneurial Self: A Foucauldian Perspective." *The Journal of Educational Enquiry* 2 (2): 58–71.

Standing, Guy. 2014. "The Precariat—The New Dangerous Class." *Amalgam* 6 (6–7): 115–19.

Strathern, Marilyn. 2005. *Partial Connections.* New York: Rowman Altamira.

Tronto, Joan C. 1993. *Moral Boundaries: A Political Argument for an Ethic of Care.* London: Psychology Press.

Tronto, Joan C. 2013. *Caring Democracy: Markets, Equality, and Justice*. New York: New York University Press.

Tsing, Anna L. 2015. *The Mushroom at the End of the World: On the Possibility of Life in Capitalist Ruins*. Princeton, N.J.: Princeton University Press.

Tsing, Anna L., Nils Bubandt, Elaine Gan, and Heather Anne Swanson. 2017. *Arts of Living on a Damaged Planet: Ghosts and Monsters of the Anthropocene*. Minneapolis: University of Minnesota Press.

Wilson, Elizabeth A. 2004. "Gut Feminism." *Differences* 15 (3): 66–94.

Wilson, Elizabeth A. 2008. "Organic Empathy: Feminism, Psychopharmaceuticals, and the Embodiment of Depression." In *Material Feminisms*, edited by Stacy Alaimo and Susan Hekman, 373–99. Indianapolis: Indiana University Press.

Wilson, Elizabeth A. 2015. *Gut Feminism*. Durham, N.C.: Duke University Press.

CHAPTER 11

Precariousness, Precarity, and Gender-Care Politics in Japan

YAYO OKANO

Precarious Japan

When planning to depart Kyoto, Japan, for the inaugural conference of the Care Ethics Research Consortium held on September 28 and 29, 2018, at Portland State University, I was not able to decide from which airport I would leave for the United States until one week before the conference started. Since September 4, when the powerful Typhoon No. 21 hit the Kansai region, including Osaka and Kyoto where I live, Kansai International Airport, which is on a man-made island in Osaka, had been paralyzed for seventeen days. When the Typhoon No. 21 hit, about eight thousand travelers and airport workers were left stranded overnight at the airport, while the two runways were submerged by high waves and the bridge connected to the airport was smashed and broken by a tanker. No one could anticipate when the airport would be operational again.

In summer 2018, Japan experienced numerous typhoons.[1] The country revealed again[2] how vulnerable it is to natural disasters and how precarious the state of its people is. The experience that summer, however, was not unusual, since preparation for emergencies and evacuations is far too familiar for the Japanese people. In fact, there is no place in Japan where residents are completely free from natural disasters.

With Japan's vulnerability to natural disasters in mind, this chapter dares to ask an ironic question: will politically heightened precarity and undoing care make for a strong nation?

To tackle this question, this chapter first briefly describes the current political situation in Japan, especially pressures to amend the Constitution. Second, it emphasizes the significance of a concept of precarity distinguished from that of precariousness by referring to Judith Butler's recent argument on precariousness. As this chapter will discuss in more detail, we as living beings are all precarious because we are indiscriminately dependent on other beings and on the environment. Precarity, however, indicates an unjust situation that has befallen some people because of a lack of basic support from society or the government. How can ethics of care fight against such violent injustice? The conclusion discusses a difficult question about how we can transform an uncaring society into more caring and democratic one.

Whose Responsibility for What and Whom? The Current Political and Social Situation in Japan

Anti-Constitutionalism and the Long-Standing Ambition for a "Real" Army in Japan

On February 3, 2014, at the budget committee of the House of Representatives, former prime minister Abe presented his long-cherished view of the Constitution when he addressed how he understood the Constitution:

> I know that there is a belief that the Constitution constrains the state power. . . . However, that understanding of the Constitution was mainstream in the era of absolute monarchy. Now the Constitution describes a country's future and outlines its ideals. (Abe 2014a, 42)

Nine days after making this statement, Abe also argued that he, as prime minister, could make the final decision on the interpretation of the Constitution. Former prime minister Abe often revealed his unique vision of, or rather antipathy toward, the Constitution during heated debates over Japan's inability to exercise collective self-defense under the Constitution, especially Article 9, which defines the "renunciation of war" based on the reflection of the defeat in the Second World War. Article 9 declares that "land, sea and air forces, as well as other war potential, will never be maintained,"[3] and therefore it has symbolized pacifism in postwar Japan, which converted from the aggressive and expansionist Imperial Japan before the defeat of war. However, to people such as Abe, Article 9 seems to have been the symbol of an inferior country and enforced by the Allied Powers.

After his first cabinet resignation in 2007, Shinzo Abe won the Liberal Democratic Party (LDP) presidential election again in 2012 and became the ninety-sixth prime minister.[4] During the presidential election, he confirmed his commitment to amending the Constitution, especially Article 9, to establish the national defense "army." Since becoming prime minister in December 2012, Abe has persistently attacked the current Constitution, which inevitably reminds us of Japan's history of colonialism, invasions of Asian countries, and war crimes.

In fact, for the LDP, the current Constitution has been a symbol of the nation's shameful history of U.S. occupation after the defeat of the Second World War—an occupation whose policies "oppressed unjustly our idea of nation and patriotism and excessively fragmented and weakened the state power of Japan" through the revision of the Constitution and the educational system (the LDP 1955).[5] This is why the LDP has been so eager to revise the Constitution since the party was founded in 1955.

However, former prime minister Abe's ambition for amending the Constitution is aimed not only at Article 9, which has been the target of the LDP's attack on the Constitution, but also the Constitution as a whole (cf. Okano 2018). Article 9 represents one of the three principles of the Constitution of Japan: pacifism. The two other principles are the sovereignty of the people and the respect for fundamental human rights.

As Abe holds a unique view of the Constitution, regarding it as an "outline of the ideal form of state," the LDP's Draft for the Amendment of the Constitution published in April 2012 (hereafter the LDP Draft) shocked many scholars and citizens[6] because it denies not only Article 9 but also all fundamental principles of the current Constitution. The LDP Draft erased the current preamble, which reflects the atrocities caused by Japan's modern wars.[7] Abe once expressed disdain for this section of the Constitution, describing it as being "strangely humble" (Abe 2013, 127) Instead, the preamble of the LDP Draft proclaims that "the Japanese people defend the country and homeland with honor and a strong sprit, and while respecting fundamental human rights, to respect harmony and to create the nation by helping one another through the family and society as a whole" (Liberal Democratic Party 2012).

Contrary to the current preamble and to Article 1 defining the people's sovereignty, the LDP Draft reads that the Emperor becomes the head of state. Fundamental human rights are restricted by the public interest and public order in Articles 12 and 13 of the LDP Draft. The main point of the LDP's thorough revision of the Constitution is most evident in their deletion of Article 97, which upholds the inviolability of fundamental human rights, considered to be "the fruits of the age-old struggle of man to be free." Furthermore, the LDP Draft added a new provision that allows the state to constrain human rights in times of emergency as declared by the prime minister (Article 98).

Given the consolidation of the state's power and the weakening of human rights found in the LDP Draft, former prime minister Abe's long-held desire to amend Article 9 to establish the national defense army, which can fight against enemies abroad under the supreme command of the prime minister, should be carefully scrutinized. On the one hand, the preamble of the LDP Draft describes the Japanese people's obligation to defend the state through helping each other; on the other hand, the prime minister will be able to exert supreme power to declare an emergency of the state and to command the army. What does this challenge to the Constitution indicate to Japan, whose land and geographic environment are too precarious for people to protect themselves? What are the implications for those such as Abe, who are eager to evoke a sense of international crisis?

As I have already pointed out, Abe often publicly asserted that the Constitution is so "disgraceful"[8] that it leaves peace for Japan dependent on others' faith of peace and finds that it includes what he perceives as petty sentences of apology directed at Western powers. However, curiously enough, his imaginary enemies are not the United States or other Western countries but rather China and North and South Korea, which were once colonized by Japan. According to Abe, under Article 9, essential elements of Japanese sovereignty have been lost because Japan constitutionally lacks the right of belligerency. However, it should also be noted that Japan has been one of the top ten countries in terms of annual military expenditure.[9] Thanks to his strong initiative, military spending has been growing since Abe returned to power in late 2012.

What does Abe want to achieve by amending the Constitution to establish a "real" army? Does he sincerely want to protect people's welfare and safety? To answer this question, I shall turn my attention not to military threat but rather to natural disasters and socioeconomic crises.

Precarious Japan and People Forsaken

As mentioned earlier, during the summer of 2018, Japan had many natural disasters. In Osaka, an earthquake killed four people, including a schoolgirl who was buried under a street wall on June 18. Then, in early July, Typhoon No. 7 struck, lasting for four days and causing severe landslides in many regions such as Hiroshima. More than two hundred people died or went missing because of heavy rainfall. On August 18, Typhoon No. 20 hit the western part of Japan, followed by another, Typhoon No. 21, which hit Osaka, Kyoto, and other Kansai cities on September 4. I myself was unable to decide which flight to take until the last minute. In Japan, people have suffered such severe disasters periodically. The question now is how our representatives, including the prime minister, responded to such precarious conditions in this country.

On July 5, when Typhoon No. 7 was approaching Hiroshima, former prime minister Abe spent the evening with other LDP members at an election campaign party for the upcoming LDP presidential election at the end of September 2018, which he went on to win. Yukio Edano, the leader of the Constitutional Democrat Party, described the typhoon as "a large-scale disaster next to the 2011 Tohoku earthquake and tsunami." Ten cities were hit by unprecedentedly heavy rainfall.

So, what happened to Osaka? On September 7, when the people of Osaka were suffering from no water, electricity, and gas lines in their cities, having still not recovered from Typhoon No. 21, the Osaka governor of those days, Ichiro Matsui, traveled to Okinawa to support a candidate in Okinawa's prefectural election of governor. On September 9, he took a flight to visit Europe to lure attendees at the World Expo and ironically to champion "the disaster-resilient Osaka." Needless to say, his flight was not from Kansai airport but rather from Nagoya airport away from the Kansai region.

Japan has been exposed not only to natural disasters but also to economic stagnation. Since the bubble economy collapsed in 1989, Japan has struggled with the retrenchment of its economy, stagnant labor markets, and shrinking populations, as well as increasing social anxiety (Allison 2013, 30).[10] Because the structural reform launched in the mid-1990s adopted neoliberalist rhetoric, workers in Japan have been facing deregulation of labor conditions in order to pay the price necessary to stimulate the national economy. The reform of the labor market in Japan directly affected and worsened the welfare of the people because the Japanese model of social protection has been characterized as "welfare through work" (Miura 2012).[11] Mari Miura once described its characteristic as "employment protection," which "functionally substituted income maintenance" (2012, 2). "Welfare through work," however, does not function for all types of workers but only for regular workers. While maintaining the breadwinner regime, Japanese employers can enjoy labor market flexibilities. For example, various types of non-regular workers exist outside of the framework of labor law that protects regular workers, such as part-time workers, those with fixed-term contracts, or indirect employment. During recessions, employers can restrict as well as dismiss these non-regular workers. "Japanese employers essentially have a free hand . . . with respect to the use of non-regular workers, which counterbalances the rigidity of employment protection" (Miura 2012, 26).[12]

Because of a series of deregulation of the temporary labor market, the ratio of non-regular workers increased from 20.2 percent in 1990 to 34.4 percent in 2010 (Miura 2012, 74) and 38.3 percent in 2019 (Statistics Bureau of Japan 2020). According to the Ministry of Internal Affairs and Communications (2018), 55.5 percent of working women were in non-regular employment in 2018. It is often still too difficult for Japanese women to work, caring for children and doing housework at the same time. Therefore, 60 percent of them leave their workplace after marriage, as well as after the birth of their first child (National Institute of Population and Social Security Research 2015). Youth, women, and those who have fewer academic credentials are more likely to become non-regular workers.

The Japanese government did not offer alternative programs to alleviate labor precarity such as heightening social spending or redistribution through taxes to protect people from poverty but rather deregulated labor law to increase non-regular jobs, which unsurprisingly resulted in deepening the gap between highly protected regular workers and lower paid non-regular workers. Since the late 1990s, new social risks such as the emergence of the working poor and those who lack an adequate safety net have been generated by the system of "welfare through work" itself.[13] Now many people in Japan, especially women, suffer from a lack of social protection.

Hiroko Takeda points out a "political" function of the family in Japan: "The family in post-war Japan has constantly shouldered the responsibility of mediating economic and social risk via domestic work by women as a part of the state mechanism of governing the population. Tax and social security were organized from the 1960s onwards so as to 'appreciate' housewives' indirect contribution to the national political economy through unpaid work" (2008, 162). It is no exaggeration to say that women's income has been lowered politically to induce women to take on more caring responsibilities at home.

While politicians in Japan are now preoccupied with being "responsible," to use their own term, by campaigning for reforming the Constitution, seizing the chance of commercial enterprise such as World Expo, and showing off power, the general public are made "responsible" for recovering from natural disasters and providing social protection by themselves, and women especially are pressured to be responsible for the national political economy through unpaid housework and care as well as being a low-cost workforce.

While politicians such as the former prime minister are eager to strengthen the national power by having a "real" army, people are forced to take heavier burdens in order to protect their own welfare. According to Osamu Watanabe (2014), Japan changed the direction of its policy from a kind of welfare state to a neoliberal state in 1990 after the end of the Cold War. Watanabe characterizes the distinguishing feature of the Abe administration as the trinity of ambition for a military superpower, neoliberal reform, and historical revisionism. He calls the great power to which Abe aspires "a global competitive state" (14) where the interests of multinational enterprises are prioritized, and the international order should be protected by a military power for those enterprises to seek profit safely.

Watanabe (2014) underlined that the Abe government reformed the taxation system to lower corporation tax and, at the same time, to increase consumption tax from 5 percent in 2013 to 10 percent in 2019. With this tax reform, the Abe government also reduced fiscal spending, especially spending on social security, such as medical care expenditure and pensions, although the government increased military expenditure and proposed the amendment to the Constitution to have a full-fledged army fighting for the national interests, that is, the profit of large companies. Watanabe argued that the historical revisionism provides the ideological justification of becoming "a global competitive state" as well as cultivates patriotism, which "is based on the strong faith in an authentic history" (140).

Why Is the Concept of Precarity So Critical to Precarious Japan?

As I have described, although the precarious situation caused by Japan's natural environment cannot be controlled, the consequences of natural disasters are worsened by the policies and practices of its political leaders. To make matters worse, many women suffer in Japan because of the political system itself, where both labor regulations and the social welfare system make families, namely women, function "as an 'absorber' of economic and social risks" (Takeda 2008, 161). Whether precariousness is worsened or bettered depends on how carefully people respond to it.

As Judith Butler argues in *Frames of War* (2009), precariousness is our shared bodily condition, which can lead to, when it is recognized, a radically egalitarian democratic reform. Before I discuss the significance of precarity, I briefly explain why apprehension of "a new bodily ontology" (Butler 2009, 2)[14] is a way to transform the Japanese political formation. Here, I use the term "vulnerability" instead of "precariousness" to articulate how significant a new bodily ontology is to rethinking democratic politics.[15] To explore this relationship, I draw on the discussions of vulnerability in the ethics of care developed since the publication of Carol Gilligan's *In a Different Voice* (1993).

Since Gilligan contrasted ethics of care to that of justice, emphasizing a particular image of the self and human relationship as connection, interdependence, and vulnerability (cf., Gilligan 1993, ch. 2), some feminist philosophers have examined the normative significance of vulnerability to develop a new ethical and political theory (e.g., Kittay 1999; Mackenzie, Rogers, and Dodds 2014; Tronto 2013; Walker 2006; Wallbank and Herring 2014).[16] In what follows, I refer mainly to

Groenhout's (2005) argument to explain how important an understanding of human corporeal vulnerability is in transforming democratic politics.

All human beings, from the start of their life, depend on others in order to survive and grow. We all are born totally vulnerable—to other humans as well as to the social and natural environment. Therefore, we all need care by others, especially when we are young and when we are old and frail. We all have physical and emotional needs, which only others can meet, typically in the relationship between a newborn baby and her care giver(s). However, in many cultures and societies, especially Western ones, values are placed not on dependency and vulnerability but rather on a rational intellect, namely, having self-control and power over one's life and body. Also, those who engage in caring for the dependent are often undervalued because of the nature of their caring practices. According to Groenhout, "not surprisingly, then, we find that most philosophers have ignored care and caring relationships, and those who have mentioned them tend to treat them as subhuman" (2005, 25).

Although care practices are indispensable for sustaining the human world, those who are in caring relations have been tended to be regarded as subhuman and excluded from the public sphere. Making those who are in caring relations a public concern is the first step to a more inclusive and democratic society.

Taking corporeal vulnerability seriously enables us to realize that we all are physical beings who are exposed to others with particular material resources and limitations. Even those who are in the same circumstance experience it differently and uniquely. Therefore, they have particular needs because of their distinguished bodily conditions. A society that values care practices would advocate "a pluralist democratic social structure" where "no single voice is allowed to speak for all" (Groenhout 2005, 33). Our diverse corporeality shows that our difference should be concerned equally, and we all should be responsible for making social environment as livable to everyone as possible.

There is a distinction between "precariousness" and "precarity." While vulnerability or precariousness leads us to rethink how society can respond to particular needs of embodied individuals and create a better social condition for caring relations, precarity is not shared but rather constitutes politically induced unequal conditions of impairment.

According to Butler, precariousness is a feature of life, and there is no life that is not precarious. However, she does not fail to emphasize that there might exist a secured life without precariousness "in fantasy, and in military fantasies in particular" (2009, 25). By contrast, precarity is a politically caused condition where some are more secured and their needs are properly addressed, while others are ignored, disavowed, or arbitrarily exploited. Precarity is a symptom of institutional failures and a sign of unequal or unjust treatment of certain populations, who are unjustly exposed to poverty, violence, and even death.

Applying Butler's argument to the context of Japan, it is interesting enough to explore how, when, and for what the precariousness of a certain population gets exploited and thus reaches precarity so that resistance to such exploitation as well as reform of unjustly allocated care for precariousness becomes possible. Such an inquiry responds well to the important caution that emphasizing vulnerability may lead to unwarranted paternalism, which may deprive some vulnerable people of their potential for freedom.[17] As Narayan noticed as early as in 1995, "notions of differences in vulnerabilities and capabilities should be recognized as contested terrain, requiring critical attention to who defines these differences as well as their practical implications" (1995, 136). We can find many historical cases where the discourses of vulnerabilities were used for the justification of patriarchal domination, such as colonialism.

During the heated debate on the amendment of Article 9, for example, Abe used a picture of a mother with two infants, apparently fleeing the war on a U.S. vessel. With this emotional picture as an example, Abe questioned why the Japanese government under the current Constitution could not protect the U.S. vessel rescuing innocent and vulnerable Japanese from the warfare between North and South Korea. He stressed his responsibility to protect the peaceful livelihood of the Japanese people as follows:

> Resolutely securing the lives and peaceful livelihood of the Japanese people under any circumstances—that is the tremendous responsibility conferred upon me as Prime Minister.
>
> This is not some kind of abstract or ideological discussion such as whether or not the right of collective self-defense is permitted under the Constitution. It is a discussion on what should be done under the

> Constitution to secure the lives and peaceful livelihood of the Japanese people in any situations that could happen in reality.
>
> For example, suppose a conflict suddenly arose overseas. And suppose that in the conflict, the United States, which is our ally and has capability, came under attack in the sea near Japan when rescuing and transporting Japanese nationals trying to escape from where the conflict had occurred. Although this would not be an attack on Japan itself, the Self-Defense Forces (SDF) would protect the U.S. vessel in order to protect the lives of the Japanese nationals. What makes this possible is the Cabinet Decision made today.
>
> I cannot possibly believe that the Constitution of Japan, which was created in the hopes of bringing happiness to the people, requires me to renounce my responsibility to protect the lives of the Japanese people in such situations. (Abe 2014b)

At the conference, Abe kept displaying this image of a mother and her children as if those who need his protection backed his claim. Although he criticized the argument to preserve Article 9 for being abstract or ideological, his hypothetical example was also unrealistic. Although there have been two exceptional cases where Japanese people have escaped areas of conflict with the help of foreign governments and armies, the Japanese government usually charters aircraft or asks private airlines to provide special flights. If Abe is seriously concerned with the lives of Japanese people "under any circumstances," he could have told people not to seek help from those involved in combat because they are most likely to be attacked by the enemy country, but rather to approach a more neutral third party.

As Abe has often claimed, the amendment of Article 9 has been his dearest wish as a politician. To achieve this long-cherished goal, he even created unlikely scenarios with phrases such as "being fully prepared for contingencies." In his story, mothers and their infants are associated with the fixed imagery of the powerlessness, provoking a paternalistic desire to protect, control, or even subjugate. Abe appears to be applying what Iris Young once criticized as "the gendered logic of masculinist protection" in which those who are in the position to protect the vulnerable in fact subordinate and control them under the name of "responsibility" or even "love" (2003, 6).

In his appeal to the image of the vulnerable, not only children but also mothers are figured as the powerless, as if they could not fight or resist for their children, or even stand by themselves without the protector(s). However, mothers are in fact not powerless at all. As Ruddick (1989) once argued, mothers do think, judge, act, and even fight for what their children need through their own struggles. To resist such paternalistic lure to describe the vulnerable as those who always need others' protection, we have to distinguish precariousness or vulnerability from precarity. Vulnerability should not be "disjoined from resistance, mobilization, and other forms of deliberate and agentic politics" (Butler 2016, 22).

In fact, the most vulnerable people in Japan, such as mothers and children, who Abe thinks best justify the country's collective self-defense right, have to survive on their own in the absence of political attention or adequate social support (Nahara 2018). More than 80 percent of single mothers in Japan work hard, sometimes burdened with three jobs. However, most of them live on less than half the national median income, that is, they live below the poverty line. Of course, their children also suffer from poverty, fewer educational opportunities, and narrower prospects. Less than half of them receive alimony. There is not enough public support for parenting. Even if they can get job, that does not necessarily make their lives easier. Japan is the one country among OECD members where working single mothers are more likely to live below the poverty line than jobless single mothers.

What happened to other precarious people in Japan? Abe once declared that the Fukushima Daiichi Nuclear Power Plant was "under control" so that Japan could host the Olympic Games in Tokyo in 2020 (Sieg and Lim 2016). In order to prove his pledge that Fukushima was safe, the government aimed to reduce the number of Fukushima evacuees to zero by 2020, cutting the housing subsidies. Fukushima evacuees were forced to choose either financial hardship or returning home, which they believed was still harmful to their health. In contrast to the image of insecure and vulnerable mothers with infants who usefully represent the country's contingency, Abe has never tried "being fully prepared for contingencies" after the disaster at the Fukushima Daiichi Nuclear Power Plant. Instead, he maintains "the myth of safety," which has been created by politicians and the economic world who propagate that the nuclear power plants are clean, safe, and economic.[18] "The myth of safety" has hindered people from recognizing how politically the nuclear power plants were introduced into a country[19] that once experienced the unprecedented tragedy of nuclear weapons and is also at high risk of large-scale earthquakes.

Highlighting the concept of "securitization," critical security studies argue that "security issues are the political outcome of the illocutionary force of security agents and that one of the most effective ways of analyzing security issues is through the discursive practices in different security sectors" (Robinson 2011, 42). By securitizing a particular issue, the Japanese government selects who is to be protected for their vulnerability, as Abe showed in his conference. While Abe securitized the relation with Korean peninsula with a visible image of the "mother and her children" rescued by military forces, he rejected listening to the needs or claims of those made insecure by economic difficulties and literally frightened by radioactive contamination. People who deviate from the ideal protectee are often exposed to political pressures and even devastated (cf. Peterson 1992).

The Japanese government does not "protect" the welfare of some vulnerable people and even ignores or silences their sufferings, such as single mothers and Fukushima evacuees. On the contrary, former prime minister Abe emphasized Japan's insecurity only from a military viewpoint or for the sake of the nation's prosperity. Here, Joan Tronto's (2013) idea helps us interpret what is happening in Japan. The Japanese government surely wants to abdicate its caring responsibilities so that it can engage in other "valuable" activities such as protection and production.[20]

Japan has been in a vicious circle of impoverishing people's welfare and, at the same, heightening insecurity, anxiety, and precarity among people. With the neoliberal rhetoric of self-responsibility, Japanese political policies shift responsibility for protection and production to individuals. Those who are in power appear to be the protector, who in fact "use the need for protection as a justification for other forms of bad treatment" (Tronto 2013, 76). Under the ideology of self-responsibility, while more people are forced to take responsibility for what they in fact have no responsibility, such as natural disasters and poor pay, privileged people in economic and political terms seem to gain more power to decide how to allocate caring responsibilities (cf. Tronto 2013, especially ch. 2).

Precariousness, Resistance, and Democracy

Most single mothers work hard and try to widen their opportunities and cultivate the capabilities of their children as well as themselves. People deprived of their hometown, intimate relationships, and jobs by escaping Fukushima struggle for a safer environment for all Japanese people and reforming the government's energy policy that is dependent on nuclear power. Ruiko Mutō, one activist who speaks up for the needs of Fukushima escapees, filed a lawsuit against Tokyo Electric Power Company and the Japanese government for damages stemming from the Fukushima Daiichi Nuclear Power Plant disaster.[21] Only six months after the accident, she addressed 60,000 people in Meiji Park, Tokyo. Her speech captures not only evacuees from Fukushima but also those who forced to make inevitable choices in order to survive:

> To flee, or not to flee. To eat, or not to eat.
> To hang out the wash, or not.
> To make children wear masks, or not.
>
> To plough our fields, or not.
>
> To protest to someone, or remain silent. . . .
> What we are realizing now is that facts are hidden,
> the government does not protect us,
> the accidents have not ended yet.
> Do not take us for fools,
> Do not rob us of life.
>
> We are ogres of the North
> quietly burning
> the fuel of our anger.[22]

Muto said that people in Fukushima, whether evacuated elsewhere or remaining, support each other through sharing their suffering, responsibilities, and hope. She described their actions as ranging from negotiation with the government and legal suits to evacuation, sending children to convalesce, decontamination, education on nuclear power, and so on. Such wide-ranging actions as sharing their sufferings, activities, speaking against people in power, and resisting subjugation and judgment are the result of their capacity to recognize and share their own precariousness.

As Butler cautions, people in precariousness are often used for reinforcing the current norms, which are already gendered, stratified, and nationalized, and for concealing how their precariousness is in fact constructed by these social and political norms and therefore nothing but precarity.

People who stand up against the nuclear power plants sternly question the health of democracy in Japan. They ask why, how, and who decided to build and expand nuclear power plants in such a precarious country as Japan. They strongly question how seriously the government take its responsibility to protect people's lives and why people in Fukushima were forsaken for Tokyo Electric Power Company as well as the national interest. They demand that the government make clear to the public its decision-making process. They tell the government to listen to their voices and needs. What people demand of the government now above all is to politicize or rather democratize the process of securitization.

Not fantasizing or romanticizing but carefully looking at and listening to the situations of precarious people and what they actually experience leads us to realize a way to break the vicious circle of an uncaring, insecure, and imaginary protective society. The number of unprecedented events have taught people in Japan a unique but indispensable lesson—that we are all equally situated in this uncontrollable land as equally vulnerable and interdependent beings, and therefore we are equally responsible for building a society safe for all lives and resisting people's precariousness being exploited by those who are in power. Under the neoliberal regime in Japan, some people more precarious than others in a gendered society are also in crisis of precarity. However, as precarious and interdependent beings, they can realize that precarity is indeed created by political power, and therefore they can start to gathering and speaking out to fight against the exploitation, the lack of safety and protection, and the uncaring politics.

Notes

1. For a general understanding of Japan's socioeconomic situation as well as Japanese psychological anxiety after the bubble economy burst in the late 1980s, see Allison (2013).

2. The earthquake on March 11, 2011, in the Tohoku region and the subsequent accident at the Fukushima Daiichi Nuclear Power Plant demonstrated not only how vulnerable Japan is to natural disasters, but also how unprepared Japan is for the worst situations that natural disasters might cause. The second section of this chapter describes in more detail what is happening now to those who lived in Fukushima.

3. Under the Constitution, despite the fact that Article 9 prescribes the renunciation of war, the possession of war potential, and the right of belligerency by the state, since Japan is an independent nation, the Japanese government unchangeably interpret that these provisions do not deny Japan's inherent right to self-defense and that "the Constitution allows Japan to possess the minimum level of armed force needed to exercise that right." Therefore, previous governments assured that any exercises of collective self-defense whose purpose is to defend other nations from attack should not be allowed under the Constitution (Ministry of Defense n.d.).

4. On August 28, 2020, Abe announced his resignation because of health problems.

5. Even though the home page of the LDP has an English version, there is no translation of its mission.

6. Regarding the scholars' involvement with the movement against the Constitutional amendment initiated by former prime minister Abe, see Okano (2018).

7. The preamble reads that "we, the Japanese people, desire peace for all time and are deeply conscious of the high ideals controlling human relationship, and we have determined to preserve our security and existence, trusting in the justice and faith of the peace-loving peoples of the world."

8. Abe said on a broadcast on the internet that "honestly speaking, it is a disgraceful constitution, since it was not drafted by the Japanese people" (Asahi Shimbun 2012).

9. For example, Japan was ninth among the highest military spending countries in 2019 (Statista 2020).

10. According to Allison, the sudden change of socioeconomic climate led to a dramatic increase in the number of suicide deaths, reaching about 32,000 in 2003. The white paper for suicide countermeasures in 2016 indicated that suicide was the leading cause of death among young people between fifteen and thirty-four years old (Ministry of Health, Labour and Welfare 2016).

11. According to Miura (2012), "social protection system" is a wider category than "social security system," which means the institution of social insurance and pension. The former includes labor regulations, social assistance, community-based services to the vulnerable, child protection, and so on.

12. For example, the Temporary Work Agency Law was revised in 1999, which opened the door widely to a low-cost and flexible workforce (Miura 2012, 72).

13. The social protection system in Japan aims to protect citizens from poverty, unemployment, illness, injury, disability, and infirmity by offering them stable employment and promoting a certain type of family. By such characterization,

Miura points out that regular workers are likely to be protected well socially with the welfare and benefits given by their companies and that the highly protected labor conditions for regular workers are maintained by the large number of potential non-regular workers, mostly women with dependent children. Because of the government's reliance on the conventional system of social protection, social safety nets such as health-care insurance or employee pension do not function for "those who work under short-hour contracts and/or fixed-term contracts" (2012, 91).

14. Butler explains that this new understanding of bodily ontology emphasizes "the body is a social phenomenon: it is exposed to others, vulnerably by definition." She insists that we reconsider the concept of social responsibility based on this "socially ecstatic structure of the body" (Butler 2009, 33).

15. Since September 11, 2001, Butler has argued that vulnerability and precariousness are interchangeable terms. In *Precarious Life,* when Butler (2004, ch. 1) makes the point about the general condition of our lives, she refers to vulnerability. Butler articulates the point in her conversation with a Greek philosopher, Athena Athanasiou, where she said that we have to "understand the difference between precarity as an existential category that is presumed to be equally shared, and precarity as a condition of induced inequality and destitution. The latter is a way of exploiting an existential condition, since precarity, understood as a vulnerability to injury and loss, can never be reversed (this I tend to call precariousness)" (Butler and Athanasiou 2013, 20).

16. Gilligan also argues for the inseparable connection between ethics of care and democracy by seeing "the ethics of care, grounded in voice and relationship, as an ethics of resistance both to injustice and to self-silencing." She continues to write: "It is a human ethic, integral to the practice of democracy and to the functioning of a global society. More controversially, it is a feminist ethic, an ethic that guides the historic struggle to free democracy from patriarchy" (2011, 175).

17. For example, Butler suggests that some scholars are concerned with the emphasis on "vulnerability" because "it will become captured by the term and women will end up being portrayed in ways that rob them of their agency" (2016, 22).

18. "A Reuters analysis calculates that as few as six more reactors are likely to restart within the next five years" (Saito 2018).

19. As early as 1952, just before the U.S. occupation after the defeat of the Second World War, some law makers visited nuclear research centers in the United States. Right after U.S. President Eisenhower delivered the speech of "Atoms for Peace" at the UN in 1953, Japanese law makers, the economic world, and some media companies decided to introduce nuclear power plants into Japan. They made an effort to use Eisenhower's phrase "Atoms for Peace" in contrast with nuclear weapons. With an increase in the anti-nuclear movement, especially after the Bikini Atoll accident in 1954, when a Japanese fishing boat was contaminated by a nuclear weapons test, ironically the peaceful use of nuclear power filtered and diffused into Japanese society. "The fundamental principle of our foreign policy" was issued in 1969 and kept strictly secret by the LDP government. The document was finally made public in 2009 when the Democratic Party was in government. The principle said that Japanese government should emphasize the peaceful use of nuclear power in order to hide the true will to possess nuclear weapons. The principle

recommended maintaining economic and technological potentiality to produce nuclear weapons.

20. According to Tronto's definition that "caring be viewed as a species activity that everything that we do to maintain, continue, and repair our world" (Fisher and Tronto 1990, 40), masculine activities such as military protection and production as a bread winner are also care work. However, due to the dichotomy and spacious split of the private and the public, military protection and economic production are not considered as care work, and instead, those who engage in such work can gain a pass out of caring responsibility. See especially Tronto (2013, ch. 3).

21. There are about thirty cases to be filed, all related to the Fukushima Daiichi Nuclear Power Plant disaster, and of which named the government as the defendant (Asahi Shimbun 2019).

22. Part of her speech was translated by Norma Field (2016). For her whole speech, see Mutō (2011).

Works Cited

Abe, Shinzo. 2013. *Atarashii Kuni e: Utsukushii Kuni e Kanzenban* [*Toward a New Country: Toward a Beautiful Country*]. Enlarged version. Tokyo: Bunshun-Shinsho.

Abe, Shinzo. 2014a. "The 186th Session of the House of Representatives Budget Committee No. 3 February 3, 2014." http://kokkai.ndl.go.jp/SENTAKU/syugiin/186/0018/18602030018003.pdf.

Abe, Shinzo. 2014b. "Press Conference by Prime Minister." July 1, 2014. https://japan.kantei.go.jp/96_abe/statement/201407/0701kaiken.html.

Allison, Anne. 2013. *Precarious Japan*. Durham, N.C.: Duke University Press.

Asahi Shimbun. 2012. "'To Be Honest, It Is a Disgraceful Constitution' said Abe, the LDP President." *Asahi Shinbun*, December 14, 2012. http://www.asahi.com/senkyo/sousenkyo46/news/TKY201212140595.html.

Asahi Shimbun. 2019. "Court Absolves Government of Blame in Nuclear Disaster." *Asahi Shinbun*, March 15, 2019. http://www.asahi.com/ajw/articles/AJ201903150041.html.

Butler, Judith. 2004. *Precarious Life: The Powers of Mourning and Violence*. London: Verso Books.

Butler, Judith. 2009. *Frames of War: When Is Life Grievable?* London: Verso Books.

Butler, Judith. 2016. "Rethinking Vulnerability and Resistance." In *Vulnerability in Resistance*, edited by Judith Butler, Zeynep Gambetti, and Leticia Sabsay, 12–27. Durham and London: Duke University Press.

Butler, Judith, and Athena Athanasiou. 2013. *Dispossession: The Performative in the Political*. Cambridge: Polity.

Field, Norma. 2016. "From Fukushima: To Despair Properly, To Find the Next Step," *The Asia-Pacific Journal: Japan Focus* 14, no. 17 (September 1). https://apjjf.org/-Norma-Field/4951/article.pdf.

Fisher, Berenice, and Joan Tronto. 1990. "Toward a Feminist Theory of Caring." In *Circles of Care*, edited by E. K. Abel and M. Nelson, 35–62. Albany: State University of New York Press.

Gilligan, Carol. 1993 [1982]. *In a Difference Voice: Psychological Theory and Women's Development,* with a new preface by the author. Cambridge, Mass.: Harvard University Press.

Gilligan, Carol. 2011. *Joining the Resistance.* Cambridge: Polity Press.

Groenhout, E. Ruth. 2005. *Connected Lives: Human Nature and an Ethics of Care.* Lanham, Md.: Rowman & Littlefield.

Kittay, Eva Feder. 1999. *Love's Labor: Essays on Women, Equality and Dependency.* New York: Routledge.

The Liberal Democratic Party. 1955. "The Mission of the LDP." https://www.jimin.jp/aboutus/declaration/.

The Liberal Democratic Party. 2012. "The LDP's Draft for the Amendment of the Constitution." https://jimin.jp-east-2.storage.api.nifcloud.com/pdf/news/policy/130250_1.pdf.

Mackenzie, Catriaona, Wendy Rogers, and Susan Dodds, eds. 2014. *Vulnerability: New Essays in Ethics and Feminist Philosophy.* Oxford: Oxford University Press.

Ministry of Defense. n.d. "Fundamental Concepts of National Defense." Accessed September 1, 2020. https://www.mod.go.jp/e/d_act/d_policy/.

Ministry of Health, Labour and Welfare. 2016. *The White Paper of Suicide Countermeasure.* https://www.mhlw.go.jp/wp/hakusyo/jisatsu/16/index.html.

Ministry of Internal Affairs and Communications. 2018. *Labor Force Survey.* https://www.stat.go.jp/data/roudou/sokuhou/nen/ft/pdf/index1.pdf.

Miura, Mari. 2012. *Welfare through Work: Conservative Ideas, Partisan Dynamics, and Social Protection in Japan.* Ithaca, N.Y.: Cornell University Press.

Mutō, Ruiko. 2011. "Bye-bye Nuclear Plants." Filmed September 21, 2011, at Meiji Park, Tokyo. https://www.youtube.com/watch?feature=player_embedded&v=5xdszFXI2J0.

Nahara, Yoshiaki. 2018. "In One of the World's Richest Countries, Most Single Mothers Live in Poverty." *Bloomberg,* January 25, 2018. https://www.bloomberg.com/news/features/2018-06-24/the-children-of-japan-s-single-mothers-are-living-in-poverty.

Narayan, Uma. 1995. "Colonialism and Its Others: Considerations on Rights and Care Discourse." *Hypatia* 10, no. 2 (Spring): 133–40.

National Institute of Population and Social Security Research. 2015. *Marriage and Childbirth in Japan Today: The Fifteenth Japanese National Fertility Survey.* http://www.ipss.go.jp/ps-doukou/e/doukou15/Nfs15R_points_eng.pdf.

Okano, Yayo. 2018. "Prime Minister Abe's Constitutional Campaign and the Assault on Individual Rights." *The Asia-Pacific Journal: Japan Focus* 16, no. 3 (March). https://apjjf.org/2018/5/Okano.html.

Peterson, Spike. 1992. "Security and Sovereign States: What Is at Stake in Taking Feminism Seriously?" In *Gendered States: Feminist (Re)Visions of International Relations Theory,* edited by Spike Peterson, 31–64. Boulder, Colo.: Lynne Rienner.

Robinson, Fiona. 2011. *The Ethics of Care: A Feminist Approach to Human Security.* Philadelphia, Pa.: Temple University Press.

Ruddick, Sara. 1989. *Maternal Thinking: Toward a Politics of Peace.* Boston: Beacon Press.

Saito, Mari. 2018. "Treading Carefully, Japan's Nuclear Industry Makes a Comeback." *Reuters,* November 2, 2018. https://www.reuters.com/article/us-japan-nuclear-industry-insight/treading-carefully-japans-nuclear-industry-makes-a-comeback-idUSKCN1N66A1.

Sieg, Linda, and Megumi Lim. 2016. "Abe's Fukushima 'Under Control' Pledge to Secure Olympics Was a Lie: Former PM." *Reuters,* September 7, 2016. https://www.reuters.com/article/us-japan-nuclear-idUSKCN11D0UF.

Statista. 2020. "The 15 Countries with the Highest Military Spending Worldwide in 2019." https://www.statista.com/statistics/262742/countries-with-the-highest-military-spending/.

Statistics Bureau of Japan. 2020. *Labor Force Survey, 2019.* February 14, 2020. https://www.stat.go.jp/data/roudou/sokuhou/nen/dt/pdf/index1.pdf.

Takeda, Hiroko. 2008. "Structural Reform of the Family and the Neoliberalisation of Everyday Life in Japan" *New Political Economy* 13 (2): 153–72. https://www.tandfonline.com/doi/abs/10.1080/13563460802018224.

Tronto, Joan. 2013. *Caring Democracy: Markets, Equality, and Justice.* New York: New York University Press.

Walker, Margaret. 2006. *Moral Repair: Reconstructing Moral Relations after Wrongdoing*. New York: Cambridge University Press.

Wallbank, Julie, and Jonathan Herring, eds. 2014. *Vulnerabilities, Care and Family Law.* Oxon, UK: Routledge.

Watanabe, Osamu. 2014. "The Truth of the Abe Cabinet." In *Ambition for "a Great Power": The Abe Cabinet and Crisis of Japan,* edited by Watanabe et al., 1–172. Tokyo: Otsuki Shoten. [Watanabe Osamu, "Abe Seiken towa Nanika" in Wathanabe hoka, *Taikoku eno Shyunen: Abe Seiken to Nihon no Kiki.*]

Young, Iris Marion. 2003. "The Logic of Masculinist Protection: Reflections on the Current Security State." *Sings: Journal of Women in Culture and Society* 29 (1): 1–25.

Conclusion

Care as Responsive Infrastructure

MAURICE HAMINGTON AND MICHAEL FLOWER

> Neoliberalism's authoritarian (re)turn has been marked by the wholesale rejection of political compromise, concession, and consensus as means of managing dissent, while those holding on to power instead seek to make a virtue of ever more strident defenses of an idealized status quo ante, based on unabashed acts of appropriation and dispossession coupled with the intensified exclusion and domination of subordinate social groups.
>
> —Jamie Peck and Nik Theodore, "Still Neoliberalism?"

> That the relentless effort of Americans to think of human beings as autonomous interest maximizers who also occasionally want to feel good ignores is a truth that most human societies, including our own not so long ago, were quite aware of: namely that being beings are not autonomous atoms, that human beings exist in and through relationships and institutions or they do not exist at all.
>
> —Robert Bellah, "Understanding Caring in Contemporary America"

This project of juxtaposing care and precarity began in late 2018. In the subsequent years of the book's development, new and powerful sources of precarity emerged. A worldwide pandemic struck, and racial unrest arose. These new challenges did not diminish other existing threats such as the march of destructive climate change, widespread unhealthy eating patterns,[1] environmental degradation, and inequitable wealth distribution. However, coronavirus disease 2019 (COVID-19) and the worldwide protests inspired by the Black Lives Movement brought new layers of precarity to the fore. An analysis of these emergent concerns reinforces the essential premise of this book: *life's precariousness is exacerbated by individualistic and market-based responses that fail to integrate empathy and care for people and the natural world.* A review of the evolution of recent events reveals how much of the world's precariousness is human made and preventable. In this final chapter, we point to a hopeful response based in care. As at least a partial antidote for neoliberalism run amok are abiding systems of caring support that we describe as infrastructure. The goal is to achieve what Fiona Robinson describes as human security through the lens of care. She claims, "A recognition of the full implications of care ethics as a lens through which to view security leads to the revision of our objectives beyond the delivery of rights narrowly understood, toward recognition of responsibilities and need for care" (2011, 61). The understanding of infrastructure employed here includes but extends beyond material welfare. Without denying that material well-being is needed by many precarious communities, there is also a social and affective dimension needed for caring infrastructure. Lauren Berlant, who describes infrastructure as "that which binds us to the world in movement," claims there is a political imperative to reinvent infrastructure constantly for "managing the unevenness, ambivalence, violence, and ordinary contingency of contemporary existence" (2016, 394). For Berlant, dynamic infrastructure takes the long view, "generating a form from within brokenness beyond the exigencies of the current crisis, and alternatively to it too" (393). Robust infrastructure is an instantiation of care embedding inquiry, connection, and action in a configuration of relations and resources. In this manner, infrastructure can facilitate what Vrinda Dalmiya describes in chapter 3 of this volume as political solidarity, thus helping to mend some of the destructive divisions that have emerged in many countries today. Infrastructure is a social vaccine that does not guarantee immunity from precarity but, if well conceived and supported, may mitigate the harm of viral neoliberal practices.

Precarity is a state of insecurity that can be so profound as to place one's life and future under siege. Political theories of care seek systemic solutions to widespread insecurity through the instantiation of the systemic support of care's flourishing. For example, Daniel Engster describes collective caring as one of the three ways of providing care (the others being direct care and caring for caregivers). He refers to collective care as "supporting institutions and policies that directly help individuals to meet their needs, develop or sustain their basic capabilities, or live as much as possible free from pain and suffering" (2007, 35–36). Infrastructure can provide sustainable security and collective care. To this end, we discuss *infrastructure* broadly as constituted by three interrelated categories: preventative infrastructure, interventionist infrastructure, and responsive infrastructure.

Infrastructure is not a generally provocative topic, seldom garnering the limelight. A term that first appeared in the late nineteenth century, infrastructure describes an underlying base or foundation, especially for an organization or system. Infrastructure is commonly employed today to describe support systems utilized to undergird our social and economic activity such as roads, a water system, the electrical grid, the education system, networks of hospitals, and so on. Some theorists have categorized infrastructure into "hard" infrastructure, or the physical manifestation of the support system, and "soft" infrastructure, or the people, practices, and policies needed to maintain the support system. Our approach entails investing in and valuing both forms of infrastructure in service to a caring social commitment.

Market-based neoliberalism is often found to exist in tension with infrastructure. On the one hand, the means of wealth accumulation and extraction rely on infrastructure: systems of productivity and exchange, including transportation systems, communication systems, health systems, and education systems. However, such systems are not always well suited to be monetized, thus reducing the profit motive to support them within a neoliberal paradigm. Furthermore, monetization can introduce elements of exclusion and restriction to aspects of infrastructure. A road can be built with public funding derived from taxes, or it can be financed through tolls. The burden of paying for construction of a road is different in each case, but so is access to the road. Someone who may not be able to afford the daily commute on a toll road might experience longer drive times. A neoliberal or capitalist or libertarian approach likely views the taxation needed to support infrastructure to be a drag on the marketplace and a barrier to wealth accumulation. However, shifting the burden of infrastructure cost to individuals means those individuals may or may not be able to afford the cost of those social goods.

For the present discussion, infrastructure is viewed in expansive terms as an important social good that contributes to the amelioration of precarity. Most infrastructures have egalitarian and connective aspects, although none of them provide unfettered utilization. Ostensibly, a national park system supports access to wilderness for all, as well as protects ecological systems. A national highway system provides a physical means of connecting locations if one owns a vehicle. A national mail service provides a low-cost means of physical communication, and the internet provides a fast means of electronic connection. These examples are not immune to monetization, but the profit motive is often muted through subsidization to make these social goods more generally accessible than private goods. The social and relational aspects of robust infrastructure are often not valorized within the neoliberal paradigm.[2] For example, the industrialization of medicine rewards health-care workers for volume of examinations as opposed to deeper interactions that take time and attention. We envision a model of infrastructure that maintains a commitment to care over profit.

Infrastructure is an economic good, which means that it has utility or benefit for society. In the context of precarity and utilizing the lens of care ethics, we also wish to claim that infrastructure also has the potential to be a moral good. Modern Western moral philosophy, given the compelling legacy of Kant, has been focused on seeking the right in the struggle between right and wrong action as opposed to a quest for the good (Murdoch 1970, 52). Although care theory has implications for normative questions, it is primarily directed at the good of care (Mortari 2015, 77). Care is a moral ideal (Noddings 2013, 4)—one that cannot reach perfection but that can still be a good even when imperfectly offered.[3] What we are suggesting here is that infrastructure is an important political and social manifestation of a caring good—one that allows care to flourish in a way that mitigates precarity. The approach and examples that follow emphasize soft infrastructure (e.g., resources and skills of caring) but are not disentangled from hard infrastructure (e.g., mechanisms of responding to community needs). At its best, infrastructure propagates care in meaningful and inclusive ways that diminish harm and meets social needs.

Lessons from Crises

A crisis is a relative and subjective term that has a great deal to do with perception and the social imaginary. The COVID-19 pandemic appeared to be a novel event (even the underlying virus is referred to as "novel" because it has not previously manifested). The COVID-19 pandemic seems unique because we are a generation removed from the 1918 influenza pandemic, but that crisis claimed the lives of between forty and fifty million people over two years—a mortality total that dwarfs the devastation of COVID-19 (LePan 2020, n.p.). Furthermore, the COVID-19 pandemic captures attention because of its event-like status. Just as the deaths from a plane crash garner more media attention than the daily deaths from international starvation,[4] although the latter is quantitatively much larger, so too does COVID-19 acquire more urgent attention than longer more systemic pandemics such as the HIV/AIDS pandemic, which has claimed between twenty-five and thirty-five million lives worldwide since 1981 (LePan 2020, n.p.). Of course, the social and political meaning attached to HIV/AIDS is far different from that of COVID-19.

In reviewing more than one hundred articles on the COVID-19 pandemic from around the world published in the first half of 2020, Andries Baart, social scientist, practical theologian, father of presence theory, and contributor to this volume, draws several conclusions (pers. commun., July 22, 2020) that reflect the nature of the crisis but also reinforce the thesis of *Care Ethics in the Age of Precarity*. Here is a summary of his conclusions, with a few exemplary observations. First, although the COVID-19 pandemic ostensibly poses a potential threat of infection, health complications, and death to everyone in the world, it does not impact everyone equally. Some are more vulnerable than others. David Everatt, Head of Wits School of Governance, University of the Witwatersrand, describes the South African context with words that resonate elsewhere: "We are so fundamentally unequal that this virus (like HIV before it) is going to disproportionately affect the poor. And the poor are overwhelmingly Black. So the prejudice that welcomed COVID has created its own truth" (2020, n.p.). The worldwide pandemic does not translate into an equal threat to all. Rather, the pandemic dramatically highlights the complexity and persistent nature of privileges in society.

Second, relatedly, precarious conditions including, but not limited to, poverty exacerbate the threat of infection, health complications, and death. Jude Mary Cénat, Assistant Professor of Psychology at the University of Ottawa, straightforwardly claims "precarity as a major factor in the spread of the disease," pointing to low- and middle-income countries: "India, Mayotte, Kenya, South Africa, Ivory Coast, Dominican Republic, Nigeria, Ecuador, Bangladesh, Democratic Republic of the Congo and others" (2020, n.p.). Even within wealthy countries, there are variations in the experience of the pandemic due to dramatic differences of social resource availability. In a vicious circle, the pandemic also leads to the creation of increased non-health-related precarity. A United Nations University World Institute for Economics Research report indicated

> there could be increases in poverty of a substantial magnitude—up to 400 million new poor living under the $1.90 poverty line, over 500 million new poor living under the poverty lines of $3.20 and $5.50. Further, the global income shortfall below each poverty line could expand by up to 60 per cent; the daily income losses could amount to $350m among those living under $1.90 per day and almost $200 million among the group of people newly pushed into extreme poverty . . . the location of global poverty is likely to shift towards middle-income countries and South Asia and East Asia. (Sumner, Ortiz-Juarez, and Hoy 2020, abstract)

So, the precariat are more vulnerable to the disease, and their situation is more likely to be rendered even more precarious by its presence.

Third, the COVID-19 pandemic shines a light on systemic precarization: practices by various jurisdictions that create greater vulnerability than might otherwise exist. A number of scholars and political observers have described how economic austerity measures such as those enforced by the European Union, the International Monetary Fund, and other international agencies reflect neoliberal values but weaken the support networks needed to confront crises. For example, Greece underwent nearly a decade of financial austerity to repay the loans that kept its economy afloat. That repayment came at a heavy price in societal well-being. In 2014 alone, the health budget was cut by 60 percent (Ladi 2020, n.p.). Fortunately, as the pandemic traveled to Greece, the government took decisive action to diminish the

COVID-19 spread, but a robust health-care system would have certainly improved the circumstances. As geographer Matthew Sparke describes, "Austerity and other policy shifts associated with neoliberalism have come to be embodied globally in ill-health" (2017, 287). Austerity regimes are only one manifestation of the neoliberal paradigm that foments precarity, but they are a powerful example of valuing finances over the well-being of society.[5]

Fourth, the COVID-19 pandemic has highlighted the need and value of care in society over and above other interests. The marketplace has proved relatively ineffective against the global pandemic. The fundamental interdependence and relationality of humanity is brought to the fore as we become acutely aware that *our* survival requires that *others* be cared for. Health-care workers are those most explicitly in need of care—and celebration—but so too is the care of those who provide food and other essential services. The cooperation of scientists across the globe is necessary if they are to make a vaccine available. Even the nature of the disease is a testament to mutual dependency; as inconvenient as it may be, wearing a mask is a means of demonstrating care for others by controlling airborne transmission. Furthermore, the pandemic has highlighted the need for caring leadership. In a *New York Times* article, Amanda Taub investigates why women-led nations seem to be faring so much better than male-led countries in regard to the pandemic. Her analysis did not lead to a conclusion of gender determinism but rather a valorization of care. Taub quotes human geographer Alice Evans on the need for caring leadership: "What we learned with COVID is that, actually, a different kind of leader can be very beneficial. Perhaps people will learn to recognize and value risk averse, caring and thoughtful leaders" (2020, n.p.). In a moment of exasperation over the leadership in the White House, the then U.S. presidential candidate, Joe Biden, addressing the murder of George Floyd, stated, "The Presidency is a duty to care" (Nilsen 2020, n.p.). Such acrimony is not unusual in presidential campaigns, but framing national leadership in terms of caring is rare, given the presumption of rugged individualism in the United States.

Fifth, the COVID-19 pandemic offers a unique opportunity for the world to rethink and make changes in values, policies, and practices in the service of enlarging care for one another. One of the insidious aspects of neoliberalism is that the drive for productivity makes it difficult to have the time necessary to reflect on the major superstructures of society. However, the nature of the pandemic and its interference with the ability of people to meet and work, as well as the requirement to stay home, has afforded a "Great Pause," which many are using to reflect on themselves and the context of their lives (Maçães 2020, n.p.). Although many long for a return to normalcy, some are viewing the world through a more caring lens and are considering replacing more and more of the neoliberal framework. For example, Australian organization scholar Layla J. Branicki suggests that the pandemic points to rethinking how we approach crisis management. She characterizes the traditional and common approach as "rational crisis management," which privileges the quantifiable and definable through "utilitarian logics, masculine and militaristic language, and the belief that crises follow linear processes of signal detection, preparation/prevention, containment, recovery and learning" (2020, 1). A care-based approach to crisis management is dynamic, relational, and context driven, whereby crises are viewed as interrelated, with attention given to qualitative as well as quantitative elements:

> Rational crisis management tends to see crises as episodes in isolation—both in the sense of isolation from broader contexts in which they arise and in the sense of separation from other, related, crises that co-occur. In this view, crises are temporally and socially specific. In contrast, feminist crisis management would see crises as multiple and contextualized, as enduring and overlapping phenomena that are enmeshed and embedded within each other to a significant extent. Crises compound and confound each other within webs of relationships informed by care. (Branicki 2020, 9).

Crisis management is not the only sphere reconsidered during the Great Pause. There has been speculation about reimagining education, work, transportation, and social safety nets.

The body of material supporting the five points above center on the COVID-19 pandemic, but of course another crisis emerged in the aftermath of a relentless pattern of racial violence perpetrated by police, primarily in the United States. The death of George Floyd and the subsequent rekindling of the Black Lives Movement sparked protests around the globe. This is a very different but not unrelated crisis.

A Crisis as Old as Humanity

Although COVID-19 entered the social imaginary in 2019 as a crisis of unique and urgent precarity, racism and its associated precarities have been a companion of humanity throughout recorded history. As George Lipsitz remarks, paraphrasing a comment Malcom X made in 1964, "Racism [is] like a Cadillac. . . . The General Motors Company brought out a new model of their car every year . . . but [they are] still Cadillacs" (1995, 701). The aggregate toll of death, violence, physical damage, and mental anguish that results from racism is immeasurable.[6] The response to this growing toll, the fight for Black liberation, has erupted numerous times throughout the history of the United States. The call for a reckoning associated with the international Black Lives Matter protests has arisen in the midst of current unrelenting racial violence and police brutality. Looking back only a few years, one can locate the act of violence that led to the Movement for Black Lives. It began as a response to the acquittal of George Zimmerman who murdered Trayvon Martin in 2013. In that year, three Black organizers—Patrisse Cullors, Alicia Garza, and Opal Tometi—founded an intersectional and inclusive movement under the banner of #BlackLivesMatter. The non-hierarchical organization includes an ambitious philosophy:

> **We are expansive.** We are a collective of liberators who believe in an inclusive and spacious movement. We also believe that in order to win and bring as many people with us along the way, we must move beyond the narrow nationalism that is all too prevalent in Black communities. We must ensure we are building a movement that brings all of us to the front.
>
> **We affirm the lives** of Black queer and trans folks, disabled folks, undocumented folks, folks with records, women, and all Black lives along the gender spectrum. Our network centers those who have been marginalized within Black liberation movements.
>
> **We are working** for a world where Black lives are no longer systematically targeted for demise.
>
> **We affirm our humanity,** our contributions to this society, and our resilience in the face of deadly oppression. (Black Lives Matter, n.d., n.p.)

The simple declaration of care for the precarious, "Black Lives Matter," became a divisive political rallying cry, with some even accusing the organization of being a terrorist group (Khan-Cullors and Bandele 2020, 6).

The reckoning tide of social imagination shifted with a violent viral video. On May 25, 2020, George Floyd died on a street in Minneapolis, Minnesota, after being pinned to the pavement as a white police officer, Derek Chauvin, knelt on Floyd's neck for nearly eight minutes. This event became an important symbol of how people of color in the United States and elsewhere live in an ongoing state of crisis or continuous precarity. Although the Black community was outraged, the event was not unfamiliar, given so many cases of similar violent oppression. As the video and reactions to it spread, it was white America that appeared to have had an epiphany regarding the severity and pervasiveness of racial oppression. Time will tell if the epiphany endures and brings about systemic change.

For all of social media's drawbacks, the question of whether the George Floyd murder caught on video prompted an epiphany is an intriguing one. Philosopher Sophie Grace Chappell describes epiphanies as "(1) overwhelming (2) existentially significant manifestation of (3) value, (4) often sudden and surprising, (5) which feels like it "comes from outside"—it is something given, relative to which I am a passive perceiver—which (6) teaches us something new, which (7) 'takes us out of ourselves', and which (8) demands a response" (2019, 95). In other words, an epiphany can be a moral disruption that causes us to care. In this case, what was common knowledge in the Black community—a pattern of racially based police brutality—suddenly caught the social imaginary of mainstream discourse. In contemporary parlance, "woke culture" is a social awareness of social justice and racial justice issues. Will the awareness take hold and grow, or will the machinations of neoliberalism cause racial concern to recede into the background of national conversation as it has done so many times before in the United States and Europe? Will the world stay woke?

Lawyer Sean Hill argues that the Black experience in the United States challenges the temporal notion of precarity and will thus require more systemic changes than that of a response to a crisis. Hill critiques the connection between precarity and neoliberalism because Black precarity predates neoliberalism and continues to endure: "Precarity, according to [Guy] Standing (2011), is a relatively new phenomenon, the result of countries rejecting the policies of the Keynesian welfare state in favor of neoliberalism's calls for fewer government interventions on behalf of the proletariat" (2017, 95). Hill acknowledges that neoliberalism has expanded and deepened all forms of precarity (97), but the existence of the Black community as a perpetual precarious class means that efforts at mitigating precarity must acknowledge the differential positions from which the precariat arise. He points to the intersectional and inclusive approach of the Movement for Black Lives as a necessary dimension of coming to grips with contemporary precarity.

Given Hill's concerns, we propose a robust investment in infrastructure as a manifestation of a society's commitment to care for its members characterized by long-term thinking, inclusion, and sensitivity to different contexts. We frame this investment in terms of preventative, interventionist, and responsive infrastructure. Although the framing may be different, such a mandate for social investment is not new. In an analysis lamenting the traditional analytical juxtaposition of race and class, Daniel Martinez HoSang and Joseph E. Lowndes recall that Martin Luther King proposed a Poor People's Campaign but was murdered before he could see it through. HoSang and Lowndes point out that the Campaign "demanded an expansive state premised on a recognition of the interdependence of everyone in the polity, rejecting the myths of settler sovereignty, autonomy and producerism" (2019, 164). Today, we live in a time of divided progressive campaigns that are somewhat at odds with the movement envisioned by King—a movement encompassing a multiethnic and multiracial effort directed at combatting the insecurity of poverty.

Preventative Infrastructure: "No One Could Have Predicted This"

Of the three forms of infrastructure offered here, preventative infrastructure is perhaps the most significant. Building preventative measures demonstrates care and helps develop and secure trust. Care is often described as both a practice and a disposition. It also elides means and ends, for in the process of working toward care, one communicates caring intent that radiates care to others. In other words, in establishing budgets and taking steps toward enacting preventative infrastructure, a polity is expressing a care for its membership. Preventative infrastructure is also perhaps the most difficult infrastructure to establish because investing in it runs counter to the immediate gratification favored by market-based neoliberalism. Deep and effective care has a long-time horizon that expresses to the one cared for that the caregiver will be there for them in the future. This kind of care is a relationship, not an exchange. A polity that invests in preventative infrastructure is manifesting care for its citizens. Hurricane early-warning systems, pandemic planning and response teams, and conflict resolution training are all examples of tangible investments in preventative infrastructure. However, there are other investments in preventative infrastructure that are less tangible that can be just as valuable as the tangible ones. Education regarding social power and privilege, the history of white supremacy, and the struggles of diverse people are all investments in building a social infrastructure that can help prevent violence and oppression. In this manner, we are suggesting that the infrastructure necessary to resist precarity is not just tangible systems but the capacities, habits, and skills of citizens in society.

Part of that preventative habit development is a rich investment in the arts and humanities. The humanities are understood here in broad and inclusive terms and not simply reinforcing a canon of Western European experience. Comprehensive knowledge of world history, philosophy, literature, and art is an important basis for understanding the human condition in its emotional and performative varieties. Despite the brunt of neoliberal criticism that sees them as nonessential, unproductive, and inefficient, the arts and humanities can help provide crucial linkages of understanding when direct experience of others and their context is not possible. This represents an important knowledge base, including propositional knowledge and social-emotional knowledge, as well as the critical and creative skills that comprise a caring infrastructure. Indeed, there is no crisis for which society would not benefit from these skills in order to weather and mitigate the resulting impacts. Poetry can help us have a personal and visceral connection to others' experience of racial injustice, for example (Hamington and Rosenow 2019, 102–3). Theatre and performance can help a community work through crisis and engage in resistance (Fisher 2020, 8–12). A knowledge of history can help us see patterns in the past that have connections to the present, whether that be of previous pandemics or of a country's history of white supremacy. An understanding of philosophy assists one in parsing out the claims made by those in authoritative positions, as well as discerning operant truth in the face of noisy, contradictory claims amidst stress and anxiety. The arts and humanities can help members of society develop habits of the mind. In other words, a robust interdisciplinary education including science and math is an intangible infrastructure that fortifies society to address its challenges.[7]

A preventative infrastructure describes systemic efforts to thwart and mitigate the sources of precarity. A society that cares for its members will seek to establish the means for them to survive and thrive without the presence of threats. There is nothing exceptional about this concept, as countries have built basins and dikes to prevent flooding, provided vaccines to prevent disease, required suppression systems in buildings to prevent fires, and so on. However, what we are suggesting here is a systematic national conversation regarding the causes of precarity and creating preventative measures that are widely available with a minimum of barriers. Most developed countries have mitigated health-care resource concerns by providing universal health care. In these countries, preventative infrastructure has proven effective for decades.

Preventative infrastructure in service of care includes psychological, emotional, and mental training or what might be called "soft infrastructure." In this manner, social resources include human capabilities such as inquiry, empathy, and habits of action that are the elements of care. For example, emotional and ethical training for children could provide a valuable resource for society to develop citizens that are curious, empathic, and willing to act on behalf of others. At the University of Verona's Melete Center of the Philosophy for Care, Luigina Mortari and Marco Ubbiali have engaged in the MelArete project (care *meléte* and virtue *areté*). Aimed at school-age children, the goal of MelArete is to encourage children to reflect on their personal experiences in order to explore the essential meaning of important ethical concepts, such as good, care, virtue, courage, generosity, respect, and justice. Based in a care ethical framework, field research was conducted with children and teachers in Italy. From that research, age-appropriate materials were developed for grade school classrooms to explore these ethical ideas. The program utilizes animal stories and student-created art to reflect on moral ideals and emotions. The result of the program is that children are better able to "recognize the different components of a virtuous action (thought, emotion, consequences, choice), acted or seen; and they could recognize the ethical 'call' inside dilemmas of everyday life" (Mortari and Ubbiali 2017, 275). This is just one of many possible examples of effective capacity building that stems from education. Accordingly, education is an important social infrastructure. However, it has also suffered under the current neoliberal regime. Examples of this suffering include shifting more of the financial burden of college education from the state to student tuition, cost-cutting measures that increase class size to the detriment of the learning experience, creating an expendable teaching workforce, as well as the political manipulation and narrowing of studies (with emphasis on professional pathways). Education and other forms of preventative infrastructure can help members of society develop the habits of mind and skills to address unforeseen precarity as it presents itself.

Interventionist Infrastructure: *"We Are Here for You"*

When preventative infrastructure fails to stop a source of precarity, a second form of infrastructure is ready to intervene on behalf of those in need during a crisis. This is what we refer to as interventionist infrastructure. If fire suppression systems are a tangible example of preventative infrastructure, then fire departments are examples of an interventional infrastructure. Interventionist infrastructure is a familiar concept given the presence of fire departments, ambulance, disaster shelters, emergency medical services, and grief counselors. However, the range and consistency of interventionist infrastructure is limited. Homelessness, drug addiction, and mental illness are conditions that many societies do not have adequate intercessions for. Without assistance, individuals experiencing these conditions are made to feel disposable—uncared for. On the other hand, timely and trustworthy rehabilitation programs express a desire to make everyone whole in a shared experience of care.

Presence—being there for the one in need—is a theme among those who theorize about the quality of care. In developing her thoughts about care and social policy, Nel Noddings draws on the caring power of presence. She claims, "That constant response, 'I am here,' is the foundation of a relation of care and trust. . . . Projected onto the social scene it represents the assurance that every community should offer its members in a time of need" (2002, 129).

The worldwide Black Lives Matter protests are a product of the precarity involved in the presence of police, particularly in the United States. For many communities of color, it is not clear if a police officer is friend or foe, given the rates of violence perpetrated against Black and brown citizens. This is a broken infrastructure. One model for reform is a program found in Eugene, Oregon, titled CAHOOTS (Crisis Assistance Helping Out on the Streets). Eugene is a university town, and together with its neighboring city of Springfield, the population is around 250,000, mostly white, but with a large homeless community. CAHOOTS was started in 1989 by White Bird Clinic, a Federally Qualified Health Center that receives funds to provide primary care services in underserved areas. CAHOOTS is an alternative to simply sending the police to respond to emergency calls. When someone calls the 911 emergency line in the Eugene-Springfield area, a trained operator will divert non-violent cases to CAHOOTS.

> The program mobilizes two-person teams consisting of a medic (a nurse, paramedic, or EMT) and a crisis worker who has substantial training and experience in the mental health field. The CAHOOTS teams deal with a wide range of mental health-related crises, including conflict resolution, welfare checks, substance abuse, suicide threats, and more, relying on trauma-informed de-escalation and harm reduction techniques. CAHOOTS staff are not law enforcement officers and do not carry weapons; their training and experience are the tools they use to ensure a non-violent resolution of crisis situations. They also handle non-emergent medical issues, avoiding costly ambulance transport and emergency room treatment. (White Bird Clinic Media Guide 2020)

Arriving in a van with their White Bird logo on the side, responders dressed in casual uniforms portray an ethos of care. Unarmed except with their five hundred hours of training in crisis management and de-escalation techniques, CAHOOTS professionals made more than 24,000 responses in 2019, representing about 17 percent of all emergency calls (White Bird Clinic Media Guide 2020). Eugene-Springfield still has challenges to face when it comes to law enforcement, but CAHOOTS and the other White Bird Clinic services represent a model of care infrastructure for those who might otherwise not receive it. White Bird Clinic press materials indicate that CAHOOTS saves the community millions of dollars annually in reduced police interventions and ambulance rides, but the real value is in the sense that the community cares about its troubled members and is willing to act in a humane manner on their behalf.

When members of a society do encounter crisis, precarity can be greatly diminished if they know and trust that there are people who will assuredly come to their aid. This is caring infrastructure.

Responsive Infrastructure: *"What Do You Need?"*

Infrastructure should be a part of an ongoing dialog between community members and government leaders. Although some infrastructure is intended to prevent precarity and other infrastructure is aimed at assisting those who become more precarious, responsive infrastructure refers to the mechanisms necessary for ongoing inquiry and discovery of what community members need—in other words, how are people empowered to prevent precarity? Prevention, intervention, and responsiveness are not mutually exclusive forms of social infrastructure, but they are all needed in a society that cares for its members.

Responsive infrastructure describes mechanisms of humility and listening that remind us that the precariat have agency. This form of infrastructure is probably the least well developed and most unfamiliar. Typically, citizens may vote or elect officials in favor of infrastructure building, but after that has occurred, standard hierarchies tend to take over, and input is limited and often perfunctory in nature. Julie Ann White describes the phenomenon of paternalistic care in regard to the welfare state: "The authority of the provider of care came to be naturalized in the public sphere just as parental, particularly paternal authority had been in the private sphere, both assuming authority in relation to a class of dependents" (2000, 4). White is concerned that social practices of care become largely controlled by a professional class that ends up interpreting the needs of the vulnerable (14). Authentic and meaningful responsiveness is intended to provide infrastructures of care with a means of engagement, inclusion, and collaboration for those who need it.

Occasionally, community leaders emerge to lead the charge for infrastructure support in their community, but seldom are there established listening systems, particularly not for those who are disenfranchised. What do the homeless want to make their lives less precarious? The working poor? Single parents? Refugees? Transgendered individuals? Undocumented workers? What mechanism do we have for finding out their expressed needs and caring for them? Often, leaders will make assumptions about voiceless constituents, but few have systematic means of direct inquiry. A caring infrastructure must have feedback and input channels that are more than perfunctory.

Responsiveness has been a significant theme among care theorists. Joan Tronto characterized responsiveness as one of her four essential elements of care. She describes responsiveness as signaling that care addresses human (and nonhuman) vulnerability—a notion that runs counter to neoliberal fantasies of autonomy, independence, and equality (1993, 135). Tronto also points out that responsiveness entails attentiveness and a vigilance to the potential for abuse because of vulnerability. Valorizing responsiveness within systems of care is one means to provide a check on unwarranted paternalism maintaining focus on the one who is cared for. In her description of a duty to care, Sarah Clark Miller is careful to protect the agency of those cared for: "the duty to care is non-paternalistic in that moral agents who enact the duty are to promote the happiness of those in need by advancing their self-determined ends" (2012, 8). Given the many demands of social delivery systems and the seemingly bureaucratic nature of many of them, one might ask whether a commitment to an attentive responsiveness is practical.

In one example of building responsiveness into infrastructures of care, Dutch researchers indicate that responsiveness is possible. Merel Visse, Tineke Abma, and Guy Widdershoven describe the theoretical basis of their investigation:

> A political care ethics puts the assignment of responsibilities and the inclusion of multiple perspectives of people at the centre of care. It honours the expressive-collaborative nature of care practices. It is responsive to political positions of vulnerability, fragility and resilience of those whom it concerns. From this, the interest in deliberative approaches is growing. Deliberative approaches aim to elicit, articulate and connect the voices of people with policy. Responsive evaluation is an empirical approach helpful to fostering mutual understanding, deliberation and inclusion. It aims to carefully understand perspectives

> of a variety of people and facilitate a dialogue between people on their experiences with a caring practice. (2015, 164)

Visse, Abma, and Widdershoven (2015, 171) inserted themselves in a complex infrastructure of care intended to help families experiencing multiple problems such as mental health issues, financial challenges, and poor living circumstances. They utilized multiple methods, including interviews, observations, and group conversations, spending a great deal of time to investigate perceptions of responsibilities, care, and need. The researchers created an atmosphere of mutual learning between case workers, administration, and clients, thereby creating a "a moral ecology of inclusion and deliberation, based on trust and solidarity concerning the division of responsibilities as the core of democratic care" (180). Responsiveness can be the basis for new projects of social care while also improving existing infrastructure, as Visse, Abma, and Widdershoven have demonstrated.

One intriguing approach to creating responsive infrastructure is through the lens of design thinking. In some ways, infrastructure represents caring by design: a preplanned and properly resourced approach to promoting the well-being of society. Design thinking was originally the purview of engineers, but it is now being taught in business schools as well. Design thinking is an iterative process and practice of creatively and inclusively solving challenges through the generation of innovative and competing solutions that explicitly seek to empathize with a user experience. Although primarily used in service of market solutions and empathizing with consumers, there have been some efforts at describing the resonance between design thinking and care (Vaughan 2018; Hamington 2017). Responsiveness to the user is part of the design thinking process, and it can be applied to thinking through social systems of care in light of precarity. The recent crises provide us with yet another opportunity to reflect on building responsive infrastructure into our society as well as caring by design, each with the aim of diminishing precarity.

Care and the Social Compact

Polities participate in the social imaginary through a shared fiction known as the social contract. This imagined contract implies that government provides for the good of its constituents who in return agree to be governed and taxed and to abide by the leadership and laws of the government. Social order and security are two of the commonly understood goods of government, but another, albeit less valorized good, is care. Social contract theory has a long and well-established body of literature in politics. However, the metaphor of a contract, like many modernist understandings that favor neatly defined categories, projects a dichotomy of two-party contractual arrangements that belies the ambiguity of political realities. Particularly in democracies, the government is comprised of elected members of society beholden to their constituency and to the charge of their elected office. These parties are not independent agents drawing up an agreed upon exchange, but rather two aggregate and dynamically enmeshed identities tied to one another through a variety of relationships. Although the current political moment appears impossibly entrenched, the history of change—sometimes dramatic change—reinforces Maggie FitzGerald's idea found in chapter 8 of this volume that rather than a fixed universe, a different political universe can be enacted.

Philosopher Naomi Zack recognizes the limitation of the imagined current social contract and favors its reinvigoration as a compact. In *Reviving the Social Compact,* Zack describes the outcome as a more inclusive and comprehensive entanglement of parties for the common good that exists independent of government: "The citizens before during, after, and altogether apart from government have a social compact among themselves. The social compact is an imagined agreement between each individual and the whole collective for the benefit of all" (2018, 5). While the notion of a contract is grounded in enlightenment ideas of free, independent agents agreeing to an exchange that is enforceable by law, for Zack, a social compact exists prior to any social contract and suggests a higher level of moral commitment to the good of the whole. For example, a government might provide rules defining citizenship that a broader social compact would extend to non-citizens such as undocumented immigrants (172). To make this case, Zack uses the language of care as a marker of good citizenship: "Caring about what others experience, good citizens are concerned to welcome new members into the whole, a concern that translates into responsible hospitality to immigrants" (174). For Zack, "good citizenship requires a moral dimension, as well as knowledge and action" (175)—a description that fits closely with the elements of care.

An effective social compact entails trust. For many communities, the trust that their society or nation cares about and for them has eroded. To varying degrees in different countries, this erosion of trust is discernible among people of color, the homeless, refugees, indigenous peoples, undocumented immigrants, poor rural white communities, migrant farm workers, LGBTQ identified people, and the differently abled. As Berlant notes, "The commons wants terms in which trust would become more robust. In liberal capitalist contexts, and as our mirror in austerity politics has insisted, this will involve rethinking work as well as labor, and the political as well as politics" (2016, 409). Earning trust requires time to overcome the memories of misdeeds and malfeasance. Building trust is like building a caring relationship: it needs presence, long-term commitment, interactive inquiry, attuned empathy, and responsive action. Once built and trusted, an infrastructure of care can mitigate part of the psychic burden of precarity, making for a vigorous social compact. Ideally, in such an environment, one might suffer tragedy and loss but with the realization that someone has their back and that they are not alone. Recognizing our mutually shared vulnerability, need, and ability to aid one another may bring about the paradigm shift toward care that the late Elena Pulcini addresses in chapter 5 of this volume. A worldwide pandemic and the renewed call for the reckoning of a too-long history of racism are reminders to all, including the otherwise privileged, that life is precious and precarious, and we need to maintain enduring methods for taking care of one another. Market-based and individualistic solutions will not provide adequate care for social beings.

Notes

1. Caloric consumption is probably a surprising addition to this list, given the media attention focused on other worldwide threats, but the World Health Organization (WHO) describes obesity and overweight health problems as not just a developed-country issue but a worldwide problem that has exceeded the collective health challenges associated with underweight populations. The WHO claims 1.9 billion people were overweight in 2016, which has been linked to cardiovascular disease, diabetes, musculoskeletal disorders, and some cancers. (WHO 2020, n.p.). The number of annual deaths from being overweight has reached pandemic proportions, with an estimated 2.8 million casualties yearly (WHO 2017, n.p.). There is a market-based neoliberal element to obesity (Schrecker and Bambra 2015, 23–41) further highlighted by the relationship between industrialized factory farming practices and pandemics (Pocock 2020, 6).

2. In chapter 10 of this volume, Dionne goes so far as to argue that the tension between care and neoliberalism exists at an ontological level.

3. Certainly, much harm has been done in the name of care. Poor efforts at care that do not engage adequate inquiry, humility, and responsiveness can result in damage, but such dangers do not mean that care is only achieved under conditions of perfection.

4. Approximately nine million people perish every year from starvation, and this number may increase in the face of pandemics (Mai 2020, n.p.). This equates to almost 25,000 starvation deaths worldwide per day, which rarely receives media consideration.

5. There are some who suggest that modern economic austerity efforts are ineffective in achieving their aims of an improved economy and unnecessarily cruel to the populaces who must live through them (Blyth 2015, 41–56; Krugman 2015, n.p.).

6. In the argument that the U.S. federal government should pay reparations to the Black community consistent with the reparations paid to other harmed communities in the United States and elsewhere, the challenge of placing a monetary value on the harm of racism is a contentious project. For an example of this complexity, in their argument for the Brookings Institute favoring Black reparations, Rashawn Ray and Andre Perry include a payment to descendants of slaves, tuition remission, loan forgiveness, housing grants, and business grants to address disparities in these areas (2020, 4–6). Although acknowledging that reparations would not resolve all the problems of the Black community, William Darity and Kirsten Mullen (2020, n.p.) argue that $800,000 granted to each Black household would bring greater parity with the average white household. Reparations are perhaps a narrow means of viewing the severity of racially driven precarity, but it does provide an opportunity for an accounting of the problem.

7. The claim that arts and humanities education is a form of social infrastructure that can promote care is not to be confused with an idealistic pacification of society. For example, a well-grounded education in ethnic studies and the history of policing might foment further unrest and protest until a more just path is found. The Black Lives Matter movement might have garnered earlier and more widespread sympathy if the general public had a better grounding in the context of the Black experience in some countries.

Works Cited

Bellah, Robert N. 1994. "Understanding Caring in Contemporary America." In *The Crisis of Care: Affirming and Restoring Caring Practices in the Helping Professions,* edited by Susan S. Phillips and Patricia Benner, 21–41. Washington, D.C.: Georgetown University Press.

Berlant, Lauren. 2016. "The Commons: Infrastructures for Troubling Times." *Environment and Planning D: Society and Space* 34 (3): 393–419.

Black Lives Matter. n.d. "About." Accessed July 20, 2020. https://blacklivesmatter.com/about/.

Blyth, Mark. 2015. "The Austerity Delusion: Why a Bad Idea Won Over the West." *Foreign Affairs* 92 (3): 41–56.

Branicki, Layla J. 2020. "COVID-19, Ethics of Care and Feminist Crisis Management." *Gender, Work, and Organization* 27 (5): 872–83.

Cénat, Jude Mary. 2020. "The Vulnerability of Low-and Middle-income Countries Facing the COVID-19 Pandemic: The Case of Haiti." *Travel Medicine and Infectious Disease* 37: 101684.

Chappell, Sophie Grace. 2019. "Introducing Epiphanies." *ZEMO* 2:95–121.

Darity, William, and Kirsten Mullen. 2020. "Black Reparations and the Racial Wealth Gap." https://www.brookings.edu/blog/up-front/2020/06/15/black-reparations-and-the-racial-wealth-gap/.

Engster, Daniel. 2007. *The Heart of Justice: Care Ethics and Political Theory.* New York: Oxford University Press.

Everatt, David. 2020. "Numbers Can Kill: Politicians Should Handle South Africa's Coronavirus Data with Care." *The Conversation,* April 21, 2020. https://theconversation.com/numbers-can-kill-politicians-should-handle-south-africas-coronavirus-data-with-care-136587.

Fisher, Amanda Stuart. 2020. "Introduction: Caring Performance, Performing Care." In *Performing Care: New Perspectives on Socially Engaged Performance,* edited by Amanda Stuart Fisher and James Thompson, 1–18. Manchester, UK: Manchester University Press.

Hamington, Maurice. 2017. "Integrating Care Ethics and Design Thinking." *Journal of Business Ethics* 155 (1): 91–103.

Hamington, Maurice, and Ce Rosenow. 2019. *Care Ethics and Poetry.* Cham, Switzerland: Palgrave Macmillan.

Hill, Sean. 2017. "Precarity in the Era of #BlackLivesMatter." *Women's Studies Quarterly* 45 (3/4): 94–109.

HoSang, Daniel Martinez, and Joseph E. Lowndes. 2019. *Producers, Parasites, Patriots: Race and the New Right-Wing Politics of Precarity.* Minneapolis: University of Minnesota Press.

Khan-Cullors, Patrisse, and Asha Bandele. 2020. *When They Call You a Terrorist: A Black Lives Matter Memoir.* New York: St. Martin's Griffin.

Krugman, Paul. 2015. "The Case for Cuts Was a Lie. Why Does Britain Still Believe It? The Austerity Delusion." *The Guardian,* April 29, 2015. https://www.theguardian.com/business/ng-interactive/2015/apr/29/the-austerity-delusion.

Ladi, Stella. 2020. "Greece: Despite a Decade of Health Cuts, Coronavirus Death Rates Appear Comparatively Low." *The Conversation,* April 17, 2020. https://theconversation.com/greece-despite-a-decade-of-health-cuts-coronavirus-death-rates-appear-comparatively-low-136293.

LePan, Nicholas. 2020. "Visualizing the History of Pandemics." *Visual Capitalist,* March 14, 2020. https://www.visualcapitalist.com/history-of-pandemics-deadliest/.

Lipsitz, George. 1995. "'Swing Low, Sweet Cadillac': White Supremacy, Antiblack Racism, and the New Historicism." *American Literary History* 7 (4): 700–25.

Maçães, Bruno. 2020. "The Great Pause Was an Economic Revolution." *Foreign Policy,* June 22, 2020. https://foreignpolicy.com/2020/06/22/the-great-pause-was-an-economic-revolution%E2%80%A8/.

Mai, H. J. 2020. "U.N. Warns Number of People Starving to Death Could Double amid Pandemic." https://www.npr.org/sections/coronavirus-live-updates/2020/05/05/850470436/u-n-warns-number-of-people-starving-to-death-could-double-amid-pandemic.

Miller, Sarah Clark. 2012. *The Ethics of Need: Agency, Dignity, and Obligation*. New York: Routledge.

Mortari, Luigina. 2015. *Filosofia della cura*. Milan: Raffaello Cortina.

Mortari, Luigina, and Marco Ubbiali. 2017. "The 'MelArete' Project: Educating Children to the Ethics of Virtue and of Care." *European Journal of Educational Research* 6 (3): 269–78.

Murdoch, Iris. 1970. *The Sovereignty of Good*. London: Routledge.

Nilsen, Ella. 2020. " 'The Presidency Is a Duty to Care': Read Joe Biden's Full Speech on George Floyd's Death." https://www.vox.com/2020/6/2/21277967/joe-biden-full-speech-george-floyd-death-trump.

Noddings, Nel. 2002. *Starting at Home: Caring and Social Policy*. Berkeley: University of California Press.

Noddings, Nel. 2013. *Caring: A Relational Approach to Ethics and Moral Education*. 2nd ed. Berkeley: University of California Press.

Peck, Jamie, and Nik Theodore. 2019. "Still Neoliberalism?" *South Atlantic Quarterly* 118 (2): 245–65.

Pocock, Lesley. 2020. "Pandemics and a New Age of Reason." *Middle East Journal of Business* 13 (2): 3–35.

Ray, Rashawn, and Andre Perry. 2020. "Why We Need Reparations for Black Americans." https://www.brookings.edu/policy2020/bigideas/why-we-need-reparations-for-black-americans/.

Robinson, Fiona. 2011. *The Ethics of Care: A Feminist Approach to Human Security*. Philadelphia, Pa.: Temple University Press.

Schrecker, Ted, and Clare Bambra. 2015. *How Politics Makes Us Sick: Neoliberal Epidemics*. New York: Palgrave Macmillan.

Sparke, Matthew. 2017. "Austerity and the Embodiment of Neoliberalism as Ill-Health: Towards a Theory of Biological Sub-Citizenship." *Social Science and Medicine* 187:287–95.

Standing, Guy. 2011. *The Precariat: The New Dangerous Class*. New York: Bloomsbury Academic.

Sumner, Andy, Eduardo Ortiz-Juarez, and Chris Hoy. 2020. "Precarity and the Pandemic: COVID-19 and Poverty Incidence, Intensity, and Severity in Developing Countries." https://www.wider.unu.edu/publication/precarity-and-pandemic.

Taub, Amanda. 2020. "Why Are Women-Led Nations Doing Better with COVID-19?" *The New York Times*, May 15, 2020. https://www.nytimes.com/2020/05/15/world/coronavirus-women-leaders.html.

Tronto, Joan. 1993. *Moral Boundaries: A Political Argument for an Ethic of Care*. New York: Routledge.

Vaughan, Laurene. 2018. *Designing Cultures of Care*. London: Bloomsbury.

Visse, Merel, Tineke Abma, and Guy Widdershoven. 2015. "Practising Political Care Ethics: Can Responsive Evaluation Foster Democratic Care?" *Ethics and Social Welfare* 9 (2): 164–82.

White Bird Clinic Media Guide. 2020. "What Is CAHOOTS?" https://whitebirdclinic.org/what-is-cahoots/.

White, Julie Ann. 2000. *Democracy, Justice and the Welfare State: Reconstructing Public Care*. University Park: The Pennsylvania State University Press.

World Health Organization. 2017. "10 Facts on Obesity." https://www.who.int/features/factfiles/obesity/en/.

World Health Organization. 2020. "Obesity and Overweight." https://www.who.int/news-room/fact-sheets/detail/obesity-and-overweight.

Zack, Naomi. 2018. *Reviving the Social Compact: Inclusive Citizenship in an Age of Extreme Politics*. Lanham, Md.: Rowman & Littlefield.

Contributors

Andries Baart is visiting professor in the Department of Psychiatry, University Medical Center Utrecht, the Netherlands; professor of aging and generational dynamics at North-West University, South Africa; and professor emeritus of the University of Humanistic Studies, Tilburg University, and Catholic Theological University Utrecht, the Netherlands. Most recently, he is the coeditor of *The Ethics of Care: The State of the Art*, coauthor of *Praktijkboek Presentie* [Practice Book Presence], and author of *De Ontdekking Van Kwaliteit: Theorie En Praktijk Van Relationeel Zorg Geven* [The Discovery of Quality: Theory and Practice of Relational Caring].

Vrinda Dalmiya is professor of philosophy at the University of Hawai'i, Mānoa. She is author of *Caring to Know: Comparative Care Ethics, Feminist Epistemology, and the Mahābhārata* and coeditor of *Exploring Agency in the Mahābhārata: Ethical and Political Dimensions of Dharma*.

Emilie Dionne is a sociopolitical scientist, feminist thinker, and qualitative health researcher at the VITAM Research Centre in Sustainable Health (Centre de recherche en santé durable) in Quebec City and adjunct professor in the Department of Sociology at Université Laval.

Maggie FitzGerald is assistant professor in the Department of Political Studies at the University of Saskatchewan.

Michael Flower is emeritus professor of interdisciplinary science studies at Portland State University.

Sacha Ghandeharian received his PhD from the Department of Political Science at Carleton University, specializing in political theory and international relations.

Maurice Hamington is professor of philosophy and affiliate faculty in women, gender, and sexuality studies at Portland State University. He is author of *Embodied Care: Jane Addams, Maurice Merleau-Ponty, and Feminist Ethics,* coauthor of *Care Ethics and Poetry,* and coeditor of *Care Ethics and Political Theory, Applying Care Ethics to Business,* and *Socializing Care: Feminist Ethics and Public Issues.*

Eva Feder Kittay recently retired as distinguished professor of philosophy at Stony Brook University/SUNY. She is author of *Learning from My Daughter: The Value and Care of Disabled Minds* and *Love's Labor: Essays on Women, Equality, and Dependency,* among other books, and coeditor of *Cognitive Disability and Its Challenge to Moral Philosophy, Frames, Fields, and Contrasts,* and *Women and Moral Theory.*

Carlo Leget is professor of care ethics at the University of Humanistic Studies in Utrecht, the Netherlands, where he also holds an endowed chair in palliative care. He is author of *Art of Living, Art of Dying: Spiritual Care for a Good Death.*

Sarah Clark Miller is associate professor in the Department of Philosophy at Penn State University, where she is also affiliated with the Bioethics Program and the Department of Women's, Gender, and Sexuality Studies. She is author of *The Ethics of Need: Agency, Dignity, and Obligation.*

Luigina Mortari is professor of human sciences and epistemology of qualitative research at the School of Medicine at the University of Verona. Her books include *La philosophie du soin: Éthique, médecine et société, Filosofia do cuidado, Prendre soin de soi: L'art d'exister entre intériorité et ouverture au monde,* and *Le savoir du cœur: Penser les émotions, ressentir les pensées.* She is coauthor of *Gestures and Thoughts of Caring: A Theory of Caring from the Voices of Nurses.*

Yayo Okano is professor of political philosophy at Doshisha University, Kyoto, Japan. Her books include *Kea Surunoha Dareka?* [Who

Cares?], coauthored with Joan Tronto; *Senso ni Kousuru* [Against War]; and *Feminizumu no Seijigaku* [The Politics of Feminism: Introducing the Ethics of Care to the Global Society].

Elena Pulcini (1950–2021) was professor of social philosophy in the Department of Social and Political Science, University of Florence, prior to her untimely death during the production of this book. Her publications include *Il potere di unire: Femminile, desiderio, cura*; *The Individual without Passions: Modern Individualism and the Loss of the Social Bond*; *Care of the World: Fear, Responsibility, and Justice in the Global Age*; and *L'envie: Essai sur une passion triste*. She is coauthor of *Emotions and Care: Interdisciplinary Perspectives*.

Index